THE BALLAD OF ROY BENAVIDEZ

THE LIFE AND TIMES OF AMERICA'S MOST FAMOUS HISPANIC WAR HERO

WILLIAM STURKEY

BASIC BOOKS

New York

Basic Books
Hachette Book Group
1290 Avenue of the Americas, New York, NY 10104
www.basicbooks.com

Printed in the United States of America

First Edition: May 2024

Published by Basic Books, an imprint of Hachette Book Group, Inc. The Basic Books name and logo is a registered trademark of the Hachette Book Group.

The Hachette Speakers Bureau provides a wide range of authors for speaking events. To find out more, go to hachettespeakersbureau.com or email HachetteSpeakers@hbgusa.com.

Basic books may be purchased in bulk for business, educational, or promotional use. For more information, please contact your local bookseller or the Hachette Book Group Special Markets Department at special.markets@hbgusa.com.

The publisher is not responsible for websites (or their content) that are not owned by the publisher.

Print book interior design by Amy Quinn.

Library of Congress Cataloging-in-Publication Data
Names: Sturkey, William, author.
Title: The ballad of Roy Benavidez : the life and times of America's most famous Hispanic war hero / William Sturkey.
Description: First edition. | New York : Basic Books, 2024. | Includes bibliographical references and index.
Identifiers: LCCN 2023040320 | ISBN 9781541600263 (hardcover) | ISBN 9781541600270 (ebook)
Subjects: LCSH: Benavidez, Roy P. | Hispanic American soldiers—Biography. | Vietnam War, 1961-1975—Veterans—United States—Biography. | United States. Army. Special Forces—Biography. | Medal of Honor—Biography.
Classification: LCC U53.B39 S84 2024 | DDC 959.704/34092 [B]—dc23/eng/20240128
LC record available at https://lccn.loc.gov/2023040320

ISBNs: 9781541600263 (hardcover), 9781541600270 (ebook)

LSC-H

Printing 1, 2024

For Roy,
and all those like him who serve

Dedicated to the memory of Army Spc. Donald Samuel Oaks Jr.,
1982–2003

CONTENTS

Brief Note on Sources and Language   xi

PROLOGUE   1

CHAPTER 1:   RAWHIDE   15

CHAPTER 2:   FIELDS   39

CHAPTER 3:   A LEAP OF FAITH   63

CHAPTER 4:   COLD WARRIOR   85

CHAPTER 5:   LAND MINE   111

CHAPTER 6:   SOJOURN   133

CHAPTER 7:   FEARLESS   161

CHAPTER 8:   HOME   191

CHAPTER 9:   HONOR   213

CHAPTER 10:   A HERO   245

CHAPTER 11:   SECURITY   279

CHAPTER 12:   GLORY DAYS   307

CHAPTER 13:   TO BE AN AMERICAN   339

EPILOGUE   365

Acknowledgments   375
Abbreviations of Sources   381
Notes   383
Index   431

Roy's Texas. Map by Kate Blackmer

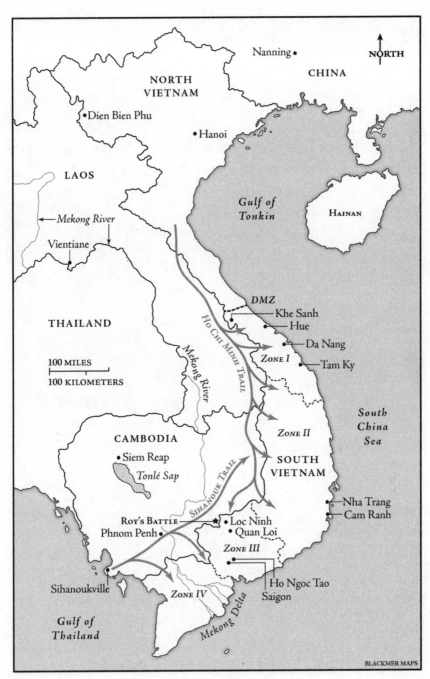

Roy's Vietnam and Cambodia. Map by Kate Blackmer

BRIEF NOTE ON SOURCES AND LANGUAGE

THE BALLAD OF ROY BENAVIDEZ RELIES HEAVILY ON ROY BE-navidez's own public speeches and writings, especially the two memoirs he coauthored after his rise to fame. Published in 1986 and 1995, Roy's autobiographical books offer unique access to his innermost thoughts about his family, childhood, and the events that most profoundly altered his fate. Like all memoirs, Roy's books were deeply affected by the passage of time, as memories can change and fade across the decades of a person's life. Roy's memoirs were also shaped by the historical context of his rise to fame in the 1980s. Years of experience taught Roy that there were things his audiences wanted him to say and others that might have been less appealing to hear. These factors resulted in some relatively minor inaccuracies, omissions, or exaggerations, whether intentional or accidental. Nevertheless, these memoirs are used here as a guide to help trace the broader chronological contours of Roy's story and as a window to understand his reactions to the circumstances that shaped his life. When possible, the timing and description of events have been verified for accuracy through other sources and relevant firsthand accounts.

This book uses the terms "Hispanic" and "Latino" to describe Roy's race. Generally speaking, *Hispanic* refers to cultures associated with Spanish-speaking places, and *Latino* is used to describe people whose families descend from Latin America. But the terminology for people like Roy can be even more complex. At various points in history, other people might have referred to someone of Roy's background as Tejano, Chicano, Yaqui, Native American, Latinx, Mexican American, or even Mexican, as his family was identified in the 1930 census. This book settles on the terms Hispanic and Latino for historical accuracy and because those are the terms Roy himself used most often to describe his racial and ethnic identity.

PROLOGUE

THE DEFINING MOMENT IN THE LIFE OF ROY BENAVIDEZ came on May 2, 1968. The thirty-two-year-old Army staff sergeant was stationed at a remote post in South Vietnam, roughly eighty miles north of Saigon. At about two o'clock in the afternoon, he was huddled in a prayer group around the hood of a jeep when he saw two men running through the camp. Alarmed, Roy hustled to a nearby communications tent where he and a handful of servicemen gathered around a radio receiver. Over the static, they could make out the sound of rapid gunfire and men screaming in distress. A covert reconnaissance mission somewhere out in the surrounding jungle was going terribly wrong.[1]

Roy rushed to the airstrip, where he saw a "badly shot up" helicopter returning from a failed attempt to rescue the reconnaissance team. Moments later, another chopper came hurtling over the treetops, thumping onto the helipad in a rushed landing. The second helicopter was pierced by so many bullets that Roy "didn't see how it could fly." Twenty-year-old Michael Craig, a

1

door gunner in the second chopper, had been shot in the chest. Roy and others pulled Craig from the aircraft and set him on the ground. Roy cradled the wounded man as they waited for medics. Craig was losing breath and struggling to speak. He managed to utter, "Oh, my God, my mother and father," before dying in Roy's arms.[2]

In 1968, Roy Benavidez was on his second tour of duty in Vietnam. He was a career military man, a "triple-volunteer" as it was known, meaning he had volunteered for the Army, Airborne, and Special Forces. Roy had first joined the Texas National Guard in 1952 and the United States Army in 1955. He had served across the globe, having previously been stationed in South Korea, Germany, Panama, Honduras, and Ecuador.[3]

Roy's first tour in Vietnam began in 1965 and lasted just over four months before he was nearly killed by some type of land mine. After a remarkable recovery, he returned in 1968 as a member of the elite Army unit known as the Green Berets. Standing only five feet eight and weighing less than 170 pounds, Roy was not physically imposing to the untrained eye, but as a member of the Green Berets, he belonged to one of the most lethal fighting forces in the world. And now he was part of a secretive mission code-named "Daniel Boone," an operation described by the Joint Chiefs of Staff as an "on-the-ground means of determining location and size of enemy organizations in sanctuary in Cambodia," a place where American soldiers were not officially supposed to be operating at that point in the Vietnam War.[4]

For years, the American military brass had been deeply concerned about enemy troops and supplies infiltrating South Vietnam from Cambodia. This was a legitimate problem for the American mission in Vietnam. North Vietnamese troops stored munitions and food in rural areas just across the border, knowing full well that United States forces couldn't interrupt their activities in the noncombatant nation of Cambodia. The communist forces could launch attacks into South Vietnam and then safely retreat back across the border to regroup.[5]

By December of 1967, communist operations in Cambodia had become such a problem that General William Westmoreland, the American military commander in Vietnam, requested seventy-two hours of "high intensity" B-52 tactical airstrikes on suspected enemy positions. This request was denied because of domestic and international concerns. The presidential administration of Lyndon B. Johnson was deeply worried that news of American action in Cambodia could cause domestic political turmoil or even trigger a military response from Russia or China. If the United States were to enter Cambodia, it would need a very good reason.[6]

Meanwhile, Cambodian officials refused to acknowledge that communist forces were operating in their country. American diplomats made overtures to members of the international community, but teams of inspectors from Canada and India couldn't find evidence of a significant communist presence. North Vietnamese soldiers were indeed operating in Cambodia, but most of their activities took place in rural, isolated stretches of the jungle that were inaccessible to foreign diplomats. The United States military needed more evidence if it was to justify military intervention into Cambodia.[7]

Operation Daniel Boone was conceived in 1966 to gather such evidence. Orchestrated by a branch of the military known as Military Assistance Command, Vietnam-Studies and Observations Group (MACV-SOG), Daniel Boone was a series of top-secret missions involving the insertion of twelve-man units over the border, or "across the fence" as servicemen often called the operations, to study and observe enemy movements in Cambodia.[8]

As was their aim, these special units saw the enemy often. At the end of 1968, a Department of Defense memo reported that more than 80 percent of these reconnaissance missions encountered enemy forces. Over 50 percent required "emergency extraction" due to close contact with the enemy. It was extraordinarily dangerous work. "When the choppers took off to take team members on some mission," Roy Benavidez recalled, "you never knew if you'd see them again."[9]

On one of Roy's first missions that spring, his unit began taking "some pretty heavy gunfire" and called for extraction. When the rescue helicopter arrived, Roy attached himself and a wounded soldier to a nylon harness known as a "McGuire rig," a secure rope dropped from choppers during urgent extractions. As the rescue craft flew off with Roy dangling below, the McGuire rig began twisting so uncontrollably that the ropes started rubbing together. The friction began to fray the harness, threatening to sever the only lifeline holding the men hundreds of feet above the jungle floor below. As bullets chased the helicopter into the sky, a soldier named Leroy Wright leaned out from the main cabin to disentangle the line, saving Roy and the other man from plummeting to the earth. The other man later succumbed to his wounds, but Roy survived. He later described Leroy Wright as a "real angel" who had saved his life.[10]

On May 2, 1968, Leroy Wright was the leader of the reconnaissance team stranded in the jungle. "I felt my heart sink," Roy recalled of learning about Wright's squad. "Those were my brothers." And so when another extraction helicopter prepared to take off, Roy rushed to the airstrip and jumped onboard, desperate to help his compatriots who were hopelessly surrounded by hundreds of North Vietnamese soldiers somewhere out in the Cambodian wilderness.[11]

After arriving at the scene, Roy jumped from the helicopter and sprinted across a clearing filled with gunfire to reach the trapped unit. He was shot numerous times, but he made his way to the survivors and managed to help them organize a defensive perimeter while treating the wounded men's injuries and calling in supporting aircraft strikes over the radio. After roughly six hours of intensive combat, another helicopter was finally able to reach the clearing and extract the men. Roy was the last American to leave the field alive. All told, Roy saved the lives of at least eight soldiers while incurring more than thirty puncture wounds to all parts of his body that left him hospitalized for nearly a year and disabled for the rest of his life.[12]

Roy Benavidez never again saw combat, but he remained in the military until September of 1976, when he was forced to medically retire. By the time he was honorably discharged, Roy had earned the Parachutist Badge, two Good Conduct Medals, a National Defense Service Medal, an Armed Forces Expeditionary Medal, four Overseas Service Bars, a Vietnam Service Medal, a Republic of Vietnam Campaign Medal, a Combat Infantryman Badge, Vietnam Jump Wings, an Army Commendation Medal, a Badge with Rifle Bar, four Purple Hearts, and a Distinguished Service Cross. Because of the secrecy of his May 2 mission, however, it would take thirteen years for the full details of his most heroic actions to become known to the public. Only then would Roy emerge as a major national hero. In December of 1980, after over six years of lobbying, Roy Benavidez was approved for the Medal of Honor, the highest decoration in the American military. He received the award from President Ronald Reagan at the Pentagon on February 24, 1981.[13]

After receiving the Medal of Honor, Roy Benavidez became an American military legend who lived out the rest of his days as a national hero. For the final seventeen years of his life, he was America's most recent living recipient of the Medal of Honor. He became an icon of military pride and patriotism at a time when the United States armed forces were trying to restore their image in the wake of the Vietnam War. In the 1980s, Roy represented the qualities the military wanted to promote, and he crafted a public persona that emphasized those qualities. He was an unflinching patriot and a shining example of service and courage.

Throughout the 1980s and 1990s, Roy delivered hundreds of speeches around the world. He spoke at military installations, schools, municipal buildings, and civic and veterans organizations—Rotary clubs, American Legions, and Chambers of Commerce. When Roy was not delivering speeches, his life was filled with an endless stream of parades, media appearances, ground-breakings, and military ceremonies. Roy's activities took him into the halls of American power and prestige. He met presidents Ronald Reagan and George H. W. Bush on numerous occasions and regularly crossed paths with major American celebrities as well as Texas political luminaries such as H. Ross Perot, Ron Paul, and former first lady Lady Bird Johnson. During those years of fame, he testified in front of Congress, visited the White House twice, and was invited to every presidential inauguration between 1985 and 1997. One of America's most famous war heroes, Roy was in constant demand. As he once joked to a Rhode Island audience, "I'm busier than a one-armed paperhanger with jock itch."[14]

In his home state of Texas, Roy was practically royalty. In 1981, the Texas Press Association named him "Texan of the Year," and Texas governor Bill Clements hosted an honorary "Roy Benavidez Day" at the state capital. Two years later, the Texas State Senate designated May 14, 1983, as "Roy P. Benavidez Day in Texas" and renamed the National Guard Armory in Roy's hometown in his honor. Roy was similarly feted with Roy Benavidez Days in the cities of San Antonio, Houston, Galveston, El Paso, Corpus Christi, and Mercedes. The state's political leaders loved being photographed with him and regularly invited him to participate in their fundraising dinners and commemorative events. Roy was a highly demanded speaker, and he traveled all over the state, serving as grand marshal in parades and offering remarks at all kinds of important events—graduations, veterans' gatherings, holiday celebrations, and more.[15]

Since his death in 1998, Roy continues to be celebrated by members of the military community. Army posts across the South have various streets, ranges, and training programs named after Roy Benavidez. The United States Military Academy at West Point has a "Benavidez Room" containing Roy's military portrait and a $10,000 bronze bust of him donated by the class of 1997. In 2001, the United States Navy christened a vehicle cargo ship named the USNS *Benavidez*. That same year, Roy Benavidez became the first Hispanic American honored with his own GI Joe. To this day, Roy remains respected across the globe by others who have fought and served. Some of America's most famous military heroes—including the famed "American Sniper" Chris Kyle and "Lone Survivor" Marcus Luttrell—have for decades marveled at his incredible heroics.[16]

Roy has also long been championed by major American politicians, especially Republican leaders, who have been enamored by his courageous actions on May 2, 1968. Former United States senator John McCain opened his 2004 book, *Why Courage Matters*, with an anecdote about the "superhuman heroics of Roy Benavidez." Former secretary of state Colin Powell wrote about Roy in his memoir, as did Ronald Reagan's secretary of defense Caspar Weinberger, who called Roy's Medal of Honor ceremony "one of the bright spots of the [Reagan] Presidency." Roy drew the praises of both President George H. W. Bush and his son President George W. Bush, who called Roy "a man of great courage and determination." As of this writing, Roy's Medal of Honor remains prominently displayed in the American Heroes Gallery at the Reagan Presidential Library in Simi Valley, California.[17]

But Roy was so much more than a war hero, especially among Hispanics. His rise to prominence in 1981 made Roy one of the country's most famous Latinos at the beginning of an era many pundits dubbed "The Decade of the Hispanic." As one of the most famous Hispanics of the 1980s, Roy was among a small number of Latino icons whose fame crossed over into mainstream American society. He was also a very different type of Hispanic idol, one famous not for his voice or beauty but for his patriotism and service. In some ways, he was the embodiment of a dream long deferred, a Hispanic soldier broadly accepted by the American public in exchange for his military contributions. Generations of Hispanic veterans had previously tried to make such a bargain, but the Latino heroes of World Wars I and II returned home only to find continued racial discrimination. Roy, on the other hand, was lionized as a national hero at a moment when Hispanic influence was expanding in all corners of American life. Latino audiences followed his life in the spotlight and cherished him as a representative of their people.[18]

When Roy first became famous, Dr. Leonardo Carrillo, a professor of ethnic studies at Texas A&M-Corpus Christi, wrote and mailed to Roy a poem titled "Ballad of Roy Benavidez." It's a traditional Mexican corrido, one that retells the public version of Roy's story—that of a poor boy who rose to prominence through heroism under fire. Like other corridos, the "Ballad of Roy Benavidez" tells an epic tale of a man's courage and rise to social prominence, building on an oral tradition of storytelling that dates back hundreds of years. The final line reads "we must not lose hope."[19]

The legend of Roy Benavidez has meant a great many things to a great many people—from hardened military hawks to Chicano academics—who have repackaged and reused it for their own purposes. To some, he is an interesting character who accomplished a remarkable feat of violent heroism. To others, he is an icon of the military or of an entire race, and an inspirational man whose American journey holds the promise to unlock some deeper meaning about perseverance, sacrifice, and citizenship. For most, Roy's story lies somewhere in between. Like all myths and legends, portions of the story of Roy Benavidez have been told and retold time and time again. But his entire story has never been told before now.

The Ballad of Roy Benavidez is a book about an extraordinary American life. Although Roy has been widely celebrated for his actions in the Cambodian jungle, the story of those wartime heroics does not fully capture the richness or complexity of his American journey. Roy was more than just a warrior, and his story can teach us much more about American history than just its military exploits. To truly understand Roy's life, it is essential to incorporate the backstory of his Hispanic family and look beyond the pomp and circumstance of America's endless military celebrations to examine the pre- and postwar experiences of working-class veterans.

Roy was born Latino and poor in Great Depression–era Texas. He came from a family with deep Texas roots. His ancestors had lived in East Texas since the 1820s, well before Texas joined the United States. Roy's family had been pioneers and landowners in East Texas, but they were forced from their lands by the racial discrimination that accompanied Texas independence from Mexico and entrance into the United States. Roy's ancestors lost nearly everything and were reduced in status from major landowners to migrant farm laborers. By the time Roy was born in the 1930s, his family was among the millions of Hispanics who worked on other people's farms for very little pay. Decades of racially discriminatory federal and state policies blocked Latinos from the very same opportunities—land grants, property, education, and access to government welfare programs like Social Security—that undergirded prosperity for millions of white families, many of whom, in turn, profited handsomely off the labor of poor Latinos. Roy spent much of his childhood in and out of school, working in the cotton and sugar beet fields of Texas and Colorado. And his youth in Jim Crow–era Texas was plagued by racial harassment and disadvantages.

Military service provided Roy with unique opportunities. The same American nation that allowed for such stark, systemic racial inequalities was also capable of providing enticing incentives for those willing to serve in its military. Like many American veterans, Roy joined the armed forces because he saw no better path toward upward mobility and equality. Military service provided Roy with not only a good career but also a strong sense of national belonging. "I felt more a part of something than I ever had in my life," he explained of joining the Army. "Nobody cared if the other was black, brown, or green. . . . I was equal." As Roy later wrote, "The United States of America had given me freedom and an opportunity to succeed. . . . I believe that only in America could I, a young Hispanic-Indian American, have risen to my place."[20]

But such opportunities came with an extraordinary price. The promise of social advancement was affixed to the physical hazards of global warfare. Roy bore the wounds of that violence. In 1974, he described himself as "a walking roadmap [of] scars." His family and closest friends remembered him plucking pieces of shrapnel from his skin and scalp, finally freeing the pieces of metal he carried home from Southeast Asia after years embedded in his body. Roy's 1968 battle left him with excruciating pain every day for the rest of his life. But the violence he witnessed also made him grateful to have lived at all. He constantly reminded his audiences that "the real heroes are those who never came back, those who gave their lives for this country."[21]

As a Medal of Honor recipient in the early 1980s, Roy at times became a political prop. Ronald Reagan, just a month into his presidency, staged a moment of grand political theater when he learned of the outstanding Latino Medal of Honor recipient.

In February of 1981, recently inaugurated President Reagan held a stately ceremony at the Pentagon and bucked tradition by reading the award citation himself, adding for the audience that Vietnam veterans had come "home without a victory not because they'd been defeated, but because they'd been denied permission to win." For many in the military, Reagan's actions and rhetoric that day signaled the restoration of pride to an American military that was still reeling from the tragedy of the Vietnam War. Colin Powell attended and remembered the Benavidez ceremony. "That afternoon marked the changing of the guard for the armed forces," Powell later wrote. "The military services had been restored to a place of honor." Reagan scored major political points that day, and throughout much of his presidency, by presenting himself as the servicemen's greatest advocate since the war in Vietnam. But Roy was not merely a passive recipient of praise. Just two years later, he used his own prestige to advocate for himself and millions of other veterans when Reagan's policies threatened his livelihood.[22]

In February of 1983, Roy Benavidez received a letter from the Social Security Administration notifying him of the discontinuance of his disability benefits. He had been on disability since retiring from the Army. In notifying Roy of the end of his benefits, the letter coldly stated, "It is concluded that you retain the ability to lift a maximum of 50 pounds; you can frequently lift and carry 25 pounds." "It is not possible for you to return to military service since you have retired," read the letter, "however, other types of work are readily available for you in our economic environment."[23]

Seven years earlier, an Army physician had diagnosed Roy with pulmonary disease, shortness of breath, severe chest wall pain, a degenerative cervical spine, osteoarthritis of the lumbar spine, chondromalacia, anterior and osseous nerve palsy, frequent nose bleeds, and sloping sensorineural hearing loss. Roy had incurred an estimated thirty-seven puncture wounds while fighting for his country. Excluded by birth from the greatest promises of American life, Benavidez had made the ultimate sacrifices to earn full citizenship and respect. Yet, there he was in 1983 being instructed to get back to work, told by his government that neither his life-threatening injuries nor his remarkable act of valor were enough to entitle him to Social Security disability benefits. "I was emotionally crushed," Roy wrote, "that my country would question my integrity in this manner." Roy went to Washington to defend his honor and his income. In doing so, he was placed in direct conflict with the very same administration whose public military pageantry often overshadowed the more complicated realities of its treatment of veterans.[24]

Historians of the 1980s have written dozens of books and articles on changes to America's memory of the Vietnam War and the deconstruction of the nation's welfare state. The Reagan era unlocked a new stance toward the war, one of unapologetic military boosterism that helped give shape to a restored form of hardline global anti-communism in the 1980s. Military spending increased as resources were redirected from a welfare state whose excessive anti-poverty programs, Reagan and his advisors argued, had led to the economic downturn of the 1970s. These central tenants of the Reagan presidency represented great and enduring changes to American society. But few historians have ever noticed the short, chubby Hispanic man wearing a Medal of Honor around his neck who appeared prominently in both episodes and served as a powerful connector between the two. Roy was not the determining factor in either trend, but his story became a major inflection point in each development. During the spring of 1983, the war hero became the living embodiment of a nation struggling over the questions and nature of the changing welfare state.

The Ballad of Roy Benavidez tracks the journey of Roy P. Benavidez across more than sixty years of an incredible American life, tracing Roy's path against the backdrop of Texas history, Hispanic American history, the Cold War, and beyond. It seeks to move beyond the innumerable examples of Roy Benavidez battlefield hagiography to tell a more complete story, one far bigger and more beautiful, complex, and heart-wrenching than anything anyone has ever said about Roy Benavidez and that day of explosive violence in May of 1968.

This is not just a story about a man but a book that seeks to capture the essence of marginalized citizens struggling to belong in a militarized nation. Told through the lens of a disadvantaged boy who became a legendary hero, this story lays bare the framework of the wide range of tragedies and triumphs that characterized American life in the twentieth century for poor people like Roy Benavidez. It is a tale about the interconnected meanings of race, citizenship, and military service in modern American society—one that uses the lore of a particular individual to interrogate the ways America celebrates its most revered heroes, balanced against what it asks of them in return.

CHAPTER 1

RAWHIDE

Roy's parents, Salvador Benavidez Jr. and Teresa Perez, met at a community dance in rural Texas in the year 1934. They were both in their early twenties, born just months apart in 1911. Salvador was tall and lean, strong from his days working as a ranch hand. He was handsome but unconventionally so. His narrow, clean-shaven face held dark eyes, oversized ears, and a large pointy nose. Teresa stood a head shorter and was beautiful by any standard. She had full lips, deep-set dark eyes, high cheekbones, and wavy black hair that she wore short.[1]

Salvador was a charmer. His lanky frame and peculiar features were offset by a bubbly personality. He was confident and outgoing, and he loved to dance. Salvador was "graceful," his family recalled, and "much sought after as a partner." He also possessed a beautiful singing voice. The young man sang old Mexican ballads that had been passed down through generations of Hispanic farmworkers—songs such as "La Noche Serena" and "Las

Cuatro Milpas" that told romantic tales of lost love and life on the old Mexican haciendas.[2]

Teresa was much more reserved, perhaps because she came from a much smaller family. Whereas Salvador grew up in a large household of eleven siblings and adopted cousins, Teresa lived with just three brothers and a sister-in-law. She also lacked the machismo of her male peers. Her family wrote much less about her personality, mostly just that she was beautiful and hardworking.[3]

The pair met at the Lindenau Rifle Club, a single-story, board and batten building that sat at the bottom of a grass-covered hill in DeWitt County. Founded in 1901, the club allowed only male members, but the structure itself housed a variety of community events. The building was constructed in 1926 by German immigrants who modeled it in the fashion of traditional European social dance halls. For years, the Lindenau Rifle Club served as a gathering place for people who lived on the surrounding farms.[4]

Salvador and Teresa spent most of their lives in DeWitt County, home to about thirty thousand residents. He was born there and raised on a ranch not far from the dance hall. She had lived in DeWitt since migrating from Mexico as a young girl. Their courtship began in 1934, but it's likely they had crossed paths before. Theirs was a small Latino community, and their families shared many connections.

Salvador's people were ranchers and farmhands who tended crops and cattle. Teresa's family lived in Cuero, the nearby seat of DeWitt County, where they held jobs in the local service industries. Her brothers worked in a bakery and as general laborers. Teresa would later become a domestic worker, cleaning the homes and minding the children of the city's white elite. Neither Salvador nor Teresa had ever attended a proper school, nor could they read or write English. Their people were blue-collar workers, the *vaqueros* and *mucamas* whose labors powered local life in that part of Texas.[5]

DeWitt County, Texas, is a beautiful land of sprawling ranches and gently rolling grass-covered hills. It sits in a prairie along the Guadalupe River, sandwiched between the Texas Hill Country and the Gulf Coast. DeWitt is the wildflower capital of Texas, a place covered in bluebonnets and golden tickseed. It is also cattle country, both back then and now. The land is packed with tens of thousands of cows who spend their days munching grass in the shade of thick post oak trees. The foliage provides endless refuge for grasshoppers and cicadas who fill the air with their high-pitched songs. At dusk on a clear day, a view from atop one of DeWitt's rolling hills reveals a sun-streaked vista of low-hanging clouds and vast grasslands stretching as far as the eye can see.[6]

Salvador's father, Salvador Benavides Sr., came to DeWitt County near the turn of the century to work on one of the ranches (back then, the family still ended its name with "s"; the "z" wouldn't stick until the late 1930s). He was a newcomer to the county but not the state. In fact, Salvador was part of the third generation of his family to live in Texas. His people were Tejanos—native Hispanics of Mexican descent who lived in modern-day Texas years before it joined the United States.

THE BENAVIDES FAMILY FIRST ARRIVED IN TEXAS IN 1828 WHEN Plácido Benavides emigrated to Victoria from Tamaulipas, Mexico, with his three brothers—Ysidro, Eugenio, and Nicholas, the great-great-grandfather of Roy Benavidez. At the time, Texas was still part of Mexico, a remote but massively sprawling outpost largely occupied by Native American tribes. The Mexican government was eager to see the area occupied by settlers and offered "extraordinary inducements," writes one historian, in the form of land grants to attract emigrants "to settle in Texas." These newcomers included the famous Texans Stephen F. Austin and Samuel Houston, as well as Plácido Benavides.[7]

The Benavides brothers came to Texas to help organize Victoria, which was part of a new colony established by the wealthy empresario Martín de León. Plácido worked as de León's secretary and later served as the town's commissioner and its first schoolteacher, important roles that brought him local prominence. In 1832, he married one of de León's daughters, further cementing his status among the city's landowning elite. The other brothers also owned land, and their family was well-known and prosperous in the growing young colony. But their status was soon altered as Texas's sovereignty changed.[8]

Texas's new white settlers quickly turned against the same Mexican government that had gifted them the land. Their primary concern was over the issue of human slavery. Some of the white farmers brought with them enslaved Black people from the American South and chafed at new legislation that threatened the institution of slavery in Mexican Texas. First came an 1824 law limiting the importation of enslaved people. Next was an 1827 decree that restricted the enslavement of children and regulated the number of enslaved people an heir could inherit. Then, in 1829, Mexico abolished slavery. Texas slaveowners found loopholes by forcing enslaved people to sign indenture contracts and successfully lobbying for exemptions in their territory, but the threats to slavery—coupled with new constitutional reforms imposed by Mexican president Antonio López de Santa Anna—ultimately compelled wealthy white Texans to rebel against Mexico. "Texas must be a slave country," insisted Stephen F. Austin.[9]

When the Texas Revolution began in 1835, Plácido joined the rebellion against Santa Anna. In addition to disputes over the future of slavery, many residents of Mexican Texas were outraged by Santa Anna's invalidation of the 1824 Mexican Constitution, a move that gave the president almost complete control over the legislative and judicial branches of government. As an influential local leader, Plácido was appointed first lieutenant in a cavalry

unit in the new Texas militia. He also helped supply the young
army with horses, cattle, and food.[10]

In the fall of 1835, Plácido's unit was part of a force that captured the city of Goliad. Later that autumn, he and his men
served near San Antonio, helping procure and distribute supplies while also monitoring the movements of the Mexican army.
His most famous contribution to the Texas Revolution came on
March 2, 1836, when he escaped an ambush and charged ahead
to Goliad to warn soldiers of the approaching Mexican army. For
this act, he earned the nickname the "Paul Revere of Texas."[11]

But soon after Texas won its independence in 1836, Plácido
and his brothers began to face questions about their loyalty. Like
all Texas revolutionaries, Plácido supported the overthrow of
Santa Anna, but he preferred that Texas remain in Mexico rather
than form its own independent nation. Race also fueled some
growing animosity toward the Benavides brothers and other
landowning Tejanos. Thousands of white Americans had poured
into Texas during and immediately after the revolution, bringing
with them racial and anti-Catholic prejudices and a strong desire to establish and maintain Anglo-Saxon supremacy. Some of
the leading figures in the Texas Revolution, including Stephen F.
Austin and Samuel Houston, had openly called for more white
settlers to lay claim to Texas. "Texas should be effectually, and
fully, Americanized," argued Austin in 1835. That same year,
Houston insisted that Anglo immigrants "will never mix with
the phlegm of the indolent Mexicans." In the eyes of many of
these white settlers, the Texas Revolution had been a war against
Mexico and a battle, at least in part, to snatch control of Texas
from people of Hispanic descent.[12]

As Martín de León's biographer wrote, the new Texas settlers "distrusted and hated the Mexicans, simply because they
were Mexican, regardless of the fact they were both on the
same side of the fighting during the war." The Anglo Americans

also questioned Tejano views on slavery and worried that these Hispanic Texans might threaten the ambitions of settlers who wanted to bring enslaved people to work on their farms. Some Anglo settlers openly sought to push Tejanos out of the new nation, using race to justify stealing property and driving people from the land.[13]

Plácido Benavides and his brothers encountered "war-crazy people," writes one historian, "who overran the town of Victoria." Fearing for their families, the brothers fled to Louisiana along with the de León family. While they were gone, white settlers began to move onto their property and claim it as their own. Plácido died in Louisiana in 1837, exiled from the very place he had just fought to liberate. The rest of the brothers eventually returned, including the youngest brother, Nicholas, the great-great-grandfather of Roy Benavidez.[14]

Upon their return, Nicholas and his brothers faced an onslaught of anti-Tejano racism around Victoria. People of Mexican descent were constant targets of theft and violence. Thieves broke into their houses and stole their horses and cattle. Some Tejanos were threatened or attacked by roving gangs of thugs. In 1843, Nicholas's sister-in-law lost her brother when a group of Tejanos was ambushed and murdered just west of Victoria. Another massacre of "eight unknown Mexicans" occurred nearby in the following decade.[15]

In 1845, Texas became the twenty-eighth state in the United States. Three years later, the Mexican-American War ended with the Treaty of Guadalupe Hidalgo, resulting in the transfer of California and parts of modern-day Arizona, New Mexico, Utah, and Nevada to the United States. At the time, about 100,000 ethnic Mexicans lived in those areas. The Treaty of Guadalupe Hidalgo gave those people United States citizenship and all the rights protected by that status. But the entrance of those territories into the United States also drew hundreds of thousands more white settlers who brought with them vile, racist rhetoric and a desire to impose new laws that protected the rights of white landowners over those of Hispanic families, some of whom had lived in Texas for generations.[16]

In the early 1850s, the famous intellectual Frederick Law Olmsted toured Texas and recounted flagrant prejudice toward Mexican American landowners near Victoria. "Mexicans were regarded in a somewhat unchristian tone," he described, "not as heretics or heathen to be converted with flannel and tracts, but rather as vermin, to be exterminated." "White folks and Mexicans," Olmsted reported of one Anglo woman's remarks, "were never made to live together, anyhow, and the Mexicans had no business here." Some Anglos spoke openly of driving them out. "They were getting so impertinent, and were so well protected by the laws," an Olmsted interviewee concluded, "that the Americans would just have to get together and drive them all out of the country." And that is precisely what ensued, albeit largely through the legal system instead of the battlefield.[17]

The entrance of Texas into the United States created several means by which Anglos could legally displace Tejano families. First, although Tejano landowners who remained in Texas after 1845 became citizens of the United States, their property titles did not always hold up in court. After Texas became a state, Anglo settlers increasingly began to dispute the property claims of traditional Tejano families. The interpretation of documentation was key, as courts in the United States did not accept the same types of property distinctions previously recognized by Spanish or Mexican property law. Older claims to the land might have been based on boundaries defined by rivers or boulders rather than units of English measurement. These types of claims were difficult to certify, especially when they were written in Spanish and/or related to a changing landscape. Even when landowners could produce documentation, the authenticity of these records could still be drawn into question. There were also cases with competing claims based on forged documents and still others where squatters claimed land they were illegally occupying. Sometimes large landowners didn't even know that people had started living on portions of their property until new claims were filed in court. Thus, landed families were often forced to procure documentation or hire attorneys and surveyors to draw up new titles. Tejano landowners could win these disputes in court but still lose chunks of land because they often paid for legal services by parceling out a section of the very same land under question. Therefore, even an illegitimate dispute could cost a landowner acreage.[18]

Second, Tejano families lost a great deal of land in tax sales. With changes in government, newly elected officials used revised property assessments to impose exorbitant tax rates on landowners. A bad harvest or mismanaged funds could force a family to sell property just to meet these new tax obligations. Failure to pay these property taxes could lead to the foreclosure of property, which was then auctioned off at sheriffs' sales, where foreclosed land was commonly bought by Anglos for prices far below the assessed value. It is impossible to measure the full extent of premeditation and fraud involved in these processes, but the Anglo judges, sheriffs, and tax collectors who controlled this system were clearly well positioned for grift.[19]

Third, the death of a Tejano landowner exposed family property to repossession during the complex legal process of probate. Probate proceedings required families to have Anglo attorneys familiar with American laws. In this role, these lawyers were paid to oversee estate administration, which involved assessing the value of the estate, settling the estate's debts, and then distributing the estate among beneficiaries. This exposed intergenerational familial wealth to a variety of means by which a family could be defrauded, including unexpected charges of taxes, court fees, or attorney fees—which could also be settled with land transfers. The other problem was that many of these traditional families did not possess a notarized last will and testament. Even if they did, the authenticity of such a document was vulnerable to legal challenge if it had not been filed in an American court. Many long-standing Tejano families were unfamiliar with the probate system and thus unprepared to protect their own property when passing it to an heir. "Thus," writes historian David Montejano, "when a money-poor clan lost its patriarch, it usually lost its inheritance." And that inheritance was often land.[20]

Fourth, market forces and new competitors also played a role. The new growers entering the marketplace weren't merely just yeoman farmers. Many of the new competitors were large transnational corporations funded by English and American investors. These corporations had access to seasoned attorneys and capital, which enabled them to buy out smaller farmers and invest in advanced farming techniques that improved crop production. Small farmers, be they Tejano or white, simply didn't have the same access to investment capital to compete with international conglomerates who drove down the prices of commodities. Some family farmers could borrow capital to improve their productivity, but these loans left them exposed to recessions. Large agribusiness firms bought land from both Anglo and Tejano farmers, but during economic downturns, Tejano farmers sold roughly twice the acreage of their white counterparts.[21]

All told, these methods of land redistribution were legal. As one Texas historian has snidely argued, "the hacendado class, as a class, was stripped of property perfectly legally, according to the highest traditions of U.S. law." Of course, there were also extralegal means, including threats or violence. "If the owner won't sell," went one popular saying at the time, "his widow will." Whatever method was employed, the combined result was the transfer of hundreds of thousands of acres of land from Tejano to Anglo ownership. As one of the Benavides brothers griped, "those who came to the land after its annexation . . . robbed the old pioneers of their hard-earned homes."[22]

Nicholas Benavides and his brothers tried to hold onto as much of their property as possible. White settlers had begun to establish homesteads on their land, and Nicholas fought in the courts to secure his lost property. He also filed a new land claim with the Texas legislature to protect his original holdings. Desperate, he took whatever action he could to reclaim his property. At one point, he paid squatters $215 just to vacate a parcel of his land on which they were illegally residing. But Nicholas and his brothers were ultimately helpless against the tidal wave of land-hungry Anglo settlers eager to answer the call to make Texas more white.[23]

The Benavides family lost their land in Victoria not through a single dramatic swindle but rather by way of a series of transactions that chipped away at their holdings. Between March of 1853 and December of 1860, the family was engaged in six separate transfers in which nearly 1,200 acres of their land was deeded to new owners. In every single transfer, the recipient of Benavides land was Anglo.[24]

In 1862, Nicholas Benavides packed up his family and left Victoria for good, moving more than two hundred miles south to the border county of Hidalgo. Nicholas died soon after the move, leaving control of the family property to his oldest son, Eugenio. The second son was named Nicholas like his father. In 1868, a Hidalgo County tax assessment listed Eugenio's property as including 4,428 acres of land, 93 horses, and 312 cattle—valued together at $3,114. Two years later, census records reported Eugenio's net worth to be $3,900. Having fled Victoria during an oncoming tide of racism and displacement, Eugenio and his siblings had reestablished themselves as successful ranchers in Hidalgo County.[25]

But the same forces of displacement stalked the Benavides family to the border. Tax sales, property disputes, and complex legal proceedings—the same processes that had cost Tejano families land in Victoria a generation earlier—reshaped the demographics of property owners in Hidalgo County. In 1852, the percentage of land owned by Tejano families was 83.5 percent. By 1900, that figure had dropped to a mere 29 percent.[26]

Most of the land transactions of the era were relatively small, but several examples of questionable land acquisitions stood out. One Anglo sheriff in Hidalgo County auctioned off seven thousand acres of repossessed land over a two-year stretch for an absurdly low amount of $32.15. In 1877, another Hidalgo County sheriff auctioned three thousand acres for $17.15. Yet a third used his position to acquire sixty thousand acres of land between 1890 and 1900. One wealthy Anglo rancher operating in Hidalgo and Cameron Counties was able to acquire roughly four hundred thousand acres. A historian who examined all land transactions in Hidalgo County between 1848 and 1900 found that every tract of land sold by a family with a Hispanic surname was purchased by buyers with Anglo surnames.[27]

Like other Tejanos, the Benavides family struggled to hold their land in Hidalgo County. That border region in those days was a frontier, often unstable and filled with violence. Cattle thieves and small posses routinely harassed ranching families on both sides of the border, and there was at least one report of Eugenio fighting off "a band of Mexican cattle thieves." It was also a place of rapid Anglo migration, with waves of eager Americans pouring into South Texas looking for land.[28]

In the 1870s, the Benavides family began dispensing their acreage through multiple property transfers. These transactions are not well-documented because the property records from that era in Hidalgo County are incomplete. Some of the legal documents, especially those concerning tax sales, are illegible or lost. But it's clear that the Benavides family faced any number of potential pressures—tax sales, fraud, market-based downturns, or even violence—that could have coerced them to sell. At least one of their major transactions is well-documented. In 1876, the Benavides family sold over one thousand acres to a man named Thaddeus Rhodes for only $50.[29]

Thaddeus Rhodes arrived in Texas from North Carolina in 1846, the year after the Lone Star State was admitted into the United States. He initially settled in Brownsville before moving to Hidalgo upon the formation of the county in 1852. Having run a small business in Brownsville, Rhodes managed to secure the position as Hidalgo's first county clerk. He went on to enjoy a long career as an administrator in Hidalgo County, later becoming a commissioner, postmaster, and judge before retiring in 1890. Rhodes also started his own cattle ranch.[30]

For nearly forty years, Rhodes played a major role in the legal proceedings of Hidalgo County. As an official of the state, he worked closely with the tax assessors and sheriffs who largely controlled local property transactions. According to an 1873 investigation, he was notorious for his involvement in sheriff's auctions, particularly those where Tejano property was sold at low prices to Anglos. His name is all over records from the era. He made legal judgments in probate cases and land disputes, and he served as executor of the estates of several Tejano families. He was also rumored to have housed a "band of robbers," wrote one commentator, who lived on his ranch under his protection and harassed and stole from other cattlemen. Rhodes's role as a local clerk and judge put him in a prime position to expand his own landholdings. By 1880, his ranch had grown to seventeen thousand acres, most of it acquired by way of tax sale auctions and various purchases from Tejano families.[31]

That same year, the Benavides family did not appear in the local tax rolls. The records are incomplete, but the end result is clear. After

1880, the Benavides family owned no land in Hidalgo County, despite having held more than four thousand acres just twelve years before. From Victoria to Hidalgo, this family of Texas landowners had lost the bulk of their holdings within two generations. Their offspring drifted across the region's farms, looking for new places to live and work in the absence of a permanent home of their own.

In another reality, perhaps this family of Texas pioneers would be remembered alongside some of the legendary figures of the Texas Revolution, such as Austin or Houston, and their ancestors would have built enormous ranches on land they'd owned since before Texas shook free of Mexico. For many American families, wealth and power comes from time on the land. But the Benavides family never had such an opportunity to plant deep roots. As it was, this family who might have otherwise been Texas royalty was scattered to the winds of the prairie.

SALVADOR BENAVIDEZ SR.—THE SON OF THE SECOND NICHOLAS and the third generation of his family to live in Texas—was born near the Mexican border in 1880. Much of his youth was spent working on different ranches across Texas. At about the age of twenty, he took a job in DeWitt County, adjacent to Victoria County, where his ancestors owned land nearly forty years before. It would take Salvador another twenty years to become a landowner himself.

Soon after Salvador Benavidez moved to DeWitt County, he met a young woman named Ysabel Cisneros, the daughter of an immigrant farming family. They were both twenty years old when they wed on December 2, 1900. Salvador and Ysabel's first child was born on April 22, 1902. They named him Nicholas, like his grandfather and great-grandfather. Seven more children followed. The fifth, Salvador Benavidez Jr.—Roy's father—was born on October 11, 1911.[32]

DeWitt County was settled by land grant recipients in the 1820s, but its modern economic foundations were truly laid in the cattle drive craze of the 1860s and 1870s. As legend has it, in 1866, a DeWitt County rancher named Crockett Cardwell amassed some 1,800 head of cattle and hired experienced frontiersmen to guide the cows north along an old Shawnee hunting trail to St. Joseph, Missouri, the nation's westernmost major railhead at the start of the Civil War. If the cattle could reach St. Joseph, then they could be loaded onto railroad cars and shipped to the great metropolises of the Northeast, where millions of hungry citizens awaited the beef.[33]

The gamble paid off. Word of that first expedition spread quickly and inspired scores of similar cattle drives. In 1866 alone, cowboys drove more than 250,000 cattle from Texas to the Great Plains. In the years to come, millions more cattle would journey from Texas to Kansas, Colorado, and Missouri along now-legendary cattle trails such as the Western, the Shawnee, the Goodnight-Loving, and the Chisholm. That mythical era lasted only a few short years before the coming of railroads made the drives obsolete.[34]

DeWitt's first tracks were laid in 1873, part of a boom that saw Texas railroad mileage grow from five hundred to 11,300 between 1860 and 1890. The tracks created fresh opportunities in DeWitt that attracted thousands of new residents. From just over 6,400 people in 1870, the county's population grew to 21,311 by 1900. Many of these new arrivals were European immigrants. In the early 1900s, about half of DeWitt County's non-Black residents were either immigrants themselves or the child of at least one foreign-born parent.[35]

Texas, with its open ranges and vast acreage, attracted hundreds of thousands of European immigrants who wanted to try their luck at farming and ranching. The Lone Star State never matched the high immigration levels of northern states such as

New York or Illinois, but Texas by the turn of the century had by
far the highest rate of foreign-born residents of any state in the
South.[36]

DeWitt was largely populated by Germans. The immigrants
maintained many of their traditions and named new settlements
after German towns and people—Hochheim, Nordheim, West-
hoff, Lindenau—but their way of living became distinctly Texan.
Whatever jobs they had held in Germany, in DeWitt they became farmers and ranchers. Almost everyone in the county was
connected to the land. Cows outnumbered people, and chickens
and turkeys outnumbered cows. The farmers grew mostly corn
and cotton, and they sold eggs, milk, butter, and meat.[37]

To run their farms, DeWitt's immigrant ranchers sought experienced laborers. With few machines yet available, they recruited poor people who did not own land. Farmworkers could
be of any race, but at that time an increasing number of Texas
landowners preferred Latinos as agricultural laborers. The state's
poor white and Black residents fell out of favor with some ranchers who believed them to be either "lazy, thriftless, and unreliable," as one DeWitt County planter described Black workers, or
too demanding of higher wages and better living conditions in
the case of white workers. One white landowner in East Texas
explained that white sharecroppers, "being of the same race and
breed," might expect "equal right with you, but the Mexican
understands that he is to do what you tell him." "The whites,"
explained another planter, "want screened houses, toilets, bed
springs, a table and a stove. The Mexican asks only [for] wood
and water." Another Texas farmer went so far as to claim that the
Latino body was "specifically fitted for the burdensome task of
bending his back to picking the cotton and the burdensome task
of grubbing the fields."[38]

Salvador and Ysabel Benavidez were among the Hispanic
farmworkers of DeWitt County. They worked as sharecroppers,

meaning they lived and worked on a section of a landowner's property in exchange for a share of the crop. Such arrangements were common across the American South. They were exploitative, almost always favoring the landowner. Because sharecropping families were poor, they often had to borrow from landowners or local merchants to obtain the supplies needed to start planting. After starting their tenancies deeply in debt, tenant farmers often struggled to fulfill their annual obligation to the landowners. Things were tight even in a good year. Bad years could prove to be disastrous. Any number of misfortunes—droughts, insects, or the whims of commodities markets—could spin vulnerable sharecropping families into deep pits of indebtedness that could take years to escape. And powerful planters typically controlled local processing mills, mercantile stores, and the courts, using the economic and legal structures of their society to further cheat tenants by altering weight scales or paying off judges.[39]

By the time Salvador Benavidez Jr. was born in 1911, more than half of DeWitt County's 2,746 farms were operated by tenant farmers, almost all of whom were engaging in growing cotton or corn, or raising livestock. The Benavidez family lived just northwest of the county seat at Cuero, out on the wide-open rolling hills. Poor sharecropping families like Salvador's usually lived in wooden shacks without electricity or indoor plumbing.[40]

Most farmwork revolved around the cotton harvest. In DeWitt County, cotton is planted in early spring and harvested in September and October. Everyone in sharecropping families worked in the fields. Kids couldn't drive the plows, but they could drop seeds. And everybody could pick cotton. Picking was a communal effort, involving all ages and genders. In fact, *most* Texas cotton at that time was picked by women and children. One of Salvador's relatives who grew up picking cotton remembered, "We used to pick cotton when we were old enough to walk down to the cotton field, make little piles, . . . three or four years old."[41]

When the cotton bolls were not in bloom, Latino families living on the East Texas prairie spent their working hours tending gardens, overseeing livestock, and completing the endless array of chores needed to maintain their farms. For young boys like Salvador Jr., their work included collecting eggs and milking cows. Many families also raised sheep, meaning that the younger boys would also have helped clean and shear the sheep for their wool.

The lives of Hispanic farmworkers were also deeply affected by race. Race, after all, was the reason many of them were so poor in the first place. And their daily experiences were contaminated by racial prejudice. Anti-Latino racial discrimination was part of the broader system of Jim Crow that separated white and Black people in the rest of the American South, but it was a little bit different than Black-white racial segregation. In many ways, anti-Latino racism was more complex, as the racial boundaries could be a bit more fluid. People of Mexican descent were usually legally classified as "White," but visibly darker skin and language discrimination left them susceptible to racial prejudice and disadvantage.

Like the Benavidez family, many Hispanics had been living in Texas for generations. But the decline of the Tejano upper class—characterized by the loss of land in the late nineteenth century—cast its descendants into a life of farm labor. In the eyes of many Anglos, this made them no different than Mexican immigrants. Some older white Texans understood a distinction between old Tejano families and new Mexican immigrants, but newcomers tended to group together all Hispanics based on surnames or the visible appearance of skin color. A Tejano family who had lived in Texas for over a century could face racial discrimination and xenophobia from white settlers who had only been in Texas a few years.[42]

Unlike Black residents, Hispanics in Texas were often able to attend the same churches or even schools as white citizens. But they faced severe discrimination in public accommodations and housing. This could vary by locale. In some places, Latinos might be able to attend school with white children but not allowed to sit next to them in the movie theater. In others, the arrangements could be reversed. It was also common for housing covenants to prohibit the sale or rental of a property to any "Mexican or person of Negro blood." People passed through the sometimes fluid color barrier, and some Latinos did very well for themselves. But generally speaking, the laws and culture of Texas prevented Hispanics from equal access to education and jobs, the traditional mechanisms of social uplift in America. They were rendered into a lower class and blocked from the greatest promises of society.[43]

Public discrimination was backed by violence. One need not look far from Cuero for large demonstrations of racialized intimidation. In 1923, the *Cuero Record* observed a "Massive KKK [Ku Klux Klan] initiation that was held in the road between Yoakum and Cuero," just a few miles from where the Benavidez family lived. The Klan grew across Texas in the 1920s, its statewide membership reaching an estimated one hundred thousand. Dallas was said to have the highest per capita Klan membership of any city in the United States. One historian has called Texas in 1924 "the number one Klan state politically."[44]

It was against the backdrop of these conditions that Salvador and Ysabel Benavidez welcomed eight children between 1902 and 1918. Their opportunities were constricted by racism and poverty, but their lives were also bound by love and the inner happiness of their family. Salvador and Ysabel impressed a great sense of familial duty upon their children. Their family was incredibly close, and they cared deeply for one another, forging bonds that became essential for the survival of their children as death began to reshape their lives.

In the fall of 1918, a global influenza pandemic brought great tragedy to the Benavidez family. That November, Ysabel contracted the flu. She died on November 16, 1918, just nine days after giving birth to a baby girl. Ysabel was only thirty-five years old when she passed away, one of about 2,100 Texans and 675,000 American citizens who lost their lives to the great influenza pandemic between 1918 and 1920. Ysabel's untimely death left her eight children, ranging in age from sixteen years to nine days, without a mother. It is somewhat miraculous that she was the only one in her immediate family who died from the virus. Yet, the flu did claim the lives of Salvador's brother and his sister-in-law, who perished within three weeks of Ysabel's death.[45]

A year and a day after Ysabel's death, Salvador married her older sister, Angelita, who was eight years older than Salvador. Their marriage appears to have been one of familial duty. Salvador and Ysabel's eight children needed a mother, and Angelita was unmarried and living nearby. She was forty-seven when she formally joined the family, replacing her lost sister as Salvador's wife and the children's mother. Angelita, who never bore children of her own, raised her sister's kids. She and Salvador also adopted their three orphaned nephews.[46]

Salvador Benavidez Jr. was just seven years old when his mother died. But he was nevertheless surrounded by a big, loving family. His father and adopted mother did manage to achieve some measure of success. In 1920, after nearly twenty years of farm labor, his father acquired 1.25 acres of land on which they lived and farmed. It had taken more than forty years for that branch of the Benavidez family to again become landowners, although the single acre was a far cry from the vast four-thousand-acre ranch their family once held.[47]

Salvador Jr. spent his youth living and working on farms around DeWitt County. His early days were filled with picking cotton, milking cows, and managing the herds. On most days, when the work was done, there wasn't much else to do on the farms but eat, sing, and tell stories under the bright stars of the open prairie. Families like his grew their own food and lived together in large extended communities, gathering to eat meals of huevos rancheros, frijoles, burritos, chilaquiles, enchiladas, and tamales. In the evenings, the workers sang songs about farm life and love affairs—"canciones rancheras" and "canciones románticas"—or ballads known as "corridos" that told stories of heroes from the past. Sometimes, the singers would be accompanied by guitars or accordions. One writer who toured Texas in the 1930s recalled a night scene at one of those ranches. "The hour of 2 A.M. is magic," the author described. "Cowbells softly tintling, crickets softly playing, frogs in the river cheeping and croaking, workmen's voices raised in happy songs of Mexico." In his youth, Salvador learned the old ranching songs from the men who worked around him. He also grew up hearing tales of his ancestors, the tough fighters and cowboys who helped Texas win its independence and worked on its legendary ranches.[48]

As Salvador Jr. aged into adolescence, he encountered other youths at Our Lady of Guadalupe in Cuero, the county's first Catholic church built for Hispanics. Salvador also had time to socialize during occasional trips into town or time spent lounging and fishing in the nearby Guadalupe River. The young ranch hands of rural DeWitt County would also gather at the trading posts and picnic shelters that dotted the countryside. The Benavidez family lived near a little spot called Mustang Mott, which was named after a grove where wild horses once ran. Mustang Mott had a small grocery store where one could buy a cold beer. Farmworkers gathered there to purchase supplies and to drink and gab over games of dominoes. Local youths also congregated at the dance halls and rifle clubs established by German immigrants in the small villages of Nordheim and Lindenau.[49]

It was during one such night in 1934 that Salvador Jr. met Teresa Perez at the Lindenau Rifle Club. That evening, the pair sang and danced, chatting and laughing with their friends and families. A spark was lit, and love soon followed. Eventually, they decided to marry. But their plans met a brief obstacle when Salvador's family expressed reservations over a particular aspect of Teresa's heritage.[50]

Teresa Perez had been born in Monclova, Mexico, on July 12, 1911, and arrived in Texas with relatives as a child. She was a descendent of Yaqui Indians, whose homeland is in the northwestern part of modern-day Mexico. Many details of Teresa's life are difficult to pin down, but her Yaqui ancestral identity was essential, as it later played an important role in her son's personal identity. "My heritage," Roy later wrote, "is Mexican and Yaqui Indian." In reconstructing that heritage, Roy emphasized the legendary ferocity of Yaqui Indians. They were the people, he wrote, who "had killed and eaten whole armies of Aztec and Toltec" and who Hernán Cortés "wisely chose to avoid" while "conquering most of Mexico." This identity would prove crucial throughout Roy's life. It was the most important aspect of an otherwise tenuous connection with his mother's people. That ancestry was also the reason why his parents almost didn't marry.[51]

Teresa's background is much murkier than Salvador's, largely because she moved from Mexico without her biological parents. She first appears in a mysterious entry in the United States Census records in 1920. The document lists a young Teresa living with a sixty-year-old woman named "Nicolosia" who is recorded as her "mother." But that woman was not Teresa's mother. Teresa's mother's name was Eusebia Ortiz, and it does not appear that she nor Teresa's father, Agapito, ever lived in the United States. The 1920 census also lists a boy named Manuel as Teresa's brother. That much is accurate. Manuel was her brother. In the next census, taken in 1930, Teresa and Manuel were living in Cuero with their older brothers, Sisto and Martin. Four years later, she met Salvador Benavidez Jr. at the Lindenau Rifle Club.[52]

According to Roy, Teresa's Yaqui background created some apprehension among Salvador Jr.'s family. "Because of my mother's background," he wrote, "the Benavidez family's reaction to my father's announcement that he intended to marry my mother was severe." Salvador Sr. "could hardly have been more shocked," Roy suggested, "if his son had announced his intentions to marry one of the daughters of the German settlers." But these initial concerns were not enough to break the bond of young love that united Roy's parents. Their romance persevered and the couple planned to wed.[53]

Salvador and Teresa were married at Our Lady of Guadalupe on Sunday, October 7, 1934. They began their lives together during the middle of the Great Depression. Cotton and oil prices in Texas had crashed along with the stock market. To the north, millions of acres of topsoil were blown away by massive dust storms during one of the worst ecological disasters in North American history. For Texans, the average per capita income declined from $476 in 1929 to $290 in 1934 (over $8,000 and $4,800 today, respectively). Hispanic sharecroppers were among

Salvador and Teresa Benavidez on their wedding day, October 7, 1934. Courtesy of the Benavidez family.

the most vulnerable and poverty-stricken groups. Nevertheless, Salvador and Teresa were also the progeny of resilient families who had survived decades of challenges, and they charged ahead with their plans, hoping for better days to come.[54]

The newlyweds left their relatives' homes and started off on their own, working as sharecroppers on a plot of land not far from Salvador's parents. They lived in a little unpainted wooden house with a side garden, where they grew vegetables and raised chickens. Salvador milked their cow, and Teresa churned its milk into butter. Those first months of marriage must have been exciting. The dreams of young lovers present a horizon's worth of possibilities, be they rich or poor, Hispanic or white.[55]

Roy Benavidez was born on August 5, 1935. Salvador and Teresa named their first son Raul Perez Benavidez, but for most of his life the boy went by Roy. Baby Roy was baptized at Our Lady of Guadalupe on November 3, 1935. A second son, Rogelio, arrived soon after on September 1, 1936. Salvador, Teresa, and their boys were at the dawn of their lives together when Salvador suddenly became very sick.[56]

In December of 1936, Salvador Benavidez Jr. was diagnosed with tuberculosis. The doctor who examined him estimated that he had been sick for about a year. His family concluded that he had contracted the disease by drinking spoiled milk, a culprit as likely as any other. Tuberculosis was particularly dangerous for Latinos living in Texas, who as late as the 1940s died at roughly seven times the rate as their white counterparts.[57]

By the time Salvador saw the doctor, he had lost thirty pounds from his 152-pound frame, leaving an already lanky man looking drastically malnourished. In addition to weight loss, other symptoms of tuberculosis include coughing, chest pain, and fever. The doctor recommended that Salvador be sent to the Texas State Tuberculosis Sanatorium, a large state-run facility located about three hundred miles northwest of DeWitt County. Salvador was admitted without payment because he owned nothing. The county and the state would cover his fees. But his physician was not optimistic. The doctor observed "extensive" infection in both lungs and offered a final prognosis of "not good."[58]

Created in 1911, the Texas State Tuberculosis Sanatorium was a self-sustaining facility that operated on a large, isolated campus in Tom Green County. It had the capacity to treat more than one thousand patients at a time, most of whom remained in residence for about nine months. At the sanatorium, hospital officials promised that with plenty of rest, good food, light exercise, and regular lectures about how to manage their condition, patients would recover.[59]

Thankfully, Salvador survived and returned home to his wife and young children. But he never fully beat the disease. Just fourteen months after his initial diagnosis, Salvador was rediagnosed with tuberculosis. The family once again fingered bad milk as the culprit, but he had never actually been cured, meaning he had lived with the disease for about three years. This time, the same doctor noted that he "probably could recover" because of "good institutional care." Salvador returned to the sanatorium in February of 1938.[60]

Salvador completed his stay and returned home, but it was not long before he became very ill yet again. Roy, just shy of three years old at the time, claimed to remember an episode of his father's illness. He recalled his Aunt Isabel coming to their home to help care for him and his brother. "She rocked us," he recalled, "to try to make us feel secure while mysterious events were taking place."[61]

Salvador Benavidez Jr. died of tuberculosis on November 7, 1938, at the age of twenty-seven. His family buried him that same day in a small, sparsely marked cemetery on the grounds of a ranch where they worked. Salvador and Teresa had been married for just over four years, their promising life together cut tragically short. Salvador's sons, only two and three years old, would barely remember their father.[62]

CHAPTER 2
FIELDS

Teresa Benavidez was twenty-seven years old when her husband died in 1938. She decided to move her small family into Cuero where she could look for a job to support her boys. A village of about 5,500 residents, Cuero was described by one local author as "a quiet, sleepy little town." The city was led by a handful of wealthy residents who owned ranches in the countryside and lived in stately homes in the center of town. Nearly everyone else lived in small, one-story wooden houses scattered about the city. Cuero had a quaint downtown that wrapped around the DeWitt County Courthouse, the city's most impressive structure. Built in the 1890s, the three-story courthouse is made of light brown sandstone bricks and adorned with red sandstone trimmings, polished granite steps, and a clock tower that "gives the entire building an air of stateliness and dignity," as one local resident bragged. Along with some cotton compresses and stockyards, the rest of Cuero consisted of a handful of churches, grocery stores, and small shops.[1]

Cuero's one claim to fame was its internationally recognized "Turkey Trot." This annual event started in 1912 when city officials hatched a plan to celebrate the beginning of poultry season. That autumn, a group of business leaders in the local Commercial Club called for nearby farmers to bring their turkeys to market at the same time. The farmer who drove the most turkeys was promised a one-hundred-dollar prize. City leaders encouraged store owners to design festive floats to parade behind the procession of birds. The Commercial Club also planned a carnival and concert, and they even invited the governor. That November, Texas governor Oscar B. Colquitt led a brass band and a legion of turkeys through the streets of downtown Cuero to the packing plant, where they were slaughtered and dressed for sale. Locals were thrilled with the event, and their visiting guests were impressed. The *Austin Statesman* called the inaugural trot "One of the most spectacular and peculiar civic festivals ever held on this continent."[2]

The annual tradition quickly grew from a single parade to an entire "Turkeyfest weekend," complete with a pageant, marching bands, carnival, dance, rodeo, and football game. In later years, it was estimated that as many as fifteen thousand turkeys trotted through the streets of Cuero during the celebration. Tens of thousands of people would pack the sidewalks to watch the procession, pitilessly munching on turkey sandwiches while cheering on the birds. Locals took great pride in the ceremony. "We want to impress the fact that the birds really strut," emphasized a Cuero reporter. Turkeys considered "too valuable to march" rode to their deaths on festooned floats. Cuero earned the moniker "Turkey capital of the world," and DeWitt County emerged as the leading producer of turkeys in the state of Texas.[3]

Other than the Turkey Trot, not much else of great consequence happened in Cuero. It was the type of place where the rumored sighting of a mountain lion on the outskirts of town

could generate front-page news for days. Most local develop-
ments were guided by civic organizations such as the Chamber of
Commerce and the Rotary Club. By the late 1930s, these groups
were spending the bulk of their time scheming proposals to access public funding programs made available through President
Franklin Roosevelt's New Deal.[4]

The odds were stacked against Teresa and her boys. A widowed immigrant, Teresa had little education and spoke very
poor English. She couldn't count on much help from the outside
world. Most of the relief programs offered by the New Deal of
the 1930s were not meant for women like Teresa. She was among
the group of single mothers who were "pitied but not entitled," as
one historian called them—poor service workers excluded from
the vast catalogue of benefits provided by the federal government
during the Great Depression.[5]

Teresa took a job as a domestic worker. Many non-white
women were trapped in such jobs because they were essentially
barred from other blue-collar work, either by gender or race.
Other employers wouldn't hire them. At that time, most domestic workers in Texas earned less than $200 per year. And the job
didn't come with any benefits or security. Women who worked
in agriculture or domestic jobs were intentionally excluded from
Social Security legislation so that wealthy Southerners could
maintain access to a cheap labor force. And Teresa was an immigrant, meaning that she had lesser access to state-level benefits,
never mind the fact that her boys were fifth-generation Texans.
Besides perhaps her church and her working-class brothers, Teresa and her boys had no support—they were on their own.[6]

Soon after moving to Cuero, Teresa began a love affair with
a man named Pablo Chavez, a widower who had lost his wife
in 1937. Chavez was about ten years older than Teresa and held
a steady job at the local cotton gin. Their romance seemed like
a natural fit, uniting two widowed Catholic Latinos in a small

community. The courtship led to a pregnancy, which prompted a swift marriage in September of 1940.[7]

Roy was five years old when his mother remarried. With Teresa increasingly occupied by her work and new husband, Roy began to experience life beyond the confines of his family home. "I found a world," he remembered, "that offered a small boy a bounty of opportunities for adventure." One of Roy's fondest memories of those days was spending time at the home of his neighbor Lula Jackson, a Black woman who sometimes babysat Roy and his brother Rogelio. Jackson would feed the boys and entertain them with stories from her life. Roy described her as "a big, warmhearted black woman who cooked the best beans and corn bread I've ever tasted." Roy and Rogelio tagged along with Jackson to small gatherings of local Black residents who came together in cooling evening temperatures to talk, eat, and sing. Lula Jackson was the first Black person Roy ever really knew, and he later credited her for helping him gain an appreciation for people of another race.[8]

Roy had fun running around Cuero. He remembered seeing the Turkey Trots as a boy. "The square around the old stone courthouse would be lined with the pickup trucks and Model-T Fords," he recalled. For him, the most vivid memories of the Turkey Trot were not of the carnival nor the parade but rather the trail of feces left behind by the birds. Roy later called it "their revenge on the town," remembering, "turkey excrement stinks as bad as any filth I encountered as a soldier in foreign countries."[9]

The young boy also loved playing in the cotton mill where his stepfather worked. It was close to his home, and Roy and some of his friends would sneak over to climb into the loft and jump onto leftover piles of cotton. World War II began when Roy was six years old, and he and his friends imagined themselves jumping out of planes, just like the paratroopers they saw in newsreels at the movie theatre. Roy later wondered if those loft jumps "were some kind of prophecy of my fate."[10]

In the fall that Roy's mother remarried, he also started attending school to learn English. Like many Latino children, the five-year-old had grown up in a Spanish-speaking household. Teresa never had an opportunity to learn English herself and wanted to ensure that her son could speak the language of his native land, especially as he prepared to enter grade school the following year.[11]

At school, Roy loved to entertain his friends by playing pranks on other classmates. He had a mischievous side, seemingly from birth. The young boy was full of energy and had a difficult time sitting still. This childish vigor led to his first bout with trouble. One day, Roy and a classmate had the idea to stick a long blade of grass through cracks in the outhouse to tickle the bare butts of their female classmates. The boys had a good laugh, but the mischief also earned Roy a whipping from his teacher. "[She] made me wish I'd found another form of entertainment," he recalled.[12]

The following year, Roy enrolled at St. Michael's Catholic School in downtown Cuero. St. Michael's, the city's Catholic church for white residents, was housed in a two-story, white-painted, wood-frame building. Black kids could not attend St. Michael's, but Hispanic and white students learned there together. The school was crowded and hot, with eight grades packed into three classrooms. Nuns lived next door and ran the school. Students spent their days sitting attentively in front of blackboards and enjoying long recess periods. Roy didn't say much about his memories from St. Michael's, only that he "found ways to annoy the nuns" and that he could "still feel the redhot pain that came when they twisted my ears."[13]

At St. Michael's, Roy dutifully learned the three R's—reading, writing, and arithmetic—but outside of school he encountered a fourth: Race. Roy began to learn about race through personal experiences with exclusion. The little boy liked movies, and he'd often complete small jobs for neighbors to earn a few cents to buy a ticket. But kids who looked like Roy couldn't just sit any-where in the movie theatre. When Roy purchased his ticket, he was directed upstairs to the balcony for "Mexicans." He wanted to be closer to the screen. On occasion, the energetic little boy managed to sneak past the attendant to sit in the white section, but he was usually spotted by the ushers who told him to move to the balcony. "Okay, muchacho, get up," Roy remembered the attendant saying. "Go on upstairs where you belong."[14]

There is no healthy way for a young child to digest these types of humiliating experiences. Roy's early trials with race would stay with him the rest of his life. It wasn't just the movie theater, it was restaurants and stores, too. There were all sorts of rules dictating where he could and could not go. As a child learn-ing about segregation, he began to become very embittered and started developing a hostility toward the white kids whose priv-ileges he desired. "I resented—and envied—the white kids who had new shoes or who could afford to buy an ice cream cone," he explained. "I was a spic, a tamale-eater, a greaser; nothing more—except angry."[15]

Around the same time that Roy began school, he also started to work. He didn't hold a formal job; he was much too young for that. But Roy found ways to earn extra money to purchase snacks and movie tickets. He hung around downtown Cuero to pick up odd jobs. Adults would give him a few coins for running errands or completing chores. He also started collecting empty soda bot-tles to exchange for pennies. Sometimes, the owner of the small convenience store where he made the exchanges would offer him a bonus in the form of an apple or banana.[16]

By age seven, Roy was regularly looking for work at the local stockyards. The men who managed the animal pens would pay the enterprising kid a few pennies "for running errands or clean-ing up," Roy recalled. He watered the cows and mucked out stalls, meaning he used a shovel or pitchfork to scoop out piles of hay, feed, and dung. It's no dream job, but it's not a bad gig for a kid. One can get used to the smell, and the work was a bit more reliable than looking for empty bottles on the roadside. Roy also helped load cow manure onto the trucks of people who came to buy fertilizer.[17]

There was one story from the stockyards that Roy was fond of telling. He was seven at the time, lingering near the cow pens in the hope of finding a quick job. A cowboy walked over and promised Roy a quarter if the boy would run into the cow pen and grab one of the bulls by its testicles. An angry bull can kill a grown man, let alone a boy. But a quarter was a lot of money for a kid who normally worked for pennies. Roy accepted the challenge. As a crowd of cowboys leaned against a fence, he scrambled underneath a post and crept behind an unsuspecting bull. "I yanked the bag," Roy remembered, and he dashed back under the railing before the bull could identify the culprit.[18]

Roy received his quarter and earned compliments from the men. As he held that quarter, he began calculating the number of ice cream cones and movie tickets he could purchase. The cowboys congratulated him, saying he was "tough as a boot" and a "crazy little frijole," Roy recalled, as he swelled with pride. "The experience changed me," he remembered. "The way they looked at me meant more than the quarter."[19]

Roy's interactions with the cowboys helped expose him to the worlds of grown men. He was a resourceful little boy, gleaning notions of belonging and respect from the men just as easily as he scooped their coins. Had his dad lived, Roy would have learned these lessons from his father. Instead, he watched the cowboys, absorbing the things they said and learning the actions they valued as he stitched together lessons about male behavior from the most unwitting of teachers. Even as a child, he began to understand that others valued boldness and courage. Just seven years old, Roy was becoming a tough little kid, independent and enterprising, with a growing awareness of his race and place in society.

Roy's life soon took another dramatic turn. With little warning, he was sent to stay with his uncle Nicholas, the oldest brother of Roy's deceased father. Nicholas and his wife, Alexandria, lived with their seven children on a farm in Wharton County, about eighty miles east of Cuero. Roy did not seem to understand at the time that this move was intended to be permanent.[20]

In Great Depression–era Texas, it was quite common for children to change homes. These quasi-adoptions were even more frequent among farming families who could use the extra labor. In fact, just a generation before, Roy's grandfather had adopted the children of his own deceased brother. It's easy to understand why Roy's aunt and uncle might have welcomed their nephew into their family. Their entire family worked in the fields, and they could use the extra hands. Some landowners wouldn't even rent to childless families.[21]

It's more difficult to understand Teresa's motivations. Certainly, it was no easy task to raise children while working hard and struggling financially. But the other consideration, and the one great unknown, was Teresa's new husband, Pablo Chavez. Chavez left behind no record of his own, but the timing of his entrance into the lives of the Benavidez family suggests a correlation with Roy's exit. Pablo and Teresa were married in a civil ceremony in September of 1940. Teresa was pregnant at the time, as she had a daughter named Maria Guadalupe Chavez barely five months afterward. This marriage, however, was not convalidated in the Catholic Church until October of 1943, just prior to Maria's baptism. Roy was sent to live with Uncle Nicholas sometime between the birth and baptism of his baby sister.[22]

It's certainly possible that Pablo cared little for his new wife's sons or saw them as an inconvenience. Roy himself acknowledged that his childhood antics may have frayed his stepfather's nerves. But Roy never said much else about Pablo, despite speaking often about his childhood. His only observation in a 1995 memoir was, "My stepfather was not cruel to Rogelio and me, but neither did he pay us much attention."[23]

Uncle Nicholas and Aunt Alexandria were older than Roy's own parents. They had married in 1924, a decade before Salvador Benavidez Jr. met Teresa Perez at the Lindenau Rifle Club. Nicholas and Alexandria's oldest son, named Salvador like his uncle and grandfather, had tragically died of a staph infection in June of 1940 at the age of sixteen. At that time, the couple had seven other living children, five sons and two daughters, all under the age of sixteen.[24]

Roy was devastated about his move. The seven-year-old boy had lost his father at the age of three, and now he was being sent away from his mother and brother for reasons he could not have possibly understood. Nicholas and Alexandria were kind and generous, and they wanted their biological children to treat Roy as an equal member of the family. "Dad lined us up," remembered one son. "He said, 'Look this is the way it's going to be. I'll be the same to one as I am to all. No favoritism or nothing. . . . I'm going to treat y'all equally.' . . . And that's the way it was." But Roy had no idea what was happening. He was scared, and he missed his mother.[25]

Roy ran away. On at least two occasions, he fled his new home in search of his mother. The first time, he slipped out of the house and somehow made it all the way to Cuero, crossing an eighty-mile stretch of dirt roads, sprawling ranches, and thick patches of forest. He must have hitchhiked, as that is the only plausible explanation for how he could have successfully navigated such a distance. Uncle Nicholas realized that Roy must have gone in search of his mother and drove to Cuero, where he found Roy hiding under the porch of his old home. When Roy ran away a second time, Nicholas brought Rogelio with them, and the two boys were reunited in Uncle Nicholas's home in Wharton County.[26]

Wharton County is not all that far from DeWitt, but it sits in a different region of Texas. Unlike the rolling hills of DeWitt County, Wharton lies in a flat strip of land known as the Coastal Prairie. It is among the best places in North America to grow cotton. The climate is warm and humid, and its great expanses of flat farmlands are watered by a series of rivers and creeks.[27]

Uncle Nicholas and Aunt Alexandria lived in a rural section of Wharton County known as Danevang. Founded in the 1890s, Danevang was a farming community of Danish immigrants who came to Texas by way of Minnesota when representatives from their group struck a deal with the Scottish-owned Texas Land & Cattle Company to acquire about twenty-four thousand acres. The firm agreed to finance each transaction and sell the land only to members of this Danish community, thus ensuring that only a certain type of people could own land in that section of Texas. The settlers loaded their wagons and headed south to Wharton County where they founded Danevang, meaning "Danish Meadows."[28]

It's not completely clear why Roy's Uncle Nicholas and Aunt Alexandria left their native DeWitt County for Wharton, but the context of the 1930s farm economy offers some clues. In Texas, as in all of the Cotton Belt, federal policies inaugurated by the 1933 Agricultural Adjustment Act incentivized thousands of cotton farmers to evict sharecroppers. To counteract falling crop prices during the Great Depression, the federal government began making direct payments to landowners who agreed not to bring their cotton to market. The goal was to stabilize commodity prices by curtailing overproduction. By 1939, the federal government was paying Texas cotton growers nearly $50 million per year to leave fields unplanted. Many of the landowners receiving these subsidies no longer needed as much labor and thus began evicting tenant families who worked their land. Between 1930 and 1940, the number of tenants operating Texas farms declined from 301,660 to 204,462.[29]

In DeWitt County, cotton farmers reduced their production by half between 1934 and 1939. Wharton County farmers, on the other hand, increased the amount of cotton they produced, thereby increasing their need for farmworkers. Uncle Nicholas, who had grown up on a sharecropping farm in DeWitt, remained a sharecropper when he came to Wharton. His family lived on a wide-open prairie surrounded by cotton fields.[30]

The magnitude of Texas cotton might surprise some. When people think of the source of American cotton, they often tend to think of Deep South states like Mississippi, Alabama, and Georgia. These places once led the nation in cotton production, especially during the antebellum era. But Texas cotton caught up in the decades after the Civil War. With greater access to capital, labor, and land, Texas by 1890 surpassed Mississippi as the nation's leading cotton producer. A decade after achieving that benchmark, the Lone Star State was producing more cotton than Mississippi, Alabama, and Georgia *combined*. In 1900, Texas produced one-third of all cotton grown in the United States and one-fourth of all cotton in the world. Its dominance in the industry has only grown since. Cotton may not be king in Texas, but Texas is the king of cotton.[31]

Some Texas cotton farmers came to prefer Hispanic migrant laborers over sharecroppers because they provided similarly cheap labor without the same expectations as tenant farmers. Permanent farmworkers—even sharecroppers—might request housing, decent working conditions, or even schools. Migrants, on the other hand, just did the work and left. Plus, landowners could pay migrants less. Nomadic workers who travel great distances are desperate to earn cash and typically more willing to work in inferior conditions to recoup the time and money they already spent getting to the fields.[32]

In the early 1900s, the popularity of Latino migrant workers spread from Texas to other parts of the United States. Landowners from across America began to recruit these laborers from labor distribution centers in San Antonio. The city became, as one historian has noted, "a virtual Ellis Island for the tens of thousands of newcomers from Mexico." By the 1940s, large numbers of Mexican and Mexican American laborers were taking jobs in places as far from the border as Minnesota, Pennsylvania, and Colorado. Texas farmers, many of whom believed they had a "natural right" to Mexican labor, were so concerned by the possible loss of labor that they lobbied for the creation of special licenses and taxes that would restrict the activities of out-of-state labor agents. In some counties, an out-of-state recruiter was required to pay as much as $5,000 for a license and a tax of $2,500.[33]

When Roy joined Uncle Nicholas's family, he became one of an estimated one million migrant laborers operating at that time in the United States. The family worked plenty at home, but cotton work is seasonal and requires less than half a year's worth of actual working days. In the months that require less labor, tenant farmers could find work away from their own farms, especially if they were willing to travel.[34]

In the spring of 1944, Roy's adopted family left their homes and headed for the sugar beet fields of northeastern Colorado. The school-age kids were pulled out of classes before the academic year ended so that the family could make it in time for sugar beet season in April. They packed their truck and wagon full of housewares, "bedding, cooking vessels, and dishes," Roy remembered, and set off for Colorado, traversing over a thousand miles of dusty roads in a journey reminiscent of the Joad family in *The Grapes of Wrath*. This was before the construction of America's interstate highway system, when the winding byways weaving through the states were still slow and unreliable. One of the sons remembered the family traveling only "35, 40 miles an hour, because there was no highway." At night, they'd camp on the side of road, cooking their meals by fire and sleeping underneath the bright stars of the wide-open skies of West Texas and rural Colorado. The family was on their own, but they were not necessarily traveling alone. Thousands of other Hispanic migrants packed the roads as part of a mass migration from South Texas to Colorado's sugar beet fields.[35]

For decades, Colorado's Great Western Sugar Company had been recruiting Latino laborers directly from Texas and New Mexico. Hispanic workers were crucial to its production process. The company employed up to sixty full-time Spanish-speaking labor agents at a time, each charged with enticing laborers to work in the fields near one of its thirteen mills in Colorado. The Great Western Sugar Company produced handbills and posters and used door-to-door canvassing to recruit Texas laborers. They even had a little booklet describing pleasant working and living conditions in Colorado. In some Texas communities, the company would show short films depicting positive scenes of life in the fields. Workers who came to Colorado were contracted out at the Great Western Sugar Company's "Field Labor Distribution Center." At Fort Collins, the company built little "colonias" for workers they were trying to convince to stay permanently. Their need for labor single-handedly led to a rapid increase in the Latino population of Colorado, which by 1930 had nearly sixty thousand Latino residents.[36]

America's historic relationship with Hispanic labor is rife with contradictions. During the 1920s, the United States had passed new immigration laws—principally the Johnson-Reed

Immigration Act of 1924—that were designed to limit the number and types of immigrants allowed into the United States. Fueled by nativist sentiment, these laws capped the total number of immigrants who could enter the country each year and established a quota system based on the ratios of historical immigration from each country, thus allowing larger numbers of immigrants from places like Germany and England. This new legislation created the term "illegal alien" and enhanced immigration enforcement mechanisms, including the creation of the United States Border Patrol in 1924. But Mexican immigrants were exempt from numerical quotas because of the intense desire for Mexican labor.[37]

Things changed in the 1930s when the United States economy collapsed during the Great Depression. As millions of Americans faced financial destitution, nativist arguments combined with economic exigency and new federal farm policies to convince American immigration officials to ramp up efforts to deter and expel Mexican immigrants. With greater immigration enforcement mechanisms and a declining demand for foreign labor, large numbers of Mexicans and even American-born Hispanics were deported in the 1930s. This process of "repatriation," as it was called, resulted in the expulsion or departure of an estimated four hundred thousand Mexicans and Mexican Americans from the United States, including roughly 250,000 from Texas.[38]

The start of World War II sparked a renewed demand for labor. And so, the United States once again reversed course and scrambled to recruit more Hispanic workers. In 1942, the United States and Mexico signed the Mexican Farm Labor Program, commonly known as the Bracero Program. Under this agreement, the United States admitted more than 4.6 million Mexican laborers over the course of the next twenty-two years. These Braceros were promised housing, transportation, and minimum wages. They contracted directly with the federal government, meaning that taxpayers subsidized the labor costs of large agri-businesses. As one historian has observed of the Bracero Program, "The government functioned as a national labor contractor for southwestern growers at taxpayers' expense."[39]

Braceros not only filled a wartime labor shortage; their presence also created a labor surplus that undercut any potential demands for better working conditions among America's existing agricultural labor force, which is why many early Latino organizations opposed the program. And the Braceros were not the only workers coming from Mexico. By the late 1940s, an estimated five hundred thousand additional undocumented Mexican workers were crossing the border every year. Many joined the throng of Hispanic laborers who sought sugar beet work in the foothills of Colorado.[40]

Back in Roy's day, sugar beet cultivation was extremely labor intensive. Because they produce several plants from one seedpod, sugar beets need to be "thinned" regularly to prevent overcrowding. Teams of workers moved through the fields, "crawling and squatting," to remove excess growth. Thinning was incredibly time consuming. It could take an individual worker more than twenty hours to finish a single acre. And that doesn't even include the actual harvest, when workers move back through the fields, plucking full-grown beets out of the ground, lopping off their crowns with a sharp blade, and then tossing them into a pile or wagon. With Colorado farmers growing about 140,000 acres of sugar beets per year, they needed a lot of laborers. Every spring, the fields of northern Colorado filled with tens of thousands of Latino farmworkers working against the picturesque backdrop of the Rocky Mountains.[41]

Most migrant sugar beet laborers were paid piecemeal by the acre, an arrangement that favored growers who preferred to pay for completed work rather than hourly individual labor. The 1937

Sugar Act attempted to establish minimum wages for sugar beet workers, but even these were extremely low and only loosely enforced. Pay did improve during World War II, when sugar beet rates increased from an average of $22.48 to $35.13 per acre. A family's earnings were directly tied to its size. Larger families could usually complete more work and therefore earn a higher income. It's impossible to pinpoint exactly how much Roy's family earned, but in 1949, when conditions were a bit better than in 1944 (the year Roy arrived in Colorado with his aunt and uncle), the average migrant farm laborer earned about $550 a year.[42]

Life in the sugar beet migrant camps was rough. The workers labored from "'can see' to 'can't see,'" Roy explained, meaning sunup to sundown. They lived in little wooden shacks with few amenities. Roy's family brought their own supplies to avoid renting from employers who charged exorbitant prices for items such as dishes and bedding. Many of the rental units had dirt floors and only a couple small windows. Some didn't have stoves, electricity, or indoor plumbing. Dozens of people shared a single outdoor toilet. A doctor inspecting these housing conditions in northern Colorado concluded, "It's below the lowest possible standard of 30 or 40 years ago, let alone today's standard."[43]

Hispanic workers also faced rampant discrimination in Colorado towns. The state's farmers depended on the migrant laborers, but its white citizens typically didn't welcome these workers into local businesses or public schools. They prevented Mexican Americans from opening their own shops and desegregating residential neighborhoods. An organization named the Colorado State Vigilantes issued handbills in the 1930s that warned "all Mexican and other aliens to leave Colorado at once," and a Colorado branch of the Ku Klux Klan organized in the 1930s to intimidate Latinos with public marches and cross burnings.[44]

Nevertheless, Roy expressed some fondness for his time in Colorado. "I loved looking at the mountains off to the west," he recalled. "They were incredibly beautiful to a flatland kid from South Texas." The family also enjoyed a sense of community among the migrant workers. The farm laborers would gather to celebrate weddings and births, joining their temporary neighbors for large suppers of tortillas, meat, beans, peppers, and tamales. Roy warmly remembered nights under the stars listening to country music on the family radio. The radio also brought news of the war. During that first spring, Roy remembered hearing about the 1944 D-Day invasion of Normandy. The following year, he and his family heard news of President Franklin Roosevelt's death and the end of World War II.[45]

When the work in Colorado finished in August, Roy's large, adopted family returned to Texas for cotton-picking season. Texas is such a large state that the timing of its cotton harvests varies quite a bit depending on locale. The first round occurs in the coastal region near Corpus Christi, where the cotton fields stretch as far as the eye can see. Most migrant cotton pickers started there before venturing west toward El Paso and the Rio Grande River Basin. From there, they headed north into the cooler High Plains of the Texas Panhandle, where they picked all summer and into the fall.[46]

Picking cotton in Texas is extraordinarily difficult, especially in the summer. To pick cotton, a person must crouch down or bend at the waist and reach into a prickly pod to pluck out the soft white bolls of the cotton plant. "You'd pick standing up until your back hurt..." described one such picker, "and you'd get down on your knees and go along until your knees got to hurting so bad you couldn't stand it." Cotton pickers can't wear gloves because the work requires the sensation of touch to feel out the bolls. Imagine repeating that task over and over, eight to ten hours a day, under a blistering Texas sun in temperatures over one hundred degrees. "Ain't no two ways about that heat," remembered one of Roy's adopted brothers. "You put that sun aside and keep on going. . . . It was bad all the way around, but you got to put up with it." "It seemed that each row was longer than the next," Roy recalled.[47]

Uncle Nicholas tried to improve the experience for his family. He was a "master psychologist," Roy wrote, who would devise little contests for the children. He pushed the young ones to compete with their oldest brother, and he incentivized working on Sundays by offering the kids half the proceeds earned by their daily haul. Roy was highly motivated to help provide for his adopted family. "I soon started noticing the closeness of the family," he wrote. "I found myself wanting to be part of that team, and I began to take pride in my contribution."[48]

Cotton pickers at the time earned less than sugar beet workers. For chopping back weeds, Texas cotton workers received between $2.25 and $5.25 per ten-hour workday. Picking a hundred pounds of cotton netted a laborer no more than $2.50. The pay might have been higher but for the constant influx of documented and undocumented workers recruited from Mexico to work in the fields. And, of course, cotton pickers had no benefits, vacations, or pension. Housing conditions were so bad in the Lower Rio Grande Valley that one witness reported seeing people "living in shacks that I wouldn't put a horse in." As the rest of the nation rapidly mobilized during World War II, migrant farm laborers fell even further behind other Americans whose working conditions were improving. As one postwar government study concluded, "In a period of rapidly advancing job and employment standards, we expect them to work at employment which, for all practical purposes, has no job standards."[49]

Texas, like most states, experienced an economic boom during World War II as the state's defense industries were flooded with orders and the oil industry generated unprecedented revenues. Texas was also home to 175 military installations that housed roughly 1.5 million troops who came to train. The majority of

Mexican American workers were unable to access the best defense industry jobs, constituting only about 5 percent of defense employees.[50]

Nevertheless, poor Hispanic migrant farm families served a major function in the American economy during and after World War II. Their labor was essential in ensuring the productivity of American agriculture during a labor shortage created by the war. The cheap labor of migrant workers kept agriculture profitable while also contributing to the American economy and war effort in a time of crisis. As a boy, Roy remembered World War II, thinking "the distances between us and Europe and Japan were unfathomable." But he, like millions of other Americans, played a crucial role in helping America's farmers produce the goods America needed to make war.[51]

At the same time, the social safety net programs of the 1930s and 1940s were written to exclude farmworkers. In addition to being ineligible for Social Security because they were agricultural workers, migrant laborers were also prevented from claiming state-sponsored relief benefits because of increased residency requirements imposed by states to exclude itinerant workers. "Thus," concluded one report, "State by State, county by county, township by township, nearly every unit of government seeks to evade responsibility for these migrant workers." The beneficiaries were the farm owners who continued to enjoy government-protected access to cheap labor, be it foreign or domestic.[52]

Roy's family spent as many as eight months on the road before returning home to Wharton County in December, just in time to celebrate the upcoming holiday season. They came home happy to be together with a little time off work. Those Christmases were good times, when the family was the most flush with cash from their days working in the fields.[53]

When Roy was at home, he and Rogelio and their adopted siblings went to public schools where they continuously fell further behind their peers. They simply didn't have as much time to learn. They left school early every spring and returned late each fall. Roy grew frustrated over performing so much worse than his classmates. When one of his elders would tell him, "Getting an education is the most important thing in your life," Roy desperately wanted to respond, "I believe you, just let me stay home and go to school." But migrant work was how the family earned its income. There was nothing Roy could do. He later wrote, "Being in the fields was more fun, for when we entered school we were far behind the other children. The teachers put us off to the side, where we rarely caught up with the rest of the class."[54]

In addition to falling behind academically, the Benavidez kids continued to experience a lot of racial tension. The local white kids were the descendants of immigrants from Denmark, Austria, Bohemia, Czechoslovakia, and Germany. Their families had been able to buy land at a time and place when and where Latinos could not, as was dictated in the terms of the Danes' contract with the Texas Land & Cattle Company. The social and political norms of Texas in the 1930s and 1940s taught local white kids that their whiteness made them superior to their Latino and Black counterparts. Black kids couldn't even go to the city's best public schools.[55]

It wasn't all bad. Sometimes the boys playfully teased each other and traded taquitos for cheeseburgers. But race was omnipresent. The school segregated its water fountains, meaning that Hispanic students were required to go outside just to get a drink of water. Imagine the humiliation and the teasing. The classrooms themselves were also often segregated, with white kids sitting in one section and Latino kids in another. And then there were the relentless racial epithets and insults. White kids would call the Benavidez children names like "spic," "taco bender," or "greaser." "I resented it deeply," Roy remembered. "It wasn't enjoyable at all," agreed his cousin Eugene. "They didn't like Mexicans." The cruelest irony, of course, was that none of the Benavidez children were Mexican. Their family had lived in Texas for over one hundred years and had fought for its independence decades before the ancestors of most white families came to the area. The reason they were poor is because their predecessors never enjoyed the community-based opportunities for land ownership that benefited European immigrants, whose acquisition of affordable land in Wharton County sustained generations of their families and continues to do so to this day.[56]

Roy's uncle Nicholas and aunt Alexandria tried to help their children navigate life in that difficult society. Aunt Alexandria worked hard to combat stereotypes of Hispanic children. Poor as they were, the family could not always afford to buy new clothes. But she made sure that their garments were clean, and that torn clothing was quickly mended, telling her kids, "We might be poor, we might not have new clothes, but the clothes you got are clean and they're sewed up the way it's supposed to be." Alexandria also paid close attention to their hair, knowing that Latino kids were often accused of carrying lice into schools. "Mama always had made sure we were clean people," remembered their son Eugene.[57]

Uncle Nicholas tried to instill hope for the future, promising his children that good citizenship and hard work would one day create opportunities. "Some of the laws and practices are stacked against us," he told his kids, "but we must respect the law." Nicholas also sought to infuse in them a sense of pride in the Benavidez family heritage. He told his kids about the previous generations of Benavidezes who had been pioneers in Texas. The Benavidez name, he insisted, must be respected. Nicholas sought to ensure that their family ancestry would provide his children with a sense of purpose and place. "We will not give up our heritage," he told Roy, "but we won't let it hold us back either. We will be judged by the way we act and by the respect we earn in the community."[58]

Important as these lessons were, Nicholas and Alexandria could only do so much to insulate their children from the realities of life in such a society. In town, Roy was exposed to countless racialized insults and humiliations. He knew he could not sit in certain sections of the movie theater or purchase a hamburger at just any restaurant like the white kids. Some businesses displayed signs that read, "No Mexicans or dogs. Colored around back." He was deeply affected by a particular incident when a white man threw a handful of change on the ground in front of Roy and his adopted siblings, only to stand by laughing at the Latino kids scrambling to gather up the coins. "I needed those dimes," Roy recalled, "but I remember the pride I lost getting them."[59]

The other issue that haunted Roy was that of his mother, Teresa. During his first four years with Nicholas and Alexandria, Roy's mother was still living only about eighty miles away in Cuero. As an adult, Roy shared a great deal about the ways he was shaped by his childhood, but he was largely silent regarding the separation from his mother. Roy's feelings toward his mother are one of the major gaps in his retelling of his life. He never publicly acknowledged that his mother gave him up. Whenever he spoke or wrote of going to live with Uncle Nicholas, he said that he went after his mother died.

Roy's mother did die young. Teresa passed away in 1946 at the age of thirty-five when Roy was eleven. Like her late husband, Salvador, Teresa also died of tuberculosis. Roy wrote that he remembered being at her funeral, but he misstated the timing, suggesting in his memoir that Teresa died sometime near 1942, which would have been right before he moved to the home of his aunt and uncle. He didn't know this, but his mother had another baby a few years after he left. That child's name was Bellantres, and she died of dysentery at only six months old in June of 1945.

Roy wouldn't get to know his other half sister, Maria Guadalupe Chavez, until he became an adult.[60]

It is doubtful that Roy was confused about the timing of his mother's death. He remembered so many other aspects of his childhood and spoke of them often. Going to live with his aunt and uncle was perhaps the most consequential event of Roy's youth, and it is highly unlikely that he ever forgot the most important detail of these circumstances. The most logical explanation for the omission is that Roy was trying to protect his mother's legacy. Teresa Perez was a poor Latino laborer in Great Depression–era Texas. She is not the type of woman who is well remembered in the lore of American history. Her grave isn't even marked. Until now, the only words ever published about her were Roy's. Teresa's actual passing in 1946 places the timing of her death close enough to Roy's move to Wharton that few people would question his chronology. Whatever one might think of this discrepancy, allow it to offer a glimpse into Roy's thinking about his family and his childhood. For the rest of his life, he remained proud and protective of his mother, choosing never to disclose the truth of his adoption. In stating that he was only able to "barely remember" her funeral, he surmised, "Perhaps I remember little because I was so frightened. . . . I felt terribly alone." When Teresa died, he no longer had a lost home to chase, only a memory to love. A growing storm was churning inside him, fueled by the loss of his mother and the hardships of life in the fields and the frustrations of a preteen coming to terms with race in society.[61]

CHAPTER 3
A LEAP OF FAITH

U NCLE NICHOLAS AND AUNT ALEXANDRIA KEPT ROY AFLOAT.
They were his rock, the only source of stability the boy had
ever known. Nicholas and Alexandria were a remarkable couple.
With ten biological and adopted children, they navigated their
family through the travails of poverty and racial discrimination
in Texas during the Great Depression. Theirs was a quiet but
steady strength, rooted in an unflappable faith in God and country. Nicholas and Alexandria were disadvantaged people living
in challenging circumstances, but they believed that life in the
United States offered great promise for their children. Roy's grit,
and later his patriotism, were rooted in the foundations of daily
life with his aunt and uncle.

Not long after Roy's arrival, Nicholas and Alexandria moved
their large family from the cotton fields of Danevang into the
nearby town of El Campo. A village of about 6,200 residents, El
Campo is named for a cowboy campground that used to occupy
the area. It was a quaint community in the 1940s, filled with

transitory cowboys and oil workers and surrounded by vast fields of corn, cotton, and rice.[1]

The family moved into a one-story house on Hillje Street. The home was small and cramped. The boys shared a bedroom in the attic. In the summers, the metal roof got so hot that it burnt to touch it, even from the inside. During those scorching summer nights, the boys would lie on sweat-soaked sheets, flipping their pillows back and forth all night long in search of a dry spot. On nights when Uncle Nicholas parked a truck trailer in the drive-way, they would sleep outside in the trailer bed to escape their sauna.[2]

When Nicholas adopted Roy, he told him, "We all work, and we share what we have." Nicholas himself was incredibly hard-working. In El Campo, he worked as an auto mechanic and a barber while Alexandria ran the house full of children. "We are not rich," Nicholas told Roy, "but everything we have belongs as much to you as to anyone." "We were dirt poor," remembered one of Roy's adopted brothers, "but we survived. We ain't skipped a meal in all them years." When they weren't working in Colorado, the kids picked up odd jobs to help the family.[3]

Roy was used to working. He had worked in Cuero from the time he was in elementary school. When he came to live with Nicholas and Alexandria, it was only natural for Roy to look for jobs. Their home in El Campo was about a mile from the down-town bus station, and the enterprising young boy lingered near the bus stop to offer shoe polishes to the cowboys and oil work-ers who passed through town. He charged a nickel for a shine and sometimes received as much as a quarter in tip. A skill that would later prove useful in the Army, shoe-shining enabled Roy to contribute to his new family. He gave most of the money he earned to his adopted parents. "Aunt Alexandria was the banker," he explained. She kept an envelope of cash for each child and withdrew from their earnings when they needed supplies.[4]

Nicholas and Alexandria offered a "sterner discipline than I had been used to," remembered Roy. Yet it was also helpful to have "very clear lines" of expected behaviors. Unlike a lot of other families at that time, Nicholas and Alexandria typically didn't employ corporal punishment. Nicholas sometimes used a leather strap for severe misconduct, but according to Roy, the most striking punishments came in the form of stern lectures about disappointing the family. These "sermons," as Roy called them, were deeply distressing. Nicholas chastised poor behavior not only as individual sin but a slight against their entire clan. Roy remembered times when "I would have preferred that he whip me and get it over."[5]

Aunt Alexandria insisted that the children welcome God into their lives. She took her children to church, read them the Bible, and taught them how to pray. Nicholas "wasn't the praying type," one of the sons explained, but Alexandria more than made up for his lack of involvement with her commitment to Catholicism. She had one unforgettable ritual. Whenever any of her children would leave the house, she stood at the door to bless them with the sign of the cross.[6]

The other major adult figure in Roy's life at that time was his grandfather Salvador Benavidez Sr. Born near the border in 1880, Salvador Sr. was the grandchild of Nicholas Benavides, one of the original four brothers who had settled in Victoria during the 1820s. After years of raising his family in DeWitt County, Salvador Sr. came with his oldest son, Nicholas, to Wharton. Roy remembered his grandfather wearing a large Stetson hat and playing dominoes. He'd walk for "recreation," Roy recalled, and enjoy a beer or two.[7]

Salvador Sr. regaled Roy and his cousins with stories. The boy especially loved hearing about his deceased father, listening intently to tales about the dad he never really knew. Grandpa Salvador entertained all the grandchildren with legends about their ancestors, helping instill pride by teaching them about their family's historical roles as Texas pioneers. "We loved his stories," Roy remembered, and "gathered around Grandfather Salvador at every opportunity." Salvador also retained an endless array of Tejano parables, many of which emphasized the concepts of communal aid and self-help.[8]

One of Salvador's favorite fables involved a man selling crabs. This man had two baskets, one labeled "American" and the other "Mexican." The Mexican crabs were preferable, the vendor told buyers, because "they don't need no lid. They don't try to get out." The American crabs, on the other hand, worked together to escape. "One of them climbs up on the back of another," the story went, "and another climbs on his back, then another climbs on his back, and on and on, and pretty soon them American crabs are getting out all over the place." This inference—that American crabs (Anglos) work together to escape poverty while Mexican crabs (Latino) struggle individually—bears little resemblance to the true historical context of Hispanic poverty in Texas, but it captures Salvador's point about self-help. Roy's grandfather believed that Mexican Americans "didn't help each other as they should."[9]

Another of Salvador's favorite stories came from his time working as a cowboy. In this story, he was a young man driving cattle through a rocky terrain when he heard a man calling from a ledge beneath the path. The man had fallen and was stranded. In a parable reminiscent of the Good Samaritan of the New Testament, Salvador stopped to help. He dropped a rope from the ledge, but it wasn't long enough to reach the man. So Salvador tied the rope to his belt, anchored his legs into the earth and pulled the man to safety using his own body weight. "Remember," Salvador Sr. would say, "people sometimes need help, and when they do you must help them."[10]

Roy would later claim to have been greatly affected by the worldview crafted by his elders. His forebears tried to teach him that he could take control of his own destiny and that the foundations of family would serve to guide and support him. Every job, no matter how hard, was an investment in a more promising future. And good, honest behavior could also help secure a better future, not only in society but also in the eyes of God. Roy's elders insisted that people like them couldn't afford selfish or risky actions that might threaten their entire family. With limited access to resources, this poor family had no choice but to rely on themselves, developing a familial culture rooted in the twin pillars of hard work and integrity. Perhaps the most important lesson Roy learned was that of hope. The reason for sacrifice lay in the promise of a better life. Nicholas and Alexandria tried to protect their kids by teaching them to believe.

Nicholas and Alexandria's approach was fairly common among their peers, a group historians have labeled "the Mexican American Generation." Born in the early twentieth century, the members of this generation lived through the Great Depression and World War II, their lives overlapping the chronology of the better-known "Greatest Generation," which typically refers to white Americans born in the early 1900s. The stewards of this "Mexican American Generation" were "civic nationalists" who advocated for Latino assimilation into mainstream American life. They understood and fought against racial discrimination, but they also fundamentally believed in the promise of American society, despite significant racial disadvantages.[11]

In 1929, several leading groups of the Mexican American Generation consolidated to create the League of United Latin American Citizens (LULAC). Founded in Corpus Christi on February 17, 1929, LULAC started as a Texas-centric organization designed to serve native-born Latinos. Within eight years, it grew to five thousand members. For years, the association was led by a small number of white-collar Mexican Americans who recognized the importance of Mexican American heritage but who also emphasized advancement through acculturation and patriotism.[12]

LULAC's early leaders performed an "exaggerated patriotism," writes one historian, to stake out their claims of American citizenship. They rejected some Mexican traditions as too antiquated and even barred Mexican immigrants from joining their organization. LULAC leaders emphasized Latino involvement in Texas history, especially the Texas Revolution, highlighting the "Texas patriots of Mexican extraction," wrote one LULAC member in the 1930s, "[who] participated actively in the Military campaigns."[13]

Early LULAC leaders required members to take loyalty oaths to the United States. They adopted "America" as their song, the "George Washington Prayer" as their prayer, and English as their official language. At one point, they even considered dropping "Latin" from their name to further promote assimilation. As an organization, they also consciously declined to openly participate in partisan politics or discuss religion, hoping to dodge the ire of white Texans who might be threatened by Hispanic political activism. Years later, LULAC would lead legal battles against racial segregation, but the bulk of their messaging in the 1930s was rooted in advocating for Mexican American assimilation. Mostly, they just wanted to prove they belonged.[14]

Roy's elders shared many of LULAC's philosophies for Mexican American advancement. They also stressed assimilation and shared stories about their ancestors' roles in the Texas Revolution. Even Grandpa Salvador's story about the Mexican crabs reflected the thinking of many early LULAC leaders who believed that Mexican Americans were themselves partially to blame for their own segregation within mainstream American society. As one reporter in the 1930s observed of LULAC leadership, "These founders realized that the greatest stumbling block in the way of accomplishing these ends was the Mexican-American himself."[15]

But the performative patriotism and assimilation could not alter the very real racial restrictions facing Mexican Americans. Try as they might to claim whiteness through acculturation, white citizens just as earnestly sought to categorize them as non-white. The 1930 United States Census was the first to list "Mexican" as the prescribed race for all Latinos, even those who were native-born citizens of the United States. In some city directories, including Corpus Christi, new designations in the listings denoted Mexican Americans as "Mexican" or "English-Speaking Mexican," while listing Anglo citizens as "American," thus effectively rejecting Mexican American claims at assimilation. Even native-born Hispanics were classified as foreign.[16]

Hispanics also lacked the most basic civil rights. In most places in Texas, Latino citizens couldn't exercise voting privileges because of a system known as the "white primary" that allowed only Anglos to vote in primary elections, thus limiting the possibility for victory by any candidate who might support Latino civil rights. Poll taxes and literacy tests further prevented non-white citizens from voting. Hispanic citizens were also blocked from serving on juries. One study published in 1946 examined fifty counties where Latinos comprised between "fifteen to forty" percent of the population and reported that "persons of Mexican descent have never been known to be called for jury duty." In San Antonio—a city whose Mexican American population hovered near fifty percent—only white citizens had ever been elected to the school board.[17]

Mexican Americans also faced discrimination in public spaces, housing, and employment, not to mention the historical disparities created by land policies that displaced Tejano families from places like Victoria and Hidalgo Counties. They also had fewer opportunities for education, especially in farming communities, where children like Roy missed months of school to work. In counties dominated by white landowners, literacy rates for people of Mexican descent hovered around 60 percent. This was all systematic and intentional. As one Texas planter explained, "Educating the Mexican is educating them away from the job, away from the dirt." Mexican Americans lagged behind their white counterparts because of structural disadvantages baked into society. There were notable exceptions, but any chance for a truly equitable assimilation would have required immense societal change.[18]

As Roy's family promised better days in the future, he struggled to navigate his lived experiences in the present. Texas in the 1940s was a highly racialized society. There was no way of avoiding it. Roy's adolescence was flooded with constant, stinging experiences with racial discrimination. It's one thing to be faced with obvious disadvantages; it's another to be taunted for them. The potential for humiliation lurked around every corner, peppering his daily life with unpleasant instances that damaged his self-esteem and hurt his feelings.[19]

Roy had a biracial cousin whose father was of Austrian descent. The boy had European features, including "blonde hair and blue eyes," explained Roy. One day, the boys went out together to buy burgers, but the restaurant displayed a sign that read "NO MEXICANS OR DOGS. COLORED AROUND BACK." As Roy paused, his light-skinned cousin strutted into the eatery and bought a burger. The biracial boy plopped down in a booth, chomping on his meal, and smirking at Roy through a window "between bites," Roy recalled. The cousin eventually brought out another burger for Roy, but the experience stung him for years.[20]

Roy's childhood jobs included a position as a dishwasher. When he would take a break for his meal, the restaurant owner wouldn't allow him to eat in the dining room with white customers because he was Hispanic. The young boy ate alone in the kitchen, simmering with bitterness because he knew that the white customers whose dishes he cleaned couldn't fathom the sight of him eating near their families. "That's the way it was," he recalled, "and I resented it deeply."[21]

There was another white kid who used to tease Roy about ice cream. One day, the kid approached Roy with an ice-cream cone and mocked him with the tasty treat, knowing that Roy couldn't obtain his own. "Sure is good," the young man said. "I bet you wish you had a nickel to get an ice-cream cone." Roy could smell the chocolate, and he remembered the kid's pink tongue gliding over the ice cream. Even decades later—after Roy had traveled the globe and become a national hero—he still recalled the hurt of that kid teasing him about that ice-cream cone.[22]

White kids had more money, and Roy knew it. "The Anglos owned most of the land, held all of the political offices, and made all of the rules," he remembered. These "certain lines," as Roy described racial inequalities, "had been drawn long ago." Roy clearly saw the racial hierarchy in his society, but he wasn't aware of the historical forces that had shaped his family's station in life. Disadvantaged non-white children who lack such an understanding of history are ill-equipped to protect themselves against the inescapable arguments of natural selection—that one race enjoyed a better position in society simply because that race was naturally superior. In reality, the racial order that Roy observed in the 1940s was the result of a carefully constructed system of racial advantages set in motion a century before Roy was born. Of course, he didn't know that. All he knew at the time was that his people were on the lowest rung of society.[23]

Schooled as Roy may have been by his elders, he was unprepared to deal with the emotional pain of daily racism. Uncle

Nicholas promised, "If we got an education, worked hard, and led a clean life of discipline we would earn the Anglos' respect." But such a long-term outlook provided little solace to an adolescent boy experiencing daily racism. The humiliating insults came from all angles—peers, adults, even signs in windows. Many people today can understand the structural disadvantages of racial discrimination, but fewer can truly appreciate the deep psychological pain of those who lived through it. The most traumatic episodes were not necessarily singular events but rather the drumbeat of recurring incidents that bang into one's soul so regularly as to affect their personality.[24]

Like most youths, Roy did not have the constitution to meet every single slight with grace. He was angry in the moment. When Nicholas insisted, "Someday, someone will open a door to you," all Roy could think was, "I can't even go in the front door of the restaurant where I work." The orphaned youth was already severely wounded when he arrived to live with Nicholas and Alexandria, and his experiences in El Campo cut him even deeper.[25]

Roy's frustrations boiled over into violence. Fighting for him became an organic mechanism for coping with the psychological toll of living in a deeply racist society. It was the only way he could level an otherwise uneven playing field. He and his siblings tried to avoid fights in school because teachers might report such scuffles to Uncle Nicholas and Aunt Alexandria, but "the streets are a different matter," explained Roy. Any social slight could have sparked fisticuffs. Roy and his adopted siblings looked after one another. When a white kid picked on one of the siblings, the older boys would track down and confront the offender. Public insults didn't always result in a fight, but Roy was among the quickest to escalate to violence. One of the kids he grew up with later called him "the meanest Mexican in school and [he] would fight at the drop of a hat."[26]

Roy fought kids older and younger, taking any affront as cause to raise his fists. "By the time I was ten years old," he remembered, "I fought anybody who looked at me wrong." Fighting, he later wrote, became a "habit," his only recourse to the name-calling white kids "who had new shoes or who had money to buy whatever they wanted," he explained. The realities of race and class clashed to produce a deeply frustrated and ornery adolescent. "Some of my experiences just made me mean," Roy remembered, "meaner than I had been as a street child in Cuero."[27]

Uncle Nicholas tried to help Roy channel his energy into something more productive. He arranged for his adopted sons, Roy and Rogelio, to join a boxing gym. It seemed like an obvious outlet for Roy. Violence had become a significant part of his life. He was fighting all the time anyway, averaging by his count "about one fight per day." "I turned out to be a pretty good fighter," Roy wrote of boxing, "but I had a hard time staying within the rules." He was an experienced yet undisciplined brawler who was "wild" on offense but also extremely tough and capable of absorbing extensive punishment.[28]

Roy and Rogelio's coach once drove them to Fort Worth to compete in the Texas Golden Gloves State Championship, a statewide boxing exhibition for middle- and high-school-age amateur boxers. Held at the famous Will Rogers Coliseum, these tournaments featured dozens of fights over three nights, drawing more than 3,500 spectators. Roy remembered having "never seen so many people in one place in all my life." The crowd made him feel good, as if his energies were finally being poured into something that people valued. But Roy lost his match at the tournament, and then he further embarrassed himself afterward by grabbing his opponent in the locker room. After the post-fight scuffle was broken up, he quickly realized that he had "disgraced the Benavidez name," a cardinal sin in the eyes of his stepfather and grandfather. He never made it back to another Golden Gloves tournament.[29]

When Roy was twelve years old, his family experienced a change that seemed to confirm Uncle Nicholas's mantra about good behavior and social uplift. That year, Nicholas was appointed a deputy sheriff by Wharton County Sheriff T. W. "Buckshot" Lane. Buckshot Lane was a fascinating character. Born in 1903, he was the grandson of a wealthy slaveowner whose family remained prominent in Wharton County. Buckshot had lived in the area his entire life. Having begun his career in law enforcement as a constable in 1933, in 1940 he was elected sheriff of Wharton County. During his time as sheriff, he emerged as one of the most colorful lawmen in Texas. He wrote a regular column in the *Houston Post*, taught himself how to fly a plane, and hosted a radio show where he announced the names of suspected criminals over the air while promising to apprehend them. Lane was also involved in several shootouts, one of which reportedly left more than fifty bullet holes in his automobile. He later served in the Texas Legislature. His personal style drew attention from the national media, including features in magazines such as *Reader's Digest*, the *Saturday Evening Post*, and *LIFE*.[30]

Lane appears to have been somewhat sympathetic toward Hispanics. During the 1940s and 1950s, he was a regular correspondent with John J. Herrera, a Houston-based Latino attorney and major figure in LULAC, who later helped lead legal fights for civil rights. Herrera exchanged letters with Lane about all types of issues related to Latinos. In the late 1940s, Lane wrote to Herrera about the lack of Hispanic doctors in Wharton County, asking for help to recruit a physician for the growing number of "Latin people." He even promised to help the prospective doctor connect with a local druggist to set up an office. At some point, Lane decided to name Nicholas Benavidez the first Latino to ever serve as a deputy sheriff in Wharton County.[31]

Roy recognized the importance of Nicholas's appointment as deputy sheriff. Nicholas was a "peacemaker," Roy wrote, who had a knack for solving disputes between members of the white and Latino communities. The children were sometimes teased by their classmates about Nicholas becoming a lawman, but the mild ribbing paled in comparison with the sense of respect Nicholas gained in the community.[32]

But Nicholas's appointment did not dramatically alter Roy's trajectory. Still an angry fighter, Roy in his teen years found new allies among other similarly disaffected youths. These new allegiances came with informal pacts of common defense. He fought not only those who angered him personally but also anyone who irritated his friends. Roy was a leader among a rough group of kids. For a tough, macho kid like Roy, his peer alliances often trumped the importance of protecting the family name.[33]

On one occasion, Roy and Rogelio were pulled into "a sizeable brawl" that attracted the attention of local law enforcement. Uncle Nicholas, recently deputized, arrived on the scene. He sent the other fighters home, but he took Roy and Rogelio to the city jail and locked them in a cell for three hours. As the boys waited behind bars, Nicholas walked past them scolding and shaming, "Oh, you Benavidez brothers sure look nice in there."[34]

Roy's behavior increasingly began to worry Uncle Nicholas. He was in trouble all the time, and at one point Roy was nearly sent to the Gatesville State School for Boys, a juvenile corrections facility near Waco. Roy continued fighting, and he was caught drinking. His friends were becoming a big problem. "Booze and bad friends will get you in trouble," Nicholas told him. Roy remembered Nicholas repeating, "Dime con quien andas, y te dije quien eres," meaning "Tell me with whom you walk and I will tell you who you are." "I'll bet Uncle Nicholas said that to me a thousand times," Roy recalled. Nicholas and Alexandria must have become very concerned about the diverging path of their adopted son. Roy worked hard and respected his family, but he was also becoming increasingly wild and unpredictable.[35]

In the spring of 1950, when Roy was only fourteen years old, he dropped out of school. The move coincided with the family's annual trip to Colorado. He was tired of being left so far behind the other kids academically. The frustrated boy felt as if he didn't have a real chance for an education, so he decided to quit. That April, when Roy returned his textbook, he remembered his English teacher saying, "I'll see you in the fall." "No, miss," Roy answered, "I'm not gonna come next year." Concerned, the teacher replied, "I want you to come back. . . . Please come back. You're smart. You'll do all right if you'll keep your mouth shut and stop fighting." Roy wanted to stay but concluded that he just could not. Another of Roy's teachers remembered them both crying "tears of sadness when he came to me and said he had to leave." But that was it. Roy was done with public school.[36]

After dropping out of school, Roy spent his time in El Campo working a series of odd jobs, including gas station attendant. He was living at home and contributing to the household expenses but also still engaging in risky behaviors. "If you could have bet on me back then," Roy later wrote, "the odds were about even that in ten years I'd either be pumping gas or be in prison."[37]

Roy eventually took a job working at the local Firestone Tire store, a position that placed him in contact with a man named Art Haddock. The bookkeeper at the Firestone shop, Haddock was an ordained Methodist minister. He was about twenty years older than Roy and made an impression on the troubled youth with his kindness and patience. "Art was different from any Anglo I had ever met at that time," Roy remembered. He was kind and careful, soft with the young man but firm in his expectations, and their interactions carried none of the poison that infected so many of Roy's other exchanges with white people. Haddock read Bible passages with Roy, and he gently reprimanded Roy whenever he heard the boy swearing. Through careful and methodical patience, Haddock began to become an important figure in Roy's life, a man that the troubled youth wanted to impress.[38]

After they'd been working together for several months, Haddock began to give Roy increased responsibilities. He let him run the store at times and allowed Roy to keep the company truck overnight so that the teenager could handle emergency calls. Roy still had his temptations, but he was less enticed to drink with friends when he was left responsible for responding to service calls. By staying busy with work, he managed to reduce his "fight-per-day average," he explained, "to just one or two bouts on weekends when I was not on call."[39]

Roy's behavior was also affected by a new romantic interest. During the time that Roy worked for Art Haddock, he began to pay attention to a young woman named Hilaria Coy. Hilaria, who went by Lala, was a couple years older than Roy. She had been born in 1933 near Corpus Christi and come to El Campo in the 1940s with her parents and nine siblings. Like many Hispanics in their community, her parents were working-class farm laborers. Roy had known Lala since he was "about twelve years old," he wrote, but it was not until he was a mid-teen that he began to really focus on her romantically.[40]

Roy would see Lala at church and various social events in their community. He thought she was "by far the prettiest girl in town." She was about his same height, with green eyes and fair skin. Her hair was a bit lighter than that of most Latinos. "If you didn't look twice," Roy wrote, "you'd think she was Anglo." According to Roy, Lala had been able to pass for white when they were young, remaining in the front of the local movie theater while Roy and other darker-skinned children were ordered to the back. Unlike Roy, Lala was still in school.[41]

Roy felt that he couldn't just approach Hilaria and ask for a date; her family was far too conservative for that. So he flirted by trying to attract her attention in other ways. He showed off during community events, especially baseball games, where he added a bit of flair to his game to stand out from the other players. He waited for opportune moments to steal a brief look or exchange a nod, and he took every chance possible to speak with her. There wasn't much opportunity for one-on-one interactions, but he was nevertheless smitten with the beautiful young woman.[42]

At sixteen years old, Roy recognized that he had little to offer Lala. Her parents were conservative about their daughter dating. For Roy to approach Lala at such an age would have invited serious questions about his direction and intentions in life, and Roy had no real plans for his future. The teenage dropout contemplated what he might be able to offer a girlfriend or future wife. He had a stable job at Firestone, but he realized that it offered little room for advancement. Roy had no great passions or well-developed skills other than farm labor and street fighting. For a while, he thought he might want to become a truck driver. He also considered a career in law enforcement like Uncle Nicholas, perhaps even becoming a Texas Ranger. But Roy never seriously pursued either option. The young man was a bit unmoored in the world as he grew into adulthood, trying to imagine a future that might allow him to provide for a family.[43]

During this time, Roy began having serious conversations with his family about the possibility of joining the military. The move made sense for a number of reasons. The most obvious was that Roy had very limited prospects, and military service offered opportunities for a career where advancement was possible. The military also provided Hispanic youths like Roy with a chance to belong. For hundreds of thousands of Latinos who grew up during World War II, military service offered the best possible way to assert patriotism and claim their status as American citizens. If the strategy of the Mexican American Generation was sound, then what could offer a better path toward assimilation than joining the United States armed forces?

During World War II, roughly five hundred thousand Latinos served in the United States military, the highest rate of any ethnicity in the country. Seventeen Latino World War II servicemen were awarded the Congressional Medal of Honor, also the highest rate of any ethnic group. Unlike Black troops who operated in segregated units, Latino soldiers served alongside white troops in every theater of the war. They were among those who stormed the beaches of Normandy and Okinawa, who perished in the Bataan Death March, and who helped liberate the Philippines. Mexican American women also joined the military, working in women's auxiliary units and as nurses.[44]

Hispanics were proud to serve and desperate to belong. As one historian has argued, "For Mexican Americans, World War II involved a leap of faith: claiming the United States as your country even when it did not claim you." During the war, Mexican American organizations encouraged military service at a time of need, hoping for a boost to their status based on wartime contributions. "We are also children of the United States," insisted an organization named the Congreso de Pueblos de Habla Española. "We will defend her." Another group, named the Mexican American Movement, stated, "[The war] has shown them what the Mexican American will do, what responsibility he will take and what leadership qualities he will demonstrate. After this struggle, the status of the Mexican American will be different."[45]

"All we wanted," one Latino soldier claimed, "was a chance to prove how loyal and American we were." Another Mexican American veteran of the European theater remembered, "Most of us were more than glad to be given the opportunity to serve in the war. It did not matter whether we were looked upon as

Mexicans; the war soon made us all genuine Americans." "We wanted to prove," explained another, "that while our cultural ties were deeply rooted in Mexico, our home was here in this country."[46]

Despite their service, Mexican Americans, even veterans, continued to face discrimination during and after the war. They didn't receive the same jobs in wartime industries or opportunities for advancement in the military. The war also exacerbated existing prejudices. In 1943 Los Angeles, roving gangs of white soldiers attacked groups of Mexican Americans as part of an anti–Mexican American hysteria that gripped the city. During the war, anti-Hispanic discrimination in Texas became a source of national embarrassment. The Mexican Foreign Office wrote to the United States government to express concerns about "humiliations, as unjust as they are cruel," that Mexican officials experienced when visiting Texas. The pervasive nature of these prejudices led the Mexican government to temporarily ban Texas from receiving laborers through the Bracero Program that contracted Mexican citizens for labor in the United States. Numerous Texas legislators introduced anti-discrimination bills in the state legislature, but none passed during the war. A Mexican American citizen could storm the beaches of Normandy only to be denied the right to eat in a public restaurant back in the United States.[47]

Perhaps the most striking example of anti-Mexican American discrimination was the treatment of the war hero Macario García. A native of Mexico, García moved to the United States with his parents at the age of three. He was drafted in 1942 and injured during the invasion of Normandy in 1944. After recovering, he rejoined the action in Germany where he "single-handedly assaulted 2 enemy machine gun emplacements," read his medal citation, killing at least six German soldiers and capturing two more. For these heroics, García was awarded the Congressional

Medal of Honor at the White House by President Harry Truman on August 23, 1945. Eighteen days later, García was denied service because of his race at the Oasis Café in Richmond, Texas. The Medal of Honor recipient protested, and a conflict ensued between the war hero and the waitstaff. García was attacked and beaten with a baseball bat before being arrested on charges of aggravated assault. The case attracted widespread publicity, and the charges were later dropped.[48]

In 1948, a Mexican American World War II veteran named Dr. Héctor Garcia founded the American GI Forum in Corpus Christi. A highly decorated combat veteran of the European theater, Garcia upon his return home was struck by the devastating poverty and lack of opportunities available to Mexican Americans. He joined LULAC and began an impressive career of advocacy for Texas Latinos that would later earn him the nickname the "Mexican-American Martin Luther King."[49]

Dr. Garcia started the American GI Forum to advocate for Hispanic veterans. He found that his fellow Latino servicemen lacked hospital beds and access to Veterans Administration (VA) care. In addition, they were having a difficult time securing overdue compensation and disability checks, facing the threat of declining pensions, and had virtually no representation on local draft boards. The families of some veterans also experienced burial discrimination, as many white Texans didn't want Hispanics buried next to their loved ones, even if those Latinos had died fighting for America. Furthermore, Mexican American veterans were often unwelcomed in branches of the American Legion and the Veterans of Foreign Wars (VFW).[50]

The American GI Forum started with seven hundred members who came together at a meeting in Corpus Christi on March 26, 1948. From there, the grassroots association spread across Texas. Individual branches needed only ten members to start a chapter, and at the end of the year, there were forty chapters. By 1950, there were one hundred chapters and roughly ten thousand members. The American GI Forum emerged alongside LULAC as the two most active and influential Mexican American civil rights organizations in the United States.[51]

Along with LULAC, the American GI Forum organized "Poll Tax" drives to register Latino voters and fought to desegregate public schools and juries. The chapters also organized youth and women's auxiliaries to promote education. Their motto, "Education is our Freedom and Freedom Should Be Everybody's Business," reflected a commitment to fighting for equal educational opportunities for Hispanic students. One youth member, who later went on to become a major civil rights leader, remembered of the American GI Forum, "It gave us—sometimes for the first time—pride in our history and our contributions to American society and culture."[52]

Roy Benavidez was six years old when the United States entered World War II and ten when it ended. He remembered listening to news about the war on his radio, and he later claimed one of his boyhood idols to be Audie Murphy, the legendary Medal of Honor recipient from Texas. He came of age amid America's "Good War," as it's often called, the fight against fascism that defined the "Greatest Generation" and provided the backdrop of a surge of patriotism that touched every American citizen in the 1940s and 1950s. The United States had defeated the Axis powers and made the world safe for democracy. World War II was a point of pride for nearly every American, no matter where they stood on the social ladder. And Texas Latinos had played a major role.[53]

Roy never talked much about the American GI Forum of his youth, but by the time he entered his teen years, the organization had emerged as one of the leading Latino civil rights groups in the country. World War II veterans were the big heroes of Mexican American communities across Texas. For a young man who

had faced so much exclusion, Roy recognized that military service could offer a pathway toward full citizenship and a potential
vehicle to escape the plague of race and poverty that contaminated his youth. He also understood that he had few desirable
skills. Uncle Nicholas advised his children, "You have to prepare yourself to sell your talents to the highest bidder in the large
market that will eventually become available to you." All teenage
Roy really knew how to do was work and fight.[54]

Meanwhile, the Texas National Guard was recruiting. A
storied institution with roots dating back to the 1836 Battle
of the Alamo, the state guard was looking to bolster its membership during the early stages of the Cold War. Federal allot-
ments paid for new airfields, training bases, and armories as the
Texas National Guard expanded throughout the late 1940s and
early 1950s. Local organizations also mobilized to help. In El
Campo, the Chamber of Commerce helped raise money to purchase twenty acres of land to turn into a National Guard armory.
By 1950, the Texas National Guard counted a troop strength of
nearly twenty thousand men supported by over $11.6 million in
state and federal funding.[55]

That year, the Texas National Guard was so desperate for enlistees that they wouldn't let people leave, sometimes even after
their agreed terms of service lapsed. In 1950, the Texas adjutant
general signed an order suspending all discharges and resigna-
tions from the Texas National Guard for one year. The following year, the governor signed an executive order issuing the same
edict. The only exception came in cases where a Texas National
Guardsman left to join a branch of the federal armed forces.[56]

The Texas National Guard recruited through newspaper ads,
radio programs, and in-person recruiters who made personal appeals to young men. Some members joined explicitly to avoid the
draft. In 1950, Audie Murphy, the famed World War II hero
and actor, signed up for the Texas National Guard, despite a

lucrative film career. The Texas National Guard used Murphy's enlistment as propaganda, publishing a recruiting poster of his likeness and heroic acts alongside the phrase, "I'm proud to be a NATIONAL GUARDSMAN."[57]

Roy joined the Texas National Guard on June 27, 1952, signing up for a three-year commitment. He was only sixteen years old. Because he was so young, Uncle Nicholas had to submit a signed notarized form authorizing his legal consent as guardian. Roy was drawn to the Guard because it promised to "give me some education, an additional income, and could be worked around my steady job," he wrote. "It seemed to be the perfect solution for someone in my position." In enlisting in the Guard, the young man joined the hundreds of thousands of Mexican Americans in the 1940s and 1950s who believed that military service could offer a pathway toward a better life. The decision to enlist also made Roy the first member of his family to fight for a Texas militia since his legendary ancestor Plácido Benavides, who more than a century before had helped win Texas its freedom from Mexico.[58]

CHAPTER 4

COLD WARRIOR

W HEN ROY JOINED THE TEXAS NATIONAL GUARD AT THE age of sixteen, he stood only five feet six inches tall and weighed 129 pounds. He was no one's idea of a model soldier. But soon Roy was folded into the ranks of the millions of American men and women charged with maintaining combat readiness during the early stages of a burgeoning global Cold War. Roy joined the military at a time when the entire planet seemed on the edge of conflict. As a colonel in the Texas National Guard forewarned, "The United States is on the verge of a crisis. We must face the facts, no matter how brutal. All Americans must prepare for service."[1]

In fact, America was already at war. When Roy signed up in 1952, American soldiers were fighting in Korea to prevent the spread of communism in Asia. The United States committed troops to Korea based largely on the "domino theory," the widely accepted belief that developing countries, especially in Asia, could fall one by one like a line of dominoes to the influence of communism. A communist revolution in one country, American statesmen warned, would embolden communist revolutionaries in the next, and so on. To prevent such a communist wave, the United States in the 1950s embraced the approach of "containment" that called for American forces to stop the spread of communism nearly anywhere in the world. This foreign policy was guided by a lesson from World War II, that the United States must never again allow a potential adversary to gain control of such a vast wealth of resources in Europe and Asia as did the Nazis and Japanese Empire in the 1930s. Communism, insisted American leaders, would not be allowed to spread as had fascism in the 1930s.[2]

Roy was mustered into the Headquarters and Service Company of the 136th Heavy Tank Battalion, a unit of 156 men out of El Campo. His three-year commitment would begin with training in basic military skills including fitness and weaponry. After this initial training, he would be responsible for appearing in uniform one weekend per month and two weeks every summer to maintain his skills. For this, he was paid a few dollars per training session, increasing with his rank. The other benefit was that he would not be eligible for the draft when he turned eighteen, fourteen months after his initial enlistment.[3]

Roy was assigned to basic training at Fort Knox, Kentucky. While many cadets agonized over boot camp, Roy made light of the training by comparing it to the difficult experiences of his childhood. "It reminded me of being back in the labor camps of my youth, only easier," he wrote. "I never could figure out what a lot of the other guys were complaining about. We ate good, most nights we slept under a roof, only one to a bed, and we got a lot of exercise." The conditions were likely more challenging than Roy later let on. The previous year, military inspectors at Fort Knox had reported "low morale" and a "deplorable situation." Still, perhaps his timing was the most fortunate factor. Either way,

Roy had a point about getting to sleep in his own bed, a luxury he didn't always enjoy during his time as a migratory laborer.[4]

Roy liked the National Guard. Always outgoing, he enjoyed meeting new people and hearing stories of their lives. He was glad that his fellow soldiers came from "a variety of backgrounds" and "worked together as a team," he wrote. Such diversity helped show Roy that cooperation between people of different races was possible. "It opened my eyes to the opportunities for a half-Mexican, half-Indian dropout from South Texas," he remembered.[5]

Roy did well in the Guard. He completed boot camp and earned promotion to corporal, giving him a little extra pay and a sense of accomplishment. The promotion was his first notable achievement in life, and he was excited to come home to tell Uncle Nicholas. The boy who had known only rejection and disadvantage was proud of his success. "I was really starting to feel good about myself," he explained.[6]

Initially, the Guard was only a small part of his life. When he wasn't training with the Guard, Roy worked at the auto shop. He was earning about fifty-five dollars per week, nearly twice the average weekly income for workers in Texas at that time. The job was challenging, not just in terms of labor but also intellectually. Roy's boss and mentor, Art Haddock, was continuously pushing him to dream of more. Roy listened. The boy who had lost his father at such a young age was still impressionable, especially when it came to older men who paid him attention, and he respected and responded to Haddock's guidance. Haddock pointed out that Roy's peers by then were graduating high school and starting their careers. "This is not a bad job," Roy remembered Haddock saying, "but is it going to be a good job for you when you're twenty-nine or thirty-nine?" Roy wrestled with this question.[7]

Those were good years. Roy began feeling a new sense of optimism about his future. At one point, he was fortunate to meet

Audie Murphy, the legendary World War II hero and movie star who had joined the Texas National Guard two years before Roy. Roy had seen Murphy's biographic film, *To Hell and Back*, a dozen times by his count. He was drawn to Murphy because they were both undersized, poor Texas kids who had grown up picking cotton. Roy admired Murphy's life story and appreciated that the famed hero "talked to us as if we were his buddies." "Audie Murphy became my idol and role model," he wrote. His appreciation for the military and its soldiers deepened as he experienced life in the Guard. The military provided structure and clearly defined values of courage and integrity. Hungry for direction, Roy soaked it in.[8]

It was not all serious. Roy shared some funny memories of various gaffes during his time in the Guard. One day he came down with a bad case of diarrhea while driving a superior to a meeting. The ailment kept forcing Roy to pull off the road and scramble behind some bushes to squat. After a few such stops, the lieutenant colonel lost patience and jumped behind the wheel, speeding off as Roy was defecating on the side of the road. But Roy had forgotten to check the gas gauge, so the officer didn't get very far before having to walk himself.[9]

Roy still carried what he called "a bad attitude" that sometimes exploded in overreactions to perceived slights. "If I thought some guy was looking down at me," he remembered, "I'd try to put him down on the ground so I'd be looking down at him." Such an attitude, combined with his "smart mouth" and penchant for goofing off, got him in trouble a couple of times. He twice lost his corporal stripes for minor infractions and had to earn them back. But for the most part, he was a pretty good soldier. One of the guys who enlisted with Roy remembered him as "a little hard to manage, but generally an excellent soldier with much pride in himself, his unit and his country."[10]

Roy stayed in the Guard until May of 1955 when he was nineteen years old. During his time in the Guard, some of his fellow guardsmen would talk about the possibility of joining the regular Army. It was a heavy topic, considering that tensions between the global superpowers appeared as if they could burst into conflict at any moment. Increasing numbers of American soldiers were stationed across the globe, the first line of defense in a worldwide struggle against communism. Anyone who joined the Army in the 1950s understood that there was a good chance of seeing action.

The idea of joining the Army appealed to Roy's sense of adventure and toughness. He could see the world, his friends said, and he could help defend America from those who wished for her demise. One day, Roy's buddies insisted, he would be able to tell his grandkids about his incredible adventures. "The recruiters omitted some of the less glamorous aspects . . . ," Roy remembered, "but they convinced me that I wanted to be army and to be a special part of it."[11]

As Roy considered the Army, he imagined the possibilities of a future spent in El Campo. All he could see in that future was a life working in the fields or the tire shop, and an existence polluted by the same racial epithets and disadvantages that framed his early life. "What was there for me if I spent the rest of my life in El Campo?" he thought. "Just another poor Mexican in a small Texas town full of them." The Army offered an escape from the deepest depths of a difficult youth.[12]

Roy was leaning toward enlisting, but he felt that he couldn't make a final decision without the approval of Uncle Nicholas. One day, the pair sat down in the family living room to talk about the possibility of Roy joining the United States Army. It was a heavy conversation. Roy remembered Nicholas telling him, "I believe that the Guard has done a lot to increase your confidence in yourself; and I think that it has begun to teach you a sense of responsibility; but I want you to be certain that this is what you want to do." Roy listened carefully to the man who had raised him. He had thought a great deal about the level of commitment the Army demanded and what it could mean for his life. Roy told Nicholas that he was sure he wanted the military to be his future. A pang of emotion passed between the men. Nicholas's voice cracked when he said, "I'm very proud of you." Roy was going to join the Army, taking a potentially dangerous path in a frightening world.[13]

Roy rode a bus more than seventy miles to the military entrance processing station in downtown Houston. He entered the old United States Custom House at 701 San Jacinto Street, a gray, three-story office building where Muhammad Ali would famously refuse military induction twelve years later. Roy walked up the steps and looked for the Army desk, crossing "that creaky old wooden floor and [feeling] as if I were running a gauntlet." He described himself approaching the Army recruiter "like a cocky little rooster with all of my papers from the Guard and all of my records tucked under my arm."[14]

Roy's Army career officially began on May 17, 1955. He signed up for a three-year enlistment, starting at the rate of $86.80 per month. He was allowed to leave the Texas National Guard a month early because he was enlisting in the United States Army. He swore an oath to serve the United States "honestly and faithfully against all their enemies whomsoever." His National Guard experience did not count toward his new rank in the Army. He began again at the rank of private, meaning he was not eligible to start an advanced program such as infantry school or airborne training. He had to do basic training again.[15]

BY THE TIME ROY JOINED THE ARMY, THE COLD WAR HAD dramatically shifted. From the United States perspective, the Korean War had ended. Both regimes survived the conflict, leaving no clear winner. North and South Korea remained separate, divided at the very same 38th parallel established at the end of World War II. The war was incredibly costly. In just over three years, thirty-six thousand American troops had died. South Korea was left mired in devastating poverty, while North Korea was almost completely leveled by American bombing. But communism had been contained to the North. Although this one domino had not fallen, the United States committed to maintaining a massive troop presence in South Korea to help stave off any further potential threats.[16]

Meanwhile, another major crisis was developing in the wake of France's defeat by communist forces in Vietnam. Since the 1880s, the French had held and managed the colony known as French Indochina, a territory that included modern-day Vietnam, Cambodia, and Laos. For decades, France profited from Indochina by exploiting the region's resources and laborers. This control began to waver in 1940 when the Vichy government of France granted Japanese access to Vietnamese territory during World War II. The ensuing years were catastrophic for many Vietnamese citizens as Japan's war machine consumed many of their people and supplies. French and Japanese food policies during World War II led to a famine that killed as many as two million Vietnamese citizens.[17]

During those catastrophic years, a small nationalist group known as the Viet Minh began to appeal to the masses. They helped poor, starving peasants capture and distribute rice from storage sheds. They also recruited Vietnamese to a cause rooted in communist liberation ideology, promising to lead a renewed revolutionary struggle after the war to overthrow the imperial powers and establish an independent Vietnamese nation.[18]

The Viet Minh were led by Ho Chi Minh, a longtime anti-colonialist who for decades had dreamed of Vietnamese sovereignty. Minh had been active in this cause since the 1910s. In 1920, he told an audience of French socialists, "We have not only been oppressed and exploited shamelessly, but also tortured and poisoned pitilessly." "We have neither freedom of press nor freedom of speech," he testified. "Thousands of Vietnamese have been led to a slow death or massacred to protect other people's interests." By the early 1930s, Ho Chi Minh was openly calling for revolution, insisting, "If the French imperialists think that they can suppress the Vietnamese revolution by means of terrorist acts, they are utterly mistaken."[19]

The opportunity for that revolution finally emerged with the end of World War II. In September of 1945, within hours of Japan's formal surrender to the United States, Viet Minh leaders declared independence from France. In doing so, they borrowed directly from language in the United States Declaration of Independence, invoking the storied phrases of a powerful nation that had once fought its own revolution to win sovereignty from a colonial power. "All men are created equal," the Vietnamese declaration similarly read, "they are endowed by their Creator with certain unalienable Rights; among these are Life, Liberty, and the pursuit of Happiness." In another speech later that autumn, Ho Chi Minh cited the language of the Allies in World War II. "Not only is our act in line with the Atlantic and San Francisco Charters, solemnly proclaimed by the Allies," he argued, "but it entirely conforms with the glorious principles upheld by the French people." Vietnamese nationalists hoped for American support by appealing to the creed of the United States and the stated principles of the victorious Allies who had just won a global war in the name of democracy and self-determination.[20]

But the French wanted their colony back. When the Viet Minh organized to resist, the United States backed the French. As it turned out, America's foreign policy did not align with its global rhetoric of self-determination when the people fighting for freedom were socialists or communists. And so began a long war between Vietnamese liberation forces and a French military aided by the United States. The French lost that war in 1954, with peace established by an agreement to split Vietnam into two, North and South, and a plan for later elections that would unify the nation under one government. Ho Chi Minh's party was heavily expected to win that vote. By the time Roy joined the Army, the United States was staring down the possibility of a united communist Vietnam, thus triggering fears of the domino theory and the spread of communism across Asia.[21]

BEFORE ROY LEFT FOR ARMY BASIC TRAINING, HIS FAMILY threw him a going-away party. Roy was warmed by his family's send-off. These were the people who had taken him in and raised him as their own, and he was forever grateful for their love. He later reflected, "I was too immature at the time to understand the pride that people of my culture take when a member of their family chooses to serve our country."[22]

Roy boarded a train headed for Fort Ord near Monterey, California. He was taking a big step, venturing out into the world. He had never been to the West Coast and was "excited" for the "adventure." The three-day trip also gave the nineteen-year-old time to reflect. He replayed memories of other trips in his life, and he thought about the people who had shaped his journey to that point. The train was packed with other enlistees and officers, charged with "herd[ing] us like cattle," he wrote, "through the dining cars and the stops and stations along the way." Roy noticed that most of the other recruits had very different expectations for the Army. The other young men talked about its temporality, expecting "two or three years" in the service before leaving to cash in on the GI Bill by going to college or starting a business.[23]

Roy was different. He already knew that he would be in the Army for the foreseeable future. He couldn't go to college; he hadn't even finished ninth grade. The Army was going to be his life. He was banking on a long career in the military, one that would provide a secure job, bring pride to his family, and help give him a sense of belonging in a nation that offered limited opportunities. "I saw it," he wrote, "as my single chance to be successful. If I was not, I knew I could never look Uncle Nicholas in the eyes again."[24]

At basic training, the drill sergeants prepared the men for combat. They were "pretty tough characters," Roy recalled of the battle-tested instructors, many of whom were veterans of World War II and/or Korea. At that time, the United States was not officially at war, but the possibility of military intervention loomed over every new enlistee. It was still the nascent days of the Cold War, when the world seemed likely to crack open at the slightest provocation. These new recruits needed to be ready to fight anywhere on the globe, and they were trained with the seriousness and urgency of men headed off to war.[25]

Roy's basic training included lessons in weapons, aptitude, and discipline. He and the other enlistees spent hours learning how to use their service rifles, taking them apart and reassembling them over and over again. They were also instructed in the use of machine guns, mortars, and a variety of other combat weapons. Teamwork and military discipline were drilled into the cadets through an endless array of exercises and inspections. The men were challenged physically and mentally. They ran hills and did push-ups, preparing their bodies and minds for combat. "I was trained as a warrior," Roy said.[26]

The seasoned soldiers picked and prodded the new enlistees, which didn't always bode well for the short-tempered teenager from South Texas. One drill sergeant made fun of Roy's given name of Raul, the name he was given at birth and under which he was baptized. This drill sergeant mocked the name, drawling it out—"Ra-oooool"—in a loud, mocking yell. Roy hated the teasing nature of the sergeant's pronunciation. Afterward, he made sure the name Roy, not Raul, appeared on every bit of his paperwork and was used in introductions.[27]

Roy also had a dispute with a cook who routinely picked on him. Roy at one point hit the guy, causing him to fall on a hot grill. "The drill sergeant chewed me up one side and down the other," Roy remembered of the incident. He also had a "few scrapes," Roy noted, off base. One evening he got into trouble when he and a buddy got lost in the dark during a night maneuver. Roy and the other soldier were trying to take a shortcut across some fields when they were sprayed by a couple of skunks. The men were ordered to strip off and burn their clothes while their comrades howled with laughter. The pair was then ordered to march to the football field where they slept all night naked in the cold. It was funny in hindsight; "I've had a grudge against skunks ever since," Roy later quipped.[28]

Roy spent two months at Fort Ord before moving on to advanced infantry training at Fort Carson near Colorado Springs, his first time back in the state since he was a kid picking sugar beets. This next stage of training began on his twentieth birthday. At Fort Carson, Roy was able to enter a classroom again, where he relished the opportunity to become a good student, unlike the public school experiences of his youth where he remembered having "felt like a dumb 'Mezikin' kid who wasn't expected to do more than take up a chair." He'd never had a chance to do well in school before because his family's migratory farmwork stole so much of his academic year. In the Army, he was able to sit for all the classes just like everyone else. "I discovered what a real kick it was," he remembered, "to sit in the front of the class and have the first answer rather than to hide in the back and hope I didn't get called on."[29]

At Fort Carson, Roy had the pleasure of watching a famous athlete excel at his craft. Billy Martin, the New York Yankees second baseman and Most Valuable Player of the 1953 World Series, had been drafted into the Army in 1954. His training at Fort Carson overlapped with Roy's for about a month. Martin had a terrific career in baseball, winning four World Series titles as a player and another as a manager. One of his peers later called him "the most brilliant manager I ever saw." In the summer of 1955, that talent was employed as the player-manager of a ball club at Fort Carson, where he led a squad of cadets to a championship season. Reporters were all over the place, following Martin's exploits before the major leaguer returned to the Yankees later that season to help Mickey Mantle and the rest of the Bronx Bombers capture the American League pennant. Roy had some interesting ball games to watch during his recreational time.[30]

After nearly two months of training at Fort Carson, Roy received orders sending him to Korea, his first overseas assignment. But first he had a chance to visit El Campo. He took a bus over five hundred miles from Fort Carson to El Paso where he transferred to another bus that carried him more than six hundred additional miles to Cuero, the place where he was born. Roy wanted to see his half-sister, Lupe, who was just thirteen at the time. After a brief visit with her, Roy returned to El Campo a much different man than the nineteen-year-old who had left for the Army less than five months before.[31]

When Roy exited the bus, he saw the cab driver he used to work for as a translator. Roy's family had not known exactly when he would arrive, so no one was waiting for him at the station. But his old cabbie friend gave Roy a ride to Uncle Nicholas's sheriff's office. Roy walked in and waited for his uncle. When Nicholas entered a few moments later, the sheriff stopped in the doorway and stared at his nephew. Roy remembered Nicholas's expression as "unsmiling but happy." Roy knew that he looked different. Men who go to basic training as teens come home with broader shoulders, thicker chests, and sharp haircuts, appearing as if they've made a transition from postpubescent adolescents into grown adult men. As Nicholas looked him over, Roy thought he could sense his uncle swelling with pride. For Roy, making Uncle Nicholas proud was perhaps the most important thing in the world. He was no longer the skinny punk who fought other kids in the streets. "Seeing him look at me that way," Roy later wrote of the moment, "made any discomfort I had endured during training completely worthwhile." They shook hands and went home.[32]

Roy was able to spend about two weeks with his family. Those were good times. The entire clan would gather around Roy to listen to his stories of Army adventures in California and Colorado. Even Grandpa Salvador, the old storyteller himself, "begged me to tell them about my experiences." They assembled around Roy just like Roy and his cousins had once congregated around Salvador. Roy had become a point of pride in their family. He believed in himself and what he was doing. "People were looking up at me," he described, "without my having to knock anybody down first." The time with his family made Roy think deeply about his life. "God had given me a 'song in the night,'" he wrote, referencing one of the old ballads his father had sung, "after I had lost my father and mother."[33]

When his time at home ended, Roy traveled to Seattle where he boarded a boat that took him across the Pacific Ocean. After a weeks-long journey, he joined the 17th Infantry Regiment, a famous unit that was part of the 7th Infantry Division. The 7th Infantry had been in the thick of fighting during the Korean War, having suffered more than fifteen thousand casualties. When Roy arrived, the unit was stationed at Camp Casey, between Seoul and the 38th parallel. As Roy wrote, "the real shooting war had just ended" by the time he arrived. Thankfully, the roughly sixteen months he spent in Korea were mostly peaceful, yet nevertheless transformative.[34]

Roy had two primary impressions of his time in Korea. The first was that he was no longer so much shorter than everyone else. "I stood taller than most Koreans," he remembered. "I liked to walk around without having to look up at everybody." The second observation was more difficult. Roy was struck by the devastating poverty and horrible conditions facing the South Korean people. The locals had been left destitute by the preceding war. Some were literally starving. People would go to trash dumps to find discarded chicken bones that hadn't been picked completely clean. Others turned to prostitution and theft to feed themselves and their families.[35]

Roy was no novice to poverty. As the child of Hispanic share-croppers in Great Depression Texas, he grew up as a member of one of the poorest groups of people in the United States. But Roy's hard life was unlike anything the twenty-year-old saw in Korea. "The living conditions of the Koreans shocked me profoundly," he wrote. He described Seoul as a "bombed-out city" and observed that houses in the rural areas were "constructed from the refuse of the army. The roofs were often made of flattened beer cans and pork-and-beans cans." He remembered the people plucking building materials from the trash heaps and women and children collecting feces out of Army latrines to fertilize their fields.[36]

Roy also had a tough time with the winters. He had never known cold like in Korea. The men had to "hack foxholes out of that frozen, snow-covered, rocky soil," he described. The rainy season brought monsoons that created other difficulties. "We squished about our duties wearing wet socks, and most of us developed foot fungus so severe that we thought our toes were going to rot." "We couldn't decide which was worse," Roy wrote in comparing the two extremes.[37]

Roy was sympathetic toward the Korean people. There were unpleasant cases of robbery and prostitution, but he remembered the local people generously and fondly. He praised those he met as "proud" and "independent." And he was inspired by their massive, battle-tested army. "The Korean soldiers I worked with were excellent," he described. Many American GIs stationed in Korea married and had children with Korean women. Some left behind kids, the abandoned offspring serving as "a horrible reminder of the price paid for occupying foreign lands," Roy wrote. Roy himself formed a relationship with a local Korean boy named Kim. He would pay Kim to run little errands, just like the cowboys of Cuero had once paid Roy.[38]

Something else happened to Roy in Korea. He learned lessons about duty, honor, and fairness, especially when it came to race. As an active-duty member of the military, he worked alongside men of other races. "Maybe I was a little shorter, or a little darker, or had a different-sounding name from some," he recalled, "but to the other troops I was just one of them." The armed forces helped insulate him from racial discrimination. The Army was certainly not free from racism, but its structures, rooted in rank and orders, offered a unique form of equity that Roy had not experienced elsewhere in society. "I felt more a part of something than I ever had," he wrote. "I was equal."[39]

Roy's time in Korea ended in January of 1957. Upon returning to the United States, he was stationed at Fort Riley in Kansas and then allowed some leave to return to El Campo before his next assignment. While back at home, Roy reconnected with Lala Coy. In 1957, Roy was still only twenty-one years old and Lala just twenty-two. According to Roy, their romance really began to blossom during a lunch break she took from her job at a local clothing store. After that, they began spending as much time together as possible before Roy's next deployment. But Lala's family was very strict and required that most of their dates be supervised. They were rarely alone, spending their time among her family or his. Going out with "only one chaperone,"

Roy later kidded, pushed the boundaries of propriety. Supervised or not, Roy and Lala established a connection during that short time. "Our feeling for each other was something special," he wrote of those few days. When Roy received orders for another deployment, they agreed to write letters to each other while he was away.[40]

In April of 1957, Roy was assigned to Berlin. Like the rest of Germany, Berlin was divided into four spheres by the Potsdam Agreement of 1945. Russia controlled the east, and the United States, England, and France occupied the west. For decades, Berlin served as a proxy for the global struggle between capitalism and communism. It was one of many such locations, but unlike places such as Korea and Vietnam, Berlin was one of the very few sites where Americans and Soviets faced off in direct confrontation, separated by mere feet across a narrow border that was later demarked by the Berlin Wall. With roughly 180,000 United States troops in West Germany and 500,000 Soviet

Roy in Germany. Roy P. Benavidez Papers, camh-dob-017318_pub, Dolph Briscoe Center for American History, The University of Texas at Austin.

soldiers in East Germany, the occupied nation in the middle of Europe promised to be a site of major conflict if the world's superpowers ever did declare war. "It was a strange city to be in during the heart of the Cold War," Roy wrote of Berlin. "There was constant tension . . ." he recalled. "We were never at ease."[41]

That international tension motivated Roy to become what he called a "model soldier," joking, "Any misstep of mine was a direct reflection on the entire U.S. Army and could launch World War III." But he was far from perfect. Roy committed some blunders in Germany while out drinking at night. On one occasion, he claimed to have peeked under a "Scotsman's kilt" as part of a prank and was punched as retribution. Luckily, Roy quickly realized that he had deserved the blow and dismissed the attack before the conflict could further escalate. On another occasion, Roy was the one throwing punches when he struck a drunken lieutenant who had insulted him. This was a major problem because of rank. Roy was deeply concerned about the consequences, but he was ultimately spared from severe punishment by the mercy of another commanding officer. Once Roy was reported as being absent without leave (AWOL) from his unit from 6:15 p.m. to 2:55 a.m., most likely because he was out drinking with friends. He was docked a rank for that violation, going from Specialist Third Class, a rank he had achieved while in Korea, to Private First Class.[42]

Despite some setbacks, Roy's service in Germany resulted in a net positive for his career. In September of 1957, he received a letter of appreciation from a captain for his "display of effort enthusiasm and professional competence." "Your effort and hard work," the captain wrote, "reflect great credit upon yourself and your unit." He also received the Army of Occupation Medal for his time in Berlin, one of many medals to come.[43]

Perhaps the greatest personal highlight of Roy's time in Germany was his burgeoning love affair with Lala Coy. "We dated through the mail," he explained, "carrying on a pretty hot love affair." Their relationship began to develop greater depth. Roy shared with Lala the frustrations with race and class that had defined his early life. "She understood the hatred and bitterness that caused my fierce temper," he wrote. "From the first letter I knew that she knew more about me than I knew about myself." Roy grew increasingly serious about pursuing Lala as a possible wife, and he told Uncle Nicholas about his intentions. Back in El Campo, Nicholas acted on his nephew's behalf. He visited Lala's family to request that Roy be allowed to formally court her upon his return home. Lala's father, influenced by Uncle Nicholas's stellar reputation, gave his blessing for the relationship to proceed, and the pair continued to write, excited to continue their courtship in person when Roy returned from Germany.[44]

Lala also came from a working-class Latino family, but there were a few major differences between her and Roy. She wasn't as wild or angry in her youth, and her calm demeanor was a good influence on Roy. She also had more formal education. While Roy was starting his Army career, Lala graduated with the El Campo High School class of 1955. In high school, she had belonged to Future Homemakers of America, the book club, the garden club, and the school choir. She was a smart, reserved, and hardworking student. After graduation, she took a job at Zlotnik's clothing store.[45]

In April of 1958, Roy returned to the United States just as his three-year commitment to the Army was about to end. He arrived at Fort Chaffee in Arkansas just weeks after Elvis Presley had been inducted there and received one of the most famous haircuts in human history. While at Fort Chaffee, Roy underwent a physical examination. He was in excellent health. He had picked up some weight while in the Army and now measured feet five eight inches and 165 pounds. His build was still classified as medium, and his vitals—blood pressure, resting heart rate, vision, and hearing—were all normal or better than average. Overall, the physician who examined Roy deemed his health to be "Excellent."[46]

Roy was in great shape, had a steady career, and was falling in love with a woman he admired and respected. He even bought himself a car. His life was becoming ever more promising. He had pulled himself out of the tailspin of trouble that had infected his youth and found purpose through the military, the one place in American society where he finally felt equal. Most importantly, he had gained the admiration of his family, especially Uncle Nicholas. "The year 1958 was a good one for me," he remembered.[47]

Roy arrived home from Germany with "an eagerness I had never felt before," he wrote. He was excited to spend time with Lala and explore the affection growing between the pair. He was twenty-two years old at the time, the same age his father had been when he met Roy's mother at the Lindenau Rifle Club. Roy brought back from Germany a special gift for Lala, a music box he claimed to be over one hundred years old. The box depicted the Virgin Mary holding baby Jesus and played the song "Ave Maria." He told her that he would like to give the box to their first child.[48]

That spring, the young couple began their formal courtship. At first, they attended social functions that were chaperoned. Like many young people in their community, they dated in groups with friends and family, spending little time in private and almost no time alone. "Eventually," Roy wrote, "we were granted the privilege of being allowed to talk privately on her front porch." But Lala's sister would still sit by a window, "watching us lest our hearts begin to rule our heads."[49]

Roy was honorably discharged from the Army on June 9, 1958. He officially reenlisted the very next day and signed up for military police training that would take him to Fort Gordon

Roy at Fort Gordon, May 1959. Courtesy of the Benavidez family.

near Augusta, Georgia. By then, he was earning about $160 per month. For the next nine months, he trained as a military police-man. He did well and stayed out of trouble. According to Roy, he finished first in his class but was bumped to second place after ordering some cadets to throw away clothes that other soldiers had left out after a night of partying. Ironically, the wild-teen-turned-disciplinarian was incensed at his fellow soldiers for goof-ing off and neglecting protocol. He, too, still liked to have fun, but he took military duties extremely seriously. But punishing these men by tossing out their property went a bit too far. "I was still working on that temper of mine," Roy explained.[50]

As often as he could, Roy drove his Chevy the more than one thousand miles back to El Campo to visit Lala. The young couple spent hours talking. "When all you're allowed to do is talk, boy, do you talk," he explained of their closely monitored courtship. Lala listened to Roy's perspective about race and discrimination. He recalled that she was understanding but also helpful in soft-ening the deep-seated resentment he carried from his formative years. "She helped me kill all of those old dragons," he wrote of the angry storms of his youth, even though he would never fully move past the pain of those difficult days. At times, they managed a little more intimacy, sneaking in some kissing and handholding in the darkness of a movie theater. This lasted for about six more months before Roy proposed marriage to Lala, on December 30, 1958.[51]

Roy and Lala were married in a traditional ceremony on June 7, 1959, at St. Robert Bellarmine Catholic Church in El Campo. Lala wore a beautiful ball gown with long sheer lace sleeves and a crown of white flowers on top of her veil. She walked down the aisle on her father's arm, carrying an orange lace bouquet. Roy sported a fresh crew cut and was decked out in a black tuxedo with a white corsage. He looked as handsome as he ever had in his life. He could see that Lala was "smiling shyly" at him from behind her veil. They were a beautiful, beaming couple, surrounded by eighteen attendants, including the flower girl and ring bearer. More than 150 guests watched the nuptials. They celebrated afterward with a barbeque reception in the parish hall.[52]

Roy and Lala's wedding, 1959.
Courtesy of the Benavidez family.

Roy and Lala took a honeymoon to Monterrey, Mexico, about a 380-mile drive from El Campo. They stayed just outside the city near the base of the Sierra Madre Mountains, close to a waterfall known as Cascada Cola de Caballo—"Horsetail Falls." Roy remembered stopping at San Juan, Texas, in Hidalgo County on the way home, where the young couple visited the Shrine of La Virgen de San Juan del Valle and made their secret "promesas" for their marriage.[53]

After their honeymoon, the newlyweds made their home at Fort Gordon, where Roy had been stationed for about a year. During his time there, he earned marksmanship badges in rifle, carbine, and pistol. In August of 1958, he had finished his military police training and was assigned as a chauffeur to the base commander. What seemed like a cushy job was a bit more involved than merely sitting behind the wheel. Being a driver also included doing personal favors for the general and his family. "As 'driver,'" Roy wrote, "I have babysat, prepared meals, and run errands." At one point, he was assigned to be the driver for William Westmoreland, who at the time was the commander of the 101st Airborne and who would later become the head of the United States armed forces in Vietnam. Roy recalled Westmoreland asking him, "Have you ever thought of going Airborne?" Roy and Lala remained at Fort Gordon for another year and ten months, the remainder of his second three-year enlistment in the United States Army.[54]

On March 24, 1961, Roy reenlisted again, this time for six more years. He had risen to the rank of sergeant, a promotion that came with a monthly salary of more than $200 (about $1,900 today). Roy was sent to Army Airborne School, an assignment he had long desired and one that would increase his pay. Roy and Lala packed up and headed to Fort Bragg in Fayetteville, North Carolina. "I planned on being the best trooper they ever had go through that jump school," he remembered.[55]

In North Carolina, Roy and Lala lived in a tiny rental house located about thirty minutes from Fort Bragg. Roy remembered getting up every morning "before the sun came up" to drive to the base, only to return in the darkness of night. The training began with jumping off a tower. "I almost killed myself," Roy recalled of that first jump. "I felt like a drunk puppet on a string." "I never had been so tired in my whole life," he explained of those first days of airborne training.[56]

Jump school was hard, "tougher than anything I had done since joining the army," Roy reflected. He considered quitting to return to his old job at Fort Gordon. But as an advanced soldier, he was tasked with leading a platoon. As a leader, it was his responsibility to help get the younger troops through the difficult course. "I met my men and saw what they looked like," he resolved. "I knew when I saw them that I couldn't quit, and I determined that none of my soldiers would quit either." Roy and his

Roy in jump school at Fort Bragg. Courtesy of the Benavidez family.

men made it through the rigors of airborne training. They were soon up in planes and jumping out over the pine forests of central North Carolina. On May 12, 1961, he received his certificate of completion.[57]

Roy spent much of the next four years hopping out of airplanes. He was part of the 82nd Airborne, one of the most storied units in the United States military. The 82nd had been among the troops who parachuted behind enemy lines during the 1944 D-Day invasion of Normandy. In the early 1960s, they were battle ready and on alert. If the United States ever did go back to war, it was almost certain that the 82nd would be among the first units dropped into combat. Some considered it the most important unit in the entire United States military. As their commander bragged in 1962, "These are the world's best soldiers. . . . They know it, and they're proud of it." "Tough, hardy and led by battle-seasoned officers," noted a *Los Angeles Times* feature from that same year, "the 82nd is therefore preparing for warfare in any area—from the Arctic to desert to jungle."[58]

There was probably never a time when the 82nd was on higher alert than during the Cold War in the early 1960s. The failed Bay of Pigs invasion in April of 1961 and the Cuban Missile Crisis in October of 1962 pushed the United States to the brink of war with Russia. The Berlin Crisis of 1958 to 1961 also frayed relations between the United States and the Soviets, evidenced most distinctly by the erection of the Berlin Wall in 1961. That same year, the American-backed Dominican Republic president Rafael Trujillo was assassinated in Santo Domingo, spinning that country into a civil war. Other potentially volatile episodes arose in places such as Venezuela, Brazil, Vietnam, Iraq, and Algeria. By 1962, the United States military covered a larger expanse of the globe than any military in the history of the world, with roughly 850,000 people stationed in more than one hundred countries.[59]

Lala pinning St. Christopher medal on Roy at Fort Bragg, 1965. Courtesy of the Benavidez family.

Between April of 1961 and December of 1965, Roy was stationed primarily at Fort Bragg. During that time, he was able to pass the General Educational Development (GED) exam. Thirteen years after dropping out of school, Roy finally earned the equivalent of a high school diploma, a proud moment in his life that helped rectify his lack of formal education. He spent a little time in Alabama and a bit more back at Fort Ord in the spring of 1965, but Fort Bragg was otherwise home for him and Lala. "The peacetime military is a hard enough life for a wife," Roy acknowledged. "Many can't take the constant moving and the instability." "I look at the pictures that were taken of us then and realize how young and inexperienced we were," he reminisced of those first years of marriage.[60]

Toward the end of 1965, Lala became pregnant with their first child. Even with this blessing, their lives were about to become much more difficult. That autumn, Roy received new orders that would take him back overseas. He was going to Vietnam, where the United States was rapidly increasing its military presence to contain the spread of communism. At age thirty, with more than thirteen years of experience in the military, Roy was headed into his first war.

CHAPTER 5

LAND MINE

Roy arrived in Saigon in December of 1965. "As the Military Air Transport Service plane banked for its final approach," he remembered, "I glimpsed the city of Saigon through my window. . . . It ranked at the top of anybody's list of the most confusing, frustrating, and dangerous places to be in the world." Roy disembarked the plane and was greeted by an afternoon heat, hanging "heavy and dank," as he stepped onto Vietnamese soil for a short and dangerous tour of duty that nearly cost him his life.[1]

Roy and the other American soldiers boarded a bus that drove them into the city. That first night, he joined some soldiers for drinks at a hotel bar before going to bed to get some sleep before orientation early the next morning. He spent much of the next two weeks in a classroom learning basic Vietnamese and gaining familiarity with the American mission, which was to aid the South Vietnamese Army's defense against the North Vietnamese communists. These Americans were advisors, told to instruct and suggest but not to take any actions on their own.[2]

After a couple weeks in Saigon, Roy was flown to Da Nang just in time to attend the annual *Bob Hope Vietnam Christmas Show* that was performed on the base every year between 1964 and 1972. Roy remembered the audience of young men looking "more like a Boy Scout jamboree than a gathering of warriors." Cameras surrounded the stage as rain fell upon an estimated crowd of ten thousand, mostly young GIs. The men loved Bob Hope. He was one of America's most famous comedians and a man deeply committed to helping boost the morale of the troops. His own son was among the American soldiers stationed in Vietnam. And it didn't hurt that Hope always brought along beautiful women. That year's entourage included actresses Carroll Baker and Joey Heatherton. As the comedian took the stage, the men could hear gunshots in the distance, but the crowd focused on Hope. "The fatigue-clad throng howled its appreciation of his humor," Roy wrote. "It was marvelous."[3]

THE UNITED STATES HAD BEEN HEAVILY INVOLVED IN VIETNAM since 1949. American leaders and their allies had long forewarned of grave consequences if communism were to spread there. "If you lose Korea," a French general told the Joint Chiefs of Staff in 1951, "Asia is not lost; but if I lose Indochina, Asia is lost." That same year, future president Dwight Eisenhower wrote in his diary, "If they [the French] quit and Indochina falls to Commies, it is easily possible that the entire Southeast Asia and Indonesia will go, soon to be followed by India." In 1953, Secretary of State John Foster Dulles cautioned that Vietnam was "in some ways more important than Korea because the consequences of loss there could not be localized, but would spread throughout Asia, and Europe." Determined to prevent that loss, the United

States in the early 1950s backed France's efforts to maintain its colony in Indochina, providing military supplies—planes, napalm, howitzers, and more—even while committing millions of its own troops against communist forces in Korea.[4]

But the French lost anyway, having been routed at the Battle of Dien Bien Phu in the spring of 1954. France had fought a nine-year war that cost the lives of roughly 110,000 soldiers and as much as $1.2 billion a year. Meanwhile, approximately 325,000 Vietnamese fighters and civilians perished during the conflict. The subsequent peace negotiations in Switzerland resulted in the 1954 Geneva Accords, an agreement that ended the war and settled all French claims in Indochina. The settlement created the nations of Cambodia and Laos, and it divided Vietnam into two separate spheres—North and South—set to be reunified with a general election in 1956. Ho Chi Minh told his followers that the Geneva Conference was "a great victory for our diplomacy." He thanked his countrymen for their support and encouraged them to "make every effort to consolidate peace and achieve reunification, independence and democracy throughout our country." "Our country will certainly be unified," he promised, "our entire people will surely be liberated."[5]

Peace did not last long, as the intertwined fate of the two new nations was reshaped by a global struggle between communism and capitalism. Ho Chi Minh was a communist committed to reunifying his country under the banner of an independent Vietnam. And South Vietnam's greatest ally, the United States, was desperate to halt communism in Vietnam to prevent its spread into Laos, Cambodia, Thailand, and perhaps even India and the Middle East. The Vietnamese people held their own diverse opinions, but their internal disagreements would not be allowed to be resolved on their own because the great global powers believed the Vietnamese conflict belonged to the world.

In South Vietnam, America backed a prime minister named
Ngo Dinh Diem who hated the Geneva Accords and never intended to honor the reunification plans. Supported by the Eisenhower administration, he won a fraudulent election in 1955
that established him as president of a new Republic of Vietnam.
He then refused to coordinate with North Vietnamese leaders
to plan for the reunification elections scheduled for July of 1956.
The month came and went, "without incident in Vietnam and
without much international comment," writes historian Fredrik
Logevall. The two countries remained divided, with the North
eager to reunify and the South and its American allies committed to separation.[6]

Beginning in 1956, the United States began spending roughly
$300 million per year to bolster the Diem government and its
military. The legal basis for this aid was provided by the creation of the Southeast Asia Treaty Organization (SEATO) in
September of 1954, just two months after the Geneva Accords
were signed. SEATO empowered its members—namely the
United States and Australia—to use military force to prevent
the spread of communism in Southeast Asia. Under this cover,
the United States sent military advisors and supplies to South
Vietnam and even paid the salaries of officers in the Army of
the Republic of Vietnam (ARVN).[7]

The following year, Diem visited the United States, where
President Eisenhower congratulated him on his "miracle of Vietnam," referring to Diem's ability to maintain South Vietnamese
independence. The pair issued a joint statement in which Eisenhower pledged American assistance against possible "aggression or subversion threatening the political independence of the
Republic of Vietnam." Diem addressed a joint session of Congress, thanking the American people for their support in fighting
against communism. That May, 250,000 people lined the streets
of New York City to cheer on the visiting South Vietnamese

president. The mayor presented him with a medal, and the *New York Times* called him "An Asian Liberator." Later, Diem attended a banquet held in his honor where he sat alongside luminaries such as Eleanor Roosevelt, John D. Rockefeller Jr., and future president John F. Kennedy.[8]

Meanwhile, the North Vietnamese communists prepared for war. Global politics had failed them, so they decided to pursue reunification through military action. North Vietnamese leaders began to rebuild their military and prepare the nation's industries to make war once again. They also established a new command post in an isolated section of the South Vietnamese Central Highlands, where they began chopping a pathway out of the jungle that would become part of the notorious Ho Chi Minh Trail. In 1960, leaders in Hanoi established the National Liberation Front (NLF) to organize resistance to Diem from within the South.[9]

Diem was far less popular among his own people than he was with American politicians. In South Vietnam, his administration failed to capture the support of rural citizens who formed the bulk of the nation's population. The regime further alienated South Vietnamese farmers through unpopular land policies, religious intolerance, and by operating what one American observer called, "a quasi-police state characterized by arbitrary arrests and imprisonment, [and] strict censorship of the press." Diem expanded the range of prosecutable political crimes and even brought back the French guillotine for executions. In response, insurgents operating in South Vietnam began conducting acts of terrorism and sabotage to threaten and harass the Diem government. By 1960, there were serious concerns about a coup that would overthrow Diem.[10]

Back in the United States, Democratic presidential candidate John F. Kennedy attacked the foreign policy record of his opponent, Eisenhower's vice president Richard Nixon, as one of "weakness, retreat and defeat." Kennedy, of course, won the election and doubled down on his promises to fight communism in his famous inauguration speech: "Let every nation know, whether it wishes us well or ill, that we shall pay any price, bear any burden, meet any hardship, support any friend, oppose any foe to assure the survival and the success of liberty."[11]

Once in office, the Kennedy administration escalated American support of Diem. By the end of 1962, more than eleven thousand American "military advisers" operated in Vietnam, helping train recruits for the growing South Vietnamese Army. American troops and supplies poured into Vietnam to help Diem's government stave off invasion from North Vietnam and an insurgency from pro-communist forces operating within South Vietnam itself.[12]

Despite significant aid from the Americans, Diem's control increasingly waned throughout the early 1960s. There were several major problems embedded in his leadership. He was a French-trained bureaucrat and a landed Catholic citizen whose familial wealth dated back to the colonial era, thus making him an easy mark as a puppet of the West. Diem surrounded himself with tyrannical family members who did not believe in true representative government. His brother oversaw corrupt secret intelligence and police forces that ruled through torture, rape, and executions. And his army was beset with problems, including commanders who seemingly didn't want to lead and troops who didn't appear eager to fight, leading to disappointing results in the early stages of a defensive war against highly motivated North Vietnamese regulars.[13]

Diem's regime also persecuted Buddhists in a majority-Buddhist country. In 1963, government forces killed nine people during a pro-Buddhist demonstration, sparking an internal "Buddhist Crisis" that involved peaceful protests and a wave of monks who committed public suicides through self-immolation. By

September of 1963, David Halberstam of the *New York Times* reported, "The protests were clearly out of control, and there were reliable reports that at least two groups were moving toward a coup. A general fear of disintegration gripped the country." Diem was ultimately killed in a coup on November 2, 1963, throwing the nation further into chaos. By the time of Kennedy's own murder just three weeks later, nearly sixteen thousand American military advisers were serving in Vietnam.[14]

Within a week of Kennedy's assassination, his successor, Lyndon B. Johnson, promised Congress, "This nation will keep its commitments from South Vietnam to West Berlin." Johnson followed the course established by previous presidents, insisting that South Vietnam was crucial to American interests. But conditions were nevertheless deteriorating for the South Vietnamese military, whose soldiers were struggling against communist forces.[15]

The following summer, in August of 1964, the United States reported two attacks—at least one of which was falsified—on American ships in the Gulf of Tonkin waters just off North Vietnam. In response, Congress passed a resolution giving President Johnson the authority to indefinitely escalate America's military presence in Vietnam. This Gulf of Tonkin Resolution was passed by a vote of 88–2 in the Senate and a unanimous vote of 416–0 in the House of Representatives. The United States military responded by launching attacks against North Vietnamese naval bases and other installations used to support military action. Three months later, Johnson's landslide victory in that November's presidential election further paved the way to ramp up American involvement.[16]

America's war strategy in Vietnam was based on the idea that North Vietnam would eventually have to halt its invasion in the face of predominant American firepower. This idea was rooted in the experiences of World War II–era bombing campaigns when America's long-range bombers pounded the factories and infrastructure of Germany and Japan, severely limiting the Axis Powers' ability to make war. If American bombers could defeat the Nazis and Japanese, so went the thinking, then surely they could stop the North Vietnamese. The brain trust at the Department of Defense believed that the communists at some point would simply lose the materials, the men, or the will to keep fighting.[17]

In March of 1965, the United States military launched Operation Rolling Thunder, a historic bombing campaign designed to neutralize the North Vietnamese by destroying their military capabilities and crushing civilian morale. A month later, Johnson issued his famous "Peace Without Conquest" speech, declaring that the United States was in Vietnam "because we have a promise to keep." "Since 1954 every American president has offered support to the people of South Vietnam. We have helped to build, and we have helped to defend," he insisted. "Thus, over many years, we have made a national pledge to help South Vietnam defend its independence. And I intend to keep that promise." That spring, the president approved an increase of eighteen to twenty thousand American troops. One hundred thousand more were ordered in July. By the end of 1965, America was fully at war, with approximately 180,000 soldiers on the ground in Vietnam. Roy Benavidez was among them.[18]

Roy's arrival into South Vietnam came just weeks after the Battle of Ia Drang Valley. Made famous by the book and film *We Were Soldiers Once . . . and Young*, the Battle of Ia Drang was the first major direct confrontation between the United States military and the North Vietnamese Army (NVA). "The valley has no strategic importance," noted an Associated Press report. "The idea was to kill as many Communist troops as possible."[19]

On November 14, roughly one thousand American Army troops were dropped by helicopter into the Ia Drang Valley to engage North Vietnamese soldiers who had been attacking special forces camps in the area. The North Vietnamese responded by sending three battalions to meet the Americans. Most of the fighting occurred in the first few days and would prove to be some of the most intense combat of the entire war. Outnumbered by more than three to one, American soldiers fought bravely and used their immense firepower advantages to win a decisive military victory in terms of casualties. During those four days in what one commander called "the Valley of Death," 234 American soldiers lost their lives, and the enemy lost at least 1,200 more. With Ia Drang, observed a journalist in the *Chicago Tribune*, "The United States has entered another new phase of the war in Viet Nam by directly engaging massed forces of the regular North Vietnamese army in the battle of Ia Drang Valley."[20]

In Vietnam, Roy was assigned as a light weapons advisor to South Vietnamese troops. In preparation for his mission, he learned some basic information about Vietnamese culture—common words, customs, holidays, and so forth—and about what he called "nation building," which focused on distributing resources, building infrastructure, and providing political and military education. His unit was there to help teach the South Vietnamese to stand on their own against the North Vietnamese forces.[21]

Roy was stationed near Tam Ky, a small coastal city located about 450 miles northeast of Saigon. The South China Sea lies just a few miles to the east and the Annamite Mountain Range about twenty miles to the west. Tam Ky was part of I Corps Tactical Zone, the northernmost of four tactical zones established by the United States military in its organization of South Vietnam. The defense of I Corps was led by the ARVN and supported by members of the United States Marines and Army. I Corps bordered the Vietnamese Demilitarized Zone (DMZ) that separated North and South Vietnam, thus making it a hotbed of action. North Vietnamese forces could enter I Corps by crossing

the highly fortified DMZ or through trails leading into South
Vietnam from Laos.[22]

At Tam Ky, Roy and his ARVN allies were primarily facing
the military arm of the NLF. Commonly known as the Viet
Cong, NLF members included military insurgents operating in
South Vietnam to aid the North Vietnamese. Some were hold-
overs from the Viet Minh who had fought the French. Others
were drawn into the struggle by the repressive policies of the
American-backed Diem administration and/or the growing involvement of the United States military. Plenty more were con-
scripted through any number of methods.[23]

The NLF were stealthy practitioners of guerilla warfare who
typically did not follow a traditional Western order of combat.
Their membership was mostly male but included people of all
ages and genders who were involved in a wide array of activities,
ranging from direct fighting to logistical support to grassroots
political organizing. Their missions included everything from ex-
ecuting brutal assassinations to feeding farmers' animals. They
were a formidable military foe, fighting on their home turf with
tactics such as booby traps, ambushes, and sabotage. They had an
uncanny ability to blend into the civilian population. Their members hopped back-and-forth across borders, moving undetected,
and operating within close proximity to American and South
Vietnamese soldiers. They built extensive underground tunnel
systems—including one near Tam Ky—that allowed them to
maneuver daringly close to major cities and even American military installations. Still, their force could also be unstable. Their
members might work for the North Vietnamese cause one day
and then help Americans the next, as everyday civilians tried to
negotiate a daily existence amid a dangerous war. Loyalties wa-
vered as all sides—North Vietnamese, South Vietnamese, and
the United States alike—undertook economic incentives and violence to affect NLF membership. While the NLF did use an

explicitly political message to recruit, they also at times employed brutal, murderous tactics to coerce civilian assistance. Menacing the United States and its South Vietnamese allies throughout the war, the NLF were a terrifying, maddening enemy because they were so hard to identify and could seemingly appear anywhere at any time.[24]

Roy was a good soldier who wanted to fulfill his mission as part of broader American foreign policy objectives. But the nature of the American approach to the war—rooted in the sometimes abstract goal of "containment" rather than a definitive victory over the enemy—made life difficult and frustrating for the average American GI. "Democracy, communism, 'domino theory,'" he later wrote, "all those things made sense someplace. Maybe they made sense in conference rooms ten thousand miles from Vietnam, but they meant nothing there." "The history and politics of the war didn't mean much to me at the time," he wrote more than twenty years later. "They still don't."[25]

In wars, territory is usually the most important objective. But in Vietnam, the United States' policy placed more value on killing people than taking land. American servicemen could fight and kill on a hill only to concede the same hill when the killing was done. Even territory controlled by allies could be incredibly dangerous when the enemy could so readily hide among the landscape and the population. Vietnam was different than Roy expected. "Nothing that I had been trained for," he recalled, "had anything to do with what was really going down." "I don't really believe that even our training personnel had any real idea about what we were walking into," he later concluded. Amid such confusion and chaos, Roy's primary concern was staying alive and protecting the lives of those with whom he served.[26]

Roy's base near Tam Ky was a shoddy headquarters, "no more than a tin-roofed shack," he described, "which served as living quarters for the Vietnamese officers and their American advisors." Roy remembered "low-wattage light bulbs," "Army cots . . . in the corners," and "a rickety table covered with maps." At the small base, Roy and his fellow servicemen at least had cots and an opportunity "to relax and be ourselves." Otherwise, he and his comrades were out in the fields and jungles of South Vietnam, advising allied soldiers in a war zone where the enemy could appear from seemingly anywhere. Time spent in the jungle meant time that one could die.[27]

Roy was primarily involved in patrolling. He was one of about fifteen men who would walk into the countryside looking for enemy soldiers. The weather was almost always either excessively rainy or hot, and the men spent their days trudging through the jungles and rice paddies, looking for the "little soldiers in the black pajamas," as Roy sometimes called members of the NLF. It was frightening duty, marching through dangerous territory in a place where "it was often impossible to tell who the enemy was," wrote Roy. To avoid detection, he made it a point to walk quietly in a straight line, especially along the small ridges separating the rice paddies. Booby traps and ambushes happened all around them, and other men brought back harrowing stories from the fields.[28]

At times, the patrols had to camp overnight in the jungle. "There were no enemy lines and no safe havens," Roy explained, "not even in our own quarters." The enemy was all around. Nighttime ambushes may have been unlikely, but the soldiers took care to avoid drawing extra attention. Men slept on their stomachs to avoid snoring, and they hid shiny objects that might draw the interest of a sniper. "Staying alive in Vietnam meant blending in," Roy wrote, because the NLF were eager to kill American advisors. He learned not to slap at mosquitos, as it was a surefire signal of being an outsider. He stayed quiet and small, aided by his short stature and darker skin. "All my life I had been fighting against the bigotry created by these differ-ences," Roy joked. "Now they were helping to keep me alive."[29]

There were numerous close calls. One of Roy's first and most vivid memories of the war was of a day out on patrol. He and an Australian soldier named Dickie were walking with South Vietnamese soldiers on a "bright sunny day" when they paused to eat lunch underneath a large tree. As they ate, Roy remembered Dickie suddenly but softly telling him to continue eating as normal, but warning him, "We're not alone." Suddenly, Dickie jerked his rifle toward the sky and opened fire into the upper branches of the tree as a stunned Roy froze with a mouth full of food. A moment later, a dead NLF soldier dropped from the tree.[30]

One night, Roy and his comrades were patrolling deep in the mountains, searching for the enemy. They were dressed like Vietnamese peasants to blend in, as they traveled far from their compound. After a few quiet days, the unit unexpectedly spotted a massive encampment of between "eight hundred and a thousand men" in a valley a few hundred yards away. Roy spent a night "sweating while the insects chewed on me." He and his men made it out without being seen and reported the information to their superiors.[31]

Another day, Roy was planning to attend mass with a group of Vietnamese Catholics from Saigon. Sometime before, these Vietnamese allies had learned that Roy was Roman Catholic and invited him to join them at church. Roy obliged and continued attending these services for a few weeks until another American soldier warned him against regular church attendance. Establishing any sort of predictable pattern was dangerous because it left one susceptible to ambush by enemies who learned your routine. According to Roy, on the day he stayed back, the transport jeep crossed a bridge with a bomb planted underneath, and all the men were killed.[32]

Later in Roy's tour, he was once again saved by the Australian advisor Dickie. Their group was out on patrol when they came across a roadside fence just outside a hamlet. The men heard some type of whimpering coming from near the barrier. When Roy approached, he saw a small puppy dog sitting in a sack looped onto the fence. When he reached to lift the puppy from its sack, a burst of gunfire landed near his feet, halting him in his tracks. Dickie had fired his gun as a warning for Roy to stop. The Australian then walked over and "slit the little fellow's throat," Roy remembered of the poor dog. "I stood there, watching in shock." When the dog stopped twitching, Dickie cut open the sack to remove the body. When the bag was opened, Roy saw a wire connecting the dog's leg to a grenade. It was a booby trap designed to attract a sympathetic American.[33]

Roy was deeply critical of the ARVN soldiers he was there to advise. "Their army was a joke," he recalled. According to Roy, ARVN was comprised of "traitors, cowards, crazies, and only a few good fighters." The force was much maligned during the early parts of the war. One early observer of ARVN wrote that they were "an army that suffered from an institutionalized unwillingness to fight." This wasn't the whole picture—many members of ARVN were dedicated and talented soldiers who fought bravely to defend their government. More than 200,000 of them died defending South Vietnam, and their abilities would improve later in the war. But most American observers of ARVN in the early 1960s characterized them as poorly trained, undisciplined, even cowardly. One problem was that many of these soldiers lacked the political resolve of either their advisors or their enemies. The Americans in Roy's unit were career military men conducting a mission for a nation they considered to be the greatest purveyor of freedom on the planet. And North Vietnamese soldiers believed they were fighting the final salvo in a long war for national independence. ARVN soldiers, on the other hand, had borne witness to countless examples of coups and corruption and carried no such faith in their government. Roy later wrote,

"I never could see one lick of difference between the people we were fighting for and the people we were fighting against."[34]

Roy wrote of a dangerous ARVN officer named Wag. Trained in the United States, Wag was a first lieutenant with a reputation for "cruelty toward civilians and Viet Cong prisoners," Roy recalled. One day, Roy and Wag were out patrolling an area where sniper fire had been reported. According to Roy, they entered a small village, and Wag began signaling for the locals to approach. When the residents ignored Wag's command, he fired his handgun toward "30–35 villagers," Roy described, who scurried to obey the order.[35]

Through an interpreter, Roy learned that Wag was asking the villagers to identify the sniper who had fired upon his allies a few days prior. He was yelling, "berating" the locals, Roy testified, when he suddenly grabbed one young woman by her hair and dragged her out in front of the rest. She was pregnant, visibly showing, and Wag screamed at her, accusing her of carrying the baby of an NLF guerilla. He threw her to the ground and then "began viciously kicking her in the stomach with the toe of his boot," Roy remembered. Wag then turned and grabbed a young man and began stabbing him in the arms and upper torso with a bayonet. When the beating ceased, Wag pulled out his handgun, pressed it to the man's temple, and blew out the side of the man's skull, scattering the victim's brains across the dirt. Some of the villagers glanced at Roy and another American who stood watching. Roy walked away, convinced there was nothing he could have done. "I will never forget the look in those villagers' eyes," he wrote nearly thirty years later.[36]

Roy bore witness to another horrifying example of civilian murder at a refugee site near his home base. Tam Ky, like many South Vietnamese cities during the war, drew displaced rural refugees whose homes had been destroyed by the violence in the countryside or whose movements were constricted by

American war strategies. Roy tended to blame either the NLF or ARVN for such displacement, but the actions of American aircraft, gunships, and soldiers certainly also played a major role in displacing millions of rural peasants. Roy called this particular refugee site "a pitiful excuse for a camp." It made him think better about the difficult living conditions in the migrant labor camps of his youth. "We had lived well compared to the way those people were living," he lamented. And so, the American soldiers took some initiative to improve the camp. They scavenged some extra building materials and helped construct better housing and sanitary facilities for the refugees. After finishing their work, Roy and his colleagues were "feeling pretty proud of ourselves."[37]

Three nights later, the refugee camp came under attack from the NLF. Roy and his fellow soldiers awoke to gunfire near one o'clock in the morning. NLF soldiers rolled through the village attacking or kidnapping civilians and leaving fliers denouncing the war. That night, a reported thirty-three refugees were killed and fifty-four more wounded. Roy believed the attack was meant to warn other Vietnamese peasants against cooperating with the Americans or South Vietnamese government. "We were all stunned . . . ," Roy recalled. "We all knew that the people in that camp had no way to defend themselves."[38]

The next morning, Roy and his colleagues walked over to the camp. "We could see the place was in bad shape," he remembered. "The gates had been shot to splinters." The Americans heard loud cries coming from near one of the buildings. As they rounded a corner, they were stunned by what they saw. "There, on the wall of the barracks facing us," Roy wrote, "three children were nailed, crucified, the spikes in their hands and feet suspending them three feet above the blood-soaked ground."[39]

After about three months in Vietnam, Roy's first tour ended in March of 1966 when he was almost killed. His men were out in the countryside on patrol, and Roy was walking point, something American advisers were not supposed to do. As Roy recalled, there had been some type of joke in the unit about Roy's indigenous background. The South Vietnamese soldiers, familiar with American Western films, joked that Roy's Yaqui ethnicity made him a natural tracker and suggested that he should be the one leading the patrol. It was a good-natured joke among fighting men. Roy played along, agreeing to walk point on patrol, the most dangerous and exposed spot in the unit.[40]

Roy was humping along on one of those days when he stepped on some type of a makeshift land mine. NLF booby traps could be quite primitive. Some were merely sharpened sticks posted into the ground; there's no telling exactly what Roy stepped on. The device detonated like a land mine, but it thankfully did not carry such an explosive charge that would have killed him on the spot.

The charge sent several hundred pounds of force into Roy's body, ejecting him from the ground and sending him flying through the air. He landed violently into the earth, knocked unconscious by the collision. Roy had no memory of the following moments, and no one could ever provide him with a definitive explanation of what happened next.[41]

Roy woke up in the hospital. He was coming out of a long fog that had clouded his journey from that spot in the jungle onto a hospital ship, to an Air Force base in the Philippines, and finally to the Beach Pavilion at Fort Sam Houston in San Antonio. Roy was back home in Texas. He had lost some hearing in his right ear, his sense of taste had been dulled, and his mind was still groggy. Worst of all, he could not feel any part of his body below the waist. He had no external wounds, but the force of the booby trap had twisted Roy's spine "like a corkscrew," he wrote.[42]

Roy stayed in the hospital for a substantial amount of time. Lala came from El Campo every weekend to be with him. She was pregnant at the time, about four months in, having conceived the baby not long before Roy left for Vietnam. On some of her first visits, Roy was barely conscious. He didn't even remember all the times she came, and he later admitted that he took her visits for granted. As Roy's mind slowly returned, he and Lala would sit in the hospital and talk. There wasn't much else they could do. Roy could use a wheelchair, but they couldn't get far outside the walls of the hospital.[43]

Some of the men around Roy were much worse off. By March of 1966, the United States had lost roughly 2,200 men killed and another 10,500 wounded in the war. As Roy later wrote, "The human debris of Vietnam was beginning to wash up on the shores of America. . . . I saw human beings with wounds so severe it was unbelievable they were still alive." Next to Roy in the hospital were men who were badly burned and others who had lost arms and legs. As injured as Roy was, at least he was alive and his limbs were intact.[44]

But Roy was also deeply afraid. He was unable to move his legs, and the prognosis was unpromising. His doctors told him that he might never regain the ability to walk. If that were true, then Roy's time in the military was over. Grateful as he was to have survived the explosion, he was terrified at the prospect of going back to El Campo in a wheelchair. He had first joined the armed forces nearly fourteen years earlier, desperately seeking a pathway toward a brighter future. The Army had provided an escape from the poverty and prejudice of his youth. With his injury, he faced the possibility of losing his livelihood.[45]

Still only thirty years old, Roy began to imagine life back home as a permanently disabled Hispanic man. His mind raced to other peoples' perceptions and concerns about what they might say: "Bet he shot himself in the foot just so he could get that check," he imagined his white neighbors griping. "Heck, they're all the same, even too lazy to steal. Except from the gov'ment." What could he possibly become, he wondered, especially if he were no longer able to walk? "Without the Army," he wrote, "I felt that I had no future."[46]

Roy turned to God. He had been raised in a religious family, with his aunt Alexandria forming the backbone of their family's Catholicism. That time in the hospital deepened his commitment. While recovering, Roy spent a great deal of time in the chapel. He was so inwardly focused on his own predicament that he had trouble connecting with others. Roy was fixated on "what my life had become," he remembered. Sitting in the chapel, he found in God a good listener at a time when "the doctors didn't listen, and the therapists didn't listen, and when Lala just couldn't listen anymore." He later wrote that he began to understand his survival as a gift—or at least a sign—of some type of divine intervention to save him for some greater cause. "I began to believe that my life had been spared for some purpose," he remembered.[47]

As April turned into May, Roy worked through his physical therapy. His recovery started with hydrotherapy in the pool. He began to learn how to live in his wheelchair. Roy endured these lessons, but he adamantly refused to believe that he wouldn't be able to walk again, and he could not bring himself to concede that his time in the Army was finished, even as he knew that the physicians in the hospital doubted his ability to reenter the service. It seemed to him like only a matter of time until he was medically discharged and placed on permanent retirement due to disability. He imagined being "back in El Campo sitting in a wheelchair on the front porch," he wrote. He begged the doctors for their patience in making their final judgments about his future in the Army.[48]

Meanwhile, Roy began to take therapy into his own hands, supplementing his guided physical therapy with some training of his own. Every night when the lights went out, Roy waited for the nurses and doctors to leave so he could try to stand and walk. The first night, he rolled out of bed and hit the ground "with a crunch," he remembered. The head nurse "chewed me out," he wrote, and orderlies lifted him back into bed. On the second night, Roy once again hit the floor, but he then managed to use his arms to drag his body to the opposite wall, where the hospital staff found him leaning the next day. "I got my butt chewed out again," he remembered.[49]

On the third night, Roy tumbled out of bed again. He made it back to the wall and reached his hands up to grab onto adjacent nightstands, using the tables to pull his body upright into a standing position. He recalled himself "just sort of hanging there" until he tried to put weight on his feet. When he did, "a burning pain shot through my back . . . ," he remembered, "like I'd been stabbed with a red-hot knife." He again collapsed to the floor, where the hospital staff found him the following morning.[50]

This struggle continued night after night. Some of the other men in the hospital were so amused by the night crawling that they joked about placing bets on how far Roy would make it. "Every night, I got knocked down," Roy explained. "Every night I got back up again. . . . The pain was like nothing I could have ever dreamed about." But Roy continued to push forward, showing slow but steady progress. One night, he was finally able to stand. On another night, he was able to move his toes. Eventually, he managed to perform a little shuffle with his back against the wall.[51]

As Roy remembers it, the doctors came close to recommending he be discharged from the service. Even after he was able to convince them that he might walk again, they still held doubts about his ability to remain in the Army. But Roy convinced them to hold off on the formal recommendation of separation, aided by testimonies of the other hospitalized soldiers who had witnessed the progress of his night moves. At one desperate point, Roy was speaking with a doctor about his health when he managed to turn his body and stand up beside his bed to convince the physician of his progress.[52]

That May, Roy formally began therapy to help him regain the ability to walk. He later credited his painful nighttime physical therapy for his recovery. It was a remedy that teetered on the impossible, but from that point on, it became part of a mythology about Roy's grit and determination. However it happened, Roy did indeed start to improve dramatically. And that May, he walked out of the hospital with Lala on his arm.[53]

CHAPTER 6

SOJOURN

IN THE SPRING OF 1966, ROY AND LALA RETURNED TO FORT Bragg. During the months Roy was fighting in Vietnam and hospitalized in San Antonio, Lala had lived in the couple's trailer in El Campo. That trailer had moved with them all over the country, logging "more miles going from post to post than most people travel in a lifetime," Roy wrote. It was an important place of solace for their family, the one spot in a chaotic world where they could spend private time together in peace. "No matter where we were," Roy remembered of their travels, "when I opened that door I was home." They settled in a small neighborhood of mobile homes located just south of Fort Bragg and began to prepare to welcome a new baby into their family. Just over four months after Roy nearly died, he and Lala were blessed with a new life. The couple's first child, Denise, was born in Fayetteville, North Carolina, on July 31, 1966, at the Womack Army Medical Center.[1]

In the summer of 1966, Fort Bragg was abuzz with men preparing for war. By the time Roy returned, Fort Bragg was churning out ten thousand combat-ready soldiers per month. That summer, a visiting reporter described Bragg as "a maze of dirt roads" occupied by "barrel chested, broad shouldered, neat and clean officers" who conducted their duties beneath "thunderous anti-tank guns blasting at splintered targets."[2]

America's war in Vietnam was expanding. When Roy first went there in December of 1965, 181,000 American soldiers were stationed in the country. Within a year, that number would swell to roughly 385,000. Operation Rolling Thunder wasn't nearly as effective as military officials had hoped, and it was becoming increasingly clear that a quick victory was out of reach. After the US military dropped 128,000 tons of bombs in 1966, a confidential December report concluded, "There is no evidence at present that economically and politically Hanoi should not be able to withstand the long, hard war it professes to have in mind."[3]

Meanwhile, the country Roy was fighting for was undergoing immense changes. The mid-1960s saw a revolution of race in America. Black communities across the American South launched a massive civil rights movement, drawing together a multiracial coalition whose greatest gains were realized in the passages of the 1964 Civil Rights Act and the 1965 Voting Rights Act. These monumental pieces of legislation made racial segregation in public spaces illegal, thus eliminating the most visible components of the Southern Jim Crow system of racial apartheid. Hispanic kids like Roy no longer had to sit in the back of movie theaters or wait outside of restaurants that refused to serve non-white customers. Roy didn't say much about his thoughts on the matter, but these profound changes meant that his and Lala's children would not have to grow up facing the same humiliations that so deeply shaped Roy's own childhood.

The Black Southern Civil Rights Movement helped inspire similar movements among Hispanic Americans. LULAC and

the American GI Forum operated at the center of a growing
Latino civil rights movement that fought for school desegrega-
tion, higher agricultural wages, and immigrant rights. By the
late 1960s, a new generation of Hispanic activists, many calling
themselves Chicanos, had launched a more militant movement
than the previous generation, demanding not only basic civil
rights but also land reform, anti-poverty policies, and political
representation. Roy was not directly involved with the civil rights
protests of that era, but he and his family were certainly affected
by improving racial conditions in the United States. For his part,
Roy and a few other Hispanic non-commissioned officers were
involved with a group called "Club Latino" that organized Hispanic heritage events at American military bases.[4]

According to the Army, roughly eighty thousand Hispanic
soldiers served in the Vietnam War. The precise numbers are difficult to track because the Army usually counted them as white,
and Hispanic Americans themselves derived from very diverse
backgrounds. They also had divergent views on the war that
changed over time. Early in the Vietnam War, some of the major
figures in both the American GI Forum and LULAC expressed
support for American involvement. In a 1967 letter to Lyndon B.
Johnson, American GI Forum founder Dr. Héctor Garcia wrote,
"As far as I know the majority if not the total Mexican-American
people approve of your present course of action in Vietnam."
Other members of the American GI Forum publicly demonstrated in Los Angeles and Austin in support of the war. In
1968, the GI Forum helped sponsor Spanish-speaking musicians
who flew to Vietnam to perform for Hispanic troops. "Our men
are 100 percent with our government," reported one of the en-
tertainers. The GI Forum supported Latino soldiers by maintaining a list of Hispanic casualties, greeting Gold Star families,
and attending the funerals of servicemen killed in action. As in
World War II, Hispanic supporters of American involvement in

Vietnam argued that military service should translate to more inclusion at home.[5]

But there were also plenty of dissidents, especially as the war grew more unpopular in later years. The Chicano Movement that emerged in the 1960s was deeply connected to the anti-war movement and included Hispanic veterans. They, too, launched demonstrations, marching against the war and picketing Army induction centers. Anti-war Chicano activists held teach-ins, sponsored lectures, and produced pamphlets arguing for Hispanic males to resist military service. It was a significant movement, especially in California, where the most militant activists sported brown berets and depicted themselves as soldiers against the war. In 1970, the California branch of the American GI Forum broke with the national organization by passing a resolution opposing the war. Much like among the rest of the country, there was no single Hispanic American opinion on the war, with reactions ranging from full support to outright anti-government revolt.[6]

Those Latinos who fought in the armed forces reported experiences fairly typical of American soldiers. Most of them enlisted voluntarily. They had limited political consciousness going into the military but were nevertheless patriotic and deeply committed to helping their country defeat the perceived evils of communism. Like generations before them, they were patriots who thought military service would help improve their conditions at home. As a whole, they reported fewer racial conflicts in the military than they had experienced back at home, as racial conflict was mitigated by the pressing need for teamwork in the face of warfare. Non-white soldiers in noncombat jobs reported more racial discrimination than those on the front lines. Similar to other veterans, the experience of the war often soured their view of American foreign policy and made them more politically conscious. As one scholar has observed, "The great majority went to Vietnam believing they were doing the right thing and were disillusioned when they saw the reality of the war." Those who arrived later tended to be more skeptical. All Hispanic American soldiers and veterans were deeply affected by the war itself and the political context of anti-war protests.[7]

At Fort Bragg, Roy was assigned to a special detail that essentially made him an administrative assistant. He was still recovering from his injuries, so the Army tasked him with clerical office duties. He was among the many thousands of active soldiers charged with piloting documents through the immense bureaucracy of an army at war. "I was handling benefits and problems for the families of my buddies who were off fighting in Vietnam," he remembered. "It was an important job, and I was doing it."[8]

But Roy did not like the work. He was a combat veteran, a grizzled, hardworking blue-collar fighter who felt remorse that his brothers-in-arms were fighting half a world away while he was nestled safely behind a desk in the United States. The ease of his job offered him little internal peace, as he was gravely concerned about his friends at war. "I was a warrior, not a clerk," he remembered. "Sitting at that desk was like sitting in a prison for me."[9]

Physically speaking, Roy's back remained a major problem. Excruciating pain was a "constant companion," he remembered. And his mind was clouded by side effects brought on by the painkillers he took to manage his agony. Roy was on Darvon, an opioid released in 1955 to help patients manage moderate pain. Darvon is a once-popular but dangerous drug that was later banned in the United States and Europe due to dangerous side effects it can have on a patient's heart. These risks were largely unknown when Roy was taking the drug in the mid-1960s, but physicians at the time did suspect that Darvon could be addictive, and they knew that it causes brain fog, memory loss, drowsiness, and a host of other side effects that can mentally impair users.[10]

Roy was taking an excessive amount of Darvon, self-diagnosing his dosage based on the extent of his daily pain. At a time when most doctors recommended patients take no more than six hundred milligrams in twenty-four hours, Roy reported ingesting as much as 1,500 milligrams per day. He took the pills as needed, and he typically ended his working days with a visit to the Non Commissioned Officers Club, where he would have several drinks before driving home to his wife and newborn daughter. "It's really amazing I never killed myself on that short drive," he later reflected, but he needed something to manage the pain. His physical discomfort was just as crippling, if not worse, than the risks of the drug.[11]

A visit to a local doctor likely saved him. Whenever Roy was in a lot of pain, he would see a Fayetteville physician who was willing to treat him without a formal appointment. This local doctor told Roy that the pills and his drinking were creating a dangerous cocktail that could lead to addiction and other severe health problems. Roy was never one to be very careful about his own health, but his greatest fear was being discharged from the Army, so he resolved to quit Darvon. He claimed that he left pills sitting in that doctor's office and quit cold turkey.[12]

Roy needed to train. He had undergone physical therapy to learn to walk again, but his body required additional work to recover more fully. The pills were a temporary solution; he needed to build strength and flexibility to improve his condition. "Your back and legs are cramped up tighter than a drum," the doctor had told him. "The pills are just masking it. You've got to stretch those injured muscles and build them back up again." After finally being confronted with the realities of his recovery, Roy started working out. Each morning, he woke up early to run and lift weights at the gym. At the beginning, the pain was "unrelenting," he wrote, but it gradually began to improve. He would never again live completely free of pain, but the exercise helped.[13]

Roy's desk duty was untenable. He was no clerk. America was at war, and Roy at thirty-one years old was still in the prime of his fighting life. He was in a tough spot, wanting to train but also feeling as if he needed to hide the severity of his injuries to protect his enlistment. Fort Bragg was crawling with men soon off to war. The Army needed fighters, not desk jockeys. So long as he wasn't training with his peers, the threat of dischargement hovered in the back of his mind. Roy knew he had to become a soldier again.[14]

On a warm Saturday morning that September, Roy had walked out to retrieve his newspaper when he spotted a friendly neighbor who was in one of the airborne units. That morning, this neighbor was scheduled to go to a training session and cajoled Roy to join him. "Come on, Hoss," Roy remembered his friend telling him, "I see you running every morning, you're in great shape. At least come along and keep me company." Never one to back down from peer pressure, Roy agreed to go along.[15]

When they arrived at the drop zone, Roy stood off to the side while a hundred or so men began to prepare to load onto helicopters for their jumps. According to Roy, these men were office workers who had little time to train during the week and needed to complete drills on the weekend to remain jump certified and thus entitled to an extra fifty-five dollars per month in pay.[16]

As Roy watched, he thought about jumping himself. He knew his body wasn't ready. No commander would have signed off on him jumping, and he was terrified of the pain that would shoot through his body when he tried to land. But that day also presented him with the chance to do some real training for the first time in months. No one at the jump site knew the full extent of his injuries. As Roy stood there watching and thinking, an unknowing sergeant slapped him on the back and asked, "You jumpin' or what?" Roy reacted. He told the man he would jump, and the sergeant assigned him to a group scheduled to go up in about forty minutes.[17]

But Roy couldn't just board a helicopter and jump. He had been on special duty and needed the signature of a commanding officer to authorize his participation. With only a few minutes to resolve this dilemma, Roy got an idea. He sauntered over to another sergeant running the drills and offered the man a cold drink, volunteering to hold the officer's clipboard to give the man a short break. There was nothing out of the ordinary about this nice gesture, just one soldier helping out another on a hot North Carolina day. The sergeant thanked Roy for the thoughtful suggestion and walked off to enjoy his refreshment. Roy flipped through the paperwork in the clipboard until he found a "refresher slip," which he quickly completed with his own information and backdated by several weeks. He then forged the signature of an officer who had recently left for Vietnam. That falsified form gave Roy the approval he needed to jump.[18]

Roy jumped three times that day. The first jump went very poorly. His technique was awful, and he somehow managed to set himself in such an odd position that his body spun in the wind like a top. It was an egregious mistake that not even a rookie jumper should make. These were simple jumps for experienced airborne soldiers. Dropping a thousand feet from a stationary helicopter in North Carolina is much easier than jumping out of an airplane flying over a combat zone. Roy called these trainings "the easiest jump that is ever made." A sergeant rushed over and chastised Roy's embarrassingly poor jump. "He was furious," Roy admitted.[19]

After such an abysmal attempt, Roy felt compelled to execute a proper jump, and he got back in line. This time, his neighbor—the one person on the scene who did have some inkling of Roy's physical condition—ran over to question Roy. "He thought I was crazy," Roy recalled, "and he said as much." Roy went anyway.

His technique was better on the second jump, but he landed on his butt, which sent a shockwave of pain through his body. Nevertheless, he felt much better about his performance. "Even with the pain I felt like a soldier again," he wrote. The third jump was excellent. Roy was once again jump certified. He and the neighbor celebrated with a cold beer and a few gulps of whiskey.[20]

Lala was furious. "Benavidez!" she yelled, "you're not supposed to be jumping. You're going to kill yourself." Lala was rightfully worried. But she also only knew a third of it. Roy told her he jumped, but he didn't tell her he jumped *three* times. The hasty decision paid off. Roy earned the extra fifty-five dollars per month, and had taken a major step forward in convincing both Lala and himself that he was capable of going back into action. After feeling like "the walls of that office were closing in on me," by September of 1966 Roy was beginning to feel more confident in his ability to resume his full duties as a soldier.[21]

As late summer turned into autumn, Roy continued his desk job at Fort Bragg. Those months were relatively uneventful. His health was improving, and he performed his duties well. That fall, letters from his superiors commended Roy for "the cheerful willingness with which you accepted each separate duty" and "the purposeful determination with which you set about the accomplishment of that duty." "The fine quality of your leadership," wrote one captain, "is evidenced by the high esteem in which you are held by your superiors and subordinates alike." In November, Roy was invited to deliver a lecture on "personal affairs" to a group of men preparing to head overseas. He did such a wonderful job that a lieutenant colonel and a major general sent him personal notes expressing their "appreciation" and thanking him for "a job well done." But Roy remained hungry for more.[22]

Shortly before his first tour in Vietnam, Roy had applied to join the Army's Special Forces, a group of elite soldiers commonly known as the Green Berets. Created in 1952, the Green

Berets were developed specifically for the unique needs of a global Cold War. They first saw combat in Korea in 1953 and in subsequent years deployed to faraway places across the globe, fighting not just in America's well-known conflicts like Vietnam but also in remote hot spots beyond the purview of the American public. Mobilized for special missions, Green Berets were trained in unconventional warfare. Their methods involved psychological operations, guerilla mobilization, and counterinsurgency tactics. Working in stealth, Green Berets were at once fighters, teachers, linguists, and negotiators. Their motto is "To Liberate the Oppressed."[23]

In 1966, there were 10,500 Green Berets stationed in Japan, Vietnam, Germany, Panama, and Fort Bragg, which is where they trained. That year, a song titled "Ballad of the Green Berets" spent five weeks atop the pop music charts, selling approximately nine million singles and albums. The previous year, a novel titled *The Green Berets* had sold nearly three million copies and was acquired to be adapted into a film starring John Wayne. At a time when few civilians understood the nature of the fighting in Vietnam, Green Berets became the nation's first heroes of the war. Millions of radio listeners sang along with the lyrics telling the story of the "Fighting soldiers from the sky," so goes the song, and the "Fearless men who jump and die." In those years, dozens of American newspapers and magazines published feature articles chronicling the Green Berets' training and special missions. The *Saturday Evening Post* called them the "Harvard Ph.D.'s of warfare." Department stores across the United States carried replicas of their famous headwear. Few civilians knew what they actually did, but at the time, the Green Berets were probably the most famous and celebrated fighting force on Earth.[24]

Becoming a Green Beret was difficult. These were professional soldiers, typically volunteers whose entrance into the Army predated America's first major battles in Vietnam. They were older, fitter, and more learned than the average soldier. All of them were required to be jump qualified and conversant in at least two languages. Roy called them "the elite of the elite." According to him, roughly seventy percent of those who tried failed to join. He was determined to be among the 30 percent who succeeded.[25]

Roy's initial application to become a Green Beret was lost somewhere in the Army's ocean of bureaucracy. But as an office clerk, he had access to forms. According to Roy, he re-created the long-lost documents needed for his admission, forging the signatures, backdating the information, and even "aging" the documents by folding and wetting and drying the paperwork. Within a month, he was accepted into the training group at the John F. Kennedy Special Warfare Center at Fort Bragg.[26]

The Special Forces training facilities were quite nice. Just two years earlier, the facility had added brand-new headquarters and an academic building that cost a combined $2 million. Another $15 million funded new barracks, mess halls, and administrative offices. A trainee who passed through the center not long after Roy described the accommodations as "modern brick buildings resembling college dormitories." "Our quarters were immaculate," this trainee observed, "with brightly painted walls and tiled floors."[27]

Special Forces training was designed to prepare soldiers for the mental and physical stress of isolated combat conditions. The trainees spent days in the forest, humping across miles of North Carolina swamps and hills, all while carrying dozens of pounds on their backs. These trainees had to be self-sufficient and capable of surviving in the wilderness, so their gear was inspected before training missions to ensure they carried no extra supplies. Operating in twelve-man A-Teams, they had to catch and kill their own food—chickens, deer, rabbits, and goats. They'd march dozens of miles out into the dense forest to complete complex simulated missions that required precise navigation and survival skills and were complicated by impromptu challenges. The missions could change at any time, as Army sergeants presented some new unforeseen obstacle. A mock ambush or new intelligence might alter their objective and extend missions by hours or even days. This was deadly serious training. If a sentry fell asleep on overnight guard duty, the sergeants might awaken the entire unit and force them to dig six-foot graves to simulate having to bury their dead comrades. The soldiers' minds were clouded by the fog of starvation and exhaustion, and their bodies were riddled with soreness and pain. It was extremely difficult, and a lot of very athletic and intelligent men washed out. Realistically, the only reason Roy physically had a chance was because the Army was at war and desperately needed more men for these roles.[28]

Roy began his Special Forces training in February of 1967. He was a staff sergeant, so he was charged with not only learning himself but also leading men of a lesser rank. "The training was tough," Roy remembered. The men ran miles each day with weighted vests and finished with calisthenics. They "ran obstacle courses" and "made parachute jumps." They spent weeks at a time in the woods, surviving only on what they could find or kill to eat. Roy was in "a lot of pain," he recalled. "My back ached constantly. The truth was, I should have still been in physical therapy in a hospital, not physical training for Special Forces." But each day he somehow forced himself to complete the training. It was a testament to his resolve.[29]

Green Berets learned at least as much in the classroom as in the field. "My commanders," Roy remembered, "expected me to study like a college student." He felt left behind because of his lack of education. Roy had earned his GED, but he had never been in classes with so many intelligent men, some of whom held college degrees. For Roy, the classes in weapons, organizational behavior, combat tactics, meteorology, and oceanography were very challenging and required a lot of studying. There was so much to consume. Green Berets were trained for unusual circumstances in extraordinarily dangerous places. They needed to be able to operate as one-man units, capable of survival in almost any setting imaginable. Such a need required lessons in psychology, propaganda, and infiltration techniques. A Green Beret was expected to be capable of organizing a group of villagers into a team of guerilla fighters. They had to be competent teachers of not only soldiers but also indigenous civilians. Green Berets spent as much as an entire week just learning about methods of instruction. "If you cannot learn to teach," one Special Forces master sergeant advised in the late 1960s, "there's no room for you in SF."[30]

Special Forces soldiers were trained broadly, but each man also specialized in at least one major discipline. Roy prequalified to concentrate in intelligence or light and heavy weapons. He chose intelligence because "it was probably best for my army career since NCO's were usually promoted faster in that area." But he then switched to the weapons course before coming back to learn intelligence. In the weapons course, Roy learned how to use "every firearm imaginable, regardless of how basic or how lethal it was." Green Berets in the field might have to use the tools of the enemy to fight. In some of their missions, they weren't even allowed to take American weapons into combat. In intelligence, Roy learned how to gather and disseminate information about foreign troops and populations, and he studied critical tactics that taught him how to handle prisoners of war and classified documents.[31]

Roy spent twenty-five weeks training with the Special Forces Training Group and eight weeks learning his specialties in the classroom. During that time, his six-year enlistment expired, and he received a nine-month extension before committing to another six-year enlistment upon the completion of his training. In

November of 1967, Roy officially joined the Army Special Forces as an operations and intelligence sergeant. After graduation, one of the commanding officers commended Roy for "attention to duty, devotion, loyalty, and knowledge" as well as "superior abilities particularly during the period of time you worked as a platoon Sgt."[32]

At that time, Army Special Forces were operating not only in Vietnam but also in Latin America. Throughout the late 1960s, Green Berets were sent into Panama, Honduras, Ecuador, and Venezuela to provide aid to American-friendly governments who were trying to stave off socialist revolutions. Especially after the problems with Fidel Castro in Cuba in the early 1960s, American leaders sought to restrict the spread of any Marxist revolutionary movement in Latin America. Between 1964 and 1966 alone, United States Army Special Forces carried out a reported 247 missions in Latin America. "We're the work horse of the Southern Command," an unnamed Green Beret officer told a

Roy in his Green Beret uniform. Courtesy of the Benavidez family.

reporter. "We aren't putting out brush fires in Latin America, but we are trying to keep any more from starting."[33]

Green Berets in Latin America usually served as advisors for various government entities. Their duties included teaching locals how to construct infrastructure, such as roads and water systems, and how to set up safe lines of communication. The vast majority of the Green Berets sent to Latin America spoke Spanish or Portuguese or both. They operated in small teams of fifteen, making them extremely mobile. These covert actions were largely classified, but the appearance of Green Berets in places like Guatemala sporadically appeared in American newspapers.[34]

According to Roy, his first duties with Special Forces took him on brief classified missions to Panama, Honduras, and Ecuador. Bilingual and Hispanic, Roy was an ideal soldier to serve in Spanish-speaking countries. Because these missions were classified, little is known about the details of his duties, excepting that he was doing exactly what the Special Forces had trained him to do: working with American-friendly groups to thwart potential revolutions started by what they termed "unfriendly guerillas." Having been such a great fit for duty in Latin America, Roy thought he might be assigned to Venezuela long-term. "I was so sure of myself," he remembered, "I even told Lala." But the Army had other plans.[35]

THE SITUATION IN SOUTHEAST ASIA WAS MUCH MORE PRESSING. By the time Roy finished his Special Forces training in the autumn of 1967, the United States was facing a military stalemate in Vietnam and losing public support for the war. Even as troop levels increased to 465,000, Secretary of Defense Robert McNamara in November of 1967 privately warned the president, "Continuing on our present course will not bring us by the end of 1968 enough closer to success, in the eyes of the

American public, to prevent erosion of popular support for our involvement in Vietnam." It was a dim but honest view. McNamara warned the president that continuing the current strategy would result in "between 700 and 1,000 US killed in action every month" without making any real progress to show the American public. The United States was not necessarily losing the war in Vietnam, but it was also clearly not winning it anytime soon. "There is, in my opinion," McNamara continued, "a very real question whether under these circumstances it will be possible to maintain our efforts in South Vietnam for the time necessary to accomplish our objectives there." The Johnson administration did not share this analysis with the American people, but the future of the conflict looked increasingly bleak toward the end of 1967.[36]

Of particular concern to the Johnson administration was the ongoing infiltration of enemy soldiers and supplies into South Vietnam by way of Cambodia and Laos. The North Vietnamese managed to evade American forces largely by using the border regions of Laos and Cambodia to smuggle goods and troops into South Vietnam. The North Vietnamese would not have been able to continue fighting the war without these safe havens and resupply routes. The most famous of these paths was the Ho Chi Minh Trail, which by the late 1960s bore little resemblance to the familiar images of mud-soaked, barefoot porters struggling to carry supplies on their backs and bikes. By then, the Ho Chi Minh Trail had been developed into a complex series of roads on which thousands of large trucks carried tons of supplies.[37]

The Sihanouk Trail was nearly as troubling. Unlike the Ho Chi Minh Trail that ran from North Vietnam through the sparsely populated Laotian Annamite Mountain Range, the Sihanouk Trail originated in southwestern Cambodia and ran through major population centers in the middle of the country, including the capital at Phnom Penh.[38]

The Sihanouk Trail was named for Norodom Sihanouk, the enigmatic leader of Cambodia who was facing his own series of internal and external crises that shaped his relationship with the United States. Sihanouk was a monarch who first took the throne in 1941 and helped lead Cambodia through World War II and the waning days of French colonial rule before Cambodia achieved independence in November of 1953.[39]

In the wake of French rule, Sihanouk wanted to ensure that Cambodia remain neutral amid a rapidly escalating global Cold War. But the United States, which was not a signing member of the Geneva Accords, attempted to pressure Cambodia to join SEATO, the treaty created in the wake of the Geneva Accords to establish an alliance of American protectorates in Southeast Asia. Cambodia's participation in the Geneva Accords barred it from joining such a military alliance, but the United States continued to push Sihanouk, promising aid to Cambodia and warning that neutrality in a global conflict was not an option. As Sihanouk tried to navigate relationships with superpowers, he also worked to stave off internal threats from both communist and anti-communist Cambodian organizations that wanted to steer the nation into the orbit of either the North Vietnamese and Chinese communists or the United States and its anti-communist allies.[40]

Sihanouk was trapped between all sides of the global Cold War. Struggling to maintain Cambodian neutrality as war escalated in Vietnam, Sihanouk initially accepted aid from both the United States and China, but his relationship with America deteriorated in the late 1950s and early 1960s. In 1959, Sihanouk's administration believed they uncovered an American-backed plot to assassinate him when a package sent to his palace exploded, killing a member of his cabinet. According to Sihanouk, the box was traced to an American base in South Vietnam. Increasingly suspicious, Sihanouk believed that the United States CIA wanted to kill him to install an American-friendly dictator in Cambodia. He later accused the United States of trying to assassinate him on three separate occasions in 1959 and a fourth in 1963. "The CIA never stopped working behind the scenes to bring about my death," he insisted in a 1972 book titled *My War with the CIA*. In 1963, Sihanouk decided to stop receiving aid from the United States in the interest of "preserving national dignity."[41]

The following year, Sihanouk struck a secret deal with the North Vietnamese to allow the movement of Chinese military supplies through Cambodia in exchange for financial restitution and munitions. By then, he had come to believe that the American-backed South Vietnamese government would lose its war against North Vietnam, and he wanted to ensure his own regime's survival in the wake of what he considered to be America's looming departure from the region. Key to Cambodian sovereignty, Sihanouk believed, would be a good relationship with communist China and communist North Vietnam. In other words, Sihanouk thought he was betting on the winner.[42]

As the war between North and South Vietnam escalated in the early 1960s, violence spilled over the border into Cambodia. In the spring of 1964, the South Vietnamese Army orchestrated an attack on a Cambodian village that resulted in the deaths of seventeen civilians. That October, some unknown group shot down an American aircraft in Cambodian airspace, killing eight American servicemen. A United States spokesman blamed the intrusion on a "map-reading error." But by then, Cambodia's leaders had had enough. The Cambodian government openly denounced America's support of South Vietnamese incursions into their territory and displayed the American plane's wreckage in a public exhibition in Phnom Penh.[43]

In April of 1965, an estimated twenty thousand Cambodians joined demonstrations at the United States embassy in Phnom Penh. Protesters tore down and burnt the embassy's American flag and hurled projectiles through the building's windows. A few days later, Sihanouk went on Cambodian national radio to publicly announce the "breaking [of] diplomatic relations with the United States." There was a last-ditch effort, supported by the Soviet Union and China, to form a conference on Cambodian neutrality, but Sihanouk was so aggravated by the attacks on Cambodian soil and a *Newsweek* article criticizing his family, especially his mother, that he decided to break off diplomatic relations with the United States altogether.[44]

But this move created further problems for Sihanouk because it freed the communist nations to use Cambodian territory however they wanted. Although Sihanouk had allowed North Vietnamese forces to operate in Cambodia, he began to worry that a victorious North Vietnam might further infringe on Cambodian territory, thus threatening the very sovereignty he sought to protect. His only hope was that China would help settle ongoing border disputes, but Sihanouk's leverage with the Chinese government waned after he cut off diplomatic relations with the United States. The Chinese communists no longer had to worry about Cambodia becoming an American protectorate and could thus abuse Cambodia however they wanted. In trying to save his regime, Sihanouk had deeply compromised Cambodian neutrality by essentially picking a side.[45]

Meanwhile, the war was changing, causing Sihanouk to begin doubting his initial conclusions about the eventual winner. Like most people, Sihanouk had no idea how many troops the United States would be willing to commit to the defense of South Vietnam. As hundreds of thousands of American soldiers entered the ground war, Sihanouk began to consider the possibility that the communists wouldn't win after all. Floating unmoored between world and regional powers, Sihanouk's only clear path toward the maintenance of a sovereign Cambodian nation with him at the head was to seek recognition of Cambodian neutrality in the international community, even as North Vietnamese forces continued using Cambodian territory to transport weapons and stage attacks into South Vietnam. By that point, Sihanouk was virtually powerless to stop them. As a CIA report concluded in 1966, "Sihanouk has also become a prisoner, in a way, of his own past policies."[46]

In December of 1967, the CIA reported that a privately owned trucking company based out of Phnom Penh was picking up Chinese arms and ammunition at the port city of Sihanoukville and transporting these goods through the hilly jungles of rural Cambodia to Phnom Penh. After stopping at a warehouse in Phnom Penh, the trucks traveled under the cover of night with protection from Cambodian armed forces to the Vietnamese border. After crossing the border, the trucks traveled another fifteen miles inside of South Vietnam to a base where their cargos were distributed to the communist forces. This was a very big problem for the United States military. These materials were being used to kill Americans and undermine the nation's global quest against communism.[47]

In addition to Chinese weapons, the CIA in 1967 reported that ships from the Soviet Union, Cyprus, and Denmark had delivered thirty-three thousand tons of "military equipment" to Sihanoukville, including ammunition, artillery, rockets, howitzers, automatic weapons, small arms, and even several fighter jets. Other reports indicated deliveries of rice and cement. That fall, the CIA received intelligence that a Greek freighter had delivered more than ten thousand tons of "ammunition and weapons, a large number of South Vietnamese and US military uniforms, and a small amount of medical supplies." Even everyday civilians were helping the North Vietnamese war effort. Cambodian farmers were selling up to one-quarter of the nation's rice harvest to North Vietnamese insurgents and using elephants to transport crops through the jungle to the soldiers.[48]

All this intelligence raised serious questions about Cambodian neutrality. The North Vietnamese undoubtably were using Cambodia to stage military attacks. At best, Sihanouk's government was an unwitting participant in the transportation of materials to the communist forces. At worst, elements of Sihanouk's government were actively engaged in helping the NLF fight against the United States and its South Vietnamese allies. Either way, by the autumn of 1967, the United States warned the South Vietnamese prime minister, "The increased danger posed by Viet Cong and North Vietnamese use of Cambodia has caused us concern that such use is reaching an intolerable level."[49]

Yet, Sihanouk denied the presence of North Vietnamese forces in Cambodia. In December of 1967, he insisted to an American journalist, "I am skeptical about the possibility that Vietnamese forces of any size could be maintained in deserted, inhospitable areas [of Cambodia] difficult to supply with food." He admitted that NLF troops had occasionally entered Cambodian territory but asserted that they only stayed "a few hours" before leaving. He also called the Sihanouk Trail "pure fiction." That November, when three American journalists claimed to have found an abandoned NLF camp in Cambodia, Sihanouk rejected their claims and announced a nationwide ban of "all American journalists, no matter who they are."[50]

With so many internal and external forces at play, Sihanouk's Cambodia was, as he put it, "caught between the hammer and the anvil." The only body that he knew wouldn't try to depose him was the International Control Commission (ICC), the organization charged with overseeing the implementation of the Geneva Accords. Led by representatives from India, Poland, and Canada, the ICC had the authority to send observers into

Vietnam, Laos, and Cambodia to ensure the integrity of the agreements. But their reach was somewhat limited to the cities and not the vast rural areas of the Cambodian-Vietnamese border that stretches over seven hundred miles. When ICC teams did examine rural parts of Cambodia, news of their approach reached the NLF well before the inspectors arrived, allowing for plenty of time to pack up camps and erase traces of their presence. The United States was also skeptical of inspectors from India and Poland because of those nations' relationships with the Soviet Union.[51]

As Sihanouk denied the true nature of North Vietnamese forces in Cambodia, he also promised retaliation if the United States ever invaded or attacked Cambodia. "If serious incursions or bombings were perpetuated against our border areas . . . ," he promised, "we would not hesitate to send to the area everything available in the form of airplanes, tanks, and infantry." "There would be fighting," Sihanouk asserted.[52]

Even more threatening, Sihanouk insisted that fighting against Americans would lead him to request "increased aid" "from friendly powers, particularly China and the Soviet Union." He also suggested that Cambodia could appeal to China and North Korea for troops who could be used "under Cambodian command" to expel American forces. In another speech, Sihanouk promised to "lodge a complaint with the [UN] Security Council because we are entitled by the UN Charter." "I will go to the United States," he promised, "to bring about action against the Americans in their own country." "I will go there myself," he vowed, "to make a great speech to inform the world of the acts of the Americans who have come to subdue Indochina contrary to international law." "It is up to Russia," he argued, "to support Cambodia effectively and strongly by warning the Americans against attacking Cambodia." That same month, a CIA report revealed that the Soviet Union had indeed promised to come to Sihanouk's aid "if the United States should 'attack' Cambodia." Sihanouk was suggesting that the presence of American troops in Cambodia could lead to the start of World War III.[53]

Meanwhile, America's military leaders were more deeply concerned about the war they were already in. They had to find a way to stop the infiltration of goods and soldiers into South Vietnam from Cambodia. In December of 1967, General William Westmoreland, the commander of American forces in Vietnam, requested permission for seventy-two hours of "high intensity tactical air strikes" over suspected NLF sanctuaries in Cambodia. Westmoreland was endlessly frustrated that he was prevented from using American firepower to counteract the enemy's usage of Cambodia. "Had the dissenting students, editorialists, and legislators," he later sniped, "been on the receiving end of some of those Soviet rockets or other lethal hardware that came through Cambodia, as were their compatriots in uniform, their indignation might have been considerably more muted." Still, Westmoreland understood the potential diplomatic and international repercussions of such attacks, arguing that the bombing could be completed at night and remain limited to remote areas near the border.[54]

The White House considered Westmoreland's request to bomb rural areas of Cambodia but ultimately rejected the idea due to obvious "political problems involved, both foreign and domestic," wrote the chairman of the Joint Chiefs of Staff. Yet, the Joint Chiefs concluded that it was "essential that the United States increase political pressure on Prince Sihanouk to take more aggressive action to deny use of this and other sanctuary areas of Cambodia by VC/NVA forces."[55]

To "increase political pressure on Prince Sihanouk," the United States needed to gather evidence verifying the extensive nature of North Vietnamese activities in Cambodia. To gather such definitive evidence, America's leaders decided to send their own troops into Cambodia to study and observe enemy movements in the "neutral" country. But they couldn't just march a division across the border; that would precipitate an international and domestic crisis. What the American military needed was a covert force of elite warriors who could be inserted behind enemy lines and blend unseen into the countryside for days at a time while gathering evidence of North Vietnamese military activities. The United States military did indeed possess such a force, and it had been preparing thousands of men for exactly these uniquely dangerous and highly sensitive missions. Those men were known as the Green Berets, and by late fall of 1967, Roy Benavidez was one of them.[56]

WHILE ROY WAS TRAINING AND STUDYING TO BECOME A Green Beret, the Cambodian border situation was becoming increasingly chaotic. In December of 1967, as the United States was considering bombing parts of Cambodia and Sihanouk was warning his own congress that Americans were "planning to kill Cambodia," Roy was just a month out of his training. In March of 1968, he learned that he was going back to the war in Southeast Asia.[57]

Roy understood that he was returning "to a war in South Vietnam that was very different from the one I had left." Early in 1968, the North Vietnamese communists launched a major surprise attack known as the Tet Offensive, enabled largely by their usage of Cambodian territory. Between October of 1967 and January of 1968, an estimated forty-four thousand North Vietnamese troops poured down the Ho Chi Minh Trail as part of a major offensive of roughly eighty-four thousand North

Vietnamese and NLF forces who launched a coordinated attack on nearly forty South Vietnamese cities. South Vietnamese and American troops fought well and turned back the surprise attack in a decisive victory. Tet was a devastating blow for the North Vietnamese forces, who suffered an estimated forty-five thousand casualties. Just two months after the attack, General Westmoreland told the president, "Militarily, we have never been in better relative position in South Viet Nam."[58]

But the reality of Tet as a military victory didn't matter as much to a shocked American populace who interpreted the rising violence as evidence that the United States was no longer winning the war. Images of Americans fighting North Vietnamese and NLF forces in the streets of Saigon alerted the public that the North Vietnamese were much stronger than they had been told and drew into doubt the possibility of American victory. As one North Vietnamese military official later claimed, "The military victory may have been limited, but the political and strategic victory was just tremendous."[59]

A month after the Tet Offensive, *CBS Evening News* anchor Walter Cronkite traveled to Vietnam to report on the aftermath of the Tet Offensive. When he came home, he famously editorialized that the American war in Vietnam had reached an unbreakable deadlock. "To say that we are mired in stalemate seems the only realistic, yet unsatisfactory, conclusion," Cronkite told millions of American viewers. "It is becoming increasingly clear," he somberly concluded, "that the only rational way will be to negotiate, not as victors but as honorable people who lived up to their desire to defend democracy, and did the best that they could." The *New York Times* agreed, arguing, "Stalemate increasingly appears as the unavoidable outcome of the Vietnam struggle." The news media did report that the Tet Offensive had been a military setback for the North Vietnamese, but thanks at least in part to these editorials, the opinion of the American people had largely shifted to the conclusion that victory for the United States was no longer in sight.[60]

By the time Roy began preparing to return to Vietnam in the spring of 1968, the war was tearing America apart. Major political figures, including Robert Kennedy and Dr. Martin Luther King Jr., had issued public condemnations of the war, calling it unwinnable and even immoral. Hundreds of thousands of anti-war activists protested across the United States, their ranks swelled by increasing numbers of students, veterans, and even government officials. Thousands more anti-war demonstrators took to the streets in cities across Europe, including London, Berlin, and Rome, calling for the United States to get out of the war in Vietnam. President Lyndon B. Johnson was burned in effigy in the Philippines. On March 31, Johnson shocked the nation when he announced that he would not seek reelection in that year's presidential campaign so that he could focus on negotiations to end the American war in Vietnam.[61]

As Americans' view of the war devolved, Lala and Roy packed up their family's trailer in preparation for her to move back to El Campo with their eight-month-old daughter. Roy didn't write much about Lala's feelings about his return to Southeast Asia, only remembering that she "didn't complain, in spite of her disappointment." "It couldn't have been easy on her," he acknowledged, "watching her husband return to the war in Asia that was dominating the headlines on the national news every night."[62]

Difficult as war always is, the conditions in the spring of 1968 made for a very challenging deployment for men like Roy Benavidez and their families. Roy and Lala lived in a military community where people were generally more supportive of the war than the broader population. But the sentiment depicted in the national news was impossible to ignore. The nation appeared to be turning against the very war that Roy was about to rejoin.

Roy and Lala could see and feel that he was returning to a conflict that was becoming increasingly unpopular among his fellow countrymen, but even they had no idea just how different this experience would be from his previous deployments. Roy, in his second tour, would be undertaking an essential but secret mission far removed from the public view of the war and completely unimaginable to most Americans.[63]

CHAPTER 7
FEARLESS

In April of 1968, Roy reentered Vietnam at an American base near Cam Ranh Bay, a small coastal city located about 230 miles northeast of Saigon. To Roy, the American soldiers were practically unrecognizable from the men with whom he'd served on his first tour. "Gone were the short military haircuts," he observed, "replaced by long hair and sideburns. . . . These were just boys." Roy was disappointed by the lack of professionalism in this new, rapidly expanding American military. He assumed many soldiers were working class, the "kids who hadn't been able to go to college to escape being drafted to fight in a war that they neither supported nor had the skills to endure." Just hours after his arrival, he and another Green Beret started walking through the bunkers, telling the younger soldiers to cut their hair and shave.[1]

Roy's time with the novice soldiers was short-lived. Within a day, he was sent about thirty miles up the road to another American base near Nha Trang, where he encountered other men like him—grizzled, professional veterans, many of whom were in Special Forces. It was through these soldiers that Roy learned about the recent death of one of his buddies from Special Forces training, a man named Stefan "Pappy" Mazak. Mazak, who had worked with the French resistance during World War II and fought rebels in the Belgian Congo, was a hero to many in Special Forces. He had been killed earlier that month while leading his unit in an intense firefight. Roy was shocked and saddened to learn about the death of this "aging gladiator" who had attracted Roy "like metal to a magnet." "I couldn't help wondering what type of war Vietnam had become," he thought, "to claim such a soldier." He would find out soon enough.[2]

Mazak had been part of a special and somewhat mythical unit. At the NCO club, Roy had heard men whisper about a group of elite soldiers engaged in top secret missions. He was dismayed that he couldn't learn more details about Mazak's death because these types of missions were "shrouded in mystery." At the time, Roy only knew that Mazak was part of a Special Forces unit known as B-56 and that they were engaged in extraordinarily dangerous missions. He heard that "casualties in the field were so high that the command needed men as fast as it could get them."[3]

Roy was never one to shy away from action. He became interested in serving in this elite unit largely because it was filled with Special Forces soldiers. "I figured I might as well be among friends," he explained. Roy approached the B-56 commander and "announced to him my intentions to join the unit." As millions of other Americans, and even the nation itself, desperately sought a way out of the war, Roy maneuvered his way into the center of it.[4]

Roy was assigned to be a light weapons leader with the 5th Special Forces Group Detachment B-56. Also known as Project Sigma, this unit was part of the Military Assistance Command,

Vietnam-Studies and Observations Group (MACV-SOG). Only about 10 percent of Special Forces soldiers in Vietnam were assigned to MACV-SOG. This was top secret stuff. Many of those involved signed nondisclosure agreements that carried heavy fines and jail times. Men in MACV-SOG units were forbidden from keeping journals, and the letters they sent home were read and censored to remove any sensitive information about their whereabouts or activities.[5]

Formed in June of 1966, Project Sigma operated out of a small base located less than twenty-five miles northeast of Saigon. It was one of two units with a combined strength of nine officers, sixty-five enlisted American soldiers, and 660 soldiers drawn from the native population of Southeast Asia—all organized into eight reconnaissance teams. Roy's detachment was part of a group involved with Operation Daniel Boone, the cross-border campaign designed to collect intelligence of North Vietnamese and NLF activities in Cambodia.[6]

By the spring of 1968, Operation Daniel Boone had provided the CIA with extensive evidence of North Vietnamese usage of Cambodia. The CIA had good evidence of at least twenty-thousand North Vietnamese soldiers operating in Cambodia during the previous years. The communist forces were moving entire regiments through the border region on their way to fight Americans in South Vietnam. Captured documents and testimonies from enemy prisoners revealed how the North Vietnamese used these infiltration routes to resupply and reinforce enemy positions in South Vietnam. More than just a highway between nations, Cambodian territory was being used for training grounds, resting areas, and hospitals.[7]

The Tet Offensive added further urgency to the issue of enemy infiltration, as many of the weapons and materials used by communist forces during these widespread attacks had undoubtably entered South Vietnam from Cambodia. It was crucial to the

United States war effort to expose North Vietnamese usage of Cambodian territory to either compel the international community to take action or justify a possible American invasion or bombing of Cambodia. Accordingly, Daniel Boone missions began increasing in number. In 1967, MACV-SOG had sent ninety-nine such missions into Cambodia. In 1968, they would conduct 287 more.[8]

These highly classified maneuvers involved teams of no more than twelve men—the largest allowed by the Pentagon—who boarded helicopters that flew them "across the fence" to remote landing zones in Cambodia. After exiting the choppers, these teams spent days in the wilderness searching for the enemy. In addition to studying and observing enemy movements, the men involved with Daniel Boone missions also sabotaged enemy weaponry, set mines along transportation routes, tapped lines of communication, and snatched prisoners for interrogation. The information they gathered was folded into confidential reports read by top military and political officials, including the president.[9]

The Vietnamese-Cambodian border region where B-56 operated was, and is still, a tropical jungle landscape that stretches across hundreds of miles of rolling hills. In some places, the brush is so dense that it's impassable without a machete. In parts, farmers have cut back the jungle to make way for swampy rice fields fed by the many ponds and rivers that flow through the region. Other clearings are often thick with elephant grass that can grow as high as a man's chest. Muddy, hot, and sunny, the region is an ideal ecosystem for all types of big, leafy tropical trees that envelop the jungle in a canopy of green. An endless array of flora covers the understory of these Cambodian forests, making them at once a beautiful place for plants to grow and live and an ideal place for humans to hide and kill.[10]

The wildlife of southeastern Cambodia added another disturbing dimension to these missions. In the rural jungle, the men of MACV-SOG encountered any number of dangerous animals, including tigers, crocodiles, elephants, monkeys, water buffalo, hornets, leeches, apes, and what one sergeant described as "some of the largest and most colorful spiders I have ever seen." Wild crocodiles and tigers are now extinct in that area, but they were still around back then. Elephants and water buffalo can be territorial and can trample humans. The insects fed off the soldiers, attaching to their skin to suck their blood or sting them. And monkeys harassed soldiers by stealing food and even weapons. But the worst were the snakes—massive twenty-foot pythons and a host of poisonous cobras, kraits, and vipers, some carrying enough venom to kill an adult man in less than an hour. The troops inserted into the jungle always possessed the firepower to kill any of these animals, but any noises created while dealing with local wildlife could alert enemy soldiers. Silencers helped, but even still, the men couldn't always see the animals coming.[11]

While moving through this war-torn tropical landscape, the men of Daniel Boone didn't wear United States uniforms or carry anything that could easily identify them as Americans. They covered their faces in camouflage, and some donned the all-black uniform of the NLF. Needing to blend in in every way, these men didn't use scented soap or aftershave in the days before a mission. None carried American weapons. Many fought with the same Russian AK-47s used by the North Vietnamese. Each man also brought ammunition, canteens, a flashlight, a wristwatch, a compass, grenades, a camouflage stick, and a machete. Many carried whistles, smoke grenades, flares, signal mirrors, hand restraints, ponchos, sleeping bags, a variety of explosives, freeze-dried long-range patrol meals, and first aid kits filled with anti-malaria pills, codeine cough syrup, Darvon, penicillin, gauze pads, and morphine. Some brought rucksacks modeled after North Vietnamese packs so they could blend in. And every unit had radios.[12]

Most of the men involved with Operation Daniel Boone were not Americans. Seeking to limit their own involvement in such highly classified missions, the United States military recruited talented soldiers from the South Vietnamese Army and others from the indigenous tribes of the tri-border area between Vietnam, Cambodia, and Laos. Collectively referred to as Montagnards, these soldiers knew the local landscapes and languages far better than any American ever could.[13]

Regulars from the South Vietnamese Army volunteered for MACV-SOG to receive higher pay, enjoy better conditions, and play a more important role in the war than they could in the regular South Vietnamese Army. The Montagnards usually joined for the cash or to help fight for tribal sovereignty. Many of them denied allegiance to any country and refused to take orders from South Vietnamese officers. According to one observer, "The main reason [the Montagnards] liked to fight with Special Forces is because they knew they could kill Vietnamese."[14]

Once they volunteered for work with Special Forces, these native soldiers were grouped into separate units than other soldiers from Southeast Asia and trained by the CIA and Special Forces in counterinsurgency and psychological operations. Most were then sent out into the field to serve in Civilian Irregular Defense Groups (CIDGs), whose members were often known as CIDGs for short. The CIDGs who worked with MACV-SOG were typically stationed in isolated camps near remote border outposts. They accompanied American soldiers on operations into Cambodia, serving as soldiers, scouts, and translators.[15]

After Roy received his assignment, he was sent to a Special Forces base at Ho Ngoc Tao, a small encampment located just north of Saigon. While there, he began specialized training for missions into Cambodia. Hard as it was to qualify for Special Forces, no soldier was fully prepared for the uniquely dangerous missions that lay ahead. Almost none of them had ever done anything like this before, and few would complete enough missions to gain a significant amount of experience. A man who completed thirteen missions into Cambodia was "almost a statistical anomaly," wrote one veteran. "By the time he had twenty missions behind him, it was a wonder that he was still alive."[16]

Roy "started training immediately," he remembered, working on "insertion and extraction tactics." The men of B-56 would load onto helicopters to practice rapid insertions into the dense jungle. When the landing zone was in a large clearing, the helicopter would hover just a few feet above the ground and the men would jump from the chopper and scramble to a rendezvous point in the jungle. In cases when the landing zone was too dense with vegetation, the men would use a harness to rappel down one-hundred-foot nylon McGuire rigs to the jungle floor.[17]

Insertions needed to be done fast. The helicopters flew loud and low over the jungle, drawing the attention of any nearby forces. Green Berets had to escape the choppers within a matter of seconds so they could organize before the enemy came upon them. American Special Forces soldiers could generally win any firefight with a similar-sized NVA unit, but these small units could never be quite sure how many enemy troops they might encounter during an insertion. Some of the NVA encampments in Cambodia contained thousands of soldiers. If a team was inserted near an NVA battalion with hundreds or more troops, it would surely be quickly overrun.[18]

Extractions involved the same process in reverse. In a clearing, the helicopter could land, and the men would quickly climb aboard. But some of the extractions occurred in dense sections of the jungle that did not provide enough space for the forty-eight-foot rotor blades of the Huey helicopters. In those cases, the men on the ground would grab a McGuire rig and hang on for dear life as the helicopter cleared the treetops while they dangled a hundred feet beneath. It was a dangerous exercise even absent enemy fire, as lines can fray or snap, dropping a man to his death. "Coming out of a jungle in a McGuire rig," Roy wrote, "is like going from night to day in a few minutes. First, there's the darkness and dankness of the jungle, then as tree limbs snap as the soldier is pulled through them, day appears."[19]

Extractions could be harrowing. In 1968, more than 50 percent of Daniel Boone missions required an "emergency extraction" due to close contact with enemy forces. Those who encountered North Vietnamese soldiers in Cambodia had to fight as they ran. Enemy soldiers would pursue the fleeing men, firing hundreds of rounds of bullets and explosives that chased the dangling soldiers into the sky.[20]

American Special Forces units operating in Cambodia did have one distinct advantage. When confronted by the enemy, they could use their radios to call in support from aircraft that would fly over the jungle and fire machine guns and rockets on enemy positions. Helicopters were the most common form of support, but also available were American A-1H Skyraiders, planes known as "Sandy," that carried cannons, rockets, and explosives, including napalm.[21]

But even these advantages were severely curtailed by the war's realities. The number of airships available for support was limited by the secretive nature of MACV-SOG missions, as the units could fly only so many helicopters into foreign territory. Most fighter planes were too loud and large to be fully unleashed over Cambodian airspace. And artillery—employed with devastating effects in support of American troops in other parts of the war— was not available to assist men engaged in firefights in Cambodia. The Army asked for artillery support, but it was denied.[22]

The delicacy of diplomacy created a spectacularly dangerous reality for the soldiers inserted into Cambodia. By choosing to operate in such covert fashion, America's politicians and commanders ensured that these remarkable fighters would almost always be outnumbered and outgunned on the ground. Some of them never returned. They could not become prisoners, as being taken alive could lead to a major international crisis. The men of these units understood that they were to fight to the death, aided only by their training, skill, and courage.

The men of Daniel Boone were conducting operations that were quite unique in the history of American warfare. American troops had operated far behind enemy lines before, but they had rarely been so isolated in the forests of a supposedly neutral border country crawling with enemy troops. As one Special Forces veteran observed, "Not since the French and Indian War had Americans roamed such complete wilderness to combat a numerically superior foe." "You can't find this stuff in 'the book,'" noted a veteran of MACV-SOG, "because we're writing 'the book.'"[23]

When men returned from a mission "across the fence," they would hold court over drinks at an NCO club on the base. The soldiers would gather around some freshly returned team leader to listen to harrowing stories of combat told by men engaged in some of the most dangerous missions in the world. Those tales not only regaled men with wild stories of death-defying escapes but also equipped their listeners with lessons crucial to the success of future missions. Special Forces teams would crowd around tables as their comrades diagrammed the action using "beer cans, glasses, and ashtrays," remembered one soldier. In such a fashion, the officers' clubs turned into classrooms, with the next men up learning from those who had just returned.[24]

Those lessons involved small but essential details, such as ways to sleep or walk or how to hold your weapon when scanning the forest. The men shared information on diet and smells, as any foreign aroma could alert the enemy that Americans were nearby. There were different ways to cross a trail or climb a ridge, and they devised unique methods for dodging human and canine trackers in the forest. The Green Berets in Daniel Boone were constantly learning more information about the best techniques for their tasks. Each mission, regardless of success, generated new lessons that survivors passed along to other men. The enemy soldiers were also continuously learning, making the missions all the more dangerous as they escalated from 1967 into the spring of 1968.[25]

The men bonded through lighthearted pranks between the action. Soon after Roy's arrival, an anonymous helicopter pilot played a crude joke on him and some of the other men. Roy and his unit had been dropped into a village and were awaiting extraction near a large man-made latrine when a helicopter arrived to pick them up. Despite ample clearing, the chopper didn't land. Instead, its crew dropped a McGuire rig to the soldiers on the ground. With no other choice for transport, the first soldier on the ground grabbed the rigging and was lifted from the ground before the helicopter once again lowered, dragging the man through the "huge brown lake" of human waste. The other soldiers were mortified. "No one wanted to volunteer to go next," Roy remembered. But they had to go. The next few men went reluctantly, each worried that the pilot would repeat his prank. But the flier let them off easy until he got to Roy.[26]

Roy was the last to go. "Almost as soon as I was lifted, I felt the chopper descend and I knew I was going down," he remembered. The helicopter dragged him waist high through the pond of filth before pulling up and carrying him back to camp, "dripping excrement all the way." "The smell was so sickening," he recalled. Roy appreciated that the pilot probably enjoyed "a good, long laugh . . . because none of the men of B-56 were amused." Roy showered and went looking for the pilot, whom he never did find. "He better be glad I didn't," Roy jested. "It's hard to fly a chopper with broken arms and legs."[27]

In their downtime, the men of Roy's unit built what he called "our own little version of an NCO club," with a few chairs and a little television on which they watched broadcasts out of Saigon. Roy and his colleagues once raided someone else's kitchen for a special celebratory meal, and at one point he wrestled with one of the Montagnards, playfully taking the man to the ground after having his green beret knocked off his head. That action earned him the nickname "Tango Mike" or "The Mean Mexican." Some also called him "bean bandit," a racialized nickname that never quite stuck. "No one was offended by the tasteless jokes we made," Roy recalled. "We knew everything we said was in fun."[28]

Outside of these respites, most of their time in Vietnam was deadly serious. Every time a group went out there was a distinct chance they could all die. "We would watch choppers leave the pad," Roy recalled, "not having any idea where they were off to, what the mission was about, and most of all, totally uncertain as to which of our friends would return." Living under such pressure, the men of MACV-SOG became extremely close. Few of them had known each other for very long, but they all understood that these were the most fateful days of their lives, and they forged lifelong bonds.[29]

Roy served with some talented and dedicated soldiers during his second tour in Vietnam. There was Lloyd Mousseau, a twenty-four-year-old Minnesota native, and Brian O'Connor, a twenty-one-year-old from New Jersey. Both their fathers had fought in World War II. Leroy Wright, the unit's sole African American soldier, was a bit older at thirty-eight. A New Jersey native like O'Connor, Wright was a seventeen-year veteran, one of the few men in the unit who had been enlisted longer than Roy. He had a wife and two children back home in New Jersey.[30]

Like Roy, Wright was among the very few non-white men in MACV-SOG. The two had met months earlier at Fort Bragg during Special Forces training and quickly became "very close to each other," Roy recalled, fondly noting, "There was no racial distinction between us." While stationed in Vietnam that

April, they shared pictures and stories of their young families. Leroy would show Roy the drawings his two sons had mailed to him, and Roy shared pictures of Lala and Denise, who by then was just a couple months shy of her second birthday. Wright had been in the miliary for nearly twenty years and was nearing his retirement. His family was eager for his military career to end. Wright was a great soldier, and Roy was glad to serve with him. "He was disciplined, had nerves of steel," Roy remembered. "Everyone who worked with him trusted his abilities."[31]

Roy started his own combat duties as a helicopter "bellyman," a soldier who straps himself into the helicopter cargo bay just behind the pilots. In cases where extraction was needed, the bellyman would peek out from the sides of the helicopter to instruct the pilot where to position the vehicle for extraction. When the chopper couldn't land because of dense vegetation, the bellyman was responsible for securing McGuire rigs to the cabin and tossing them to the men on the ground. Bellymen also helped deliver supplies to troops on the ground. Roy's duty as a bellyman was short-lived, as he was needed for the reconnaissance missions. Soon, he too was being inserted across the fence.[32]

On Roy's first foray into the jungle, his team was charged with capturing an enemy soldier for interrogation. They started their day before dawn and spent most of their time squatting in the bush near a small path, waiting for an enemy soldier to pass. Special Forces soldiers were ordered to avoid Cambodian civilians at all costs, so they had to remain hidden from anyone and everyone, even nonthreatening passersby; although one never could be entirely sure who was a threat. They sat in the bush all day, "tormented by the nagging insects and communicating with hand signals," wrote Roy. It was hot and "boring," he recalled.[33]

After several hours, a man walked down the path carrying a rifle. Roy alerted his partner and then jumped out of the bush and attacked the man, "knocking him unconscious." The

American soldiers bound the man with hand and foot restraints and then pulled him into a thick stand of trees. When he woke, they began to question him. The captive denied knowing anything about the NLF. In fact, he said he was carrying the rifle to protect himself from communist forces. That was about all they got out of him. But that was alright because their primary job was merely to abduct the prisoner so he could be questioned by professional interrogators in a more secure area.[34]

Their ride home was scheduled to arrive soon, but they grew nervous because the presence of one suspected enemy could mean many more nearby. Soon they began to hear a helicopter moving toward them. When the prisoner heard the motor, he tried to make a desperate dash into the forest. One of Roy's fellow soldiers reacted instantly, spinning on his feet and aiming his weapon at the fleeing prisoner. But Roy was standing between the panicked soldier and the fleeing captive. In a split second, Roy ducked, landing "face first" into the ground just as a bullet whizzed past him and into the stomach of the fleeing captive. "We were all stunned," Roy recalled. "I was scared to death." When the helicopter arrived, the men loaded themselves and the wounded prisoner aboard the chopper for the flight back to the base. "I never knew if he made it or not," Roy remembered of the prisoner.[35]

On another mission, Roy and his men found themselves "in the middle of some pretty heavy gunfire" and had to call for an emergency extraction. At least one of the men had been hit by a bullet. There was no time or space for the helicopter to land amid the gunfire, so a bellyman dropped a McGuire rig. But then the bellyman was struck by a bullet and had to roll back into the cargo bay, incapacitated but having at least accomplished the task of pushing out the lifelines to the men on the ground. Roy helped the wounded soldier fit into one of the harnesses and then secured himself into another harness. The helicopter took off, climbing above the jungle canopy with the men hanging in tow below.[36]

As Roy and the wounded soldier flew over the treetops, he suddenly noticed a problem with the McGuire rig. "The ropes had become entangled and were rubbing together," he wrote. "If this continued, my injured man and I would plunge about three hundred feet to our deaths." Normally, the bellyman would help, but that bellyman was too badly wounded, having been shot during the extraction. Luckily, Roy's friend Leroy Wright was also on that helicopter, and he strapped himself in to replace the wounded bellyman. Wright leaned out from the chopper, with bullets dashing through the air, and untwisted the fraying harnesses holding Roy and the other soldier high above the ground. The wounded man later died from his injuries, but Roy made it through untouched. "Don't ever let anyone tell you all angels are white," he later joked of his savior, Leroy Wright.[37]

NEAR THE END OF APRIL, ROY HAD BEEN IN VIETNAM FOR LESS than three weeks when a special assignment came through his unit. Three Americans—Leroy Wright, Brian O'Connor, and Lloyd Mousseau—and nine CIDG soldiers were to be inserted into Cambodia to locate and surveil a contingent of NVA regulars moving south near the border.[38]

The team trained for several days before flying to the American base at Quan Loi. From there, they would travel to Loc Ninh, a remote outpost located closer to the border. Roy was on separate orders from Wright's team, but their entire unit arrived in Quan Loi on May 1, the night before the mission. They spent that evening together playing cards, "insulting each other," Roy wrote, "and having a good time."

Leroy Wright won most of the hands that night. He seemed happy, Roy remembered, joking with his friends as he swept his winnings from the card table into a hat. It seemed like a normal evening in the war, "like any other night, hanging out in the barracks," Roy described. They enjoyed some beer and food, and everyone was in a good mood. After they tired of playing cards, they played a stag film that someone had brought and then spent the rest of the evening laughing and teasing each other. It was a good night. Wright, Mousseau, and O'Connor retired early. After they went to bed, Roy hopped on a helicopter that took him to the forward operating base at Loc Ninh, where he bunked down for the night. The other men would go out the next day, Thursday, May 2.

Before dawn on May 2, the team led by Leroy Wright flew to Loc Ninh to launch their mission. They made instant coffee and loaded their equipment before boarding the two helicopters that would insert them into Cambodian territory. It was a short flight into their landing zone, but the pilots couldn't proceed directly to the location because the enemy was learning how to track these American missions. The pilots flew in irregular patterns to throw off any enemy soldiers who might be trying to anticipate the location of their landing zone. Another aviator was flying nearby in a command and control (C&C) helicopter to provide direction and oversee the insertion in the correct location.

Wright's team arrived at their landing zone without incident and dropped into a clearing in the jungle. The clearing was free of trees but covered in tall elephant grass. They scrambled off the helicopters and ducked beneath the tall elephant grass while the helicopters flew away over the treetops. Once on the ground, they were alone in Cambodia, dangerously isolated from the rest of the war. The Ho Chi Minh Trail lay just a half-mile to the west.

The men moved to the edge of the clearing and paused to gather their bearings. Every insertion carried the possibility of detection, and they needed to make sure they were not about to be attacked. Just one man in a tree with a radio could alert hundreds, perhaps thousands, of enemy troops who could quickly overrun their twelve-man team. But Wright's team was ready. This was what they had been training for. They lay still and quiet in the darkness of the jungle, watching for any sign of danger.

After about thirty minutes, the team felt confident they had avoided detection and began to move. They took out their machetes and began chopping their way through the brush. They soon reached a trail and paused to wait for traffic. They didn't have to wait long. In less than ten minutes, a group of enemy soldiers came ambling down the path. Wright saw them first and motioned to attract O'Connor's attention. The Americans froze and prepared to reverse course, if necessary. When the enemy soldiers drew closer, the Americans could tell they were woodcutters chopping a path through the forest. There were only a few of them, but they carried AK-47s. Most likely, they had friends nearby.

The American soldiers and their Vietnamese allies backed deeper into the foliage. They sat in the brush in two small groups, each crouching just a few dozen yards from one another. Unexpectedly, the woodcutters made a sharp turn and began chopping a path directly toward one of the groups. The woodcutters didn't appear to suspect anything yet, but their path was heading right toward the American unit.

O'Connor, crouched near the rear, could hear breaking branches as the woodcutters approached their position. Suddenly, he heard a short burst of gunfire from an AK-47. Mousseau and one of the CIDGs had waited until the woodcutters were right on top of them before jumping out and quickly killing the unsuspecting workers with silenced pistols. The AK-47 fire came from one of the woodcutters who had reacted too late to save his own life. The American team hid the woodcutters' bodies in the dense brush. But the sound of the AK-47 fire threatened to attract more enemy soldiers to the area. They had to move quickly to avoid detection.

Another noise came from behind them. Toward the clearing, they could make out the faint sound of what O'Connor described as "voices and commotion." It was an alarmingly fast second encounter, which suggested that enemy soldiers might have heard the machine gun fire. The team leader, Wright, considered calling for an extraction right then and there. They could hear enemy forces several hundred feet away, "talking and occasionally hollering," described O'Connor. Wright tried to get on the radio to speak with their superiors, but the signal didn't work.

The group decided to move back through the jungle in search of better reception. As they worked their way along the edge of the clearing, the CIDGs tried to make out the words of the enemy troops but struggled to hear them clearly. They didn't know if the other group were NVA soldiers or a small detachment of woodcutters. The translators thought they heard the Vietnamese word for helicopter, which could mean that the soldiers may have heard the insertion helicopter's engine and were looking for a team of Americans. Perhaps the translators heard wrong. No one could be sure. Either way, the American team had good reason for concern.

After circling back around the clearing to reassess, the American team heard additional noises moving toward them. This was all the reason they needed to call for an emergency extraction. They were able to radio the call through the C&C helicopter orbiting nearby. It was a difficult call to make so quickly after insertion, but they had no clue what was out there and wanted to evade any serious conflict. Command disagreed with the decision to leave. The team had made contact, their superiors acknowledged, but the threat of the woodcutters had been neutralized, and they had yet to face the other men moving about across the landing zone. Command denied Wright's extraction request and ordered him to proceed. The men accepted the order but still wanted to leave that area as quickly as possible.

At that point, they dashed into a small opening between the trees and ran directly into about a dozen NVA regulars. Each side froze. The Americans were dressed as Viet Cong, with their faces shaded and camouflaged. They carried no identifying markers or American weapons, disguised just well enough to make the enemy pause. One of the interpreters started talking to the enemy leader. The Americans pulled out a piece of paper and began studying it to further cover their faces. For a moment, "all seemed well," remembered O'Connor. The leader of the enemy unit started issuing orders, and the American team moved as if they were getting ready to follow some direction. Then, something happened. It might have been that one of the enemy soldiers caught a glimpse of the Americans' faces or was simply overwhelmed by intuition. No one will ever know. But in that tense moment, the Americans' interpreter sensed the change and uttered, "They know."

The Americans immediately opened fire with their machine guns, quickly killing most of the men standing in front of them before diving for cover. One of the enemy troops managed to fire off a rocket-propelled grenade that flew into the trees across the clearing. The subsequent explosion ended any hopes of concealment. The team was exposed. They had to get out immediately or they would certainly be killed.

Wright's team retreated to the edge of the clearing and set up a defensive perimeter along the wood line. They radioed in the request for extraction, which was granted. Wright lit a fuse to destroy sensitive documents he carried, telling the others, "They're no good to us now." The men in the unit, still fully intact after two separate run-ins with the enemy, crouched beneath the dense brush of the Cambodian jungle, waiting for the helicopter to take them home as any number of enemy troops bore down upon them. This extraction would be what they called "a hot one."

After a few moments, they started hearing helicopters in the distance. Four choppers—two transport ships and two gunships—were flying their way. As the helicopters approached, the men on the ground heard gunshots being fired at their escape vehicles. "It was quiet around us," O'Connor recalled, "but it sounded like they had the whole jungle firing at them." Three of the choppers turned away. One began bellowing smoke, forcing the pilot to make an emergency landing several hundred yards away. On one of the Hueys, a door gunner named Michael Craig had taken a bullet to his midsection before his pilot pulled them out of the fray.

High above, a forward air controller took stock of the situation. "Everywhere I looked," he recalled, "I saw swarming khaki uniforms. I estimated nearly 250 NVA in the open. No telling how many still in the trees." The sheer number of enemies suggested that Wright's team had been inserted near an NVA base camp, which could mean the presence of thousands of soldiers.

A single helicopter made it through the wall of fire and flew over the trees. It began to lower itself into the landing zone, about one hundred meters away from the isolated unit. Just as it began its descent, about a half dozen NVA soldiers appeared below the chopper and began waving for the pilot to land. The men in Wright's unit were stunned; their rescue craft was being duped into landing into an ambush.

One of the CIDG soldiers opened fire on the NVA soldiers waving to the helicopter. This attracted return fire from the chopper's door gunner, who didn't realize that the men standing in the landing zone were actually enemy soldiers and that the men on the edge of the clearing were the very ones they were there to extract. Other team members from the stranded unit tried to call the helicopter on their radios while some continued firing at the NVA soldiers standing in the landing zone. After a moment, the helicopter's door gunner realized the mistake and aimed his weapon at the NVA troops below, who returned fire, shattering the chopper's windshield.

As the helicopter hovered over the clearing, the men in the stranded unit tried to warn the pilot to flee, signaling with a mirror and then smoke grenades. Wright had a radio and was frantically flipping through "the frequencies to get a better channel," described O'Connor. Finally, he managed to contact the extraction team, and the chopper ascended into the air. As the helicopter lifted, the men in Wright's unit spotted more than two dozen North Vietnamese moving into the clearing underneath the chopper. Wright's men alerted those on the helicopter, who quickly turned and strafed the enemy troops with machine gun fire before their chopper flew out of the pickup zone.

After the extraction helicopter left, the men of Wright's unit scrambled to prep for their defense until another extraction attempt could be made. Every passing minute gave more time for NVA soldiers to arrive at their position in the jungle. The American team couldn't see their enemies through the tall elephant grass, but they could hear them moving and shouting. The jungle filled with "orders and commands being shouted out by the NVA units," remembers O'Connor. On the radio, Wright talked to the pilot flying high above the action. The man flying above could see troops pouring through the jungle toward the American unit. He didn't know how many there were, but there were a lot. "The big shit" is coming, Wright warned his men.

Wright wanted to move closer to the landing zone to speed their escape if and when another helicopter arrived. He ordered Mousseau and a few others to run across the clearing to a small stand of trees, while Wright and the rest applied suppressive cover fire. Wright's men would then scramble past the position of the first group while Mousseau's unit covered them in return. Mousseau's team dashed out into the clearing as the North Vietnamese unloaded rounds of fifty-caliber machine gun fire. Somehow, they made it to the trees without being hit. Wright's team followed and had just passed Mousseau's position when "the jungle exploded with auto and crew operated weapons," wrote O'Connor.

O'Connor took a bullet to the arm. Wright was hit too. "His body boomed and jerked in front of me," O'Connor remembered. "He said he couldn't move his legs." They pulled each other toward a large anthill rising just above the tall elephant grass. Behind them, two of the CIDGs lay dead in the clearing. The stranded men opened fire into the trees. Mousseau, positioned about twenty meters behind his comrades, yelled that he was hit. O'Connor looked over and saw a group of NVA soldiers moving toward Mousseau's position. Wright and O'Connor's team started tossing grenades and laying cover fire to protect their friends.

Another enemy unit charged Wright and O'Connor's position. The Americans pointed their weapons and opened fire. One of the charging NVA soldiers fell but continued to fight, rolling two grenades toward the American position. Wright caught the first grenade and tossed it into the air, where it exploded. As the second grenade approached, Wright yelled, "Get down! Get down!" and rolled onto his side to position his body between the grenade and the rest of his men. The weapon exploded, and Wright's "legs flew up as we continued firing," recalled O'Connor. "We thought he was dead." But somehow, he wasn't. O'Connor crawled toward Wright to retrieve his radio and was surprised when the wounded team leader turned his head and said, "Give me a gun."

As hundreds of rounds pierced the air between the separate teams, O'Connor grabbed a radio and started screaming for help. The air controller told O'Connor that more support was on the way. As O'Connor yelled into the radio, he glanced over at Wright and saw that his team leader had taken a bullet to the forehead. Wright was now surely dead.

O'Connor was shot again in his left ankle and right thigh. He turned to face the field so he could identify targets to the forward air controller who was communicating with air support. One of the CIDGs, whose arm was barely "hanging on to the shoulder by a hunk of muscle and skin," tugged at O'Connor to alert his attention to Mousseau, who was signaling for more ammunition. "Ammo—ammo—grenades," Mousseau yelled. O'Connor crawled over to the dead CIDGs and pulled off their ammunition clips and unspent grenades and tossed them to Mousseau. The forward air controller marked a target with smoke, and O'Connor confirmed. Seconds later, two F-100 fighter jets came screaming over the treetops and decimated the target with rockets.

With the enemy badly hit, O'Connor and his men had a moment of calm. They used the brief pause to begin patching their wounds. Air control asked for more targets over the radio, and O'Connor identified a few spots that soon lit up with explosions. This bought the stranded unit a few more seconds before Mousseau yelled, "They're coming in!" O'Connor braced himself, terrified that an untold number of NVA soldiers was about to overrun his position and kill him in the clearing. A bullet tore through his abdomen. Another hit his radio. "I was put out of commission," O'Connor later testified. He laid on the ground behind Wright's body, "firing at the NVA in the open field until the ammo ran out." "I was ready to die," remembered O'Connor.

With the firefight "increasing in intensity," the grounded men once again heard the approach of a helicopter. "My hopes," O'Connor recalled, "were that it was the strike force coming in mass to recover what was left." But just one helicopter flew over the treetops. Its pilot steered the chopper over the clearing and hovered just above the ground, as its door gunners unloaded automatic weapon fire toward the North Vietnamese positions. Somebody tossed a rucksack out of the hovering helicopter. And then out jumped Roy Benavidez.

EARLIER THAT DAY, ROY HAD AWOKEN AT THE SMALL ENCAMP-ment at Loc Ninh. The friends he had seen the night before had already arrived from Quan Loi and left for their mission into Cambodia. Roy's day opened calmly; he didn't have any pressing duties that morning. What he remembered most was the heat of the day. He had tried to sleep in, but the temperature pulled him out of bed.

Later that day, Roy walked out of his tent and came across a small prayer group. A chaplain had placed a small cross in the middle of a white cloth strewn across the hood of a jeep. Roy remembered "a small, attentive group of men" listening to the sermon. Roy joined them, pausing for a moment to take off his cap and perform the sign of the cross. He remembered the chaplain discussing the trials each man might face.

As Roy turned away from the prayer group, he caught sight of two men running toward the airstrip. Something was happening. Roy hustled to the Special Forces communication tent. "If there was action out in the field," he remembered, "the operator there monitoring the radio would be picking it up." Through the noisy crackling of static inside the tent, Roy could make out the loud sound of automatic gunfire and explosions. Someone was screaming over the radio. He heard what he described as "the voice of someone cursing and crying for help." Roy rushed to the airstrip to see how he could assist.

Roy saw the helicopters returning from the first rescue attempt. The first one was "badly shot up," he wrote, "but no one seemed to be injured." The second chopper was in much worse shape. "I didn't see how it could still fly," Roy remembered. As it landed, Roy saw Michael Craig, the nineteen-year-old door gunner who had been shot in the midsection. Craig was in critical condition, barely hanging onto his life as he struggled to breathe.

Roy and others helped pull Craig off the helicopter, and Roy sat with the dying young man, cradling him in his arms and yelling for help. "[He] was like our son or little brother . . . full of life and happiness," Roy remembered. Craig's wounds were mortal. Roy held him for those final few moments of his life, remembering Craig's final words as, "Oh, my God, my mother and father."

Roy later said that he "felt my heart sink" upon learning who was in trouble. When one of the pilots said he was going back in to help the stranded unit, Roy jumped onto the helicopter. "I can't explain what happened inside me," Roy recalled. "I just couldn't sit there and listen to my buddies die on the radio."

A pilot named Larry McKibben flew Roy's helicopter. Other choppers flew alongside to provide cover. They raced over the treetops, across the border, and into the firefight. McKibben was "zigzagging the chopper," Roy described, "and making every attempt to dodge the bullets." Roy's seat jerked and lurched as the chopper dashed through the bullet-filled sky. "We flew into the firefight like a runaway rollercoaster," he recalled. Fastened to the vehicle with only his seat belt, he repeated the sign of the cross over his face and heart. A clearing appeared in the jungle below, and the helicopter began to descend. As bullets pounded the walls of the chopper, Roy tossed a medical kit out onto the ground. With the helicopter hovering about ten feet off the earth, he leaped out and rolled into a crouch amid the tall grass as the air "vibrated with the roar of combat."

Roy paused for a second amid the tall elephant grass before grabbing the medical kit and taking off toward the stranded men. He had caught a glimpse of their position from the helicopter, so he knew where they were trapped, about eighty yards away. Roy began to run as McKibben pulled the chopper out of the clearing. High on adrenaline, Roy was just a few seconds into a sprint when a bullet tore through his calf, knocking him to the ground. He got back on his feet and ran through even more gunfire to reach the stranded unit.

When Roy reached the men, "there was blood everywhere." Everyone was wounded. They sat, shot up and bleeding, in a small stand of trees amid the tall elephant grass. As Roy remembered, "The fact that these men were still alive was a flat-out miracle."

He found Mousseau sitting up against a tree trunk, covered in blood and shot through the shoulder and the eye. "One side of his face looked as if someone had sledgehammered it," Roy recalled. But Mousseau was still fighting, returning the enemy's fire to hold them at bay. "The other side could have overrun these guys at any time," Roy later testified, but he suspected that the height of the elephant grass prevented the NVA from fully appreciating the vulnerability of the stranded unit. Of course, the enemy troops were probably also terrified by the sheer firepower that could appear from overhead whenever they moved.

Roy grabbed Mousseau's radio and called for the helicopter pilot McKibben to come back to get them. He glanced over to O'Connor, who gave a thumbs up, indicating that he was okay for the moment. Roy didn't see Wright, and he assumed the worst. McKibben flew over the clearing with guns blazing from his chopper. The North Vietnamese hit the helicopter with a barrage of bullets, and they sprayed additional gunfire toward the stranded men. A bullet punctured Roy's thigh, the pain "spreading like a small hot fire through my legs," he remembered.

Roy tossed a smoke grenade into a clearing to mark a pickup zone. He snatched a fallen man's AK-47 and sprayed the enemy position with a hail of bullets before ducking back below the tall grass. O'Connor told Roy about Wright. Roy thought the deceased team leader had been carrying classified documents that should not fall into enemy hands, so he made a note to retrieve the papers before they left.

The survivors began moving toward the smoke grenade marking the pickup spot. As they moved, Roy and O'Connor spotted movement in the grass and lobbed grenades that exploded near two NVA soldiers, knocking them off their feet. Some of the CIDGs made it to the helicopter and managed to board. As the rest of the American unit slogged toward the chopper, Roy circled back to Wright's body to grab the documents and a radio. Once he saw his friend, he knew he couldn't leave his body behind in that jungle. Roy bent down and hoisted Wright's body over his shoulder. As he rose, a shot hit him in the back. He collapsed and blacked out from the pain.

Roy awoke a moment later. He looked to the clearing and saw the rescue helicopter lying on its side, "a smoking ruin" on the ground. McKibben was in the cockpit window, shot through dead, his lifeless body leaning against the seat-belt straps. Roy quickly discerned that the pilot had been killed by enemy fire, causing the chopper to crash nose-first into the ground. Another member of the helicopter crew, Nelson Fournier, had been killed by the crushing weight of the chopper. Two other crew members were badly injured, and the CIDGs who had crawled aboard now crawled back out. Eleven men crouched in the field next to the downed helicopter, stranded in a no-man's-land across the Cambodian border in the middle of a firefight with hundreds of enemy soldiers.

The helicopter was leaking jet fuel, and Roy was worried it might explode, so he ordered the men to crawl through the tall grass toward another stand of trees. When they reached their destination, Roy began organizing the battered men into a defensive perimeter. The noise of gunfire and explosives filled the clearing. Roy wiped away "tiny shards of shrapnel" that had landed in the outer skin of his skull. Blood covered his face and dripped into his eyes. He pulled out the medical kit and began injecting the wounded men with morphine and patching their injuries however he could. Roy took another bullet to his butt. He picked up the radio and called in supporting airstrikes. Moments later, helicopters and fighter jets zoomed overhead, firing guns and rockets into the enemy positions. The air support bought precious time for the men on the ground as the enemy temporarily stopped firing in order to take cover.

Roy and one of the CIDGs spotted the bodies of a few dead NVA soldiers and crawled into the clearing to drag the deceased men back to their position near the trees. They stacked the corpses in front of them, using the bodies as "human sandbags," O'Connor later wrote, to shield themselves from the enemy gunfire. Another bullet ripped through Roy's leg. He got back on the radio, transmitting more locations to the air support who came to their aid with a "blast of rocket fire from overhead." The men of the stranded unit were growing inebriated from the morphine. The scene was wildly chaotic, and they struggled to hold onto their wits, their senses dulled from the morphine and the pain. O'Connor, whom Roy had injected three times, "was cross-eyed from the dope." Roy continued attending to the men's wounds while calling in airstrikes. He struggled to concentrate, knowing that the wrong coordinates could bring the overwhelming American firepower down on them instead of the enemy.

The men of the stranded unit were clustered in two groups about forty feet apart, lying on the ground just below the tall elephant grass. Their situation was incredibly dire. Bullets flew in from every direction. It seemed as if they were surrounded and could be overrun at any second. "We were in the middle of hell," Roy wrote. "Every movement brought a hail of gunfire. Men were crying and screaming for help. I was one of them. We were going to die."

The fighter pilots saved them. The jets screamed over the field, pounding the enemy positions with rockets and bombs. The planes flew so low that the men on the ground could feel the heat from their engines. Parts of the forest caught fire from the heat emitted by the afterburners. More helicopters arrived, spraying the tree line with thousands of rounds of automatic weapons fire. The jungle erupted into a concert of gunfire and explosions. Roy likened the air support to a "swarm of killer bees."

Out of the chaos, a lone helicopter touched down in the clearing about thirty yards from the stranded men. Its pilot reported seeing "wreckage and bodies laying over the entire landing zone." A member of the crew jumped out, and he and Roy started dragging their comrades toward the vehicle. Roy could barely see through the blood covering his face. The chopper's door gunners unloaded their weapons into the forest. Even the pilots, armed only with pistols, desperately shot at the NVA positioned near the tree line.

After getting some of the men onto the chopper, Roy turned back to search for more. He located Mousseau and staggered back to grab his friend. With both hands, he picked up Mousseau and slung the wounded man over his shoulder. But just as he did, an NVA soldier ran up behind him and slammed the butt of a rifle into the back of Roy's head. Roy spun and dropped his friend, coming face-to-face with the enemy combatant. The enemy hit him again, this time in the mouth, knocking Roy to the ground. Roy leapt to his feet and unsheathed his knife. As he rose, the NVA soldier stabbed a bayonet into Roy's forearm. Roy struck the enemy soldier with his hand, knocking the man to his knees. Then he plunged his knife into the man's abdomen. The man desperately waved his bayonet, "slicing my arm to ribbons," Roy wrote, "as he sawed it back and forth." Screaming, Roy mustered one more burst of energy, thrusting his knife deep into the man's ribs. The enemy soldier fell onto him and died.

Roy left the knife in the man's body and began to move. He found another gun lying on the jungle floor and pulled Mousseau back over his shoulder. He reached down and helped pull one of the CIDGs off the ground, and they all ran to the chopper. Roy held his hand over his stomach to hold in parts of his intestines that had started spilling out of a gaping wound in his abdomen. As he neared the rescue helicopter, he saw two enemy soldiers moving toward the chopper and shot them dead. A crew member from the rescue helicopter helped carry O'Connor, who told Roy that one of the Vietnamese CIDGs was still lying in the field. Shooting as he ran, Roy followed a trail of blood back to the position of the interpreter and helped him to the helicopter. He then looked around and spotted three more bodies, unsure if they were dead or alive, and picked them up and carried each to the helicopter and dropped them into the chopper's cargo bay. Everyone who might be alive was now onboard.

As the helicopter began lifting from the ground, Roy turned once more toward the clearing and fired his weapon into the jungle. Covered in blood and cradling his outpouring intestines, he strafed everything in sight, filling the field with one more spray of bullets. As he shot, sets of hands reached out from the helicopter and pulled him into a cabin filled with blood. With gunfire panging against its walls, the helicopter lifted out of the clearing and sped away over the treetops, just as Roy slipped out of consciousness.

CHAPTER 8

HOME

Roy awoke in a Saigon hospital "bandaged like a mummy," he recalled, with "tubes sticking in every opening in my body." He was in agonizing pain, aided only by "heavy doses of narcotics." His eyes opened to a grim scene. The hospital ward was filled with men whose bodies had been torn apart by the violence of war. A young man in a nearby bed had lost all his arms and legs. Other soldiers, covered with casts and bandages, lay suffering across the infirmary. Roy remembered a nurse succumbing to the emotion of treating so many badly wounded young soldiers. "Why do you keep doing this to these men?" the nurse screamed to God. Bound to his hospital bed, Roy struggled to hold on to his own life. He "faded in and out," he recalled, "while the doctors, nurses, and medics fought to save my life with surgery after surgery."[1]

Back in Texas, Lala received a telegram from the secretary of the Army. The notification informed her that Roy had been "slightly wounded in Vietnam," having suffered "multiple fragment wounds to the face, the neck and the abdomen." "Since he is not repeat not seriously wounded," the telegram emphasized, "no further reports will be furnished." Roy had asked the Army to notify his family as soon as possible. "I couldn't write to Lala," he later explained, "but I was worried because I knew she had probably gotten a telegram telling her I was injured. Man, I didn't want her to know how bad I was beat up."[2]

There was no way she could have known. The telegram was deeply misleading. Roy had not been "slightly wounded in Vietnam"; he was in critical condition because of injuries suffered fighting in Cambodia. Still, whatever the reason for the miscommunication, Lala knew at least that Roy had been wounded and that he was alive. She did not know just how close he had come to death or that he would never be the same.

Roy had barely made it out of that jungle. As he would later emphasize, it was a "miracle" that he survived. The pilot who flew him out, a man named Roger Waggie, had pulled out of the clearing as a hail of gunfire chased his helicopter into the sky. The chopper's cargo bay was filled with severely wounded and dying men, strewn across a "cabin floor ankle-deep in blood." The helicopter was pockmarked with bullet holes, and its navigational equipment had been destroyed. Panicked and disoriented, Waggie initially flew in the wrong direction over Cambodia before jet pilots managed to turn him around toward the American base in South Vietnam.[3]

When the helicopter arrived back at Loc Ninh, other soldiers rushed over to help the wounded men off the chopper. As they unloaded the helicopter, they discovered that Roy had mistakenly loaded three dead North Vietnamese soldiers onto the extraction vehicle. Roy himself was in very bad shape. They pulled him off the chopper and rested him on the ground, where he lay covered in blood, fading in and out of consciousness in a state of paralyzing shock. One of the first medics to approach Roy thought he was already dead. The medic retrieved a body bag and was preparing it for Roy's body when Roy suddenly spit a mouthful of blood into the man's face.[4]

During his time on that Cambodian battlefield, Roy incurred a total of thirty-seven puncture wounds. He had been struck by seven bullets. Both arms were sliced by the enemy combatant's bayonet, and it looked as if he could lose his left arm. His jaw was broken. His intestines were exposed through a laceration in his abdomen. He had taken shrapnel to nearly all parts of his body, including his skull and chest. Some of the material was dangerously close to his heart. Other pieces had penetrated his lungs. The pilot Waggie asked the medical staff about Roy's condition and remembered being "informed that SSG Benavidez was severely wounded and was not expected to live." Another man who asked about Roy reported "They didn't expect him to live—he was a bloody mess."[5]

Others were already dead. Leroy Wright. Michael Craig, the door gunner in the first extraction attempt, had been killed. Larry McKibben, the pilot who first flew Roy into the landing zone, had died that day in his chopper. So had the helicopter crewman Nelson Fournier. And many North Vietnamese soldiers had also been killed. It was later estimated that roughly two hundred men lost their lives that day in the jungle. Lloyd Mousseau fought through grenade and gunshot wounds to escape the field alive, but he succumbed to his injuries while being transported to Saigon. Roy was riding in a helicopter with Mousseau, squeezing his hand and "praying for another miracle," when his friend died. But Roy's actions saved the lives of at least eight men.[6]

Hours after the action in that Cambodian clearing, additional troops traveled to the area to search for survivors and retrieve the bodies of their deceased comrades. The first group to arrive was able to confirm that no one was left alive, but they quickly fled the area after taking some gunfire. The next day, another unit came to recover the bodies of the dead Americans and their CIDG allies. A member of this retrieval team later told Roy that he had counted about thirty foxholes and saw "more dead NVAs than he had time to count."[7]

Roy was joined in the hospital by Brian O'Connor, the only survivor among the three Americans involved in the original May 2 mission. Roy was in his hospital bed when he recognized O'Connor lying across the ward. "He looked to be in about as bad a shape as I was," Roy remembered. "Neither of us could move or talk, but each morning we would wiggle our toes at each other to prove that we had made it through another night."[8]

During those first days in the hospital, Roy and O'Connor were visited by Lt. Col. Ralph Drake, the commanding officer of the B-56 Sigma unit. Roy couldn't speak when Drake first started visiting, but he remembered the officer touching him on the shoulder. When Roy could finally muster some words, he asked Drake about the status of the documents he had tried to retrieve from Leroy Wright. Drake couldn't believe that Roy, who appeared to be on the verge of death, was at that point worried about those documents. He assured Roy that the materials were safe and encouraged the wounded soldier to focus on his recovery.[9]

A few others visited, including some of the pilots involved in the extraction and supportive efforts on May 2. Since the battle, the fliers had been piecing together their shared memories to gain a sense of the order of events. As they talked, the full extent of Roy's contributions began to become clear. They were awed by Roy's bravery against such overwhelming odds. One later remembered, "Almost everyone involved in the operation on the ground agreed that Benavidez was instrumental in saving their lives."[10]

After a few days, Roy woke to find that O'Connor was no longer across the ward. There was no explanation, and Roy didn't bother to ask. His own surgeries and pain medication had left his mind too muddied to exert much thought on the matter. O'Connor had been so badly wounded that Roy assumed he'd died.[11]

Roy spent about ten days in Saigon before being transported to a hospital in Japan. This was a good sign. "By then," he wrote, "I was able to stand—barely—for very short periods of time." In Japan, Roy underwent a variety of procedures that left him in "constant pain." He didn't know the full extent of the operations, and no one in his family was present to offer consent or keep records. Such concerns were secondary, as the doctors desperately worked to save his life and finally managed to stabilize his condition. In Tokyo, Roy was barely lucid, but he also began to fully realize that he was going to live.[12]

After about a week in Japan, Roy was told that he was being sent home to Texas. The medics loaded him onto a stretcher and took him out to the helipad for the flight to the airport. Roy, mustering whatever pride he could gather, "insisted" that he be allowed to walk the final steps to the helicopter. He had entered the war in the prime fighting condition of his life and wanted the symbolism of at least leaving the hospital under his own power. Roy slowly limped over to the helicopter, where a well-meaning medic tried to help him aboard. But the man had no sense of the full extent of Roy's injuries. When the medic grabbed Roy's midsection to assist him into the chopper, Roy was met with excruciating pain and, instinctually, punched the medic in the face. Roy couldn't hit very hard at that moment, so the medic wasn't seriously wounded, but the man immediately realized his mistake and apologized. "I just wanted to get the hell out of there," Roy recalled. A few hours later, he was sleeping in a plane over the Pacific Ocean.[13]

AFTER ROY'S BATTLE ON MAY 2, DANIEL BOONE OPERATIONS shut down for three days so that the unit could replenish the lost men and aircraft. Eighteen men—a big number in the small unit—were either dead or wounded. After the brief lull, the missions resumed as communist activities in the region continued escalating through the summer. CIA reports from August of 1968 detail increasing enemy infiltration into Cambodia as well as intelligence reports documenting additional emergency extractions and major conflicts between Special Forces and North Vietnamese and NLF troops in Cambodia.[14]

Communist usage of Cambodia remained a major problem for the American military through the end of 1968. By that autumn, Sihanouk had once again become convinced that the North Vietnamese would win the war, and he exercised a "double standard," observed one intelligence report, toward American and communist usage of Cambodian territory. While openly hostile toward the United States for its operations near the border, he refused to undertake any substantive action that might stymie the movements of North Vietnamese troops in Cambodia. In fact, his subordinates were working directly with the North Vietnamese. As late as October of 1968, the CIA reported that high-ranking Cambodian officials were still meeting with NLF leaders to coordinate the movement of supplies and troops to communist forces in South Vietnam.[15]

As expected, the broader American war effort reached a critical juncture in 1968. May of that year was a cauldron of chaos for the American military in Vietnam. In the week after Roy's battle, 562 US soldiers were killed in combat, making it the deadliest week of the entire American war in Vietnam. That month, the North Vietnamese launched another coordinated offensive of roughly sixty thousand soldiers, an aggressive follow-up to that winter's Tet Offensive. A lieutenant colonel who had defected from the North Vietnamese Army informed American officials of the oncoming attack, leading to decisive military victories for the United States and South Vietnamese Army. The

North Vietnamese lost more than twenty-four thousand soldiers, compared to 4,223 combined deaths among South Vietnamese and American forces. Despite convincing victories in the field, May of 1968 was the deadliest month for American troops in Vietnam.[16]

May 1968 was also the same month that the United States and North Vietnam began formal peace negotiations in Paris. The North Vietnamese communist forces were still in the middle of a series of offensive maneuvers that by October of 1968 would cost their side more than 150,000 soldiers killed, compared to about 12,500 men lost by the United States. The communists' 1968 offensives failed to achieve their longtime dream of sparking a general uprising, nor did they secure any long-standing significant military objectives. Militarily speaking, North Vietnam at the end of 1968 was nowhere close to its goal of defeating the American-backed Republic of South Vietnam on the battlefield.[17]

But the North Vietnamese did believe they were winning the war in the minds of the American public. Gallup polling in the summer of 1968 indicated that the majority of Americans believed it had been a mistake to send American troops to Vietnam. The North Vietnamese, despite heavy losses in 1968, viewed the Tet Offensive as a major victory, citing President Johnson's withdrawal from the 1968 presidential election as evidence. Johnson's announcement stunned the world. A senior South Vietnamese diplomat called it "a turning point that is to [the] benefit of North Vietnam." The North Vietnamese had plenty of their own problems, but by May of 1968, they expected to win because American support for the war was floundering.[18]

When the Paris peace talks began on May 10, 1968, both sides settled in for a long, drawn-out negotiation. The two sides were very far apart. The United States was committed to the preservation of an independent Republic of South Vietnam, and

North Vietnam was committed to a unification of the two nations under communist rule. That was the entire point of their war: to unify Vietnam after over a century of intervention from Western powers. The United States could spend months, even years, negotiating through bombing pauses and troop reductions, but what the Americans did not fully understand was that North Vietnamese leaders envisioned themselves as part of a century-long struggle for independence. Mere months or even years were but small epochs in a much longer revolution. Time was on their side. "Hanoi," the CIA reported, "believes time is running against the Allied side." Hanoi was right, especially with the impending turnover in the American presidency. The war continued, even as the diplomats spoke of peace.[19]

As THE WAR BORE ON, ROY WAS BACK IN THE UNITED STATES recovering at Brooke Army Medical Center (BAMC) in San Antonio. This was his second stay at the enormous facility. After surviving two very close brushes with death, he was home in Texas with Lala; his baby girl, Denise; and the rest of his family. Roy hadn't lived in Texas since joining the Army thirteen years earlier. His time at BAMC would be his longest stint in the Lone Star State since he was a teenager. His family and friends who had stayed in Texas came to see him in San Antonio.

At thirty-two years old, Roy still had a great deal of life in front of him. Although he would live, many questions remained about his future. As with Roy's previous injuries, the damage done to his body on May 2, 1968, threatened to disrupt the only career he had ever known. The wounds he incurred would forever restrict his physical abilities. Roy would never live another day without pain or with normal lung functionality. Just a few months before his injuries, he had been running around the forests of North Carolina with a pack of equipment strapped on his back. That training had paid off in Southeast Asia, but he could never move like that again. The body that once qualified him for membership in the most revered fighting force in the world was the same body that could no longer perform basic physical tasks like climbing stairs without losing his breath. Roy certainly could never go back into combat, a severe limitation for an enlisted man in an Army at war. Grateful as he was to have survived, his ongoing physical recovery was shrouded by doubts about his future quality of life and his ability to provide for his family.[20]

Roy spent those hospital days recuperating and talking with Lala. He was "in a little bit worse shape," he told a nurse, than his last extended stay at BAMC, but at least he was awake long enough to interact with Lala. The last time Roy had been at BAMC, he had been unconscious for some of her early visits, and this time he was grateful to have his wits about him. Most important of all, he was alive.[21]

A month into Roy's arrival at BAMC, he was promoted from staff sergeant to sergeant first class, his first rank promotion in nearly four years. The recommendation had been submitted on June 3 by Lt. Col. Ralph Drake, and the promotion went into effect on June 20, raising his base monthly pay by nearly forty dollars.[22]

A few weeks later, a lieutenant came through the hospital ward distributing medals to some of the men. Most of these commendations were Purple Hearts, the medal American soldiers are given when wounded in combat. Roy thought the man was a bit too informal in distributing the medals, later writing, "He was passing them out like prizes at a carnival show. It was certainly nothing like I would have expected for these men who had taken a bullet or worse for their country."[23]

Roy received his own Purple Heart, and then the officer handed him something else—a little black box. Roy opened the box and was shocked by the contents. Inside was a Distinguished Service Cross, the second-highest medal for combat valor available in the United States military. He didn't know this at the time, but Lt. Col. Drake had submitted the names of Roy, Lloyd Mousseau, and Larry McKibben for this prestigious honor. Leroy Wright was nominated for the same award a year later. They all received it, albeit posthumously for all but Roy.[24]

The Distinguished Service Cross is a great honor. It was established during World War I to award combat soldiers for "acts of heroism [that] must have been so notable and have involved risk of life so extraordinary as to set the individual apart from their comrades." Just over one thousand veterans received the Distinguished Service Cross during America's war in Vietnam, roughly four hundred of them posthumously.[25]

It was rare for men in MACV-SOG units to receive such an award. They were involved in plenty of heroic activities, but the secret nature of their missions disincentivized most commanders from making formal recommendations for decorations. Medals are part of the public record and must include the location of the action being recognized. Because the United States didn't want the world to know about its activities in Cambodia, citations had to be sanitized to remove any direct acknowledgment of actions across the border, and the men who signed nondisclosure agreements were understandably limited in their ability to provide additional testimony. Some commanders simply didn't make any recommendations that might draw unneeded attention to the activities of MACV-SOG.[26]

Lt. Col. Drake must have felt very strongly about the actions of Wright, McKibben, Mousseau, and Roy to recommend them for the Distinguished Service Cross. But the language of each citation was intentionally deceptive. In each of them, the location of the action is listed as "the Republic of Vietnam." Roy later pointed out the discrepancy in his 1986 memoir, writing,

"Interestingly enough, there was no mention in the citation of Cambodia." "But that was okay with me," he continued. "I knew where I almost died, and I knew why the army didn't want to mention it." "I thought nothing—at that time," he wrote, "of the government's decision to shift the scene of action a bit to the east."[27]

There was another, more pressing problem with Roy's Distinguished Service Cross. The lieutenant charged with passing out the awards didn't hold the appropriate rank to present that level of decoration. Roy, who could be a stickler for the formalities of the Army, reminded the officer that the Distinguished Service Cross needed to be presented by a general and "not handed out like a cereal premium by a second lieutenant," he wrote. One of the hospital orderlies backed him up, insisting to the officer that Roy was correct in observing the proper procedure for awarding that level of commendation. The lieutenant took back the medal and left.[28]

Roy finally received his Distinguished Service Cross on September 9, 1968, when General William Westmoreland visited soldiers in BAMC. The former commander of MACV, Westmoreland had been relieved of his duties in Vietnam and sworn in as the new Army chief of staff in the spring of 1968. America's leading officer in Vietnam was by then much maligned in the public, but Roy still held "a general feeling of respect and admiration for the man," he remembered. "He was a fine commander as far as I was concerned." Roy was glad it was Westmoreland who would give him the award.[29]

Roy had met Westmoreland more than ten years beforehand when he briefly served as the general's driver at Fort Gordon in Georgia. Roy remembered that meeting well and was surprised when Westmoreland said he did too. "I was impressed with him as a soldier," Westmoreland remembered in 1968. "I told him he ought to go airborne and I recruited him right on the spot."

The reunion between the general and the enlisted man drew the attention of the media. The Associated Press picked up the story, and it was reprinted in several newspapers across Texas with a picture of Westmoreland pinning the medal on Roy as Lala watched. Another picture shows Roy and Westmoreland shaking hands during the ceremony. Roy later tracked down a copy and had the general sign it.[30]

A little over a week after Roy was awarded the Distinguished Service Cross, he received a letter from the pilot Roger Waggie in Vietnam. Roy didn't know Waggie well, but he had written to the pilot twice in the preceding months to express his gratitude for Waggie's heroics on May 2. Waggie's written response took months to arrive and offered a grim assessment of the situation in Cambodia. Waggie told of more American soldiers and pilots who had been lost since the events of May 2, including Waggie's roommate, who was one of six pilots killed on a single disastrous day that August. "Hope you understand my situation and forgive me for not answering promptly," Waggie explained. "We are having a lot of action here. Seems like they are everywhere." Roy lay in his hospital bed, feeling deeply sympathetic toward the men fighting the war he had just left.[31]

Roy stayed in the hospital for nearly nine months, an extraordinarily long time even for a soldier suffering multiple combat wounds. His medical records indicate many severe injuries but do not include a detailed explanation of each procedure. There are several viable reasons for such a lengthy stay. Most pressing would have been the threat of infection presented by any of his thirty-seven puncture wounds. Roy also had severe lung damage that gave him trouble breathing and left him exposed to possible respiratory failure. His condition also elevated his risk for pneumonia, which might have been even more deadly than normal given the state of his health. Then there was the sheer volume of his surgeries and time spent in rehab. There is no telling what setbacks Roy encountered, but his condition gradually improved.[32]

Roy finally left BAMC in February of 1969. One of the first things he did was get in a car and drive to Houston to visit the family of the pilot Larry McKibben. McKibben, only twenty years old when he was killed, was the man who bravely flew Roy into that clearing on May 2. Roy embraced his parents and discussed McKibben's role in saving the lives of Roy and the other men.[33]

After he was discharged from the hospital, Roy was assigned to Fort Devens, a Special Forces training base located about thirty-five miles northwest of Boston. While there, he served as a light weapons infantry leader. He also claimed to have made one more jump, only to be met with unbearable pain. After that, his parachuting days were over. Roy remembered Massachusetts in February and March as "bitterly cold," especially during some of the training maneuvers in the Green Mountains of Vermont. He later wrote that the "cool nights and mornings made my wounds ache to the point that at times I was almost incapable of functioning." The cold was particularly bad for the nerve damage in his forearms and hands. Roy managed to make it through to the summer, but he was concerned about the oncoming autumn and winter, so he requested a transfer.[34]

In August of 1969, Roy received a new assignment. Having requested a transfer out of Massachusetts, Roy had learned in the *Army Times* magazine that an old contact, General Robert Linvill from the 82nd Airborne, was taking over command of the 1st Infantry Division at Fort Riley, Kansas. Roy claimed to have put in a call to Linvill, who helped facilitate a transfer for Roy to become the general's driver in Kansas. "It seemed to be the best I could hope for," he remembered of his new orders.[35]

In August of 1969, Roy, Lala, and Denise packed their belongings and headed to Kansas. Fort Riley sits in the northeast part of the state, about 130 miles west of Kansas City, in the grassy prairie known as the Flint Hills near the college town of Manhattan. It wasn't a particularly warm place, which didn't necessarily help with Roy's pain in cold weather. But he figured, "At least the summers would be pleasant."[36]

Being a driver offered Roy an easy assignment after years of difficult ones. He was thirty-four years old and had been in the military his entire adult life. He had already experienced a remarkable Cold War military career, serving in hotspots like Korea, Berlin, and Latin America, and fighting in Vietnam and Cambodia. He had completed extensive and dangerous training programs and served in the fabled 82nd Airborne and the legendary Green Berets. Life as a chauffeur took him away from the hottest action of the American military, but it was also comparatively easy and peaceful.

Roy had previously served as a driver in his early twenties. A decade later, the job felt different. He was no longer a naive kid driving around commanders. By then, Roy had the stature and reputation of a grizzled combat veteran. He had earned that cushy job, even though other men were still fighting. He took his duties seriously, but now he could relax a bit and slip into a new role as a smart, gregarious, mid-career soldier that everybody liked.

In 1969, Fort Riley was slated to hold about twenty thousand soldiers. It was home to a large military correctional facility, built to house the growing number of young men convicted of violating various military codes, especially going AWOL. The base has a famous history as the one-time home of the 7th Cavalry (the last horse in the Army's cavalry died the year before Roy arrived). It was the place where General George A. Custer trained his men in the years before their demise at Little Bighorn. Tourists can still visit a replica of his old house on the base. Otherwise, Fort Riley was a nondescript training base, although it could get rowdy at times. Every summer, the base housed thousands of ROTC college students whose antics peppered the local newspaper with reports of speeding violations and alcohol-related arrests.[37]

Roy kept a low profile in Kansas. His name popped up only once in the local media when he was interviewed at a Veterans Day parade in Wichita. When a local reporter asked him to explain the importance of Veterans Day, he said, "Why the answer is right here in a show of patriotic spirit like this," referring to the forty-two marching units participating in the parade. "That's what Veterans Day is all about—having a community like this where you can be free." A woman also interviewed commented, "I was thankful we had a good parade and there were no demonstrations," in reference to the widespread anti-war protests that by then were sweeping the country. Other than that brief clip, Roy kept his head low.[38]

Roy and Lala's family continued to grow. On November 20, 1969, they welcomed another baby girl named Yvette. She was born at 12:20 p.m. at the Irwin Army Hospital at Fort Riley. Roy's new job allowed him to be more present as a father. His duties as a chauffeur and later as an operations sergeant at Fort Riley provided more time to spend at home with Lala, Denise, and Yvette. Besides a couple short training missions to West Germany, Roy remained in Kansas. "Family life," he wrote of his time at Fort Riley, "was finally a reality. I enjoyed every minute of it."[39]

Roy continued working to advance his career. He applied to Warrant Officer Candidate School, which would have put him on a different career track than that of the typical enlisted man. His glowing letters of recommendation highlighted not only his contributions as the commanding officer's driver but also excellence in other administrative and logistical support duties. General Linvill observed, "I know of no soldier who is more dedicated to the military or to the principle of military discipline." Another brigadier general wrote, "I don't know of an assignment that Sergeant Benavidez has had in recent years that has not been performed in a thoroughly outstanding manner." A colonel who worked with Roy at Fort Riley emphasized his "dependability and dedication." And Col. Richard E. Cavazos, who later became the Army's first Hispanic four-star general, highlighted Roy's "inexhaustible efforts, devotion to duty, and outstanding leadership." Unfortunately, Roy was not selected for Warrant Officer Candidate School. It would be one of the great disappointments in an otherwise illustrious career in the Army.[40]

DURING ROY'S YEARS AT FORT RILEY, THE AMERICAN WAR IN Vietnam changed drastically. Richard Nixon assumed the presidency in January of 1969, his prospects enhanced by internal dissention in the Democratic Party and his own promise to achieve "Peace with Honor" in Southeast Asia. His administration took over the management of the war and the ongoing peace talks. Allied troop numbers reached an all-time high during the first month of the Nixon presidency, as the new commander in chief vowed to maintain troop levels until progress had been made in negotiations.[41]

Conditions in Cambodia rapidly deteriorated. Like its predecessors, the Nixon administration quickly realized the enormous problem of enemy usage of Cambodia and began to take even more aggressive action. In March of 1969, President Nixon formally approved a secret bombing campaign targeting communist positions in Cambodia. As the *New York Times* observed, the Nixon administration was "willing to take some military risks avoided by the previous administration." Over the next fourteen months, the United States dropped 110,000 tons of bombs over Cambodia.[42]

By the time Roy was released from the hospital, America's relationship with Prince Sihanouk was again improving, largely because of Sihanouk's problems within his own country. By then, it had become widely recognized in virtually every diplomatic circle that communist forces were using Cambodian territory. Sihanouk could no longer reasonably deny this fact. He also faced major financial problems as the Cambodian economy was hampered by farming debt, declining rubber prices, and high urban unemployment. In July of 1969, Cambodia and the United States formally resumed diplomatic relations for the first time since 1965.[43]

After years of fighting external forces, by the summer of 1969 Sihanouk faced serious threats from within Cambodia. On his right sat conservative leaders who wanted to align more closely with the United States to fight against communism. And on his left were Cambodian communists who wanted to ally with the North Vietnamese and Chinese. Cambodian communists had been active since the 1950s, but for years operated only underground. In 1967, they launched an uprising in the western part of the country, spinning the nation into a civil war, even as the Cambodian government continued to aid North Vietnamese communists. Sihanouk, facing pressure from every possible direction, began to lose his grip on the country.[44]

In early 1970, Sihanouk left Cambodia amid growing unrest and was replaced in a coup by his prime minister Lon Nol. Soon after, Cambodian citizens engaged in a wave of protests against the North Vietnamese embassy in response to widespread news of communist usage of Cambodian territory. Unlike Sihanouk, Lon Nol ordered North Vietnamese forces to leave Cambodia at once and began rebuilding the Cambodian military to resist communist forces. Lon Nol's government ended Cambodian neutrality, officially joining the United States' side of the Vietnam War. Cambodia recognized the Republic of South Vietnam and cut off relations with the North. A break in relations with China followed. Soon thereafter, Cambodia and the United States agreed to defense pacts that brought nearly $50 million in military aid to Lon Nol's government during the spring and summer of 1970.[45]

That May, President Nixon announced that American soldiers would be entering Cambodia for two months to disrupt communist usage of Cambodian territory. Despite Nixon's insistence that this limited action did not constitute a full-fledged invasion, the American anti-war movement erupted in the first week of May 1970 as millions of protestors demonstrated against American action in Cambodia. College campuses exploded with protests, highlighted by shootings at Kent State University that resulted in the killing of four students and the wounding of nine other demonstrators. Ten days later, two more students were killed and twelve wounded at Jackson State College in Mississippi. During that tense month, hundreds of thousands of demonstrators took to the streets across the United States, especially on college campuses. Students at nearly 1,350 colleges participated in protests that May. Over 350 campuses experienced student strikes, and hundreds of college administrators decided to end the spring semester early. This was precisely the type of domestic fallout the Johnson administration so feared when first planning covert actions in Cambodia in the mid-1960s.[46]

The American-backed invasion of Cambodia did help quell some of the communist infiltration into South Vietnam, but it also set off another international crisis. China and North Vietnam had interpreted the 1970 overthrow of Sihanouk as a plot sparked by the United States to install an American-friendly dictator in Phnom Penh. Hanoi radio insisted, "It is clear from the recent coup in Cambodia that the United States is plotting not only to counter the Vietnamese people's fight against

US aggression and for national salvation, but also to subvert the independence and sovereignty of Cambodia." Ultimately, the Cambodian coup and invasion helped further mobilize international communist support for Cambodia's communist nationalists. Despite heavy American bombing and financial assistance to the other side, those Cambodian communists were eventually victorious, and in 1975, Lon Nol's government fell, giving control of Cambodia to a group known as the Khmer Rouge, led by the genocidal dictator Pol Pot.[47]

BACK IN THE UNITED STATES, ROY IN 1972 HAD A FORTUITOUS run-in that offered him a chance to return to Texas. Lieutenant General Patrick F. Cassidy, commander of the Fifth United States Army, was touring Fort Riley when he happened upon Roy. When they met, Roy was wearing his Distinguished Service Cross. Cassidy took note, having earned his own Distinguished Service Cross for heroics performed during the invasion of France in World War II. The pair had crossed paths years before in Germany, but Roy wasn't keen on reminding the general about their previous meeting because it involved an incident where Roy had a physical confrontation with a superior officer. During their chat, Cassidy learned that Roy was from Texas, and he asked the thirty-six-year-old war hero if he would like to return to serve as his driver at Fort Sam Houston in San Antonio. "Naturally, I accepted," Roy wrote. "Lala and I could hardly wait to take our children back to Texas, where they would be near our families."[48]

In May of 1972, after nearly three years at Fort Riley, Roy, Lala, Denise, and Yvette came home to Texas, this time for good. Notwithstanding the time he spent recovering in the hospital, it had been seventeen years since Roy had last lived in his home state. Three months later, Lala gave birth to a boy they named

Noel. He was born on August 26, 1972, at BAMC, the same San Antonio facility where Roy had twice been hospitalized.[49]

Roy and his young family lived in military housing on Fort Sam Houston, where he played an essential role in Lt. Gen. Cassidy's daily life. In later recommending Roy for promotion, the lieutenant general wrote that Roy's duties "went far beyond the normal duties of driving. . . . He served as host, guide, advisor, and personal representative." "In every respect," Cassidy noted, "his appearance, deportment, and overall performance was of the highest order, and he reflected credit upon the Fifth Army and its commander." Roy also continued to enhance his skills by completing weapons testing and a series of sub-courses.[50]

As Cassidy's driver, Roy received widespread praise from other superior officers who later wrote letters of recommendation in support of a promotion. Lt. Gen. James Hollingsworth, a veteran of World War II and Vietnam, judged Roy to be "one of the most outstanding noncommissioned officers I have ever encountered." "His exceptional leadership and managerial expertise," wrote another general, "has served to inspire his subordinates and won the respect of his superiors." A colonel who worked with Roy

Roy and Lala with their children, 1974. Courtesy of the Benavidez family.

commented, "He discharged that role with such aplomb, spirit and professionalism that he was a constant inspiration to every other driver. . . . His enthusiasm was contagious and his dependability unmatched."[51]

Roy drove for Lt. Gen. Cassidy at Fort Sam Houston for about a year before Cassidy's retirement. When the general retired in 1973, he gave Roy an opportunity to select his next assignment. Roy decided to stay in San Antonio and work with Special Forces as a senior enlisted officer. The Benavidez family, by then five in number, would stay in Texas for the foreseeable future.[52]

That same year, the United States came to terms with the North Vietnamese for a ceasefire that would end America's involvement in Vietnam. Both sides agreed to respect the boundaries created by the 1954 Geneva Accords. In exchange, the United States consented to pull out its remaining troops from Southeast Asia. It was a short-lived pact. Within two months of the removal of American forces, hostilities resumed between the South Vietnamese and North Vietnamese. Two years later, the North Vietnamese captured Saigon, fulfilling their long-standing dream of a unified Vietnam free from Western control. The following year saw the creation of the Socialist Republic of Vietnam.[53]

When the war ended, Roy thought of the men with whom he had served. "My thoughts and those of the other servicemen were of the MIA's and POW's still there," he wrote years later. "My mind was not able to absorb the impact of Vietnam at that time. My emotions and reasoning ability about this subject were in deep conflict." For Roy and many others who served, the war would never be over. He would forever attach his identity to that service in Southeast Asia.[54]

That December marked the end of Roy's most recent six-year enlistment, and he reenlisted in the Army for another five-year term. His reenlistment drew the attention of a local reporter for the *San Antonio Express*, who published a feature on Roy's career with the headline, "'Walking Roadmap' Re-ups for 5." "I'm a walking roadmap, scars everywhere," Roy told the reporter. He was clearly in the twilight of his career, but the thirty-eight-year-old wanted to remain in the service for as long as he could. Plus, Roy still had another battle in him, one rooted in fighting for recognition for the physical sacrifices he had made fighting on behalf of his country. This quest would consume him, and one day, it would complete him.[55]

CHAPTER 9

HONOR

O N February 25, 1974, Roy mailed a letter to Texas con-gressman Henry B. González, requesting his "assistance in upgrading a Service Award." "I cannot understand why I was not awarded a higher award," Roy wrote. "During this period I have noticed that higher awards have been given to service members for less conspicuous actions." While acknowledging some un-certainty about the award, Roy hinted to the Hispanic politician that race might have played a role in his being overlooked. "To my knowledge," Roy noted, incorrectly, "there are no living Mex-ican Americans with the Medal of Honor for Viet Nam service and we wonder why" (there in fact was one). "I have given this matter a great deal of thought," he continued, "and have come to the conclusion that I should follow this route." With this inquiry, Roy was asking the San Antonio–based politician to help him advocate for his Distinguished Service Cross to be upgraded to a Congressional Medal of Honor. And so began the next great pursuit of his life.[1]

The Congressional Medal of Honor is the most prestigious decoration available to soldiers in any branch of the United States Armed Forces. Established during the Civil War, it is given only to combat war heroes "who distinguish themselves through conspicuous gallantry and intrepidity at the risk of life above and beyond the call of duty," explains the Department of Defense. These honors are exceedingly rare. As of this writing, only 268 have been awarded to soldiers who fought in the American war in Vietnam, equating to roughly one per every ten thousand who served. The process itself involves extensive documentation and requires the approval of high-ranking Army officials, Congress, and the president of the United States.[2]

The Medal of Honor is awarded during a formal ceremony with the president of the United States. Those who receive the award are entitled to special privileges including an additional monthly pension, lifetime travel on military airplanes, burial at Arlington National Cemetery, preferred admission for their children into every service academy, and an invitation to every presidential inauguration for the rest of their lives. Perhaps the greatest aspect of this unique honor is that it formally certifies each recipient as one of the greatest soldiers in the history of the United States. It is an exclusive and illustrious brotherhood to which Roy believed he deserved to belong.[3]

It was harder, in general, for men involved with Operation Daniel Boone to receive major awards like the Medal of Honor due to the confidential nature of their missions. MACV-SOG units were notoriously underrecognized. Most of their activities were classified, and the Army in 1974 or 1975 destroyed MACV-SOG after-action reports that included crucial evidence. The men in these units, having signed nondisclosure agreements, couldn't always stipulate the location of their activities. Some even flat-out refused awards to avoid drawing attention to their wartime activities. Eyewitnesses were limited because of the small numbers of Americans involved in these special operations. Roy's decision to push for a higher award was unique among veterans of MACV-SOG and would have met disapproval from many other soldiers. Several men of MACV-SOG received the Medal of Honor, but they were not supposed to pursue it on their own.[4]

Roy wrote that he had first started thinking about the Medal of Honor while stationed at Fort Devens in 1969. According to him, some of the soldiers there had heard rumors of his exploits. Others heard the tale directly from Roy, usually over drinks at the NCO club, where stories from Vietnam flowed as freely as the booze. Roy's peers marveled that he had not been awarded the Medal of Honor. "Some of them thought I had received it," Roy recalled, "and others said they heard I was recommended for it. I never thought too much about it," he claimed of the time.[5]

There was less such talk during Roy's years in Kansas, but the Medal of Honor discussions picked up again when he returned to Texas and began spending more time with other Special Forces veterans. By then, Roy's heroics had become the stuff of legend, and of speculation and gossip. There was a rumor that Lt. Col. Ralph Drake, the commander of Roy's unit in South Vietnam, had nominated Roy for the Medal of Honor, but no one was sure what had happened after that. Roy's buddies pressed him on the issue, insisting he should have received the medal. At the very least, they prodded, he should try to find out what happened with the nomination. One of these interested soldiers knew Ralph Drake and where he was currently assigned. So Roy and the soldier called Drake on the phone.[6]

Roy had not seen Drake since May of 1968 in Saigon, when the commander visited him and Brian O'Connor in the hospital. Drake thought Roy had died and was shocked to hear his voice on the phone six years later, in the spring of 1974. Roy fought back tears, remembering those traumatic days in the hospital and recalling "the concern and compassion this hardnosed Special Forces colonel had shown for me as I had lain half-dead in that hospital bed in Saigon."[7]

The conversation with Drake cleared things up. Roy had not been recommended for the Medal of Honor. Drake had considered it, but he was restricted by the nature of the battle itself. A Medal of Honor approval requires eyewitnesses. Only four Americans (counting Roy) had been present on the ground. And at the time of Drake's initial recommendation, two of them had already died and the other two were barely holding on to life. There were simply no other American eyewitnesses who could provide the testimony needed to pass each level of review. Plus, Drake was extremely busy at the time, running his unit during some of the most intense days of the war. But when Roy called in 1974, Drake was ready to act on his behalf.[8]

On April 9, 1974, Lt. Col. Ralph Drake submitted a letter to the new commander of the Fifth Army. Drake explained that he had recently reviewed the original Distinguished Service Cross citation and realized that "two very important aspects of this extraordinarily heroic action were not included." These "two very important aspects" were the fact that Roy voluntarily boarded the rescue helicopter and that he was the last to leave the field. "Had the completely voluntary nature of these extraordinary and repeated acts of heroism been known to me," Drake insisted in 1974, "I would have recommended SFC Benavidez for the Medal of Honor." "These new facts," Drake argued, were "adequate basis for a review and upgrading of his award." If only it were that easy.[9]

The Army has a procedure to upgrade medals. It happens in cases when new information becomes available or to remedy a clerical error or failure in judgment. The Army Board for Correction of Military Records (ABCMR) oversees commendation upgrades. Individual soldiers and veterans can apply for reviews on their own behalf. Interested parties can also submit applications to correct the records of others. Either way, it is the applicants who are responsible for proving to the board that an injustice has occurred, and all decisions must be approved by the secretary of the Army.[10]

In Roy's case, this first step alone seemed nearly impossible. His upgrade would require new eyewitness testimony. The only eyewitnesses on the ground that day either were deceased or their whereabouts were unknown. There was virtually no chance of finding one of the CIDGs who had worked with Special Forces that day. Their testimony likely wouldn't count anyway. Some American pilots and Special Forces soldiers had seen parts of the action, but no one could account for all of Roy's time on that battlefield.[11]

Roy's quest faced several other challenges. At that time, the Army could issue a Medal of Honor only for acts conducted within the two previous years. Roy's heroics had taken place six years beforehand, meaning he was about four years too late. There was a little bit of good news. By the time Roy began his inquest in 1974, the military was already in the process of lobbying Congress to pass new legislation that would extend the period of eligibility. That legislation was signed into law by President Gerald Ford on October 24, 1974, but it only extended the eligibility by an additional two years. Even if Roy could convince the Army to approve the upgrade, he would still need another act of Congress to even be eligible for the award.[12]

The political climate of the mid-1970s was also unfavorable. When Roy began advocating for the medal, America was in the early stages of a national malaise commonly known as "Vietnam syndrome." After years of war and domestic political upheaval, American citizens were weary of talk about Vietnam. The United States had pulled out of South Vietnam just a year before, and the American public was still digesting the fallout from the war.

By then, many citizens were familiar with the government se-
crets exposed in the Pentagon Papers and the cover-up of horren-
dous episodes like the bloody My Lai massacre where American
troops murdered hundreds of South Vietnamese civilians. And
although the United States had left South Vietnam, the conflict
clearly wasn't over. In 1974, news broke of heavy fighting between North and South Vietnam, suggesting that the United
States had been duped into abandoning its former South Vietnamese allies in the face of imminent communist aggression.
"Real peace is nowhere at hand," reported the *New York Times*
early in 1974. Yet, Congress rejected further efforts to offer military aid to the South Vietnamese. Many Americans just wanted
to forget about the entire fiasco.[13]

Meanwhile, at the same time Roy started his pursuit, the
Watergate scandal unraveled. The impeachment hearings for
President Richard Nixon began a month after Lt. Col. Drake
submitted his recommendation to upgrade Roy's medal. It was
a poor atmosphere in which to ask anyone to revisit Vietnam, let
alone to examine the details of questionable, perhaps even illegal, incursions into Cambodia. The Army and federal government certainly didn't want any additional unnecessary attention
or controversy.[14]

Drake's initial request was quickly rejected by an Army official
who cited three major problems. First, they couldn't find Drake's
original Distinguished Service Cross recommendation, making
it impossible to compare the original document with the new
information he provided. Second was the two-year time limit to
recommend soldiers for a Congressional Medal of Honor. And
third, Drake himself was not eligible to provide new information
because he was not an eyewitness. As the personnel official explained, new evidence would need to include "statements of eyewitnesses, extracts from official records, maps, diagrams or other
documents amplifying the stated facts."[15]

After that first response in April of 1974, Roy and a small number of supporters pursued their goal through a two-pronged strategy. The first involved tracking down the pilots who had been involved in the battle on May 2, 1968. On that day in Cambodia, Roy's unit had been supported by the 240th Assault Helicopter Company, and he and his allies went looking for the men in that unit who had been flying above his battle. None of these pilots could provide the type of on-the-ground eyewitness testimony requested by the Army, but Roy and his supporters hoped that their statements, if taken together, would be enough to verify Roy's heroics. The second part of the strategy was to build a broad base of influential supporters who might be able to help steer Roy's case through the bureaucracy of the Army.

Over the next several months, Roy, with the help of Drake and several other Army contacts, was able to locate dozens of men who were in some way involved in the events of May 2, 1968, even if only tangentially. Some declined to participate, "holding their pain close and refusing to let it loose," Roy presumed. But eight pilots did submit notarized affidavits to Army officials. Together, these statements helped illuminate parts of Roy's actions on that fateful day. Unfortunately, none of them told the whole story, as each participant had only witnessed portions of the action. Many of the statements were supplemented with descriptions of what the men had heard from others, not necessarily what they saw. The pilots had been in the sky. Much of what they knew about what happened on the ground came from what they heard over the radio or from stories told after the fighting.[16]

Meanwhile, Roy's old commander Lt. Gen. Cassidy also wrote to Congressman González, who had met with Roy the previous year in his San Antonio office and promised to help. Cassidy's letter explained the reasons for appeal and encouraged the San Antonio politician to interject on Roy's behalf. "I feel sure you would want to support this recommendation," Cassidy suggested, "and a letter from you to the Secretary of the Army would be very helpful in this respect." Cassidy also wrote to his friend Lt. Gen. Harold Moore—the man who would later become famous for the book *We Were Soldiers Once . . . and Young*—who was then the Army's deputy chief of staff for personnel. Cassidy asked Moore to "glance at the enclosed papers and then forward them to the appropriate office for action."[17]

As THIS PROCESS BEGAN TO UNFOLD, Roy EXPERIENCED SOME major life changes. On May 1, 1975, his Uncle Nicholas died of a heart attack in El Campo. Seventy-three years old, Nicholas left behind his wife of fifty-one years, Alexandria, and nine biological and adopted children who by then were adults with their own families. Roy had not spent a lot of time with his uncle since he enlisted in the Army, but the childhood lessons he'd received from Uncle Nicholas shaped every aspect of Roy's life. Nicholas and Alexandria had been the stabilizing factors in an otherwise tumultuous and unpromising youth. There was no telling how his life would have turned out without them. Roy appropriately called Nicholas "the uncle of a lifetime." Because Roy was stationed in nearby San Antonio, he was able to make the 160-mile drive to El Campo for the funeral. Roy remembered, "The respect in which the citizens held him was evident, for many people gathered to pay tribute to his memory."[18]

Meanwhile, Roy continued his advising duties at Fort Sam Houston. He was also invited to participate in one of his first speaking engagements, appearing at a small Catholic school in San Antonio for a Junior ROTC field day. The principal later wrote to Roy's commander to offer praise for his speech about "respect for authority, family life, Christian heritage, and love of God and Country." The speech, reported the principal, "will surely be remembered by these students as one of the highlights of the 1974–1975 school year; it was a moving experience for our students."[19]

In July of 1975, Roy was promoted from sergeant first class to master sergeant. Lt. Gen. Cassidy had recommended the promotion the previous year. The new position bumped Roy's pay to nearly $950 per month (the historical equivalent of an annual salary of roughly $60,000). Roy was earning more money than he ever had before. He was still working to advance his career, completing courses on topics such as logistics, medical subjects, and special purpose weapons, even as he performed his normal advisory duties and worked to gather eyewitness statements for his decorations appeal.[20]

While Roy was stationed at Fort Sam Houston, his physical limitations were increasingly becoming a major problem, both personally and professionally. He had severe challenges related to the injuries he sustained in Cambodia, and those who served with him noticed his anguish. In a 1974 letter, Lt. Gen. Cassidy noted that Roy was "still suffering considerable discomfort from his wounds." "He never complained of the pain," Cassidy wrote, but the general knew it was there. There were some basic tasks that Roy simply could not do. Near the time of his promotion, an Army physician noted that Roy's limitations included "no crawling, stooping, running, jumping, marching, or standing for long periods." In other words, he could no longer perform the duties of a soldier. Because he was an enlisted man, whose request to become a warrant officer had been denied, the Army had limited use for him.[21]

In March of 1976, Roy received a letter ordering him to appear before an Army reclassification board. He didn't know exactly why. Most likely, his file had been flagged by an Army physician who was concerned about his physical limitations. When Roy reported for the hearing on March 23, the reclassification board found, "There appears to be reasonable doubt as to the ability of MSG Benavidez to perform full duties of any MOS [Military Occupation Specialties] and therefore his fitness to perform the duties of his office, grade, rank or rating." The board recommended that Roy be medically reevaluated "to determine physical fitness for retention in the military." Roy's combat injuries, which first threatened to end his career ten years earlier in 1966, were finally catching up to him.[22]

A few weeks later, Roy underwent a medical exam. He was evaluated by the Army's PULHES system, a method used to grade medical conditions across six different categories, using a scale of 1–4, with 1 being excellent and 4 indicating a serious physical limitation. Roy scored a 4 in the first category of (P) physical capacity, a 3 in (U) upper extremities, a 3 in (H) hearing and ears, and a 1 in (L) lower extremities, (E) eyes, and (S) psychiatric. His most significant problems were "chest wall pain," "nerve palsy," and "bilateral hearing loss," and he was referred to the Physical Evaluation Board for further testing. In the summer of America's bicentennial, Roy prepared for a medical examination that could potentially end his career in the Army.[23]

In mid-July, Roy received notice that the Senior Army Decorations Board had rejected his appeal for his Distinguished Service Cross to be upgraded to a Medal of Honor, despite a packet of testimonies submitted by helicopter pilots involved in the May 2 mission and supporting letters from Lt. Gen. Cassidy, Lt. Gen. Harold Moore, and Texas congressmen J. J. Pickle and Olin E. Teague. The reason given was that "the additional documents provided did not significantly add to the previously considered recommendation." This news was a setback to his quest for recognition, but Roy had more pressing matters at hand.[24]

A few weeks later, on August 4, 1976, Roy appeared before the Physical Evaluation Board. A physician had examined Roy and found a handful of significant medical problems. Among these were difficulty breathing with minimal exertion, minor to moderate left median nerve neuropathy, degenerative cervical spine, and osteoarthritis in his lumbar spine. The doctor also reported significant tenderness and knee pain near the scar where a bullet had entered Roy's leg. All of this was named in the report before the hearing even began.[25]

That morning, Roy was sworn in to testify in front of the four-person board. He had no grounds to dispute the reports of his medical condition. His body was wrecked, and he clearly couldn't perform the duties of an enlisted man. If anything, the doctors didn't fully appreciate just how bad his injuries were. In some regard, it was surprising that he had been able to remain in the Army as long as he did. "It hurts my pride even to come before the board," Roy admitted, before offering perhaps the most honest assessment of his health that he would ever give.[26]

When the board questioned him, Roy detailed his breathing problems, explaining that he couldn't walk more than fifty feet or climb a single flight of stairs without losing his breath. He told the board that a physician concluded that these limitations were the result of "an injury from foreign objects that you have in your body." Shrapnel had been lodged in his chest for more than eight years.[27]

The board asked Roy about his next problem, and he mentioned his knee. "The doctor said that I had a piece of shrapnel in the tissue," he told the examiners. "That's what the x-ray showed in my medical records and it just hurts, it just even hurts to bend it." Roy explained how his knee "just buckles up and it just cramps up on me." He could barely move his leg up and down while sitting. The other knee hurt too, just not quite as much. The medical board asked him to demonstrate his gait, and the former Green Beret limped around the room as the board watched.[28]

Next, Roy described his arms. He told the board about some of the surgeries he had undergone to repair tendons and nerves.

"I cannot lift no more than 2 or 3 pounds," he said of his left arm. With his other hand, he could barely make a fist. Some of his fingers were numb.[29]

Then there was the back problem, stemming from his first combat injury in 1966. He felt constant pain and pressure in his back. It hurt whenever he walked, he said, and it hurt whenever he had to carry a thirty-pound sack. Sometimes, he said, it hurt when he was just sitting down.[30]

The board didn't have time to discuss all of Roy's medical problems. There were too many to address. The original examination had also revealed hypertension, frequent nosebleeds, hearing loss, recurring headaches, loss of vision, and obesity. He was gaining weight partly because he was getting older, but also because his movements were so restricted by pain and difficulty breathing.[31]

After a twenty-six-minute hearing, the board deliberated for about fifteen minutes before delivering its recommendation: "MSG Roy P. Benavidez is physically unfit to perform the duties of his grade by reason of physical disabilities which are permanent." Then they issued the ruling that Roy had been fearing for more than a decade: "The board recommends that MSG Roy P. Benavidez be permanently retired." Roy signed the paperwork indicating he agreed with the recommendation. And that was it. After twenty-four years, Roy Benavidez was leaving the military.[32]

A few weeks later, Roy received his retirement orders. His last day would be September 10, 1976. Based on his injuries, Roy was deemed 80 percent disabled, an important number in defining his eligibility for disability benefits. His net pay for more than twenty-one years in the Army was scheduled to be $589 per month (the historical equivalent of an annual salary of nearly $34,000). In his final days in the Army, he was awarded the Meritorious Service Medal. On the day after his retirement,

Roy receiving the Meritorious Service Medal upon his retirement, Fort Sam Houston, 1976. Roy P. Benavidez Papers, camh-dob-017309, Dolph Briscoe Center for American History, The University of Texas at Austin.

the *Victoria Advocate* ran a front-page feature about his career, highlighting his role in the May 2 mission without mentioning that it took place in Cambodia. When all was finished, Roy and Lala packed up their family and belongings in San Antonio and moved back to El Campo.[33]

Roy and Lala bought a little ranch house and began settling into the next stage of their lives. At the time, they had three young children. Denise was ten, Yvette six, and Noel had just turned four years old. Their kids were either in school or just about to begin. Roy's long military career was over. On the other side of that journey awaited a family, financial stability, and the peace of mind of having served his country and earned his place in a nation that had not always accepted him.

Roy's active relationship with the military could have ended there, but he couldn't let go of the idea of the Medal of Honor. It was becoming an obsession. He could not get over the ambiguity in the Army's response to his appeal. The Army had never flatly said he didn't deserve the medal, only that they needed additional evidence. Roy was starting to believe that "a real injustice was being done." Something in the mechanisms of the Army was broken, and Roy believed it should be fixed.[34]

There was more to it. Roy's childhood experience as an angry, orphaned boy would forever affect his psychology. He had a chip on his shoulder. He had always been somewhat combative, fueled by an eternal frustration with racial discrimination and the loss of his parents. Medal of Honor recipients forever hold a special status among all veterans and much of the civilian population. If Roy was awarded the medal, he would earn instant respect among every member of the military community, including the more privileged officers who had attended college and rose through the Army ranks, even though they hadn't worked and fought like Roy had. He may never gain their status, but the medal promised to bring adoration and respect from men he had always strove to impress and from a nation that had long told him that he was lesser. There was also an obvious financial motivation. In retirement Roy was about to take a major pay cut, and the Medal of Honor carried an additional monthly stipend.

Roy, with the encouragement of Lt. Col. Ralph Drake, decided to continue his pursuit of the medal in retirement. Men with less impressive heroics had received the award. The key, it seemed to Roy, was finding the right eyewitness or well-positioned advocate. Roy continued to spend countless hours writing to dozens of politicians, Army officials, and other influential figures, seeking their support in his attempt to pursue the upgrade. "I made a nuisance of myself," he remembered, "buttonholing every officer of every civic club and veterans organization that would listen, urging them to write a letter for me."[35]

Retirement presented one major disadvantage to this effort. Roy had been using official channels to locate and contact potential witnesses. Leaving the Army meant losing access to those channels, office supplies, and long-distance telephone calls needed to track down eyewitnesses and lobby supporters. Roy now had to fund his own efforts while he, Lala, and their children lived on a fixed income. "The one thing I did have," Roy wrote, "was time."[36]

Roy's greatest advantage lay in the growing number of allies signing on to help his quest. By the time he retired in 1976, he had added two more important supporters who would aid his fight. The first was a Philadelphia man named Joseph D. Martin, a guy Roy had never met but who would become perhaps his most dedicated advocate.

Roy first came across Martin in 1976 when Martin wrote to Roy to ask for his autograph. The son of Scottish and Irish immigrants, Martin was about the same age as Roy. He was also a former marine with a hobby of collecting autographs from decorated soldiers, which is why he first wrote to Roy. Roy responded to Martin's first letter with an autograph and a letter in which he mentioned his appeals to receive an award upgrade. Martin quickly responded, sending Roy his phone number and volunteering to help. Roy called the Pennsylvanian, and they chatted about Roy's new mission. Martin reacted with a remarkable level of enthusiasm. He immediately sprang into action, conducting research about other Medal of Honor recipients and writing letters on Roy's behalf.[37]

Roy was not necessarily shy about pursuing the Medal of Honor, but he was tactical. He was very careful about the tone of his letters, and he worried about how other people might respond if they thought he was pursuing the medal too aggressively. The men of Special Forces were not supposed to seek such recognition. It was seen as unbecoming of them and a possible violation of protocol. Even after Roy left the military, he closely adhered to military etiquette, never asking for too much or acting out of rank. Joseph D. Martin, on the other hand, was not limited by such constraints.

Martin wrote to seemingly anyone and everyone—senators, congressmen, even two sitting American presidents—to advocate for Roy. Within days of his phone call with Roy, he sent letters to Texas congressman Olin E. Teague and Nevada senator Howard Cannon, a World War II hero. In the ensuing months, Martin mailed additional letters to Congressman John Young, Congressman Henry González, American GI Forum President Héctor Garcia, and the president of the Congressional Medal of Honor Society, Carlos Ogden. Ogden was the only respondent to outright decline to offer assistance, citing his organization's policy "not to become embroiled in matters." Martin also sent inquests to several military figures with whom he had previously corresponded. After writing every single letter, Martin walked over to his local library and made copies on the Xerox machine to send to Roy. "Any correspondence I undertake on your behalf Roy," Martin pledged, "you will get a copy of for your files and reference." Martin asked Roy to keep their correspondence confidential, and he promised to make sure to avoid implicating Roy in his letter-writing campaign. "I am trying my darnedest to get someone on your side," he assured Roy, "and feel these are the right guys for the job!!"[38]

Martin began targeting politicians who were either World War II veterans or who had large Latino constituencies. He assumed that Texas politicians in particular would be interested in helping Roy to boost their appeal with Hispanic voters. His message included an introductory letter describing Roy's 1968 heroics and then a request for assistance. In several cases, he also included copies of the pilots' statements and even shared other men's Medal of Honor citations so his recipients could make a comparison. "I do not wish to demean these CMH's," Martin insisted of the comparisons, "I am just comparing their citation to Roy's DSC citation! There is an inequity." There was little denying that Roy's feats were more impressive than those of some of the other Medal of Honor recipients. It was just a matter of convincing the military brass that they had adequate documentation verifying the actions. Martin didn't specifically mention the word "Cambodia." Either he didn't know that the May 2 battle had taken place there, or he thought such a suggestion might be too inflammatory.[39]

Joseph Martin's letter-writing campaign alone was never going to resolve all the obstacles standing between Roy and the medal, but his scattershot efforts did generate some surprising responses. People wrote back, including some congressmen and senators, who also contacted the Senior Army Decorations Board to help spark another review of Roy's case in April of 1977. By then, at least six sitting congressmen had joined the legion of supporters advocating for further consideration of Roy's upgrade. Of course, neither President Ford nor President Carter returned Martin's correspondence, but he did receive a letter on behalf of President Carter from the Army's Director of Personnel Management Systems, who put his staff in charge of compiling "all the efforts that have been made to present Master Sergeant Benavidez's case to the Senior Army Decorations Board." That compilation would later become part of the case itself. Martin's persistence did not result in the medal upgrade, but his efforts helped generate a lot of documentation and awareness among influential legislators whom Roy never would have felt comfortable contacting himself.[40]

Roy's second new supporter was an El Campo newspaper man named Fred Barbee. Like Martin, Barbee would also write to major political figures on Roy's behalf. But even more importantly, Barbee owned and operated the *El Campo Leader-News* alongside his son, Chris. This put him in a unique position to draw publicity to Roy's case.[41]

Roy met Fred and Chris Barbee in 1976, near the time of his retirement. They crossed paths when Roy spoke at a meeting of the El Campo Rotary Club. The Barbees were vaguely familiar with Roy, having read the story of his Distinguished Service Cross, but they didn't know much about his quest for the Medal of Honor. That night, Roy dazzled the audience with his patriotic sentiment and positive message, earning "a standing ovation," observed one attendee.[42]

The Barbees were particularly fond of a joke Roy told the crowd. The war hero shared that his wife had mailed him copies of the *El Campo Leader-News* while he was stationed in Vietnam. Therefore, he said, people all over Southeast Asia were familiar with "Ricky the Ricebird," the mascot of El Campo High School. The owners of the newspaper enjoyed Roy's quip and approached him to chat after the event. A friendship quickly blossomed.[43]

In the weeks that followed, Roy would occasionally visit with the Barbees at their newspaper office in downtown El Campo. Eventually, the issue of the medal came up. When it did, Fred "offered to make some phone calls," remembered Chris. The elder Barbee was a well-known publisher and former president of the Texas Press Association. He knew a lot of Texas journalists and politicians. Barbee contacted Senators Lloyd Bentsen and John Tower and Congressmen George Mahon and John Young, urging these politicians to help remedy what he called a "monumental injustice." The newspapermen also opened their offices to Roy, allowing him to take advantage of their resources—copies, paper, ink, and so on—to carry on his own lobbying efforts through the mail.[44]

Roy and his allies kept up their work into 1977, sending an encyclopedia's worth of paperwork to various Army officials, politicians, and potential allies at organizations such as the VA and the American GI Forum. Roy completed his own notarized testimony, and his buddies continued to search for additional men who had witnessed any part of the action. They found several more individuals willing to submit affidavits to the Senior Army Decorations Board.

Together, they were very successful in getting attention. One colonel noted that Roy's appeal "had been given more attention than any other case since he had been in that office." Yet, none of their efforts altered the basic fact that they still lacked an on-the-ground eyewitness. Time and again they were told by the Army that the request would not be reconsidered or approved without substantial new evidence. Everyone who reviewed the file said no—the Senior Army Decorations Board, the commander in chief in the Pacific, the Joint Chiefs of Staff, and the secretary of the Army, who had been persuaded by Congressman Young to reassemble the Senior Army Decorations Board to reconsider Roy's case. Between April of 1974 and December of 1977, Roy's appeals were denied nine times.[45]

As the disappointing news continued to roll in, Roy was struggling to balance these professional setbacks with significant personal challenges. Like many veterans, Roy was having a hard time adjusting to retirement. He had a pretty good life in El Campo, where he enjoyed spending time with his family and a small network of friends, and he had also started taking classes at nearby Wharton County Junior College. But the military had been the greatest adventure of his life, and his daily activities were dull and mundane in comparison. Roy had left El Campo as a young soldier and traveled the world in service to his country. His entire adult life had been enmeshed in the camaraderie of Army men and the thrill of military life in a nation at war. He missed the structure and the closeness he felt with his Army buddies. As one of his friends in El Campo recalled, "I can't imagine what it would be like to be a fighting man at the level that Roy was and his achievements in battle, and then to come back to sleepy little El Campo."[46]

His health was a major problem. Roy was suffering to an extent that no one knew. By most accounts, not even Roy fully grasped all that was wrong with him. His medical reports showed the physical ailments known by his doctors—the difficulty breathing, severe back pain, problems with his arms and knees, hearing loss, hypertension, and weight gain—but no one fully recognized what it was like for Roy to live every day in a body pierced and shredded by steel.

Well into the 1970s, Roy was still plucking out little pieces of metal shrapnel from underneath his skin. "Those little bits of metal would move under the skin and eventually some of it would pop out," remembered one of his friends. At times, the pieces of metal would come from his head, emerging from the outer layer of his skin with a thin streak of blood. His daughter Yvette remembers one day sitting behind her dad in the car. "As he's driving," she recalled, "I can see blood just trickling out from his head." "Oh, that's just shrapnel making its way out," Roy told her. Everyone who was close with Roy at that time had a shrapnel story. "I was with him once when he pulled a little piece of shrapnel out of his scalp," remembered Chris Barbee. "He kept kind of messing with something, and he [pulled it out and said], 'Hey, look at that.'" It was "just little, like a BB," said Chris.[47]

Fewer people saw the fuller extent of his wounds. Chris Barbee once saw Roy shirtless and was stunned by the extensive markings carved across his friend's body. "I saw his body and the scars, and it was amazing, bullet scars, bayonet wound scars, shrapnel scars . . . all the way across his legs." His kids saw them too. "I could see the battle scars, the wounds," remembered his daughter Yvette. "He had a wound from the front of his belly to the back. . . . I don't think as a child I ever asked him—I knew he was in the war, Vietnam War. I knew he had seen some things, but I never asked. I was too young, you know?" "You could see the scars on his body and all over his face," Denise remembered. "We knew, we just didn't talk about it."[48]

Even fewer people knew about Roy's struggles with his mental health. Roy carried home the wounds of war not only in his body but in his mind. He was later diagnosed with post-traumatic stress disorder, and it's very possible that he also suffered from brain damage incurred when he was wounded during his first tour in Vietnam. But Roy hid his innermost anguish. The machoistic former soldier never fully shared how the moments of astounding violence and near-death shaped his psychological state, but there were some clues. His family remembers his occasional nightmares and screams, with Lala trying to calm him back to sleep. His kids, who were still young at the time, remember small details like Roy insisting their home have mirrored windows, him walking the perimeter of the house, flinching when plates dropped in restaurants, and staring intently out the kitchen window like he was watching for something. Sometimes, Roy would take a different route home for no good reason. "You should never take the same route home," he told Yvette. "You should always switch it up because you never know who's following you." Roy's son, Noel, remembered him saying you shouldn't sleep with the curtains open because "he always said that there was a sniper out there somewhere with a bullet that had his name on it." Roy might have been partially joking, or at least they thought he was. These were "no big deal" to them as kids, said Yvette. "But as an adult, I remember little things."[49]

Roy leaned on a handful of people when he was really struggling. One of these men was Steve Sucher, a reporter at the Barbees' *El Campo Leader-News*. Roy and Steve began spending time together in 1977 and 1978, after the veteran had become friends with the Barbees. The ongoing issue over the medal caused Roy "great personal consternation and stress," remembered Sucher, who said, "His and my relationship became very personal and very close. . . . I became something of a confidant for him."[50]

For a few years, Sucher was one of the very few people who witnessed the dark nature of Roy's troubles. They would get together to drink and gossip, but their outings went beyond a handful of casual beers. Roy came from a culture of heavy drinking in the military, and he brought elements of that behavior home to El Campo. "We both drank a lot during these sessions," remembered Sucher, "so I honestly can't remember a lot of what we talked about. I can just tell you that he got down into the nitty-gritty with me on a lot of stuff."[51]

Roy had a lot of reasons to drink. Drinking offered something to do in his sedentary small-town life. He also was self-medicating his physical wounds, and it helped assuage the mental anguish of a war hero who had experienced such unspeakable violence. "Roy carried a heavy weight on his shoulders all the time," remembered Sucher. "He could be very emotionally distraught, distressed, depressed, but he had also routine moments of brilliance in the way he approached people—upbeat, positive, strong, decisive. He had the highest of highs and the lowest of lows." "He was fun to be around," Sucher described, "but he could get very dark."[52]

There were times at night when Roy would call Sucher crying on the phone. He would say things such as, "I just can't take it," remembered Sucher. "He just needed somebody to talk to. I guess he didn't want to bother his wife with this stuff all the time. . . . Maybe there were things he was able to tell me that he couldn't talk to other people about." The relationship went both ways. Both men drank a lot and were prone to depression. "He counseled me," said Sucher, "just as much as I was counseling him sometimes."[53]

In early 1978, four years into Roy's quest, Fred Barbee published an exposé in the *El Campo Leader-News* titled "Roy

Benavidez . . . *Sometimes Patience Wears Thin.*" The article was a scathing critique of the process of Roy's military decorations appeal, described by Barbee as "a runaround of bureaucratic in- nuendo and military double talk." Barbee's story included quo- tations from eyewitness statements and others from military leaders who had reviewed Roy's file and insisted he deserved the Medal of Honor. Barbee questioned the entire process, casting a shadow of doubt over the methods of the Senior Army Decora- tions Board, an organization, Barbee observed, "whose members are anonymous and whose actions are not subjected to any sort of public scrutiny." "What criteria did this group of anonymous men," he further questioned, "use in arbitararily [sic] refusing to upgrade the medal?" Barbee's article also argued that the politi- cal atmosphere surrounding the unpopular war was shaping the reception to Roy's appeal. Perhaps most provocatively, Barbee's article revealed the one aspect of Roy's heroics that Roy him- self could never tell—that the action had occurred in Cambodia. "Perhaps that is a contributing factor to the continuing 'run- around' given Sgt. Benavidez," Barbee theorized.[54]

Roy had mixed feelings. "I remember inwardly cringing," he recalled, "at Fred's words suggesting both that the action took place outside the boundaries of South Vietnam and that there was collusion on the U.S. government's part to conceal that fact." But ultimately, Roy was "delighted" that someone had said what he could not. In a sense, he had been waiting for this. When the article was published, Roy mailed "between 150 and 200 copies" to a variety of politicians and business leaders, targeting legisla- tors from Texas and those with a connection to the military.[55]

By the time Barbee's article was published, Roy and his sup- porters had generated nothing short of a minor political move- ment that spanned a remarkably diverse cast of characters. Congressman Henry González, the first politician to whom Roy had written, was a Democrat from San Antonio, a longtime liberal leader in Texas who had risen from city council in the 1950s to the United States House of Representatives in the 1960s on the growing political power of Black and Hispanic voters. He was a civil rights supporter and one of the most important liberal politicians in Texas.[56]

Other Texas Democrats in Roy's corner included Representatives J. J. Pickle, Olin E. Teague, John Young, and Senator Lloyd Bentsen. The Texas Republicans who supported Roy included Senator John Tower and later George H. W. Bush. The military men who supported Roy's cause represented a variety of political persuasions. It was truly a bipartisan effort. None of these men necessarily led the way in this fight, but they worked across the aisle as an assemblage of supporters who made inquiries to help further Roy's pursuit.

By 1978, Roy and his allies had collected statements from eight pilots involved in at least some part of the action of May 2. They also had ongoing support from several United States congressmen and senators, as well as a handful of well-known retired Army officers. Despite all of this, that September, Roy once again received notice from the Army that his case still did not warrant a full hearing because "insufficient relevant evidence has been presented to demonstrate the existence of probable material error or injustice."[57]

Some of Roy's allies seemed ready to give up. Texas Congressman J. J. Pickle had been exchanging letters with Roy about this matter since 1974, and he had used his connections in Washington, DC, to advocate for another review. In January of 1979, he convinced the chairman of the House Committee on Armed Services, Representative Melvin Price of Illinois, to appeal to the Army for a special review on Roy's behalf. The review took place, but the medal was once again denied. "It appears from the correspondence," noted Representative Price, "that M/Sgt. Benavidez has exhausted all of the remedies available to him in the

Department of Defense." Defeated, Pickle wrote to Roy, "It does not appear there is any other route that we can follow this time." "At this point, the possibility of such a change is pretty negative," the congressman concluded.[58]

But Roy still had some support. In January of 1979, his congressional district got a new representative who injected a burst of energy into this quest. Congressman Joe Wyatt Jr., himself a former member of the Marine Reserve, took up the mantle from his predecessor in advocating for Roy's upgrade. "I wholeheartedly agree that you deserve the Medal of Honor," the freshman congressman wrote to Roy, "and I want to assist you in any possible way." But Wyatt also recognized the challenges, "based on the number of Board reviews that have taken place and the Secretary of the Army's unfavorable consideration." "I must say in all fairness to you," Wyatt observed, "it does not look very promising."[59]

In June of that year, George H. W. Bush, who at the time was briefly out of public service, stepped in to help. The future president wrote to General Sam Wilson, sending along Roy's file and appealing "on a personal basis" for Wilson to "forward these papers to someone high enough up to give this another look."[60]

That same month, the Texas state office of the League of United Latin American Citizens (LULAC) passed a resolution at its annual convention "urging the United States of America to award the Congressional Medal of Honor to MSG (Ret) Roy P. Benavidez of El Campo." The organization called on its members to send letters of support to both Texas senators and the president of the United States. The following year, LULAC's president wrote to President Jimmy Carter directly, asking for his "support of Sgt. Benavides [*sic*] to the appropriate military officials."[61]

Roy located another individual living in Germany who he thought might be able to provide a convincing statement. It was a Special Forces man with whom Roy had served in South Vietnam. This man, who Roy regarded as one of the "masters of their craft," had been among those soldiers who later traveled to the site of Roy's May 2 battle to retrieve the remaining bodies. Congressman Wyatt contacted this solider to ask for a witness statement, but the man declined to provide testimony because he had not been on the ground for long enough to witness Roy's actions.[62]

Wyatt pushed in other ways. In September of 1979, he wrote to the assistant secretary of the Army, requesting "that the [Army] Board for Correction of Military Records (ABCMR) conduct a formal hearing regarding the up-grade request and allow Sgt. Benavidez and others, as determined, to appear in his defense." The assistant secretary acknowledged Wyatt's request and instructed ABCMR to review the file. Five months later, that review came back with a familiar answer: "The applicant has failed to submit sufficient relevant evidence to demonstrate the existence of probable material error or injustice to warrant a formal hearing." The Senior Army Decorations Board concurred.[63]

Despite the incredible amount of support Roy had marshaled over a six-year fight, by the spring of 1980, he and his influential allies were seemingly no closer to achieving their goal than when they began in 1974. In fact, they appeared to be even farther away because they had exhausted nearly all possible avenues without much success.

Momentum was starting to slow. This latest rejection was the twelfth such denial in six years. Roy's political connections had proved to be the decisive factor in getting the hearings in the first place, but even the support of his most powerful allies couldn't achieve the desired outcome. His collaborators seemed lost about next steps. The politicians were telling him that not much else could be done, and the letters of support from his civilian friends began to dwindle. Even the correspondence from the ever-zealous Joseph Martin began to slow down. An Army colonel who had previously noted that Roy's case drew more attention than any other observed in early 1980, "We haven't heard anything on the case for a long time." But then came a voice from the dead.[64]

On a July evening in 1980, Roy was watching television with his son, Noel, when the phone rang. He answered without taking his eyes off the screen. "Hello," he said, thinking nothing in particular about the phone call.

"Is this Tango Mike?" asked the voice on the other end of the line.

"What?" Roy asked, sitting straight up in his chair. No one in his current life referred to him by that name. It had been over a decade since anyone had regularly called him that. He had not been Tango Mike in a long time, not since he was stationed with the Special Forces in South Vietnam. Roy had a lot of buddies who were Vietnam veterans, and many of them had been in Special Forces, but these guys usually just called him "Roy." "Who is this?" he asked the caller.[65]

The man on the other end of the line was Brian O'Connor, the third American member of Leroy Wright's team who had been inserted into that Cambodian landing zone on May 2, 1968. Roy was "speechless," he remembered. "The emotions boiled over in both of us, and for minutes, neither of us could speak more than a word or two before choking up." They sat there in silence, holding the phones to their ears until they managed to harness their emotions.[66]

Roy and O'Connor had not seen each other since they laid in that hospital in Saigon, barely clinging to their lives. When O'Connor was moved one night, each man had assumed the other had died. "I had never considered finding O'Connor. No man could long live with the wounds he had," Roy explained. O'Connor shared Roy's sentiment, echoing, "There was no way you could live shot up like that."[67]

As it turned out, O'Connor was living in Fiji, where he was enjoying a peaceful existence as a potter. He had been there since 1970, after roughly two years in intensive medical care following the events of May 2. Like Roy, the Army's talented doctors had saved his life and rebuilt his body well enough so he could walk again and enjoy a decent quality of life. O'Connor was severely traumatized by the war and had chosen to live his life outside of the United States.[68]

O'Connor had been contacted by a representative of the Army who asked him about Roy Benavidez and the events of May 2. O'Connor was the sole living witness of Roy's valor, the only man on Earth who could provide the type of firsthand account that might allow for Roy's Distinguished Service Cross to be upgraded to a Medal of Honor. After agreeing to speak with the Army representative, O'Connor asked for Roy's phone number and dialed up his long-lost friend. That night, he told Roy, "I'm writing a statement on what happened that day. . . . You're going to get that Medal of Honor."[69]

It was the Army that found O'Connor. Their willingness to do so represented a major change in their approach to Roy's case. Before 1980, the onus of finding eyewitnesses and securing statements had fallen on Roy and his allies. But unbeknownst to Roy, something about his quest had changed, and people had been working behind the scenes on his behalf. The roots of this sea change lie in Fred Barbee's 1978 article.[70]

A lot of people in South Texas read Barbee's article. After it was published, letters from across the region poured into the offices of congressmen, senators, military officers, and a variety of organizations, as dozens of people wrote to express support of Roy's appeals. Probably the most important letter was sent by a man named Absalom Theodore "AB" Webber Jr., who on September 11, 1978, penned a letter to Texas senator John Tower.[71]

AB Webber was a successful forty-nine-year-old businessman and Army veteran who owned Webber Steel Products in Houston. He wrote his letter nine months after the publication of Barbee's article. "I am writing you because I feel a grave injustice has been done," Webber wrote Senator Tower. "It is the extreme of charity to say this might have come about inadvertently." Webber's three-page letter included a copy of Barbee's article and quotations from a manual outlining the criteria for a Medal of Honor. Webber laid out his argument for Roy's upgrade and then asked many of the same questions raised by Barbee in the article. It was particularly odd, he argued, that the board had never bothered to interview Col. Ralph Drake. He was incredulous about the entire process and the perceived injustice. "If this decent, brave, dedicated soldier is denied that which he honestly deserves," Webber emphasized of Roy's case, "then I am certain that you will join me in prayer that God will save this Republic." Copies of Webber's letter were also sent to Texas governor Dolph Briscoe, Texas congressman William Archer, Army Chief of Staff Bernard Rogers, Deputy Chief of Staff for Personnel Lt. Gen. Robert G. Yerks, and Lt. Gen. Edward C. Meyer, the deputy chief of staff for operations.[72]

Lt. Gen. Edward C. Meyer was an old acquaintance of Webber. The two had graduated together from the United States Military Academy in 1951. While at West Point, they had both belonged to the ski club. After graduation, both men served in Korea. Webber eventually left the military, but he maintained a close connection to the academy, serving on numerous West Point committees and regularly attending the Army versus Navy football game. Meyer was a career Army man, a highly decorated soldier who served in Vietnam and rose through the ranks throughout the 1970s. About nine months after Webber sent his letter, Meyer was named the Army's chief of staff, which put him on the powerful Joint Chiefs of Staff.[73]

On March 12, 1980, Roy received a phone call from a lieutenant colonel in the Military Awards Branch of the Army. This call informed Roy that his appeal, despite having been rejected just nineteen days earlier, would be "reprocessed and reconsidered." It was a shocking but welcome reversal. The reason wasn't explained to Roy, but what had happened was the vice chief of staff of the Army had "nonconcurred" with the decision of the Senior Army Decorations Board to reject Roy's appeal. That nonconcurrence sent the case up the chain of command.[74]

On May 6, 1980, Army Chief of Staff Edward C. Meyer wrote an "action memorandum" to his colleagues on the Joint Chiefs of Staff concerning the "Proposed Award of the Medal of Honor to MSG Roy Benavidez." The memo outlined the basic details of the case and recounted previous disapprovals of the upgrade. An earlier version of the Joint Chiefs of Staff had previously encountered this case, but none of the members had acted on Roy's behalf. This time, Edward C. Meyer did.[75]

Meyer reached a different conclusion than his predecessors. "My review of the basic recommendation and these additional witness statements," he noted, "indicate that new consideration should be given to this recommendation." Meyer recognized that it would require an act of Congress for Roy to receive the award, but he nevertheless recommended to his colleagues that they proceed. In a sentence that was later redacted for confidentiality, Meyer urged the Joint Chiefs to "approve the award of the Medal of Honor to MSG Benavidez." Lt. General Meyer was the first Army official to make such a recommendation. According to Congressman Wyatt, it was also Meyer who was responsible for ordering those under his command to figure out the name of the other men involved with the May 2 mission and then ultimately track down O'Connor. From that point on, one follower noted, "everything just started falling like dominos."[76]

As much as Meyer might have been influenced by conversations with his old friend AB Webber, he had his own motivations for recommending the award. When he became Army chief of staff in 1979, he inherited an army still beset by low morale and disciplinary problems lingering from the Vietnam War. The draft had ended in the wake of extreme resistance during the Vietnam War, and Meyer was charged with helping to modernize and elevate America's new all-volunteer Army. The military welcomed any positive publicity it could share with Americans.[77]

The Army found Brian O'Connor when Roy never could. Not only did Roy think O'Connor was dead, but he was also confused about the man's last name. In Barbee's 1978 article in the *El Campo Leader-News*, Roy had referred to O'Connor as "Conners." Army officials in 1980 searched for the right name and found Brian O'Connor in Fiji.[78]

O'Connor produced a stunning ten-page statement that revealed even more spectacular details about the battle of May 2, 1968, including portions of the day that Roy himself didn't know about. The testimony absolved any doubts that Roy Benavidez deserved the Medal of Honor. In fact, O'Connor's eyewitness statement described actions by Roy that might have been the greatest individual act of heroism performed by any American solider during the entire war in Vietnam. "It is my sincere belief," O'Connor wrote, "that MSG Benavidez deserved the CMH back in 1968 and still does this very day." "I was ready to die," he testified. "It was Benavidez's indomitable spirit and courage that made us hold on."[79]

Soon thereafter, everything else fell in order. The Joints Chiefs approved the award, as did the secretary of the Army and eventually the president of the United States, who endorsed the upgrade on November 26, 1980. It could not become official, however, until a new piece of legislation was passed by Congress to extend the statute of limitations. At this point, Congressman Joe Wyatt introduced legislation titled "For the relief of Roy P. Benavidez." There was a hearing before the Military Personnel Subcommittee of the House Committee on Armed Services. The bill made it out of committee and passed through the House on December 2. In the Senate, the bill was sponsored by Texas senators Lloyd Bentsen and John Tower, both of whom had for years been corresponding with Roy and his allies. On December 18—twelve years, seven months, and thirteen days after Roy Benavidez's actions in Cambodia—President Jimmy Carter signed into law legislation extending Roy's eligibility to receive the Congressional Medal of Honor.[80]

A few days earlier, AB Webber had called Roy at home, yelling, "The Senate just approved the bill! It's on its way to President Carter's desk for him to sign. The Congressional Medal of Honor is yours!" "My legs felt like rubber," Roy remembered, "and I thought I was going to fall flat on my face." He had done it. All told, Roy estimated that the campaign had cost him about $5,000 in the form of phone calls, office supplies, and stamps. Now, all of America was going to know that Roy Benavidez was a national hero.[81]

CHAPTER 10
A HERO

Roy's Medal of Honor ceremony was scheduled for February 24, 1981. There was much to do to prepare for the trip to Washington, DC. A few days before the ceremony, an Army officer named Captain Hayes came to El Campo to assist the Benavidez family with the arrangements. Hayes helped Roy submit the names of dozens of guests who would need to undergo background checks, and he spent hours briefing Roy on every detail of the coming ceremony. Hayes was with the family so often during those days that he started answering their telephone and greeting visitors at the front door. He even gave the kids rides to school. Fourteen-year-old Denise was tickled by the excitement. "It was mind-boggling," she remembered. "Dad was going to be treated royally."[1]

Receiving the Medal of Honor is like a coronation of sorts for American soldiers. It certifies their incredible heroics in combat and provides entry into a uniquely prestigious society with special benefits and honors. But the medal meant even more for a man like Roy Benavidez. To Roy, the Medal of Honor signified not just battlefield heroics but a triumph over the obstacles he'd faced across the broad sweep of his life. Roy couldn't wait for the trip. He knew the ceremony would be his "proudest moment."[2]

Many in El Campo were also excited. Over the years, some local residents had heard rumors about Roy's military feats, but few could have fully appreciated the extent of his heroics before the Army verified his actions with the nation's most prestigious military honor. Roy was going to the Pentagon to receive the Medal of Honor from the president. Small-town brushes with fame don't get much more regal than that.

When Roy's award was announced the previous December, a group of local elementary school students took up a collection to purchase a framed photograph of Roy for their classroom. Roy was deeply touched. "When I think about these kids," he told a reporter, "when I realize how proud my fellow citizens are of me, its [sic] brings a lump to my throat." The Pentagon let the kids keep their money by sending over a picture free of charge.

Throughout that December and January, the *El Campo Leader-News* kept readers abreast of Roy's activities. The newspaper's owners, the Barbees, had played a major role in helping Roy obtain the medal, and they remained close friends with him. "[Roy] was always making the news," Chris Barbee reflected. He certainly appeared in their paper all the time. In their sleepy little town, he was the most interesting story of 1981. Three days before the ceremony, the *El Campo Leader-News* ran a front-page story previewing the Benavidezes' trip. It showed a picture of Roy receiving a last-minute haircut from his barber and included a brief outline of his schedule. Talk of the upcoming ceremony buzzed across town, with locals discussing the event over coffees and lunches. Friends and strangers alike would stop Roy in public to express their appreciation. "Congratulations, Roy," they would say. "We're proud of you."[3]

Not everyone was happy. A few days after Roy learned about the medal decision, he and Lala attended a Christmas dinner at the local American Legion. At one point, the club commander stood to greet everyone and introduce some of the legion officials and organizers of the event. In doing so, the commander also offered a "special welcome" to Roy and Lala, noting that Roy was soon to receive the Medal of Honor. A table away, an intoxicated man started booing loudly and yelling that Roy did not deserve the award. The man's dinner party quickly shushed him, and the meal continued. The post commander later assured Roy that the man was drunk and out of line. But Roy was stung.[4]

Although most locals seemed to support Roy, he could always sense a slight chill, especially from some of his Anglo neighbors. Even though many years had passed, this was the same place where Roy was once called "greaser," "spic," and "taco bender," and forced to eat his meals in the back of the restaurant where he worked. Some of the people from that era still lived in town. Times had changed, but there were still incidents and comments that invoked the same prejudices from the past. Unlike during his childhood, Roy generally managed to hold his tongue to avoid conflict.[5]

The social slights weren't necessarily only about race. "To some," Roy explained, "my efforts [to obtain the medal] had been no more than an arm twisting political campaign to pressure the army and the federal government into taking action where none was needed." Roy's detractors did not fully understand the process or standards for receiving a Medal of Honor. They suggested he was no war hero but rather an irritating opportunist who used personal connections to secure a recognition he did not deserve.[6]

Nevertheless, Roy carried on, buoyed by the coming ceremony at the Pentagon and other honors that started coming his way. In January, the Texas 82nd Airborne Association wrote to share that their members had unanimously voted to rename their museum for him. Roy was invited to be a speaker and guest of honor at the Wharton County DeMolay Club and the annual banquet of the El Campo Chamber of Commerce and Agriculture. He also received a letter from the Special Forces center at Fort Bragg, the place where he once trained, congratulating him on the forthcoming award and informing him that they planned to add his portrait to their JFK Hall of Heroes.[7]

During the week of the ceremony, *ABC World News Tonight* sent reporter David Ensor to El Campo to film a segment about Roy and the upcoming ceremony. After a brief introduction from lead anchor Sam Donaldson, Ensor narrated the three-minute story, which included several clips of Roy describing the battle of May 2, 1968, and of Roy walking through an El Campo neighborhood. "President Reagan is rolling out the red carpet," Ensor told viewers. "By choosing to make the award himself," Ensor observed, "President Reagan seeks to send a message to Vietnam veterans in towns like this one [El Campo] around the country that he will not ignore them, and he puts the Presidency behind an effort to renew American pride in military service."[8]

ROY'S MEDAL OF HONOR CEREMONY PRESENTED THE NEW PRESident Ronald Reagan with an opportune moment. Although it was President Carter who had signed the law that enabled Roy to receive the medal, the newly inaugurated president Reagan had the pleasure of bestowing it upon Roy. Carter was a lame duck by the time Roy's medal was approved. He had signed off on the legislation based on the recommendations of his staff and the Department of Defense, but he did not push to make the award himself because, according to Reagan's secretary of defense, "the Carter Administration had not wanted to do anything that reminded people of Vietnam."[9]

President Reagan, on the other hand, was thrilled for the opportunity to present a Medal of Honor to a Vietnam War veteran. In office barely more than a month, Reagan looked forward to demonstrating his administration's commitment to the rejuvenation of the military. He learned in mid-February that Roy was due to receive the medal and jumped at the chance to hold a big ceremony. When Secretary of Defense Caspar Weinberger told Reagan that "a soldier with a trained voice" usually reads the citation, the president replied, "I have a trained voice." Weinberger checked with the Pentagon to make sure that Reagan would not be breaking protocol by reading the citation himself. It is believed that Reagan became the first president to read the formal citation during a Medal of Honor ceremony.[10]

The United States, eight years removed from its involvement in the war, remained mired in Vietnam syndrome. Much of the country still felt a sense of collective national guilt, and many felt that the Vietnam War signified a troubling decline in American military power. Vietnam syndrome remained pervasive in the years after the war's end, as countless books, magazine articles, and films depicted the American war effort in Vietnam as misguided and immoral. Movies like *The Deer Hunter* (1978) and *Apocalypse Now* (1979) cast American military leaders and soldiers as bloodthirsty maniacs who had lied to the country's public. The Iran Hostage Crisis, between 1979 and 1981, further crippled public confidence in the military and government, even among the most ardent supporters of the military who saw the response from the Carter administration as a sign of weakness.[11]

Ronald Reagan had long been a staunch supporter of the Vietnam War. In October of 1965, while running for governor of California, he declared that the United States military could use its overwhelming power to "pave the whole country [of Vietnam], put parking strips on it and still be home by Christmas." While joking in tone, his statement was horribly misguided, dripping in the very same brand of American hubris that would cause the war to go so awry.[12]

As governor of California in the late 1960s and early 1970s, Reagan defended Nixon's wartime policies. After the war, he routinely criticized Congress and President Lyndon B. Johnson for wartime strategies that, he argued, prevented American victory by forcing the military to operate "with their hands tied behind their back." Throughout his political career, Reagan insisted that the United States should have won in Vietnam, even as he offered no specifics on how, or precisely what such a victory would have meant for Americans. Unlike much of the rest of the country, he seemed uninterested in reflecting on whether the United States should have been in Vietnam in the first place. In 1975, he argued that the war was lost because America's politicians "gave up," calling the American withdrawal from Vietnam more shameful "than any single event in our nation's history."[13]

When Reagan ran for president in 1980, he publicly defended what was still an unpopular war. That summer, he took the stage in front of five thousand attendees of the VFW Convention and told his audience exactly what many of them wanted to hear. The Vietnam War was a "noble cause," Reagan insisted. "We dishonor the memory of fifty thousand young Americans who died in that cause when we give way to feelings of guilt as if we were doing something shameful." "Let us tell those who fought in that war," Reagan continued, "that we will never again ask young men to fight and possibly die in a war our government is afraid to let them win." He told the VFW that Jimmy Carter ran an "anti-veteran administration," and he promised to do more to help America's veterans.[14]

Coverage of Reagan's remarks appeared in virtually every major newspaper in America. Members of groups like the VFW and American Legion loved his message. The audience at the VFW Convention interrupted Reagan's thirty-minute speech with twenty-six ovations. Reagan's remarks drew a heap of criticism among those familiar with the war, but it was also welcomed by millions of Americans who refused to question the sanctity of the United States military.[15]

As a candidate during the 1980 election, Reagan worked to cast President Carter as weak and indecisive, likening him to the Democrat politicians who, he argued, had failed America in Vietnam. Reagan sought to separate the war's soldiers from its architects, celebrating the fighting men while blaming political leaders for their lack of success. "It is time we purged ourselves of the Vietnam syndrome," he insisted that March, "which has colored our thinking for too long." Reagan worked to build support among veterans and military boosters, appealing to the pride and patriotism of people who wanted to see America restore its predominant role in the world and renew its fight against the threat of global communism. Whereas Jimmy Carter in 1977 had stated, "We are now free of that inordinate fear of communism," the Republican party platform of 1980 argued, "The scope and magnitude of the growth of Soviet military power threatens American interest at every level, from the nuclear threat to our survival, to our ability to protect the lives and property of American citizens abroad."[16]

Reagan saw the United States of America as an arbiter of good in a dangerous world threatened by the evils of communism. The Soviets, he argued, sought a "one-world Communist state." He mocked Jimmy Carter's 1977 remarks throughout the 1980 campaign, emphasizing the need to face down communism across the globe. "The West will not contain communism," he promised, "it will transcend communism." Reagan leaned into the conflict of the Cold War, rejecting his predecessors who had argued for détente, disarmament, and a cooling of tensions with Russia and other communist nations. In a press conference held just days into his term, Reagan quipped, "So far détente has been a one-way street the Soviet Union has used to pursue its own aims." That same week, his secretary of state openly accused the Soviet Union of fostering "international terrorism." And just ten days into Reagan's term, the *New York Times* called his administration's stance "an unprecedented verbal assault on the Soviet Union by a new Administration."[17]

As promised in his campaign, Reagan sought to ramp up spending on pro-American propaganda and military expenditures. In doing so, he recognized the need to restore the prestige of the military. The pomp and circumstance of a Medal of Honor ceremony presented an opportune moment for a grand celebration of the armed forces. In office for barely more than a month before the Roy Benavidez Medal of Honor ceremony, the president couldn't wait to call the Army back to center stage.[18]

THE BENAVIDEZ FAMILY LEFT FOR WASHINGTON ON THE MORN-ing of February 22. Roy took nearly his entire family with him, along with his friends from the newspaper, Chris and Fred Barbee and Steve Sucher. The entourage of more than forty guests left El Campo in a Greyhound bus that drove them the one hundred miles to Houston's Intercontinental Airport (now George Bush Intercontinental Airport). From there, they flew into Washington National (now Reagan National) and stayed at the Crystal City Marriott in Arlington, Virginia. The Benavidez family and their friends occupied an entire floor of rooms, and the floors above and below their block were left empty. Roy and Lala's suite was "decked out in flowers and baskets of fruit and cheese," he remembered.[19]

On Monday the 23rd, Roy was fitted for two new dress uniforms while his family toured the nation's capital. Later that afternoon, he met with government officials who explained the benefits attached to the Medal of Honor. As a recipient of the military's highest award, Roy was entitled to a free seat on

military aircraft flying within the United States, a supplemental
uniform allowance, priority burial at Arlington National Cemetery, a lifetime invitation to presidential inaugurations, and several other privileges on military bases. He would also receive a
supplementary pension of $200 per month. Roy submitted the
pension paperwork the next day.[20]

That evening, Roy relaxed in his hotel room with his loved
ones. As the night wore on, family gradually gave way to some
of Roy's Army buddies who had traveled to Washington for the
ceremony and made their way to Roy and Lala's suite to greet
their friend. Some of the visitors were men involved with the
May 2 mission. Colonel Ralph Drake came. Jerry Cottingham,
the man who recognized Roy in the body bag and alerted the
medic, was there. Chandler Carter, a helicopter pilot who had
sat on standby listening over the radio as Roy directed supporting attacks, arrived from Alaska. Each of these men had completed notarized witness statements verifying Roy's heroics and
supporting his pursuit of the medal. It meant a lot to Roy for
them to be there. He described that evening as filled with "a flow
of old buddies coming to the suite to visit and shoot the bull just
like the old days."[21]

Later that night, after most everyone else had left, Drake returned to Roy's door with another guest. Drake stepped aside
to reveal that the man behind him was none other than Brian
O'Connor. Roy and O'Connor locked in an embrace, fighting
tears as they held onto one another. Each man was there because
of the other. Roy had saved O'Connor's life, and O'Connor's testimony the previous July had proved to be the deciding factor
in the Army's decision to award Roy the Medal of Honor. Although the men had spoken on the phone, they still hadn't seen
each other since May of 1968, in that Saigon hospital. "Last time
I saw him," O'Connor told reporters, "he was floating in his own
blood."[22]

That night, Roy and O'Connor spoke of those who did not survive that dreadful day in Cambodia. They spoke of Leroy Wright, Lloyd Mousseau, and Larry McKibben, who would have turned thirty-three that year. Roy and O'Connor were deeply emotional, each remembering those terrifying hours spent surrounded by enemies. Either of them could have easily been among the dead. Neither man had ever completely left that jungle. Roy and O'Connor had not actually spent a great deal of time together in Cambodia, but those moments in the field defined their lives and bonded them as closely as brothers. The war would be with them always. "O'Connor and I had something in common," Roy explained of their friendship. "We each knew that the other had been through hell."[23]

The next morning, Roy enjoyed breakfast with his family in the hotel dining room. He was briefed once again about the day's schedule. Only four years retired, Roy still appreciated the detailed plan of a day in the Army. He had always liked the organization of military life. The hierarchy made sense to him; it had provided order out of an otherwise unsteady youth. Unlike in his childhood, men in the Army were mostly judged by rank and accomplishments. It just so happened that on that day, February 24, 1981, the most accomplished man was him.[24]

The main action began just after 11 a.m. Roy traveled to the Pentagon to eat lunch with Secretary of Defense Caspar Weinberger and Secretary of the Army John March. The men shared a laugh when Secretary Weinberger followed Roy's example of piling spoonfuls of pico de gallo on top of his steak, only to be rebuffed by the level of heat the spicy topping added to his beef. "I'll never forget the look on his face," Roy cheerfully recalled of the defense secretary. After lunch, he returned to the hotel.[25]

Throughout the day, Roy could feel the weight of the moment set against the backdrop of his forty-five years of life. Here, after all, was a lifelong underdog, one of America's poorest sons, the offspring of a disadvantaged minority race, raised earning a living picking cotton and sugar beets for a nation that barely recognized his existence. Roy's experiences had long suggested to him that he was among the most undeserving groups in America. His family worked hard and carried themselves with dignity, but he came from people who had no reason to expect much recognition.

In his youth, Roy had resented his status and craved respect. The Army provided a pathway toward social mobility, but it wasn't an easy or equal path. Roy knew of many higher-ranking officers who'd entered the service under better circumstances, former high school superstars who had earned admission to West Point and gone on to become colonels and generals. Without a college degree, Roy lacked the same prospects. He had served in the Army because he saw no other opportunities; he understood that the blue bloods of the American military commanded more respect than a Hispanic eighth-grade dropout who had enlisted in his teens. But on that day, Roy would be feted by the entire government at the Pentagon. A devotee of tradition, he welcomed the attention and basked in the proceedings that brought him so close to eminency. On that day, he was more than just a war hero; he was the realized dreams of his family.

Just before one o'clock, Roy, Lala, and their children were driven to the White House to meet with the president and first lady. Roy looked sharp in his crisp new Army greens. Lala wore a blue dress suit with a white corsage pinned to her lapel. Denise and Yvette, aged fourteen and eleven, wore red jackets adorned with white corsages like their mother's. Noel, just eight years old, was smartly dressed in a dark blue suit.[26]

Roy's family met the Reagans in the Roosevelt Room and then proceeded into the Oval Office. Lala spoke with Nancy Reagan as Roy chatted with the president. It was a surreal experience. The extroverted war hero looked uncharacteristically nervous and awkward. Roy was rarely shy, but he was rendered starstruck by the commander in chief, and he quickly retreated to the decorum expected of a noncommissioned officer meeting a higher-ranking superior. President Reagan was new to this as well. He'd barely been in office a month and had certainly never been part of a military ceremony of this magnitude. The start of Roy's conversation with the president consisted of a lot of small talk and "yes-sirring and no-sirring," Roy recalled.[27]

Noel helped break the ice. As the solemn adults settled into the occasion, Roy's son began eyeing Reagan's now famous jelly bean jar. The president noticed Noel's interest and offered him a piece of the candy. When Noel nodded enthusiastically, Reagan handed him the entire jar. Roy joked that he too wanted a jelly bean, and everyone chuckled as they passed around the container. "After that," Roy recalled, the rest of their time in the Oval Office was "a breeze." A few minutes later, the group was joined by Secretary of Defense Weinberger and Reagan's advisor Ed Meese.[28]

After about fifteen minutes in the Oval Office, the president and first lady escorted the Benavidez family to the South Lawn, where vehicles were waiting to drive them to the Pentagon. Roy and Lala rode in the presidential state car with the Reagans and the secretary of defense. The Benavidez children followed in another vehicle. The quick ride in the presidential motorcade was thrilling. People along the sidewalks stopped to "watch and wave," Roy recalled. As he and Lala rode through Washington, DC, with the president, the hero's thoughts drifted back to his childhood. "It was literally more than I could conceive," he remembered, "that a little ol' barefoot Mexican-American farm-boy from Cuero and El Campo, Texas could ever find himself in such company." He "had to hold back tears," he remembered, "thinking about how far this black taxi was from that little 'jit-ney' cab in El Campo."[29]

The presidential party arrived at the Pentagon at about one thirty and was escorted to the Hall of Heroes, the long corridor filled with portraits of Medal of Honor recipients. They were greeted there by another group of high-ranking officials: Vice President George H. W. Bush and his wife, Barbara, Army Chief of Staff Edward C. Meyer, the chairman of the Joint Chiefs of Staff, the secretary of the Army, the sergeant major of the Army, and the secretary and deputy secretary of defense along with their wives. After the brief welcome, the entire party proceeded down a set of stairs into the central courtyard of the Pentagon. Roy and Reagan would enter last.[30]

It was a warm and windy winter day, with high temperatures in the mid-fifties. Neither Roy nor the president wore a coat. Everyone at the Pentagon was invited. "Every window on the Pentagon courtyard was jammed with onlookers," observed a *Washington Post* reporter. Reagan was big on appearances, and his administration sought to reestablish acts of military decorum. He ordered all military personnel to don their service uniforms for the Benavidez ceremony. The Pentagon courtyard was a sea of caps, berets, and military service flags. "I haven't seen so many uniforms around here in years," one officer told a reporter.[31]

With horns blasting and the audience cheering, Roy and Reagan descended the stairs into the courtyard. Roy stood a head shorter than the six-foot-one president. Dozens of photographers snapped pictures as the pair walked together toward the center of the courtyard, pausing for a moment as the military band played "Hail to the Chief." Then, an Army officer escorted the chief and the hero through the courtyard to inspect the Honor Guard. A throng of civilian onlookers, surrounded by cameras, clapped and waved as hundreds of uniformed men and women watched stoically.[32]

Roy, standing short and stout, looked out of place among the young, fit soldiers who were immaculately clad in their best dress

Roy and President Reagan inspect the troops, 1981. Courtesy Ronald Reagan Presidential Library.

uniforms. But on that day, he was the brightest hero of them all. And he knew it. One could see it in his walk. He strutted alongside the president with the swagger of a giant, strolling by the throng of onlookers, passing troops from every branch of the military, and stepping up onto a red carpeted platform, where chairs awaited him and the president. For the next few minutes, it was just Roy and Reagan in the middle of the stage.[33]

Roy soaked it in. He and Reagan watched performances by the US Army Drill Team and the Fife and Drum Corps, outfitted in their colonial-era red coats and white pants. Roy looked on, watching the impressive unit twirl and shoulder their weapons, the courtyard filling with the rhythmic click-clack of their synchronized gun movements. Roy seemed attentive but anxious. He fidgeted in his chair and fiddled with his program. Later, he said that his leg began throbbing during the Honor Guard inspection. As the military drills wound down, Roy and Reagan glanced at each other and exchanged a smile. Then, the secretary of defense walked onstage to introduce the president.[34]

"Mr. President," Secretary Weinberger said, "it is especially fitting that you honor us today with your presence here because of your clear and long-standing support for those who wear the uniforms of the United States armed forces. . . . And I share and support your pledge to restore the pride that we as a nation once felt, and should feel again, for those who serve all of us so selflessly and, in the case of Sergeant Benavidez, so magnificently." The audience politely applauded.[35]

Reagan then took the podium as Weinberger sat down. "Several years ago," he began, "we brought home a group of American fighting men who had obeyed their country's call and who had fought as bravely and as well as any Americans in our history. They came home without a victory not because they'd been defeated, but because they'd been denied permission to win." At this, the crowd in the Pentagon courtyard erupted in applause. They'd been craving such a message for years—through all the anti-war protests, through the endless hearings and mortifying revelations, and through the dishonorable departure from Saigon and the fall of South Vietnam. Many of those in the courtyard were members of a once-proud military who felt they had been unfairly shunned by their society. They soaked in the new president's praise. Finally, they were getting the respect they felt they deserved. Reagan paused to let them finish clapping before he continued.[36]

"There's been little or no recognition of the gratitude we owe to the more than 300,000 men who suffered wounds in that war." The president mentioned "recent movies about that war" that showed negative depictions of the American forces in Vietnam, and he stated that he wanted to help set the record straight. He highlighted "examples of humanitarianism" that "none of the recent movies about that war have found time to show." He talked about the number of schools and hospitals built by American troops. He shared stories of servicemen adopting Vietnamese orphans and building houses for lepers. For Reagan, Vietnam veterans were merely the misunderstood victims of an incompetent foreign policy and a misguided public. "It's time to show our pride in them and to thank them," he insisted.[37]

Reagan circled back to Roy. "I have one more Vietnam story," he told the crowd. At this, Roy and Secretary Weinberger rose to face the president. The pair stood just off to Reagan's right as the commander in chief read the full Medal of Honor citation himself, an unprecedented gesture for a president before Roy's ceremony. It took the president a full five minutes to read the official citation describing Roy's remarkable acts of valor. Roy stood in what he described as a "trance," swaying ever so slightly, taking deep breaths, and occasionally scanning the crowd. His face held a serious look. Roy later explained that his mind was occupied by thoughts from that day in Cambodia.[38]

This moment was a preview of a scene that would repeat itself throughout the rest of Roy's life. Honored as he was to receive the Medal of Honor, public recognition of his actions also often

Roy and Reagan during 1981 Medal of Honor ceremony. Courtesy Ronald Reagan Presidential Library.

required him to relive the most traumatic experience of his life. Roy rarely described his own heroics in public, choosing instead to let others tell the story. One can only speculate why. Perhaps he was too humble. Or maybe it was simply too painful to discuss those experiences with people who have never seen combat. But others did speak about Roy's actions in great detail. All they had to do was read the Medal of Honor citation. Those who sought to honor Roy, both during and after the Medal of Honor ceremony, unwittingly dragged his thoughts back to the violence of that Cambodian battlefield. It was another weight that Roy would have to carry, a burden of sorts that accompanied his new status as a national hero.

As Reagan finished reading the citation, a lieutenant colonel brought the medal onstage and stood behind the president. Reagan took the Medal of Honor and placed the award around Roy's neck, allowing the officer to affix the ribbon to the back of Roy's collar. The president then shook Roy's right hand and gently touched Roy's right elbow. As their hands unlocked, Reagan leaned toward Roy and pulled the hero closer. Roy was surprised. "It wasn't exactly military protocol," he later wrote. "I started to step back and salute the President, but before I could move, he reached forward and grasped me in a hug." Unbeknownst to the audience, Roy stepped on the president's shoe during their impromptu hug. But neither man seemed very bothered. When they separated, Roy stepped back and saluted. The president responded as he normally did, by placing his hand over his heart.[39]

The president looked at Roy, beaming, as the men stood for their photograph. They stood at attention, Roy in a salute and Reagan with his hand over his heart, as the military band played "The Star Spangled Banner." Pictures of the two onstage were reprinted the next day in hundreds of newspapers across the United States. Reagan was deeply affected by the ceremony. "It was an emotional experience for everyone," he wrote that night in his diary.[40]

Unsurprisingly, those in the crowd loved Reagan's sentiment and remembered the ceremony for years to come. Colin Powell, a Vietnam veteran who would go on to become chairman of the Joint Chiefs of Staff and later secretary of state, was in attendance. "That afternoon marked the changing of the guard for the armed forces," he wrote in his 1995 memoir. "We no longer had to hide in civvies. A hero received a hero's due. The military services had been restored to a place of honor."[41]

Dozens of media outlets offered similar interpretations. With headlines like "President Reagan Lauds Vietnam Vets," "Reagan Extends Overdue 'Gratitude' to Vietnam Veterans," and "Reagan: Viet Vets Overlooked 'Too Long,'" American newspapers also seemed to understand that this ceremony was meant to honor more than just a single veteran. So did Roy. "I know I'm a symbol in the eyes of the public," he told a reporter that day. It was "a high honor," he said, to serve as "a stand-in for all the millions who served over there."[42]

After the thirty-minute ceremony in the courtyard, Roy and Reagan returned to the Hall of Heroes to take part in a receiving line. Roy and Lala stood with the president and first lady as attendees approached to pay their respects. Passersby shook the hand of the president, then Roy, then the first lady, and then Lala—the working-class Hispanic couple from South Texas receiving guests alongside the president and his movie star wife. By then, Roy's nerves had steadied. He was acting more like himself, cheerful and playful, repeatedly tapping Reagan on the arm to share a comment and greeting those who passed by with a witty quip and a smile. Some people wanted to hug him, and he welcomed their embrace. Brian O'Connor came through the line and paused for a photograph with Roy and the president. The three of them shared a laugh over something Reagan said. The event lasted about ninety minutes before the president and first lady left to return to the White House.[43]

Afterward, Roy and his family were "exhausted," he wrote. They enjoyed some downtime at their hotel, where they reflected on the day's events. A few of Roy's old military buddies came by that afternoon and evening to say farewell. The next day, Roy's entourage went back to the White House for a group photograph on the White House steps. Then they all boarded a flight for Texas. Roy had no idea about the surprise that awaited his return.[44]

After Roy and his crew landed in Houston, they boarded a chartered bus that drove them back to El Campo with a police escort. Instead of taking Roy home, the bus went to El Campo High School. When Roy stepped off at about 7:45 p.m., he was met by school officials who welcomed him back from

Reagan and Roy with Brian O'Connor (center) at the Pentagon, 1981. Roy P. Benavidez Papers, camh-dob-017319_pub, Dolph Briscoe Center for American History, The University of Texas at Austin.

Washington, DC, with what they called a "public 'surprise party'" at the high school gymnasium.[45]

That morning, the entire front page of the *El Campo Leader-News* was covered with stories about Roy. The Barbees had filed their firsthand accounts of the Washington ceremony from the road. Their articles were just two of five different stories covering Roy's Medal of Honor ceremony. That morning's newspaper also featured a photograph of Roy with President Reagan and a copy of the official Medal of Honor citation. The next page included another picture of Roy departing El Campo a few days prior and another story about his heroics and honors. On the third page appeared the notice of that night's party and instructions for all who wanted to attend.[46]

Roy walked through a line of Boy Scout honor guards into the "Home of the Rice Birds," a classic red-painted multipurpose high school gymnasium with fold-down basketball hoops, encircled by concrete seating and retractable bleachers. Waiting for Roy inside the gym was a raucous crowd of around 1,500 locals who had turned out to welcome home their hero. The El Campo High School band was in attendance, along with the Northside Elementary choir. Signs handmade by students hung from the walls.[47]

The event commenced with the high school band playing the national anthem. A priest from Roy's church led an invocation before the emcee, a local reporter and radio man, took over the microphone. He began by playing a recording of President Reagan's comments from the previous day. Next, a series of local dignitaries took the microphone to address the audience. Congressman Joe Wyatt spoke, as did the Wharton County judge and attorney and El Campo's mayor, who declared the day "Roy Benavidez Day." Two local citizens presented a special poem they had written to honor Roy, and the elementary school choir sang a song honoring Green Berets. Texas governor Bill Clements was unable to attend, but he called in to the rally on a rotary phone. An extension cord allowed Roy to hold the receiver up to a microphone so the crowd could hear the governor's voice.[48]

Roy took the podium. He was thrilled and honored, practically glowing. In the years to come, Roy would appear in thousands of pictures. There is not one picture of him ever looking happier than he did in the photographs from that night at El Campo High School. "I certainly appreciate what you people have done for me, receiving me and my family this way," he told the audience. "It's really great to come back to people who really supported you. . . . And I appreciate even more those people who didn't support me in this act because they encouraged me to fight." "I'm proud to be a Texan," he told them, "and I'm even prouder to have been given the privilege to serve my country." After the event, Roy and his family returned home. Despite the ongoing celebrations, they could not have known just how much their lives were about to change.[49]

Roy Benavidez was suddenly famous. Coverage of his Medal of Honor ceremony appeared in almost every newspaper in the United States—from the *Los Angeles Times* and *Boston Globe* to smaller dailies like the *Anniston (AL) Star* and the *Palm Beach Post*. The story was everywhere. It was also broadcast on the nightly news of every major television station in the country.

The coming weeks and months were a whirlwind of recognition and adoration that helped give new purpose to Roy's life. It started in Texas. In March, the city of Galveston welcomed Roy for its own "Roy Benavidez Day." A week later, he visited the Texas Legislature, where Governor Bill Clements declared another "Roy Benavidez Day." He met with members of the Texas House and Senate, who joined him for a private lunch at one of Austin's most exclusive restaurants, followed by a special reception hosted by the governor.[50]

That spring was a good and busy one for Roy. He threw out the first pitch at the Houston Astros home opener, and his family visited the dugout to meet the team, including Hall-of-Fame pitcher Nolan Ryan. The Texas Press Association named Roy "Texan of the Year" and honored him and his family at a ceremony in Fort Worth. Wharton County Junior College, where Roy had briefly attended classes, awarded him an honorary degree.[51]

That spring, Roy began receiving dozens of invitations to speak. He spoke at rotary clubs, chambers of commerce, churches, hospitals, social clubs, and charity events. He served as grand marshal in several parades. In May, he traveled to Virginia where he spoke at an ROTC banquet at Virginia Tech before returning to Texas to speak at the commissioning ceremony for ROTC cadets at the University of Texas at Austin. "We've been having a tough time keeping up with El Campo Medal of Honor winner Roy Benavidez," noted the *El Campo Leader-News* that spring.[52]

Roy was an inexperienced but extremely effective speaker. At every appearance, his message was simple: America was the greatest nation on Earth and patriotism was its most important value. When he spoke, he usually described the broad outline of a childhood mired in poverty and discrimination and talked about how he had dropped out of school. He then explained why he joined the military and credited the armed forces with pulling him off a dangerous path. Roy always had a few military jokes or lighthearted stories to make people laugh. He told his audiences how proud he was "to be an American," which might have been the phrase he used most often. He'd often return to a handful of other sayings, such as "Quitters never win and winners never quit," and "I am not a hero, the real heroes are those who never came back." He loved to share that people often asked him if he'd do it all over again. "There will never be enough paper to print the money," he'd answer himself, "nor enough gold in Fort Knox for me to have, to keep me from doing it all over again."

Roy throwing the first pitch, Houston Astro- dome, 1981. Roy P. Benavidez Papers, camh-dob-017307 _pub, Dolph Briscoe Center for American History, The Univer- sity of Texas at Austin.

His commitment to the Army was cemented, as it was the ser- vice in that Army that first pulled him out of El Campo and now formed the backbone of his new identity as a war hero.[53]

Roy spoke with a thick South Texas accent. He had a deep voice with a twang, and his diction sounded like it came from the back of his throat. He used simple words. Few people would have called him elegant. But his timing was impeccable, and he was very funny. He commanded a room because of how he was introduced. Moderators would often share the story of his he- roics, stunning audiences who became instantly fascinated by a man who had taken such punishment and demonstrated such courage. Kids who'd had no idea about the Vietnam War would be struck by the fact that Roy had been shot seven times. An alumnus of one of the high schools where he spoke remembered, "I was in that auditorium many times in my life, and I had never heard it so quiet." Roy was a master of positivity and patriotism.

He made other people feel proud to be American. And he complimented them and assured them all that they had a bright future.[54]

Roy loved to speak with young people more than any other group. "When it came to talking to kids, man, he was driven," remembered Chris Barbee. "His mission was to tell every kid he could [get] hold of to mind their parents, stay in school, and go to church." Roy would tell young people, "After what I've been through, I dedicated my life to come talk to you students. You're the future of our country. You're the future leaders." "An education and a diploma," he told them, "is the key to success." He liked the kids, and the kids liked him. They would ask him silly questions that tested his wit—if he was scared or if it hurt when he got shot. He particularly enjoyed speaking with kids who came from backgrounds like his. He had read about poor high school graduation rates among Hispanic teenagers, and he wanted to show them a role model and encourage them to finish school. His speeches to youths were steeped in patriotism and flavored by the political messaging of the day: stay in school and stay off drugs. To the kids of the 1980s, he must have sounded like one of their D.A.R.E. officers.[55]

Roy would go on to give hundreds of talks in the years to come. He was reimbursed for his travel, but he almost always spoke for free. Even though traveling and speaking to large groups is time consuming and labor intensive, Roy did all of this, constantly and for the rest of his life, out of a sense of duty. As his close friend Chris Barbee recalled, Roy "felt the MOH carried with it a huge responsibility to continue to represent his country before young people, military personnel, and even prisoners." Roy viewed those speaking engagements as part of his duty to the United States. This sense of duty compelled him to travel across the country and eventually the world, telling his story over and over, bearing all the trauma of his experiences and the difficulties of constant travel for a disabled man to share his message with other Americans.[56]

Roy's sense of his duty also came from President Reagan, who had essentially asked him to help spread patriotism. At the Medal of Honor ceremony, Reagan had told Roy that he could help his country by telling youths about the greatness of America. A couple months later, Secretary of Defense Weinberger reached out to Roy to ask if the war hero would help with military recruitment. Roy accepted, and Weinberger informed the president that Roy would "be used in the Southwest Region Recruiting Command to speak to young people and educators on the importance of military service." This role was never formalized, but Roy took the charge seriously. Ever the soldier, he viewed his speaking engagements as an order from his commander in chief. He rarely said no to an invitation. According to one regular travel companion, Roy also came to believe that speaking to young people had become his destiny, even "his purpose in life."[57]

Roy ardently believed in the messaging. How could he not? This deeply personal faith in the military had been germinating since he was sixteen years old. He had staked his whole life to this faith in America and its military. When he spoke in the early 1980s, he was aware of the Vietnam syndrome Reagan referenced. "With old-fashioned patriotism in short supply . . . ," he later explained, "it didn't seem too much out of line for one short, fat Mexican-American to stand up and publicly state that he was proud of the uniform he wore, the country he served, and considered it a privilege to wear its highest award." He knew he was a symbol, one he hoped was capable of inspiring "the young people with whom I came in contact."[58]

Roy's approach invoked a strategy advocated by earlier generations of Latino veterans who belonged to groups like LULAC or the American GI Forum, which Roy later joined. His constant invocation of being "proud to be an American" was a reminder to others that he was one. It was an argument made before, both by his ancestors after the Texas Revolution and by Latino World War II veterans. But this time it had a chance to work.

Although Roy wasn't typically paid for appearances, he received some nice perks. In April, a group of El Campo businessmen gifted Roy a brand-new Chevy El Camino for serving as grand marshal in a local youth parade. A month later, the State of Texas gave him customized Congressional Medal of Honor vanity license plates that entitled him to "free parking anywhere in the state" and free registration renewals for life. In the years to come, that car would take the hero all over the state, and the license plate ensured that everyone knew who he was. For years, folks on the Texas highways would smile, wave, and honk, yelling thank-yous and doling out handshakes as they encountered the military hero on the road.[59]

Roy's appearances often served a political purpose. The 1981 Medal of Honor ceremony itself was the first of many examples of Roy being honored in a ceremony with deep political implications. Reagan put on such a show largely because he wanted the vote of veterans and those who supported the military. He and his advisors also sought the Latino vote. As Hispanic voters increased in number and political significance, both major political parties of the 1980s jockeyed for their support.

Dubbed "The Decade of the Hispanic" by contemporary commentators, the 1980s were revolutionary for Hispanic politics. America's Hispanic population was growing faster than any other ethnic or racial group, making them major political players, especially in large states such as Texas, California, and Florida. Between 1974 and 1981, the number of Hispanic elected officials grew from 1,539 to 3,128. In 1981, Henry Cisneros became the first Hispanic mayor of a major US city after winning election in San Antonio. As one journalist observed in 1980, "The Hispanic giant in the United States is awakening."[60]

In the early 1980s, most Latino voters, who are much more diverse than other ethnic groups, were solidly Democratic. In 1980, Reagan won more than 30 percent of the Hispanic vote, a record for a Republican, but his approval rating slipped early in his presidency. In 1982, over 75 percent of Hispanic voters said they were likely to vote Democratic in the next election, largely for economic reasons. Reagan responded by courting Hispanic voters over issues such as conservative family values, religion, education, and anti-communism, which played particularly well with Cubans in Florida. He touted Latinos as proud Americans, emphasizing the accomplishments of Hispanic immigrants and pointing toward representative heroes. He also appointed dozens of Hispanics to government positions.[61]

Ronald Reagan loved heroes, and in the early 1980s, Roy Benavidez was the president's greatest Latino hero. Reagan mentioned Roy often when speaking to Hispanic groups. He toasted Roy when hosting the president of Mexico at Camp David in June of 1981. He mentioned Roy when speaking at a White House ceremony for Hispanic Heritage Week in 1982, calling the previous year's Medal of Honor ceremony "an unforgettable experience." He brought up Roy at a Cinco de Mayo ceremony in San Antonio in 1983, crediting the Medal of Honor recipient with helping to make America "free and independent." Later that summer, he discussed Roy during an event with the American GI Forum in El Paso, and he spoke of giving Roy the Medal of Honor during a White House meeting of the National Hispanic Leadership Conference in 1984. "I had the pleasure of giving him his medal," Reagan told the group. "I don't know what had stalled it. It had been lying there, not delivered to him."[62]

There was a similar dynamic in Texas. Roy was close with a handful of Texas state legislators, who appeared with him at rallies, parades, and various events related to veterans or the military. One of the first to latch on was Frank Tejeda, a Hispanic

Vietnam veteran who served in the state legislature. So, too, did Republican governor Bill Clements, who reunited Roy and Reagan in 1982, the year after they first met, when he asked each to speak at a $1,000-per-plate fundraising dinner for his reelection. The pair shared another hug and photo op.[63]

Joe Wyatt, the congressman who sponsored the legislation that enabled Roy to receive the Medal of Honor, regularly mentioned his efforts in supporting Roy's quest when he ran for reelection in 1982. At one debate with his opponent, Bill Patman, "tempers flared . . . ," observed a Victoria reporter, "when Patman made light of the importance of Wyatt's effort to have El Campo veteran Sgt. Roy Benavidez receive the Congressional Medal of Honor." Wyatt, trembling, pointed a finger at Patman and said, "I cannot believe, Bill, cannot believe, you would make that kind of remark. A distinguished and great American. And I worked for him and I'm proud of it." Later, one of Patman's supporters accused Wyatt of using Benavidez for his own personal gain. For a period of time, the level of support one gave to Roy Benavidez was a tangible political issue in Texas.[64]

Roy was aware of his status as a symbol, but he mostly stayed above the fray of partisan politics. In his first memoir, published five years after the Medal of Honor ceremony, he admitted, "I was a proper and convenient vehicle for the incoming administration to use as a demonstration of a new attitude of respect and understanding toward those who had fought and died in Vietnam." Nevertheless, he always remained grateful to Reagan for the acknowledgment, even as he came to recognize that the theatrics of the ceremony provided political capital for the president.[65]

In the fall of 1981, Roy was busier than ever. In October, he went to West Point. The cadets were sitting down to dinner and listening to the typical announcements when a speaker called for their attention and began reading Roy's Medal of Honor citation. "You had 4,000 people in the mess hall and it went silent," recalled a member of the West Point class of 1982. "The citation just went on and on and you couldn't believe one man could have accomplished this." When Roy later spoke, "he had us spellbound," remembered the cadet. "It made a huge impression on us. There wasn't a dry eye. Of course, the applause was thunderous."[66]

From West Point to elementary schools, Roy spoke to students of all ages. Back in Texas, he delivered lectures all over the state. He was particularly in demand in Austin, where the local branch of the American Legion helped organize events with local schools. During the 1981–1982 school year, Roy gave twenty-eight talks in Austin schools, interacting with tens of thousands of students. During one two-day stretch that October, he spoke to 7,500 students. After watching Roy speak, some of the students participated in essay contests based on a prompt asking them to describe what it means to be an American.[67]

After a 1982 lecture in Burnet, Texas, a special education teacher sent a stack of letters from her students to Roy. The kids all praised Roy's speech, telling him how much they appreciated his courage and patriotism. Some of them shared lessons from his talk that they attached to their own lives. One young man wrote, "I was thinking about quitting school but you came along and after your speech I changed my mind." Another wrote, "Your speech about quitting school help me a lot to stay in school." Another student told Roy, "Your speech made me feel like a proud American."[68]

One of the greatest highlights of 1982 for Roy came in November when he traveled to Washington for the dedication of the Vietnam Veterans Memorial. Approved by Jimmy Carter in 1980 and completed with private funding in 1982, the Vietnam Veterans Memorial represented a watershed moment for the collective memory of the war. A group fundraising effort created the memorial, often referred to as "the wall," uniting stakeholders in a new discourse that prioritized honoring veterans instead of rehashing the political fights of the 1970s that could never be fully resolved. The design of the wall was a highly contentious political issue, but the completed version, unveiled during a weeklong "National Salute to Vietnam Veterans," helped refocus conversations about the war onto the sacrifices of those who fought. Many veterans appreciated the wall for the simple fact that it made them feel less invisible and more appreciated by a nation that had at times ignored their service.[69]

That November, Roy was asked by the governor of Texas to lead the state's contingent of Vietnam veterans in a parade. Roy traveled to Washington, DC, where he led the Texas delegation in a demonstration of more than fifteen thousand veterans from across the country who marched down Constitution Avenue in front of a crowd of 150,000. The parade ended with the dedication of the wall, a twin set of two-hundred-foot black granite walls engraved with the names of the men and women who died serving their country in the Vietnam War. "I'm not the hero," Roy told a reporter that day. "The names on that wall and those disabled in hospitals are the real heroes."[70]

WHEN ROY WASN'T ON THE ROAD, HE AND LALA LIVED A SIMple life in their modest house with their three kids. Their love was the old-fashioned kind. They didn't openly demonstrate physical affection in public, but they were deeply committed to one another, and they rarely fought. When they did, they argued in Spanish so the kids wouldn't know; although Roy and Lala grew up in Spanish-speaking households, their own children didn't learn Spanish, largely because Hispanic parents at that time were told to help their kids assimilate by speaking only English. The family went to church every Sunday, where they sat in the same section with their extended local family. They spent holidays at Aunt Alexandria's house, the home where Roy and his cousins grew up. The entire extended family of sixty or more would pack into the small house, exchanging stories about Uncle Nicholas and sharing memories of their days on the road picking sugar beets and cotton. Roy had been away with the Army for most of the 1960s and 1970s, but he always remained close with his brother and cousins, who were successful members of El Campo society. His brother Roger worked as a realtor for thirty-nine years.[71]

Lala cooked family dinners, preparing beef and pork, even though she was vegetarian. She occasionally worked seasonal shifts at a local craft store, but that was the extent of her professional life. Lala otherwise didn't work, nor did Roy want her to. She had her own circle of friends who played dominoes and bingo and took bus trips out of town. She was also involved with the children's school, serving as a "room mom" who helped organize activities and supplies. When Roy was gone, Lala performed the daily work of raising three kids on her own.[72]

Denise, the oldest, remembers those times. She was impressed by the Medal of Honor ceremony, especially as it briefly elevated her status in school. "We were treated like rock stars," she remembered of the night at the El Campo gymnasium. "Wow. That's pretty cool," thought the shy teen, who suddenly started getting autograph requests herself, despite being "just a nerdy freshman [who previously was] not getting much attention."[73]

But it was also tough because their dad was so busy. After receiving the medal, Roy began to travel all the time. Lala was left home "helping us with homework," remembers Denise, "taking us to various school activities that we needed to be [at], being the disciplinary person." The family sometimes traveled with Roy, which they enjoyed, but even these trips were sometimes tarred by her dad's celebrity status. Denise spent her sixteenth birthday at one of her dad's speaking events in Louisiana. "I'm sixteen years old," she remembered thinking, "and I don't need to be in some swamp camp, Fort-something in Louisiana. . . . Of course I acted against it." On another occasion, when Roy missed her birthday while traveling, Denise remembered a politician calling her to apologize for borrowing her dad. "Eventually I got over it," Denise acquiesced. "It's just going to be our lifestyle for a good while," she remembered musing at the time. "It had its good moments and its bad moments."[74]

Still, the kids were impressed by the way others responded to their father. Some people treated him like a movie star, asking for autographs and photographs. Others just wanted to shake his hand. Roy was big news in those days. When he boarded a flight, it was common for the pilot to tell the other passengers that Medal of Honor recipient Roy Benavidez was on the airplane, which always drew a cheer. During the flight, people would get out of their seats and walk over to greet him. It could get annoying, especially when someone would disrupt a family meal or private conversation to ask for an autograph. Roy rarely said no. He believed, one friend explained, that it was "his duty to oblige them with whatever they wanted. . . . Americans were his number-one priority, not his dinner."[75]

Roy's life had changed. This was a new existence. He was going to spend his days traveling around, giving talks to groups of admirers who would respond to him with standing ovations and long evenings of adoration. With all the trials Roy had faced, he was the happiest he had ever been. It's hard to imagine his life without the Medal of Honor. It certainly would have been much worse without the recognition. Roy was a hero everywhere he went. People loved him. They wrote songs about him. He made them feel good. He told them about growing up poor and about his ascension to his heroic status. He was an outsider turned insider, a man who had ascended the height of American military lore.

To many in those audiences, America was great because it was a place that had provided such an opportunity for a kid like Roy. Certainly, some members of those crowds enjoyed a level of prosperity and stability bestowed upon them from birth. But Roy's path to success had come from the other direction. He had once lived in a very different America, one in which he and his family couldn't even sit in the front of a movie theater. Roy had earned his status not through the generosity of the country but rather because of his own willingness to sacrifice his life and health for a country that only later claimed him as one of its own. Still, Roy never made that point. Instead, he fed his audiences positive stories about the opportunities promised by life in the United States. In a way, his greatest gift to the nation, both in terms of what he had overcome as a boy and endured as a man, was his capacity to suffer for America. And the people loved him for it.

CHAPTER 11

SECURITY

IN FEBRUARY OF 1983, ROY RECEIVED A LETTER THAT NEARLY knocked him off his feet. It came from the Social Security Administration. "This notice," the letter began, "concerns your continuing entitlement to benefits under the Social Security Disability program." "The law provides," the notice continued, "that an individual's disability period shall end if the person is able to do substantial gainful work." The document then referenced Roy's medical reports from his Army retirement hearings in 1976 and a conversation with a health-care provider from early 1983. "We did not obtain other reports because this information was sufficient enough to evaluate your condition." Based on this evidence, the Social Security Administration concluded, "you became able to do substantial gainful work in February 1983. Accordingly, the last disability benefit to which you are entitled is for the month of April 1983." Roy's livelihood was being cut off. He was being told to go back to work.[1]

Roy had been enrolled in Social Security Disability Insurance (SSDI) since his retirement in 1976. As with many retiring veterans, he faced a choice between his military disability pay or SSDI. The decision is complicated by a formula that takes into account an individual's rank, career earnings, and "percentage of disability." One can receive both benefits, but SSDI payment amounts are affected by other income. When Roy retired, he was deemed 80 percent disabled, and his condition was listed as permanent. His ability to work would never improve. Based on these factors, Roy had been advised that SSDI would provide more income for him and his family over the course of his retirement.[2]

Despite his fame, Roy was never wealthy. He was in high demand as a speaker but rarely charged an honorarium. His SSDI payments netted his family less than $500 per month. The medal helped him earn a better living by entitling him to an additional $200 monthly stipend, but the bulk of his income came from SSDI. Now, even this meager income was something he had to fight to protect.[3]

In 1980, the United States Congress passed a law designed to curb SSDI abuses. After a report by the General Accounting Office concluded that 20 percent of people receiving SSDI should be ruled ineligible, President Carter signed legislation requiring reviews of disability recipients every three years. In March of 1981, the Reagan Administration accelerated these reviews, eager to curb spending on social services.[4]

Ronald Reagan's 1980 presidential campaign promised to curtail government spending. Reagan and his advisors were among a wave of right-wing political leaders fighting to retract Great Society programs of the 1960s—initiatives like Medicare, Medicaid, and rental housing subsidies that expanded America's social safety net and offered unprecedented levels of aid to the poor. In fact, it was Reagan's opposition to anti-poverty programs in the 1960s that had launched his political career.[5]

Reagan blamed runaway government spending for many of the financial problems of the 1970s. "I'm trying to undo the Great Society," he once wrote in his journal. "It was LBJ's war on poverty that led us to our present mess." The federal government, he argued, should move aside to allow people to thrive or fail in a free marketplace. These ideas gained traction thanks to Reagan's ability to depict some welfare recipients as poor, lazy citizens who lived lavish lifestyles funded by government excess, a trope most commonly manifested in the idea of the so-called "welfare queen."[6]

When Reagan entered office, his administration began slashing spending on social entitlement programs. Part of its effort involved accelerating the review of people enrolled in SSDI. As one journalist observed, these reviews "became a virtual purge" of the social security disability rolls. The reviews increased from roughly 180,000 in 1981 to nearly 500,000 in 1982, with an expected 850,000 more in 1983. Between 1980 and 1982, the number of people receiving disability in America dropped by nearly 250,000, and the Reagan administration sought to remove another 300,000 more from disability rolls in 1983. Many SSDI recipients were veterans like Roy, who received their notices in the mail that spring.[7]

Roy was devastated. He felt embarrassed and hurt, even "frightened." The letter made him feel "a great sense of shock and betrayal," and he took it very personally. For Roy, those SSDI payments were the return for the wounds he suffered on the battlefield, the same injuries that prevented him from working. He was frustrated by the cold, bureaucratic tone of the letter compared to the realities of his condition. "If they had to spend a day in this body," he wrote of the unnamed Washington, DC, bureaucrat who authored the letter, "they'd have a different opinion." Maybe he could complete a day or two of labor, but he certainly could not go back to work for months and years on end. Roy decided to appeal.[8]

According to Roy, he went to his family doctor who submitted a medical report on his behalf. A few weeks later, the government requested that he see another physician in Houston. This physician tested his lungs and walking ability on a treadmill before agreeing that Roy was "unfit for work requiring any type of physical exertion over any extended period of time."[9]

But this was not the end. Roy had to drive fifty miles to Victoria to see a psychiatrist, and he was required to appear before a judge for a hearing. It was an awful experience. As part of his evaluation, Roy was asked to remove his shirt so that the judge could examine the deep scars cut across his body. When the judge then ordered him to appear before yet another psychiatrist, Roy became incensed. "I have never felt so humiliated and angry in all my life," he remembered. "It was at this point," he wrote, "that things . . . got complicated."[10]

On May 27, 1983, as Roy awaited the results of his appeal, national news broke that America's most recent Medal of Honor recipient was being removed from the Social Security Disability rolls. That morning, the *Washington Post* printed a front-page story, "Vietnam-Era Hero Falls Victim to Cuts in Social Security," reminding readers of Roy's wartime heroics and explaining the recent denial of his benefits. That same night, *NBC Nightly News* ran a segment about Roy's case. It opened with a clip showing Roy with President Reagan at the Medal of Honor ceremony and the reporter reminding viewers that "Benavidez was wounded in almost every part of his body" before transitioning to an interview with Roy in his living room. "This is just absolutely ridiculous," Roy told the audience. "It's salt in my open wounds."[11]

It was Roy who had first alerted reporters to the story. In his life as a public hero, he spoke with reporters weekly, sometimes daily. Journalists called constantly. But even as Roy spoke with reporters that March and April, he at first held his tongue about the SSDI issue. But his frustration grew as the case dragged into May. A reporter from the *Dallas Morning News* happened to catch him at a time when he was particularly upset. Frustrated, he just "unloaded," he said of the conversation. "He may have thought he was interviewing a 'madman,'" Roy remembered, "whose Social Security psychiatrists were trying to get into a straitjacket."[12]

Within days, the news of Roy's disability cutoff hit just about every major newspaper in the country. Hundreds more smaller papers reprinted versions of the story from newspaper wire services. Roy told the *New York Times* that the SSDI cutoff was "an insult to my integrity, to the military and to all veterans." "I don't want them to just look at my personal case," he told another reporter. "I want them to understand what all veterans who fought for this country's freedom suffer in trying to get their rightful benefits."[13]

As the news cascaded, Roy began receiving mail from other veterans facing similar threats to their benefits. Veterans who had served in World War II, Korea, and Vietnam wrote to Roy to share their own stories and express their appreciation for his public response to the SSDI purges. "I had never encountered so many desperate people," Roy recalled. "The letters were heartbreaking."[14]

One such letter came from a World War II veteran whose own appeal was coming up that July. "Thanks for being on WFAA [the Texas radio station]," the former merchant marine wrote to Roy. "There is a whole bunch of us, even if they stop our checks, no one will hire us, because of our disability." "You are not alone . . . ," wrote the daughter of an injured veteran from New Jersey. "Others across the country are challenging the Social Security Disability practices. I want the President to realize that he and his administration are dealing with actual people, not just case numbers." The mother of a Vietnam veteran from Tennessee wrote, "I'm glad to know you're trying to help others. . . . I can't imagine someone like you being told to go to work," she emphasized. "Stick to your guns! And try to get as much publicity as possible." A Georgia Vietnam veteran wrote, "I just finished facing the same problems with loss of Social Security Disability as you are." This man said he struggled with his mental health and was briefly "institutionalized" before finally finding work in 1983. Another Vietnam veteran from Kentucky wrote to suggest a "letter writing campaign to our Senators and Congressmen." A New Hampshire veteran wrote, "I was shocked when I read yesterday that your social security benefits had been terminated. I have gotten over all my anxieties about Vietnam and am living a fairly normal life, but when I see what has been done by some bureaucrat to you, I am truly saddened." A guy in Pennsylvania sent Roy a copy of his book, *Social Security Disability Benefits: How to Get Them! How to Keep Them!* Some people even sent cash or five- or ten-dollar checks, attempting to help Roy and his family in a time of need.[15]

Roy received one negative letter. A World War II veteran from New Jersey wrote to ask, "Why can't you work and support yourself?" "I came out of service with a disability, as did many others," stated the man, "but most of us were not willing to be cry-babies and charity cases: we hustled up educations and jobs, and didn't consider milking the system and the taxpayer." The man cruelly cited Roy's "physical condition," noting, "even though I am some older than you, and have obviously (from your appearance in the picture carried here) taken much better care of myself than you." The letter continued, "Stop feeling the taxpayer owes you something special." Roy was livid. He didn't keep a copy of his response, but he kept the letter and attached a note that read, "You really told him off."[16]

That May and June, Roy once again emerged as a major national figure as hundreds of newspapers published stories about his struggle to secure his disability benefits, stunning millions of

Americans. It was a striking contradiction that such a celebrated soldier could lose access to federal aid. The cruelest irony was that Roy needed those benefits because of injuries he suffered in the very same battle for which he was so widely celebrated. As Roy later testified, "It seems odd to me that my entitlements were terminated by the same Administration that made such a fuss to ensure that I was awarded the Congressional Medal of Honor in February, 1981."[17]

Pressure began to mount on the Reagan administration. Veterans and their families wrote to the White House, sharing stories of their own challenges with Social Security Disability denials. The daughter of a New Jersey World War II veteran pleaded with the president over the case of her father. "The main purpose of this letter, Mr. President," the woman wrote, "is to petition you to reevaluate what is being done to people like my father, Sgt. Benavidez, and countless others. . . . Please do something to halt this insane display of bureaucratic nonsense." Roy himself worried about Reagan's view. "I had just gone on national television," he reflected, "and openly defied, and probably created some embarrassment for, my commander-in-chief."[18]

The *Los Angeles Times* published an op-ed titled "So Much for Heroes," observing, "The incident is embarrassing to the President," and calling on Reagan to "reexamine Administration standards that are inflicting extreme hardship on a host of other disability recipients." "The Reagan Administration has been much too harsh," it concluded. Nationally syndicated columnist Mike Royko told readers, "When Reagan gave Benavidez his medal, he made a lovely speech about Benavidez and other Vietnam veterans, saying: 'It's time to show our pride in them and to thank them.'" "Some thanks," Royko griped. The *Philadelphia Tribune* mocked Reagan's call to show greater appreciation toward veterans, snarking, "The Social Security Administration has shown its appreciation by removing Mr. Benavidez from the disability rolls." The newspaper called for a complete halt to the "purge of the disabled."[19]

The story was indeed a major source of embarrassment for a Reagan administration that had tried to build political capital through its support of the military community and with Hispanic voters by way of its support of Roy Benavidez. As some of the news stories pointed out, Reagan had invoked Roy's name in San Antonio just weeks before the SSDI story broke, telling a Hispanic audience about "Sergeant Roy Benavidez who deserved our country's highest award." "If they place their lives on the line for us," Reagan had told his audience, "we must make sure they know that we're behind them and appreciate what they're doing." As the *New York Times* observed, "Mr. Benavidez said today that that appreciation appeared to have disappeared."[20]

The Reagan administration deflected blame, pointing out that the Social Security Disability review law had been signed in 1980 by President Jimmy Carter. A representative from the White House called Roy at home, and a Reagan spokesman publicly expressed concern over Roy's case. "The White House is sympathetic to the plight of Benavidez and all the other unfortunate victims of the squeeze created by the law," said the deputy White House press secretary. The White House promised to use its connections in the private sector to help Roy find a job, but they were quickly rebuffed by the war hero who said, "I don't want charity. I want what I'm entitled to under law, authorized by Congress." "And I don't want them just to look at my personal case," Roy insisted, "I want them to understand what all veterans who fought for this country's freedom suffer in trying to get their rightful benefits."[21]

THE PUBLICITY SURROUNDING ROY'S DISABILITY CASE WAS JUST one episode in a series of public controversies related to the

Reagan administration's mixed record on veteran policies. The president certainly talked a good game. The early days of his presidency were filled with public ceremonies and proclamations in support of the troops, and he promised to build back America's armed forces, in terms of both weaponry and public esteem. He argued against some of his own economic advisors, who seemingly despised anything resembling a social safety net, to support the rejuvenation of a new GI Bill that was eventually passed in 1984 to help attract a new class of soldiers to the military. Reagan also advocated for raises in military pay, which increased 14.3 percent in 1981, and he later worked to expand health benefits for some veterans. He was a major supporter of the Vietnam Veterans Memorial Fund, which culminated in the erection of the Vietnam Memorial wall in 1982. In his second term, he would help pass legislation making the VA a cabinet-level department.[22]

Reagan's policies helped rebuild the American military in the 1980s. The unpopular draft had effectively ended with the Vietnam War, forcing the Reagan administration to design new programs to recruit soldiers into the armed forces. Even as Reagan cut social welfare spending elsewhere, he sought to cast the military as "a special and elevated category," writes historian Jennifer Mittelstadt. "Military social welfare progressed in unprecedented fashion in the 1980s thanks to a resurgence of militarization in a nation that had long operated 'in the shadow of war.'" Reagan's policies helped revive public confidence in the military and secured his support among military leaders. By the mid-1980s, 85 percent of officer corps defined themselves as conservative.[23]

But the inducements used to recruit to the active armed forces did not necessarily benefit the millions of American veterans who had already served. The early days of the Reagan presidency saw a significant gulf emerge between the president's pro-military rhetoric and his policies concerning veterans, the soldiers no longer in uniform, especially those who had fought in Vietnam. When balanced against his lofty statements about the military, the Reagan administration's stance toward veterans appeared remarkably shallow and even at times openly hostile.

Just weeks after celebrating Roy Benavidez at the Pentagon, the Reagan administration proposed sweeping cuts to the VA. The idea of veterans' benefits is older than the United States itself and runs central to America's ability to wage war. Disabled veterans' benefits started during the Revolutionary War, and the first veterans' hospitals were created decades before the Civil War. The modern VA was established in 1930 and expanded after World War II with the explosion of America's veteran population. Every war America enters requires an expansion of the VA system to serve the soldiers who are recruited to fight.[24]

Seeking to reduce federal spending in nearly all areas except the active military, the new administration sought to reduce VA spending by several hundred million dollars. The proposed cuts included capping disability benefits, limiting unemployment benefits for veterans, reducing eligibility for survivor benefits, ending low-interest VA loans, curtailing dental care for veterans, shuttering newly created Vet Centers that helped counsel Vietnam veterans, laying off thousands of VA employees, and restricting eligibility for veterans' burial allowances. As one writer observed in March of 1981 of the funding cuts to Vet Centers, "Now Reagan is axing them—his Office of Management and Budget called for obliterating them by September—even as the president pins medals on Vietnam veterans."[25]

The proposed cuts created a great deal of confusion for veterans. Advocates worried that VA hospitals might be subject to widespread closures and layoffs, leaving veterans, especially those in the aging populations of the World War II, Korea, and Vietnam generations, without adequate health care and mental health services. None of it squared with the pro-military boosterism dripping from Reagan's messaging.[26]

Conservative commentators defended these reductions in VA support. One widely reprinted 1981 op-ed argued, "Cuts in the 1982 budget are not quite as ruthless as some would have us believe," pointing out that cutting $700 million from a VA budget of $24.5 billion "can hardly be called cruel and unusual punishment." "Everyone agrees that Americans injured while in service of this country deserve very special treatment," noted the op-ed. "However, most of the VA's budget goes not to men with service-connected disabilities but to men who left the service healthier than when they entered it." "It's the most overblown bureaucracy in the government," the article concluded. The *Wall Street Journal* concurred, opining, "There are very few better examples than VA hospitals of how the politics of compassion interferes with rational federal budget-making."[27]

Veterans' groups disagreed. Members of the American Legion passed a resolution at their 1981 national meeting opposing cutbacks to the VA. The director of the National Veterans Law Center told a reporter, "All these cuts leave the Vietnam veterans without any government-supported advocacy programs." A director of a Vet Center in San Diego griped, "With the administration pulling the rug out from under these people, there's a sense of rage and betrayal." "The lack of compassion by those people in Washington is incredible," lamented another vet in the *New York Times*. In the summer of 1981, veterans in Los Angeles conducted sit-ins and hunger strikes at local VA hospitals to protest funding cuts and a refusal by the administration to investigate the medical effects of chemical defoliants used in the Vietnam War.[28]

Many veterans were also affected by the Reagan administration's policies toward anti-poverty and health-care programs. The Omnibus Budget Reconciliation Act of 1981 was the signature

achievement of Reagan's first year. This legislation was famous
for its budgetary implications, but it was also important because
it essentially repealed the 1980 Mental Health Systems Act, a
law that provided additional funding to states for mental health
programming and facilities—services desperately needed by
veterans, one of America's most at-risk demographics when it
came to mental health, alcohol abuse, suicide, and homelessness.
The Omnibus Budget Reconciliation Act of 1981 also reduced
spending on programs like public housing and food stamps. Reagan sold his sweeping reductions as eliminating grift and waste,
but these programs did truly benefit millions of needy people,
including working-class veterans. The Vietnam War had been
a "working-class war," writes historian Christian Appy. But the
unique needs of working-class veterans were not necessarily
considered when formulating broader public policies regarding
America's working poor. Veterans were celebrated during special
military ceremonies but then seemingly forgotten all over again
when it came to making policies that deeply affected many of
their lives.[29]

The most direct target of the veterans' ire was Reagan's choice
for head of the VA, Robert Nimmo. Nimmo came to Washington, DC, from California, where he had been a state legislator
and a longtime political ally of Reagan. During Reagan's gover-
norship of California, Nimmo served for three years as his chief
fiscal officer. He was a retired Air Force colonel who had flown a
B-24 bomber during World War II. He was famous in veterans'
circles for his 1979 effort to block Jane Fonda's appointment to
the California Arts Council in retribution for her 1972 visit to
Hanoi to meet with North Vietnamese leaders. Nimmo accused
Fonda of treason and worked to deny her the appointment. In
1981, he came into the VA with a mandate to help curtail the organization's exploding budget, which was largely a consequence
of the United States fighting three major wars in the forty years

immediately preceding his appointment. He arrived at the position promising to introduce "internal budgetary controls" and "fiscal restraint."[30]

After a short grace period, Nimmo's tenure as head of the VA was rife with a series of inflammatory statements, policies, and scandals that infuriated veterans. These began when he sought repayment of services for veterans who had undergone medical treatment for health problems that he claimed were unrelated to their service. Nimmo instituted a collection process involving mailing medical bills to veterans for past services, an enormously unpopular policy, especially among veterans who couldn't otherwise afford health care. And who was to say precisely which ailments were caused by combat? Nimmo was basically following through on budget-cutting mandates from the administration, but it was he who took much of the blame.[31]

In January of 1982, just six months into his term, Nimmo publicly floated the idea of ending VA medical care for veterans over the age of sixty-five. He said this at a time when the average age of twelve million World War II veterans was sixty-two. This idea had enormous and immediate implications for the millions of American veterans of World War II and the Korean War. "What has to be recognized, I think," Nimmo told the press, "is that there are more words in the dictionary than 'more, more, more.'" A month later, Nimmo implemented a "construction freeze," stalling $2.7 billion in funds earmarked for new VA medical facilities. "I'm going to get tons of flak," Nimmo recognized.[32]

The head of the American Legion called Nimmo's comments on the construction freeze "totally irresponsible." Disabled American Veterans released a statement saying it was "amazed and appalled." Their organization's spokesperson said that Nimmo's "remarks would be more appropriate for the anti-veteran budget-cutting director of OMB than for the VA administrator." The executive director of the VFW sternly admonished Nimmo's "sentiments." "They go beyond legitimacy of concern," he said, "into the realm of dereliction; the breaking of faith with your duty to serve those who served their country faithfully."[33]

No generation of veterans was more upset with Nimmo than those who fought in Vietnam. They were affected by all these other issues and further incensed by Nimmo's stance on Agent Orange. During the war in Vietnam, the United States sprayed more than seventy million liters of chemical defoliants, most notably an herbicide called Agent Orange, across the forests of Indochina. Scientists now know that prolonged exposure to Agent Orange can lead to a variety of cancers and intergenerational birth defects. But Nimmo at the time dismissed veterans' concerns, insisting that the side effects of Agent Orange were no more serious than "teenage acne." He also refused to fund a study on the effects of Agent Orange, rejecting the legitimate concerns of millions of veterans who faced very serious health problems, even death, because of exposure to chemicals their government used in the war.[34]

At the same time, Nimmo spent excessive amounts of government dollars to fund his own luxurious amenities and travel. He redecorated his government office, spending $6,000 on "plush elegance" rugs, $4,000 on "wall treatments and bookshelves," $1,400 on a coffee table and television, and over $700 on framed pictures and an office chair. He used an additional sum of nearly $8,500 to remodel his office, adding a private bathroom so he could shower and change before heading out to fancy dinners at the end of his workday. The total cost of his office improvements topped $46,000.[35]

Nimmo also spent over $700 of the government's money per month to lease a luxury car, and he hired a chauffeur who was paid more than $8,000 in overtime pay the first year, including time on the clock when Nimmo himself wasn't even in Washington, DC. Nimmo spent an additional $10,422 of taxpayer dollars flying first class back and forth to California. And on one occasion, he chartered an Air Force jet at the price of $5,600 to carry him and his aides back to Washington, despite the availability of ten commercial flights that day. He did all this while insisting that veterans were demanding too many entitlements. As the *Washington Post* observed, "The man who is tightening the screws on the nation's veterans evidently feels that budget cuts don't apply to him."[36]

Veterans' groups were livid. The National Association of Concerned Veterans passed a resolution calling for Nimmo's "immediate resignation or removal from office." The VFW passed its own decree calling on Reagan to "reprimand" Nimmo. *Stars and Stripes* magazine asked, "How long will the Administration allow this self-humiliation to continue?" A group of seventeen congressmen openly called for Nimmo's dismissal. By August of 1982, the *Los Angeles Times* concluded that "nothing short of a full-blown war is being waged against former California legislator Robert Nimmo."[37]

The Reagan administration was deeply concerned. The president's advisors followed the news closely and kept a file on negative press toward the VA head. In an internal memo, one advisor warned, "The Administration is about to experience a major embarrassment as the result of a call by the major national veterans' organizations for the removal of VA Administrator Robert Nimmo." The advisor continued, "The democrats are ready to have a field day with Nimmo. . . . You really don't need this in an election year."[38]

Nimmo resigned shortly thereafter in October of 1982, effective at the end of the year. After an investigation, he paid back some of the money he'd spent on his office. Reagan told him that he was "sincerely saddened to hear of your decision to leave government." "You will be sorely missed by me," the president continued, "[and] by the veterans you have so ably served."

Veterans' groups did not share these positive feelings, especially after Nimmo decided to skip the dedication of the Vietnam Veterans Memorial to play golf. A week later, Nimmo capped his tenure as head of the VA with a series of interviews in which he said that disability pay was wasted on veterans who should have been working.[39]

The Reagan administration would continue to manage damage control. Shortly after Nimmo's resignation, it helped push a bill through Congress that provided a cost-of-living increase to 2.3 million veterans and 319,000 widows and dependents who were receiving compensation for wartime injuries. "This legislation," Reagan insisted, "demonstrates the Nation's continuing commitment and support for the men and women who have served in our military forces." Reagan would continue to publicly support veterans' causes throughout his administration, and his next pick for head of the VA would prove to be much less inflammatory than Nimmo. But when the Roy Benavidez story emerged just five months after Nimmo's departure, it once again riled those who were concerned about cutting spending for veterans' causes, even as the administration paid lip service to the men and women who risked their lives in America's wars. In light of all this pressure, Reagan had to act.[40]

ON JUNE 7, 1983, THE REAGAN ADMINISTRATION ANNOUNCED changes to its Social Security Disability review process. It expanded the number of people eligible for "permanent disability" to include about two hundred thousand additional beneficiaries who would be "exempted from the eligibility reviews," reported the *New York Times*. Also exempted were roughly 135,000 individuals with mental health problems. The administration promised to review future cases more randomly and infrequently, instead of through a general purge, and it pledged to propose legislation that would mandate reviews of not only people currently on SSDI but also those who had already been removed. They also changed a rule that allowed payments to continue through the first stage of the appeal process rather than cutting off recipients immediately. In announcing the changes, Margaret M. Heckler, the secretary of Health and Human Services admitted, "I had no idea that the sudden, three-year review of millions of cases we then mandated might result in hardships and heartbreaks for innocent and worthy disability recipients."[41]

The case of Roy Benavidez sparked these changes, as was widely reported in the media. On the day they were announced, *CBS Evening News* played a clip from Roy's Medal of Honor ceremony and told viewers, "Last month the White House got personally involved in the issue when it was discovered that Roy Benavidez, a forty-seven-year-old Medal of Honor winner, had his benefits threatened even though his Vietnam wounds left him unable to bend, lift heavy objects, or stand for very long. . . . With that example, and with pressure building in Congress to enact changes in the process, the Secretary of Health and Human services announced changes to the process."[42]

The *Baltimore Sun* told readers, "The Benavidez case quickened action on disability reforms," concluding that it "seemed to have the effect of accelerating the administration's 'reform' of the disability system." "White House officials," noted the *New York Times*, "had directed Heckler to correct problems in the $18 billion-a-year disability program after reading reports that her department had stopped benefit payments for Roy P. Benavidez." "The administration," agreed the Raleigh *News & Observer*, "took corrective action only after President Reagan learned about the loss of disability allowance by a Vietnam veteran on whom he had pinned the Medal of Honor in 1981."[43]

Politicians and activists had protested Reagan's disability policies since the beginning of his administration. But these calls for action were easy enough for Reagan to ignore so long as they came from Democrats and poor, disabled citizens. Roy's story put a public face on disability reviews, offering implications not just for America's poor but also its most deserving heroes. Roy had no idea how widespread these denials were when he took his story to the press, but his willingness to leverage his own celebrity and relationship with the Reagan administration brought a new level of clout to the public debate over disability benefits that the Reagan administration found impossible to ignore. As one staff member on the Senate Committee on Aging told a reporter, when Reagan learned of Roy's case and saw pictures of himself with Roy in the media, "it got him going."[44]

Critics of the Reagan administration, such as the *New York Times*, welcomed the initial changes but, in the words of the *Times'* editorial board, argued that "they don't go nearly far enough." Republican senator William Cohen of Maine said that the changes "will have little impact on the fate of severely disabled workers because they do not remedy the fundamental flaws in the review process." Pennsylvania Republican senator John Heinz introduced legislation that would halt reviews until the new policies took effect. The *Philadelphia Inquirer* joined others in calling for a complete moratorium on all reviews.[45]

Less than two weeks later, Roy was called to Washington to testify in front of the House Committee on Aging, which held a hearing in response to the issue of disability reviews. Roy appeared in front of the committee on June 20, 1983. He donned his full unform, sans the green beret, but wearing all of his medals, including the Medal of Honor around his neck. The wood-paneled room was packed with media, and Roy was once again on center stage. "I am here not only to testify for myself, but for hundreds and thousands of other veterans that have been deprived of their benefits." Roy was still awaiting the results of his own appeal. "I am here to testify because there has been a gross injustice done to me," he told the committee. "I feel ashamed, my integrity and the integrity of the United States Medical Corps in the Army has been insulted. . . . We didn't ask to go and fight a war for this country and we didn't go fight for luxury, we didn't go fight for money, we didn't go fight for popularity. . . . I ask that this committee please assist in any way, this administration to help not only me but hundreds of thousands of other veterans."[46]

Roy then submitted a statement in which he called for a "complete moratorium" on disability reviews for veterans. "I implore you," he pleaded, "not to place those warriors who have served this country in a degrading and embarrassing position such as I have been forced to endure." The power in his testimony lay in the marriage between his moral authority as a war hero and his own naked vulnerability as a disabled American veteran. "My war injuries will never get any better," he admitted. "Today, as I sit before you, it is asserted that I can work because some social security official claims I can lift fifty pounds. Since May 2, 1968, I have had two pieces of shrapnel lodged in my heart. Both my arms and legs are severely impaired. I also have a punctured lung. My pain is constant. . . . If they can do this to me, what will they do to my fellow comrades? . . . Whatever actions are taken on my behalf should be applied equally to all the many other people who now find themselves in the same predicament."[47]

Roy was joined by an attorney named J. Thomas Burch, himself a former Green Beret and a spokesman for the United Vietnam Veterans Organizations. Burch told of the effects of these reviews on "many disabled and Vietnam veterans." He also submitted some of the letters Roy had received from disabled veterans and their family members. Burch noted "some actions" undertaken by the White House "since Roy's case came to light," but he argued, "they have not done enough." He joined those calling for a moratorium.[48]

After the statements, Roy answered questions about his personal life and medical history, all in front of a panel of politicians and surrounded by cameras. These were hard questions for a proud man—strangers asking him for intimate details about his health in front of the media. Roy was poised and confident, and the politicians questioned him in a polite, respectful tone. Nearly all those who questioned Roy thanked him for his appearance. One of the congressmen, Democrat Norman Sisisky of Virginia, recognized, "I think it took a lot of courage for you to be here, and I applaud you." California Democrat Tom Lantos apologized to Roy for "the outrage that has been perpetrated upon you." "You were an American hero on the battlefield and now you are an American hero for the second time," Lantos praised. "You are an inspiration to every American."[49]

Most of the committee members were sympathetic. A few made sarcastic remarks about bureaucrats determining Roy's physical condition, hammering down on the absurdity of the process by which a Washington government employee could deem someone physically able to work without so much as ever looking at the person. There was some politicking but nothing like the hard-core partisanship that afflicted other hearings. When it was over, everyone in the room offered Roy a standing ovation. He got up and walked down the aisle, giving way to the next witness, the thirty-six-year-old governor of Arkansas, Bill Clinton.[50]

Roy's appearance put him back in the news yet again. His testimony was covered in newspapers across America, and the *New York Times* featured one of his answers as their "Quotation of the Day" for June 21, 1983: "The Administration that put this medal around my neck is curtailing my benefits."[51]

A few weeks later, Roy received a new letter from the Social Security Administration. In a document that included an extensive review of his medical history—including details about his wounds and disabilities, and reports from multiple physicians—a judge ruled that "the claimant continues to be entitled to a period of disability and to disability insurance benefits under sections 216(i) and 223, respectively, of the Social Security Act." Roy had won his appeal. In doing so, he had leveraged his own fame to help create policy changes and draw attention to the plight of America's disabled working-class citizens.[52]

On the night of July 12, 1983, Tom Brokaw told millions of viewers of *NBC Nightly News* that "Roy Benavidez, who won the Congressional Medal of Honor while a Green Beret in Vietnam, has now won back his Social Security disability benefits." The story of his winning appeal appeared in newspapers across the country, from Guam to Vermont. Reporters and opinion writers called it justice. "I'm grateful," Roy told a reporter. "I just hope that every other veteran is not overlooked."[53]

This national fight over disability benefits would continue. A representative from the Social Security office claimed that Roy's reinstatement "proves the system works." But not everyone agreed that the case of a single famous man signified a healthy review process for all. Within a month of Roy's successful appeal, a dozen disabled citizens filed a class-action lawsuit over what they deemed "improperly terminated" benefits. They were seeking a court injunction to "halt further improper terminations." By that fall, twenty-eight states had issued executive orders, moratoriums, or new review policies designed to halt or protect needy citizens from removal from the SSDI rolls. Those battles would be fought in the courts, but Roy's time with this issue was done.[54]

BACK IN EL CAMPO, ROY WAS FACING ANOTHER CHALLENGE. He was popular in his hometown, as he had been since receiving the Medal of Honor. El Campo had covered him in honors, and there was a special display documenting Roy's heroics at the Wharton County Historical Museum. Roy had well-placed friends across the city, especially his buddies the Barbees at the *El Campo Leader-News*. And he enjoyed small privileges. People gave him things and allowed him to skip lines. Sometimes, folks announced his presence at an event.[55]

He was also involved in a handful of local causes. In 1980, Roy had been among the founding members of an organization called the Community Action Committee of El Campo, a group formed to "advise the mayor and city council on conditions and needs of every El Campo community" and to help locals gain access to state and federal resources they could use for educational purposes or civic improvement. The group's goals were to help local needy families with housing, employment, and education. They ran neighborhood cleanup campaigns, helped families arrange for sewer and water line connections, and lobbied the city to make improvements in poor neighborhoods.[56]

Roy also had a reputation as a guy who could be counted on when a local family needed something. Chris Barbee liked to share a story about one December night when Roy learned that a poor Hispanic family in El Campo didn't have any heat. Roy went out and bought blankets and recruited a plumber to hook up a portable heater. "I think he did a lot of that kind of stuff that probably I don't know about, and other people don't know about," said Barbee. "He didn't do it looking for praise. It was the right thing to do."[57]

But Roy's fame, and the way he went about his life, had begun to breed resentment, especially after the Social Security disability story broke in May of 1983. That same month, the local armory was rededicated as the Roy P. Benavidez National Guard Armory. Colonel Ralph Drake came to town for a ceremony that attracted two thousand guests. The city hosted a military parade, and the state legislature once again declared it to be "Roy

P. Benavidez Day." A bunch of Green Berets from Texas joined the parade. And the Texas National Guard erected a plaque honoring "A SON OF TEXAS / WHO LIVES BY THE MOTTO / 'DUTY, HONOR, COUNTRY.'"[58]

A few weeks later, one of Roy's neighbors, a woman by the name of Kathryn Moore, published a letter in the *Victoria Advocate* accusing Roy of using the medal for personal gain and criticizing him for not working. "Ever since Roy Benavidez received the highest medal in our country," the letter began, "he has been shoving it down our throats." "It seems that his philosophy now is that the people of our city should feel honored to have him living here. . . . I wish he would stop using the Medal of Honor to get what he wants," Moore wrote. "Most disabled vets, those that get less than him, have to survive on guts and determination alone."[59]

Moore had been moved to write her letter by the latest wave of media coverage surrounding Roy's disability standoff. When she began encountering these stories in late May, along with the Armory dedication, she just "couldn't stand it any longer," she told a reporter. "I know him. I've lived across the street from him for years. I've seen what he can do."[60]

That same month, another local white woman named Billie Jean Hauser published an angry letter in the *El Campo Leader-News*. "I am writing this out of anger and frustration," Hauser began. "The media coverage given to Roy Benavidez for his heroic deeds in the Vietnam conflict was really an outrage." Hauser's argument was that the media and city leaders should pay attention to all the region's veterans and spend less time focusing on Roy as an individual. "The other soldiers who were there were just as brave but perhaps did not have the need to be patted on the back," Hauser suggested. "To honor just one man for what many did is in very bad taste."[61]

A handful of Victoria residents responded to Moore's letter. A local retired Air Force veteran directly addressed Moore. "Your unjust attack on Sgt. Roy Benavidez truly angered me. . . . Had it not been for men such as Sgt. Benavidez, past, present and future, our letters to the editor (if allowed) could very well be written in the only language allowed, Russian, German or Japanese." "While we were enjoying ourselves . . . ," wrote another local woman, "the poor veterans were fighting wars away from home, not eating or sleeping and their lives were in danger." "What right does Kathryn Moore of El Campo have to criticize Sgt. Roy Benavidez?" "I say, Roy Benavidez, stand up for your rights," wrote another Victoria woman. "Most people, like me, say you deserve it."[62]

Still, resentment festered in some quarters of the small town. Moore and Hauser were among the very few who spoke publicly against Roy. Their views weren't held by everyone, but Roy could sense antipathy in other quarters. Most criticisms directed toward him were made in private conversations, small-town people gossiping about one man receiving too much glory and speculating about his ability to work. "The resentment gets like dry grass," explained the director of the Chamber of Commerce. "When something like this comes along that tends to justify the feelings of people who don't like him, it sweeps across the community."[63]

The naysayers read stories in the newspaper about Roy traveling the country, and they saw him out walking. Because Roy was told by his doctors to lose weight and exercise, he walked religiously, every day, even in the rain. Roy walked at the high school track and at Friendship Park, a little recreational area located off a central thoroughfare in El Campo. In an era of increasing skepticism over government entitlements, the people who saw Roy walking and then read about his disability claim wondered why he wasn't working. He was their welfare queen.

What they didn't see was his body. The clothes he wore covered a body once described as a "walking roadmap [of] scars." They didn't see the "agonizing pain" that he fought through with every step around the park. They didn't see the arthritis plaguing his spine, hips, and knees, and they didn't see the tiny shards of metal that still occasionally popped out of his skin. They didn't see that he couldn't "use his left arm," a judge had concluded during his appeal, "for much more than to guide things for his right hand," or that he couldn't sit for more than an hour, or that "metallic fragments" still floated in the cells around his lungs and prevented him from normal breathing. They couldn't possibly see that his ventilation capacity was about one-third that of a normal adult male. They didn't see the years of doctors' reports that were "as thick as two Bibles," Roy once said. It was the doctors who insisted that he walk every day. He'd die if he didn't. These naysayers just saw him walking and concluded that he should get back to work. "If this man saved eight men all by himself," Kathryn Moore insisted, "surely he can master any job offered him."[64]

Roy's detractors wrote about him as if he had led some great privileged life. Roy was enjoying a moment in the sun, but parts of his life to that point had been extraordinarily difficult by virtually any measure. As an orphaned, Hispanic boy growing up in Great Depression–era Texas, he had worked since he could walk. Unlike many of them, he didn't have an opportunity to finish high school and gain a civilian's trade or inherit a family business. He found his calling as a teen by joining the military, signing up for a lifetime of fighting because he saw no other opportunity. That decision twice led him to death's door in a faraway land. And Roy *did* work. He served in the way that President Reagan asked him to, by speaking to tens of thousands of people for free, even at personal cost to himself. "If he can go to Washington and be all over the country giving speeches," said another local critic, "he can work."[65]

Some locals were weary of the attention he received. His fame made him synonymous with the town itself. Many Americans had only heard of El Campo because they knew about Roy

Benavidez. He overshadowed everybody; from an outsider's point of view, he overshadowed the whole town. "He's got the worst PR I ever saw," one anonymous interviewee told a reporter. "The paper overexposed this guy. Nobody wants to hear about it any more." The head of the Chamber of Commerce suggested, "There is something in human nature that makes it hard to watch another person get the glory. . . . He left here a poor unknown Mexican and came back a hero. Some people resent that." Other comments still targeted Roy with racist vitriol: "He's still a Mexican fighting man who bites the heads off chickens," said another anonymous interviewee. Much had changed since Roy was a boy, but he believed racial prejudice still played a major role in the bubbling resentment. "I don't mean everybody," Roy told a reporter about local racists, "I'm just talking about that 10 percent or so, those people who remember the old days and resent it that some of us [Hispanics] have made it to the top."[66]

In August of 1983, the Sunday magazine of the *Dallas Times Herald* ran a cover story on Roy titled "A Hero Without Hometown Honors." The reporter interviewed Roy's friends and foes alike, along with Roy's personal physician. Some agreed only to anonymous interviews. The journalist uncovered a stunning range of reactions toward the El Campo hero. "The feelings here go from hero worship to animosity," said a local businessman. "Roy goes to the White House and meets with generals and presidents. A little town like this kind of gets outdone." Roy told the reporter that he was thinking about leaving El Campo. "He doesn't want to," read the story, "but he's tired of fighting." "If he does leave, there are those who will say it is a result of a tragic misunderstanding between a community and its most famous citizen," the reporter concluded, "a rift fed by jealousy and pride, and deepened by television cameras, magazines, and newspapers eager to turn Benavidez into some kind of superhuman patriot."[67]

Despite some misgivings, Roy and Lala decided to stay. They wanted to remain near their families in the place where they grew up. Roy would just have to live with it. He had a thick skin but also a chip on his shoulder. Roy had good friends in town, but he was leery of the jealous whispers that stalked his life there. He was undoubtably a national hero, but there were local conflicts over his iconography. Roy had to adapt in every situation as everyone from the president to his neighbors felt empowered to batter about his identity in their judgments about his life. His outside fame didn't directly affect his neighbors; they were just weary of hearing about him for their own reasons. His paranoia about his local role was part of the reason he so enjoyed being out on the road.

CHAPTER 12
GLORY DAYS

O N November 9, 1983, Roy was featured in a Veterans Day episode of the primetime NBC television program *Real People*. Considered one of the first successful reality shows in the United States, *Real People* was a series of hour-long programs comprising short segments featuring fascinating everyday individuals. Most of the filming for Roy's segment had been completed months earlier in El Campo and Washington, DC.[1]

The episode opened with one of the show's hosts standing in the courtyard of the Pentagon recounting Roy's 1981 ceremony as "a very impressive event commemorating an almost unbelievable story of courage and bravery." The scene then changed to a clip of Roy greeting hospitalized veterans. "The men here are honored by his visit," stated the narrator, "because to anyone in the military Roy Benavidez is a living legend."[2]

This segment offered a general overview of Roy's journey toward heroism—from a migrant worker to soldier—everything

Roy on *Real People*, 1983. Roy P. Benavidez Papers, camh-dob-017311_pub, Dolph Briscoe Center for American History, The University of Texas at Austin.

leading up to the combat story of May 2, 1968. A host inter-viewed Roy in his living room, where he sat in his armchair ex-plaining his heroic actions. "There was no turning back," he said. "You either fight, doggonit, or die right there. And I was gonna fight to the last damn minute I had." The episode included inter-views with the pilot Roger Waggie, Roy's old commander Ralph Drake, and Congressman Joe Wyatt.[3]

The next portion of the episode highlighted Roy's commitment to speaking in schools. "Roy feels that the honor of receiving the medal carries with it a great responsibility," said the narrator. "To that end, he has traveled to schools all over this country to meet with and speak to the people he calls the future leaders of this nation." It showed footage of an interaction between Roy and a student who asked, "When you were running through there and getting shot and everything, did giving up ever run through your mind?" "No honey," Roy told her, "An American never gives up." The room erupted in applause.[4]

Real People also arranged for a White House meeting between Roy's family, a representative from the Reagan administration, and the hosts of the show. This portion of the episode was filmed during Roy's SSDI fiasco. The final minutes showed clips from the White House, where Roy's family met with Reagan's director of public affairs. The show also included footage of the parade and ceremony marking the rededication of the Roy P. Benavidez National Guard Armory in El Campo. The last scene in Roy's segment was of his family being honored on an outdoor stage in front of a live *Real People* audience who greeted them with a standing ovation. An estimated 13.4 million people watched the episode in its Wednesday prime-time slot. The episode was rerun twice the following year, including on the Fourth of July.[5]

The year 1983 marked the height of Roy's fame. The Social Security saga of that year kept his name in the news and further elevated his status as a national hero. Roy's case had been featured numerous times on every major network's evening news program and in widely circulating dailies including the *New York Times*, *Washington Post*, and *Los Angeles Times*. *Reader's Digest* had published a feature on him earlier that year, and millions saw the *Real People* episode. Roy was quite famous; not like a movie star or politician, but famous enough that millions of people across the country knew who he was. It was rare that he went somewhere in public without being recognized.

With his Social Security case settled, Roy went back out on the road, speaking to tens of thousands more people in 1984. There was no typical event—only Roy's message remained the same. He would arrive at a venue and greet the organizers, who almost always wanted to shake his hand and pose for pictures. Sometimes, there would be a dinner. Other times, there would be drinks and socializing. The event might take place in a classroom, a cafeteria, or even a stadium. Roy spoke everywhere. Wherever he was, he was always ready to go with his life story and positive messages about patriotism and education.[6]

Roy was most popular in schools and military installations and at veterans' events. He was busiest in Texas, especially around Memorial Day, the Fourth of July, and Veterans Day. A sampling of his 1984 events includes speaking at a Vietnam Veterans Day ceremony in New Jersey; appearing at a POW/MIA ceremony in Bay City, Texas; and speaking at the American GI Forum convention in June in Kansas City, where he spent two hours touring the local VA hospital. "I think it's great he came here," one of the patients told a reporter. Other events included a speech at the Dallas Rotary Club, flying to Washington for Hispanic Heritage Week, and another appearance in New Jersey to speak with college students. In November, he attended groundbreaking ceremonies for an armed forces reserve center in Corpus Christi that was dedicated in his honor. When a journalist asked Roy why he spent so much time on the road, Roy said, "The military molded me into the person I am today, so if the phone rings and somebody says, 'I need you here,' I leave my wife a note and go."[7]

Roy kept track of his many appointments by writing them into the date boxes of a large monthly calendar. The 1984 version is filled with scribbles detailing the places and times of his events, along with the phone numbers of local contacts. The schedule is packed with speeches to all types of groups—Boy Scouts, students, veterans, and so forth. That year, he usually had two or three speaking engagements every week, mostly in Texas.[8]

Roy didn't like to travel alone. By then, he had recruited a couple companions who drove him to events. One was the newspaper man Chris Barbee. The other was a new friend named Jose Garcia, whom Roy met in 1984 when delivering the keynote address at a LULAC event in Houston. Garcia was also a Hispanic veteran, and he had military security clearances that Barbee did not, which allowed him to travel nearly anywhere with Roy. Garcia was also retired, so he had a lot more free time than Barbee. Soon after they met, Roy asked Garcia to serve as his escort to some of the speaking events.[9]

Garcia worked as a handler of sorts for Roy. He was much better organized than Roy and helped plan trips and protect him from overbearing admirers. Roy was quite extroverted and grateful for all the attention he received. People fawned over him. They wanted to meet him, shake his hand, ask him questions, and even hug and kiss him. He spent hours after his talks meeting new people and signing autographs. Roy loved these interactions, but they consumed so much of his time, which could be a challenge if he had to run to another event. Garcia would pull him out of a crowd. He could say no when Roy was seemingly incapable of doing so himself. Roy was like a rock star catering to adoring fans, and Garcia served as his manager. When Roy had a hard time saying no, he could tell admirers, "Go talk to my escort." Jose Garcia was happy to decline on Roy's behalf.[10]

Garcia also watched out for folks who tried to take advantage of Roy. "Sometimes people would try to abuse him or take pictures with him and then use those pictures . . . for advertising for political reasons," Garcia recalled. "So I needed to let people know that they could not abuse him in any way, shape, or form, especially women who wanted to get close to him." Some people did shady things. There were cases of event organizers collecting cash at the door to hear Roy speak—ten or fifteen dollars a plate to hear Roy Benavidez over dinner—and then insisting they had no money to offer an honorarium. Some organizers invited Roy for one purpose and then asked for more of his time and energy upon arrival—piling on to Roy's duties by requesting an extra meeting, talk, or meal. Garcia was there to advocate on Roy's behalf.[11]

He also helped keep Roy out of trouble. A lot of military guys wanted to take Roy out drinking, and Garcia tried to make sure their activities didn't get too out of hand. "Every time people took him to go sit down and discuss something, everybody was drinking," Garcia remembered. "I mean, soldiers get together, they're always drinking every time." Garcia often stepped in to say no or "Don't overdo it," but Roy "drank sometimes a little bit more than I wanted to see him do." The fact of the matter is that Roy liked to party a bit on the road; he liked to cut loose and socialize, especially with his fellow soldiers.[12]

With Chris Barbee, Roy had an agreement that "what happens in the field stays in the field." They had a lot of fun on the trips. Roy loved meeting his admirers, and he was extremely social. But even beyond that, he enjoyed being out on the road, meeting interesting people and hearing their stories. "He was always going up and talking to people, you know," Barbee recalled. Strangers would approach Roy, Barbee says, almost always asking "the exact same words: 'Excuse me, sir. Aren't you

Roy with Fred and Chris Barbee. Roy P. Benavidez Papers, camh-dob-017319_pub, Dolph Briscoe Center for American History, The University of Texas at Austin.

Sergeant Benavidez?' or, 'Aren't you Sergeant Roy Benavidez?'"
"It always amazed me how many people knew Roy, knew of Roy,
and appreciated Roy," Barbee said of his old friend. "It made him
feel good."[13]

Roy had not sought the Medal of Honor to become famous.
He had first begun fighting for it in 1974 and would gladly have
accepted it then. It took seven frustrating and uncertain years for
him to finally receive the commendation he deserved. One could
argue that this itself was an injustice. Even the producers at *Real
People* told their audience they were "bewildered why it had taken
so long for him to receive his medal." The delay also cost him
thousands of dollars, both in personal funds he spent pursuing
the medal and in the missing monthly Medal of Honor stipends
he would have received throughout those years of delay.[14]

Yet the delay also cleared a lane to fame. Had Roy received the
Medal of Honor in the 1960s or 1970s, he would have been just
one of more than two hundred recipients from the Vietnam War,
and his fame likely would have faded away during the military
malaise of the 1970s. By receiving the medal in 1981, Roy got to
be a hero in the long memory of the war, in the days when the
nation once again started celebrating its military heroes without becoming overwhelmed by the collective national guilt and
moral injury left in the wake of Vietnam.

In the early 1980s, writes historian Christian Appy, "there developed a powerful need to identify heroes who might serve as
symbols of a reconstituted national pride." The soldiers were pulled
apart from the war, separated from the cause for which they had
fought. The blame for the failures of the war was pinned on the
politicians and not the military. As historian Patrick Hagopian
has observed of the era, "the idea took hold that veterans' and
society's wounds had to be healed together."[15]

The tragic Vietnam films of the 1970s were replaced by a resurgence of patriotic movies like *Rocky IV* and *Top Gun*, films

that set aside the complex issues of diplomacy in favor of a paradigm that celebrated America's cold warriors. Part of the failure of Vietnam, audiences came to recognize, became the unwillingness to celebrate those who fought it. The veteran was the victim, the forgotten hero like John Rambo—the half–Native American Medal of Honor–recipient Special Forces veteran of the 1980s film franchise—who, after being shunned by his country, asked his former commander, "Do we get to win this time?"[16]

For some, Roy was the living embodiment of a nation that had turned its back on its troops. Like Rambo, he was a Special Forces veteran who had operated deep behind enemy lines under mysterious circumstances. And he had been the victim of a government that had not only sent him into harm's way but also failed to later recognize his sacrifice. By the end of the decade some were openly calling him "The Mexican Rambo." The difference was that Roy was real.[17]

The timing of Roy's award also meant that he was alone. Other living veterans had received the Medal of Honor, but for the rest of Roy's life, he was the most recent living recipient. And his ceremony had come at a turning point—in fact his ceremony was *the* turning point—for the resuscitation of the American military in the eyes of the public. As the admirers and media circled, Roy sought to further capitalize on his own story.

One could argue that Roy had always been self-promoting, ever since beginning his quest to pursue the medal. He doggedly pursued the medal for years, aligning dozens of influential allies who worked through more than six years of Army denials to constantly advocate for Roy's Distinguished Service Cross to be upgraded to a Medal of Honor. But that pursuit was largely about proper recognition within the military. Roy mostly wanted only what he thought he had earned. He had certainly asked for the medal but not the attention that came along with it in the 1980s. The same could be said of the Social Security appeal. The

fame that accompanied his story outpaced even Roy's wildest
dreams, and it began to reveal to him just how powerful his story
could be. He always knew that his story was inspirational, but
now he was coming to imagine it could also be profitable.

Although Roy enjoyed prominence, none of his activities
generated a significant amount of income. He did most of the
events and interviews for free. His travel was usually paid for
by whoever made the invitation. Jose Garcia sometimes helped
him secure an honorarium, but Roy was so committed to this
type of service that he rarely pressed the issue of payment. But
Roy's speaking engagements were laborious. Public speaking was
work, and traveling was hard. Roy's commitments consumed
countless hours of his life. He was willing to do it; in fact it made
him happy. But at the same time, it was clear by 1983 that others
were using Roy's story for their own benefit, be it political or financial. He was grateful for the treatment and honorifics, but he
also, understandably, wanted a bigger cut of the take. Plenty of
others were clearly benefiting from his story in their magazines
and television programs. Prompted by an endless stream of suggestions from friends and strangers alike, Roy began searching
for ways to turn his life story into a book that he hoped could
become a movie.

To do this, he needed help. Roy could work a crowd, but he
didn't know the first thing about authoring a book or making
a movie. To accomplish this task, he tried to draw on some of
the many connections he had made as a celebrity. One of the
first people he contacted was Ronald Reagan, the movie star
president. It was Reagan who had helped make Roy famous in
the first place with the gaudy Medal of Honor ceremony. Based
on the president's reception to him, Roy thought they might be
able to work together in the future. "Although we spent such a
short time together," Roy wrote to the president in 1982, "I still
feel the closeness of those cherished moments." When Roy first

began considering a movie, he viewed Reagan as a natural ally. He wrote to the president seeking help with contacting a movie producer, and he asked Reagan to consider writing a foreword if Roy were to produce a book. But the president's counsel declined, noting that "the President does not participate in any commercial ventures."[18]

The following year, Roy wrote to the owner of a New York bookstore asking for help finding "a good ghost writer." "I am told it will make such a good book and movie material," he said of his life story. America's growing Hispanic population, he argued, provided a natural audience. "There never has been a book or movie written by a Hispanic American MOH Winner. 22 million Mexican Americans and the rest of this country await such a good story." He also wrote to the owner of a major New York literary agency asking if she'd be interested in representing him, but she declined, noting, "Your story is an important one, but I am currently unable to take on new projects."[19]

Roy did not have the skills to write a book himself, nor did he have a solid understanding of the publishing marketplace. He made a good point about Hispanic audiences, but the New York publishing industry seemingly wasn't very interested in attracting broad Hispanic audiences. The industry was, and remains, overwhelmingly white. White agents and editors sought books they believed white audiences would buy. Some very famous African American figures, especially Bill Cosby and Michael Jackson, used their fame to elbow their way onto bestseller lists, but mainstream publishers printed very few books about non-white subjects. There is no smoking gun that proves that race limited Roy's commercial appeal, but the prevalence of other veterans' stories—especially the mountains of books published by lesser-known white veterans—suggests there may be some connection. Regardless, Roy struggled to gain a foothold in the worlds of books and movies in Manhattan and Hollywood.

Speaking engagements came more naturally to Roy, and he continued these as he searched for more recognition in other forms of media. Roy understood how to craft his own persona with in-person audiences. He came across as an unassuming, modest soldier who just loved his country. Roy was a deeply intelligent man and a gifted speaker, capable of holding thousands of people on his every word. But he would begin his speeches by disarming his audiences, telling them he was a high school dropout and speaking with a thick accent and measured cadence. He'd recount his life story, starting with his parents and poverty-stricken childhood before describing his early days in the Army and eventually his time in Vietnam. Next, he would tell them how he recovered in the hospital, and then he'd talk about completing jump school training and joining the Green Berets. He didn't need any outline or script because he was just telling the story of his life. All public speakers perform in some regard, but Roy's persona tracked so closely to his actual personality and life story that he never strayed very far from who he truly was. He didn't have to be anyone else when he had the Medal of Honor hanging around his neck.[20]

Roy almost always wore his uniform when giving speeches, allowing the decorations to establish his credentials. His ability to speak without notes made his lectures naturally conversational in tone. He was humble and kind, deflecting credit with lines like, "I am not a hero, the real heroes are those who never came back." And he was ever so funny. He infused the grim details of his life with well-timed lighthearted quips that always drew a laugh from audiences. His humor was a gift to his crowds, a moment of levity in an otherwise weighty tale of poverty, war, and death. When explaining that he had mistakenly loaded three enemy soldiers on the aircraft during the May 2 battle, he'd pause and say, "I didn't want to leave anybody behind," and the audiences would erupt in laughter. The only thing that truly bothered him was when strangers asked, "How many people did you kill?" Of course, he didn't know the answer. He never let on that taking so many lives bothered him. His emotions around those actions were private, discussed only with others who had had similar experiences. Otherwise, Roy's message was simple, one wrapped in layered themes of patriotism and sacrifice that made his audiences feel good about their country. And he always told them, "I'm proud to be an American."[21]

Roy's brand was patriotism and service. His product appealed most to those who wanted to feel good about the United States of America. The message was always overwhelmingly positive, filled with sayings such as "An American never gives up" and "It's great to be an American, so you can never do enough to help a fellow American." He lived by the mantra of "Duty, Honor, Country," and he committed to memory the patriotic poem "Remember Me?," a sonnet about the fading reverence of Old Glory. He recited it often during his speeches.[22]

For those watching, Roy's patriotism became the stuff of legend. In 1981, one columnist observed, "I understand this man . . . is so patriotic that he actually stands at attention and salutes even while watching television in his livingroom [sic], and the American flag is shown or the national anthem played." "It's hard to know," wrote a Houston journalist, "just how to take a man so completely occupied with patriotism. You wonder if battle scarred his mind as well as his body. You wonder if he's for real." "That kind of intense patriotism," wrote another Texas journalist, "just isn't espoused by mainstream America anymore." "You might meet someone as patriotic as Roy," noted another author, "but nobody more patriotic."[23]

Roy's own life story carried immense patriotic power. He had every right to be bitter about the obstacles he'd faced along his journey, but he didn't blame anyone or anything for the conditions of his youth, instead framing his early struggles as his own individual failure. Dropping out of school, he commonly told audiences, was a personal mistake. He told them that it was his fault, at times calling himself a "a fool" for doing so. But anyone who really knew Roy's story understood that his leaving school was not his own fault. Of course, his audiences didn't know that, making his capacity to absorb blame for his own disadvantage all the more remarkable. Roy made light of his obstacles in life to make his story more digestible for others.[24]

After establishing his supposed shortcomings, Roy praised the military for his salvation, telling audiences that the United States Army—and by extension the nation itself—gave him a chance in life after the mistakes of his youth. The story of his ascension at once gave hope to similarly disadvantaged youths and reassured the most privileged people in his audiences that America was a land of economic mobility. Roy's story appealed to Reagan conservatives by emphasizing the opportunities America had to offer instead of dwelling on the inequalities he faced. People who support cutting federal programs for the poor so often commit themselves to the belief that those at the bottom simply don't have the talent or drive to succeed. In fact, they even claim that the reason people are poor is because they have become too reliant on those same programs that provide basic necessities such as food and housing. But many Americans are poor not from a lack of talent or ambition but because their families didn't have equal opportunities to build wealth. Racial segregation was not merely the separation of the races, it was also a systematic way of creating financial inequalities between white people and everyone else. It was the policies and legal practices of the United States government that made and kept Roy's family poor. But Roy only gave America credit for helping to lift him up.

Roy also carefully sidestepped the issue of race, for both his audiences and himself. By virtually any measure, race had been the single greatest factor in creating the challenges of Roy's family's lives. Roy didn't completely ignore the issue of race, but he repackaged it with sayings such as "True Americans do not look at the color of the skin, the only colors they look at are red, white, and blue." For his audiences, his messaging softened the historical realities of race that, in truth, deeply affected the fate of his family.[25]

Roy also felt compelled to explain the origins of his mindset. Like the origin story of a politician or the conversion story of a prophet, Roy was called to explain the inspiration for his extreme patriotism. Like many politicians do, Roy said that the origins of his commitment to service were rooted in a meeting with a great American icon. For Roy, this was Audie Murphy, the famous World War II hero turned movie star. For years, Roy told audiences and reporters that he had become inspired to join the military by reading Audie Murphy's book, *To Hell and Back*, and seeing the film as a child. He later recounted meeting Murphy while in the Texas National Guard, telling audiences that Murphy was his "idol and role model" and explaining that he was drawn to Murphy because they shared a similar background as poor cotton-picking kids from Texas.[26]

What Roy didn't quite let on was that Audie Murphy was more than just a source of inspiration; he was a model—a poor Texas farmworker turned famous Medal of Honor winner. Roy wanted to be like him not only as a soldier but as a public figure. Audie Murphy had the book, the movie, and the fame, and Roy wanted the same. He essentially wanted to become the Audie Murphy of the 1980s, a newer, Hispanic version, repackaged and celebrated for another generation.

Roy's approach worked in the speaking circuits. He was always in demand. There would be no film, and the books were years in the making, but he did successfully curate a very fulfilling life as a public speaker based on his accomplishments, messaging, and persona. Throughout the 1980s, the speaking engagements never stopped, and he spent much of the decade on the road, a traveling war hero for audiences across the nation.

Military folks particularly loved him. It was with them that Roy was most himself. They generally understood his experiences, and he seemed most relaxed in their presence. He counseled young men and women about their military careers, and he regularly visited VA patients during his speaking tours. One man who served as Roy's guide at Fort Meade noted, "I have escorted him in the presence of general officers, senior civilian officials and tough warrant officers and enlisted personnel. It is always the same. They all hang on his every word, they salute him, they are moved to high emotion and they seek to learn from this quiet man."[27]

In 1984, Roy's travels included several visits back to Washington, DC, for military-related events involving President Reagan during the election year. In March, Roy attended a White House luncheon where Ronald Reagan awarded the Presidential Medal of Freedom to Dr. Héctor Garcia, the founder of the American GI Forum. Roy was one of eight Hispanic Medal of Honor recipients invited to the event. They enjoyed a reception hosted by the president and were asked to weigh in on a speculative design for a new stamp honoring Hispanic American veterans.[28]

In May, Roy flew back to Washington to attend a Memorial Day tribute to the "Unknown Soldier" of the Vietnam War organized by the Reagan administration. An estimated 250,000 people lined the streets of Washington, DC, to watch the procession of a symbolic empty casket to Arlington National Cemetery, where an additional four thousand special guests, including Roy, attended a funeral service. Reagan offered a eulogy, for those "who served us so well in a war whose end offered no parades, no flags, and so little thanks," and adorned the casket with a Medal of Honor. At the ceremony, a photographer snapped a picture of Roy wiping away a tear, an image that was picked up by the Associated Press and reprinted in newspapers across the country.[29]

In late October, Roy was back at the White House for an event in the Rose Garden where President Reagan unveiled a new stamp honoring Hispanic American servicemen and women. "I've always been aware of the many contributions Americans of Hispanic descent have made to our country," Reagan said during the quick fifteen-minute ceremony. "It was my honor," Reagan reminded the audience, "to have presented the Medal of Honor, the last one awarded to an Hispanic American, to Master Sergeant Roy Benavidez." The new stamp depicted seven Hispanic Americans proudly standing in front of an American flag. It included four Hispanic veterans in uniform, three adorned with Medals of Honor, a woman in uniform, and two Hispanic youths on each flank, signifying the next generation of Latino leadership.[30]

The timing of the stamp ceremony was an obvious political stunt to many in the media. Reporters were skeptical when it was hastily announced a week before the 1984 presidential election. A widely syndicated column by journalist Dominic Sama noted, "Politics got mixed up in philately," as "there were plaints that Reagan was tampering with philately to get some Hispanic voters in his column." "The surprise move," observed a reporter in the *Richmond Times-Dispatch*, "was, in part, an 11th-hour bid to increase the administration's minority vote share." New Jersey columnist George W. Brown called it "a bid for votes from the nation's growing Hispanic population." "Politics permeates even stamp world," lamented a column in the *Akron Beacon Journal*. A *Washington Post* reporter also recognized the implications but argued that "earlier action might have provided greater political capital for Reagan."[31]

The director of the White House Office of Public Liaison warned, two years earlier, that the president's "initial upsurge [among Hispanics] has since reversed itself and is now declining at an alarming rate." "Hispanics," the same administrator warned that spring, "are beginning to view the Administration as racist and as one with little concern for the poor." Some conservative Republican Hispanic devotees existed, but they were largely Floridians of Cuban descent. Republicans were very unpopular with the rapidly growing population of Hispanic voters in places like New York, Texas, and California. The Congressional Hispanic Caucus had formed in the late 1970s, and several major Hispanic organizations formed a lobbying group named the National Congress of Hispanic American Citizens. With their influence growing, the Reagan administration tried to appeal more directly to these groups to gain support among this crucial demographic.[32]

Roy didn't say much publicly about politicians using him as political prop. He likely didn't know the full extent. In any event, his enjoyment of the bright lights and big stages seemed to trump any concerns he may have had about the matter. He certainly never shied away from an event where a politician would honor him. Roy usually voted Democrat, but he worked with political leaders on both sides of the aisle, so long as they helped promote his message and, quite frankly, him. Whatever Roy may have said about Reagan during the Social Security conflict, he never missed a chance to be by the president's side.

In January of 1985, Roy returned to Washington, DC, with Chris Barbee to attend Reagan's second presidential inauguration. Every inauguration, the Presidential Inaugural Committee hosts the members of the Congressional Medal of Honor Society, holding a special reception to honor these decorated veterans. Roy was close with many of the other Medal of Honor recipients and enjoyed these occasions with his friends. Barbee wrote about the event in the *El Campo Leader-News*. "Wherever we went," he noted, "Sgt. Roy Benavidez was recognized, and respected. . . .

Many asked for his autograph, others wanted to take his picture. Most just wanted to say 'thank you.'"[33]

In 1985, Roy began openly talking about Vietnam-era foreign policy for the first time. He had previously avoided dealing with broad questions about the war, choosing instead to focus on his own individual experience and that of his fellow servicemen. But that spring, Roy made the rare move of telling an interviewer, "It wasn't the soldiers who lost the war. It was the politicians and Congress." "We weren't defeated," he said in a statement reminiscent of a Reagan talking point, "we just weren't given permission to win."[34]

The following year, Roy finally managed to publish an autobiography. *The Three Wars of Roy Benavidez* was published on Veterans Day in 1986. "Three wars" refers to Roy's difficult youth, his fighting in Vietnam, and then his quest for the Medal of Honor. The book is a retelling of Roy's time in combat and his pursuit of the Medal of Honor, interspersed with brief flashbacks to military training and his youth in Jim Crow–era Texas. Roy wrote the book with Oscar Griffin, a Texas-based journalist, businessman, and Army veteran who had won a Pulitzer Prize for local reporting in 1963. It was published by Corona Publishing Company, a small firm based in San Antonio. A press release quoted Roy as stating that writing the book was "like being in the Army again—we worked day and night."[35]

The book provided another space for Roy to offer his feelings toward the war. It was a challenging subject. Roy's criticisms, like those of a lot of miliary boosters in the 1980s, were aimed at unnamed politicians who, he said, denied the real soldiers the ability to win. But the policies he criticized were not merely political concerns or the Cold War theories like containment or the domino theory. He criticized the nature of the war itself. Here, Roy had to tread very lightly. The fact of the matter is that the problems with the war's strategy were not solely the fault of political leaders. It was, after all, the Department of Defense and Roy's superiors in the Army who designed and orchestrated much of the war. Roy's most direct critiques were aimed at the South Vietnamese Army and the small cards with "Nine Rules" distributed to all American servicemen upon arrival in Vietnam, offering guidelines on how to "govern our conduct while in South Vietnam." "The naiveté," Roy wrote of the cards, "involved in their preparation is phenomenal."[36]

Much of the blame for the American limitations in Vietnam could have been laid at the feet of William Westmoreland, the United States military commander in Vietnam between 1964 and 1968. It was Westmoreland who influenced many of the misguided strategies that led to America's failures in Vietnam. This was no secret, and Westmoreland was emphatically criticized by others. Westmoreland was also the person who designed the "Nine Rules" cards. While Roy indirectly critiqued Westmoreland by bashing the cards, he likely didn't know that Westmoreland himself had ordered them to be produced and

Roy and William Westmoreland at veterans' parade, Chicago, 1986. Courtesy of the Dolph Briscoe Center for American History, The University of Texas at Austin.

distributed. Roy would never have knowingly publicly criticized his former commander, a posture undoubtably influenced by his own personal relationship with Westmoreland. The men knew each other. They had crossed paths several times during the 1960s and again in the 1980s. In fact, a few months before Roy's book was released, they marched together along with two hundred thousand other veterans at a "Welcome Home Veterans" parade in Chicago.[37]

Like many military boosters of his day, Roy also had to deal with the challenging problem of celebrating the American military while addressing its shortcomings in Vietnam. To suggest that the military itself had failed in Vietnam would be to indict America's armed forces as sometimes misguided, perhaps even immoral or weak. Like Reagan, Roy scapegoated politicians—the nameless, faceless softies who had limited America's ability to win in Southeast Asia. He did so as he celebrated veterans for protecting American freedoms.

But neither Roy nor Reagan ever openly engaged with the question of whether America should have been in Vietnam in the first place. While many American citizens have long rooted military service and sacrifice in the name of freedom and liberty, the hard truth is that no one from Vietnam was ever coming to the United States to threaten any American's freedom. The proof is in the past. The fall of South Vietnam and Cambodia to communist forces in 1975 did not present a direct threat to the national security of the United States or the individual liberties of its citizens. But that's not something Roy ever wanted to explore or that his audiences would have liked to hear. It was much easier for him to question the tactics of the war than its entire premise.

For Roy, the matter was also so personal. He couldn't possibly resign himself to the idea that his sacrifices and those of his friends had been made for the sake of a misguided cause. Psychologically, it would have been devastating to suggest that these sacrifices had been for naught. That would have been emotionally crushing and liable to cast doubt on the American military—the thing he believed in most in life. So Roy simplified his analysis, concluding that the war was lost by the idealistic politicians who cared too much about what other people might think. No one will ever really know what else Roy might have thought about the war. It is clear, however, why he could only critique it in a particular way.

The Three Wars of Roy Benavidez didn't get a great deal of national attention. Kirkus Reviews recommended it for "lovers of war stories and meat-and-potatoes virtues," noting, "It is direct and honest like its author." But it also dismissed the prose as "forgivable." The Associated Press ran an article mentioning the book, but its story read more like one of the many human-interest pieces on Roy rather than a review of his book. The book's best review was published in the *Austin American-Statesman*, which praised Roy's text for providing "details of one of the most incredible combat situations anyone has ever lived to tell about." "Occasional overwriting aside," the review concluded, "the book is a good read. And an inspiration for ordinary people."[38]

A handful of local promotional events took place. Roy published a related op-ed in the *Corpus Christi Caller-Times*, emphasizing the important roles Hispanic Americans have played in America's military. "I hope—no, I pray," Roy wrote, "for the day that an American will simply be an American, and no hyphens will be necessary to describe that person." The *San Antonio Daily Star* printed excerpts from the book, as did the magazine *Vista*, a Sunday newspaper insert distributed to newspaper subscribers in zip codes with large Hispanic populations.[39]

Roy received some positive letters in response to the book. One woman wrote, "In reading for nearly 20 years about the Vietnam war [*sic*], nothing that I have read has touched me quite the way your book has. Your courage and great humor shine on every page." A man from El Paso praised, "I read your book and found it to be emotionally absorbing. It was also inspiring and epitomized the true American spirit." Roy even received a note from Vice-President George H. W. Bush. "I have now read your story, and it really 'came alive,'" Bush wrote. "I will treasure the volume you sent me."[40]

But Roy's book did not meet his own expectations. It did not lead to a film, nor did it sell a large number of copies. In the months that followed, he still searched for a connection to someone in the film industry, and he wrote often to his publisher, imploring the company to find ways to sell more copies. He even convinced Jose Garcia to write to the sergeant major of the United States Army to help him with sales, suggesting that the book should be "standard Army historical literature." In 1989, an exasperated representative from the publisher responded to one of Roy's inquiries, writing, "I've explained this several times before but I'm going to try one more time: we cannot force bookstores or any other retailer of books to order copies."[41]

Meanwhile, Roy's in-person public appearances carried on as they had for years. The *Los Angeles Times* called him a "professional military hero," and the *Austin American-Statesman* noted, "The public won't leave him alone." Roy spoke at dozens of events, ranging from school assemblies to receptions hosted by small-town Chambers of Commerce and Rotary clubs. He carried around color eight-by-ten-inch photos, ready to sign for autographs. By 1989, his El Camino had 190,000 miles on it.[42]

During those years, Roy was still convinced there was going to be a movie made about his life. It wasn't only him who thought this. People around him brought up the idea of a movie or documentary constantly. His audiences asked about it often, and his friends floated the idea through their various networks. In 1987, one of Roy's old Green Beret buddies wrote to director

Luis Valdez, whose film *La Bamba*, about rock star Ritchie Valens, had achieved mainstream success. "The Hispanic community desperately needs role models," Roy's friend asserted. At one point, Roy worked with a writer on a movie script that they submitted to the Department of Defense for official approval, but the military found several problems in the description of the combat and suggested major revisions. This effort ended shortly thereafter. There was seemingly always talk of some agent or director who might be able to get the movie made, and in the late 1980s, Roy constantly told his audiences and journalists across the country that a film would be produced. Alas, it was never to be.[43]

Still, the late 1980s saw some big highlights for Roy. In May of 1987, he was inducted into the LULAC Hispanic Hall of Fame during a black-tie event in downtown Los Angeles. A few weeks later, he traveled to West Point, New York, to visit the United States Military Academy. The events of that weekend included the dedication of "The Benavidez Room," a conference room named in Roy's honor. The following year, Roy traveled to Panama over the Fourth of July along with Willard Scott, the weatherman on NBC's daily morning series *Today*. Perhaps the most special event of those years was Roy's trip to Silvis, Illinois, a town where the local Mexican American community had renamed a street "Hero Street" in honor of a small neighborhood that had sent over one hundred men and women into the armed forces, almost all of them Hispanic. Roy spoke there and served as grand marshal of their 1987 Memorial Day parade.[44]

In 1989, Roy and Chris Barbee attended the presidential inauguration of George H. W. Bush, whom Roy had known since his Medal of Honor ceremony in 1981. President Bush once told a writer of Roy, "Every time I see him I get goose pimples, realizing all of the wounds he received while defending our country. . . . Barbara and I think the world of this man."[45]

Roy addressing a group of young soldiers. Courtesy of the Dolph Briscoe Center for American History.

Barbee was particularly excited by the inauguration of "a Texas president and we were Texans and all the Texans were struttin' their stuff in Washington." Roy was among 146 of the 225 living Medal of Honor recipients who gathered in Washington for the inauguration. Barbee was honored when the president-elect and his wife, Barbara, stopped to visit with Roy. He was also thrilled when Barbara Bush, "with a glow on her face," flashed him a "Hook 'em, Horns" sign, the hand gesture of the University of Texas. "It was a grand inaugural for a Texan!" Barbee told readers back home. Roy sat on the podium during Bush's swearing in at the United States Capitol. "I tell you," he said to a reporter covering the ritual, "it puts a lump in your throat. It really does."[46]

ROY WAS LESS ACTIVE WHEN IN EL CAMPO. WHILE HIS DAYS ON the road were filled with receptions, parades, and ceremonies, at home he was more relaxed. He truly loved being a war hero, and he enjoyed the pomp and circumstance, the decorum and salutes, and the nights drinking and joshing with his military buddies. But it was also nice for him to be at home where he didn't have to play that role. It was easier and more comfortable, and he'd be under less pressure. He could goof off and have fun with his family. His youngest daughter, Yvette, called him "very funny, a gentle giant."[47]

Roy's children entered high school age in the 1980s. Denise, the oldest, graduated from El Campo High School in 1984 and matriculated at Texas Lutheran College (now University) just outside of San Antonio, where she majored in music for three years before leaving school to start her own family. She later went back to college and earned her degree. Yvette graduated from El Campo High School in 1988, and Noel two years later in 1990. The 1980s were Roy's kids' teen years, the days of high school, first loves, and self-discovery. Roy was there for a lot of it, but it was Lala who raised their children during the many days he spent on the road. When he was home, he was involved, driving them to school, enjoying family dinners, and helping them with their teenage struggles, however big or small. "I could always go to him if I had an issue or a problem," remembered Yvette, "and he always just knew the right things to say." His greatest weakness as a father was that he was gone so much, but it was also that very role of a traveling war hero that provided him so much sustenance, both emotionally and financially, and peace of mind during the time he was home.[48]

Lala was a quiet but fierce woman. She commanded discipline and respect. Denise called her mother "strict" but noted that "she didn't have to raise her voice at us. She had that look. . . . She wasn't going to take any crap from anybody, and if you did let her down, if we made her disappointed in us, you could just tell by that look."[49]

Like his Uncle Nicholas and Aunt Alexandria, who passed away in 1990 at the age of eighty-nine, Roy and Lala tried to teach their kids how to behave through their own example. They were exceedingly positive. They didn't loudly argue or complain, and they didn't gossip in front of their children. "They never said anything hateful or mean," remembers Yvette, who insists "they had every right" to be bitter toward the local people who publicly criticized her father. "I never saw him yell at anybody," Noel recalled. "I know he had disagreements, but it was just an adult conversation." It set an important example that their children continue to follow.[50]

Roy and Lala also tried to instill in their kids a strong work ethic, a difficult task when neither parent has a traditional full-time job. Their children heard stories about Roy's work as a child and of the difficult Army trainings. He didn't bombard them with constant lessons from the military, but they perceived from his heroics and esteem that he was a very hardworking man. That work, Roy and Lala insisted, would pay off in the long term. "We knew the value of a dollar," remembered Yvette, "and we knew that hard work will get you the finer things in life." The Benavidez kids, like Roy decades before, were also schooled in the significance of their family name. "We knew we had a name that needed to be respected," Yvette recalls, "and so I just didn't want to bring dishonor to the name."[51]

Noel had a tougher time with his dad than the girls. He was the youngest and the only boy, and Roy kept the closest eye on him. "He was strict," Noel remembers of his dad. "Everything had to be done the right way." Roy stayed on Noel about small things like proper manners and good grades. As someone who lectured kids about education and good behavior, he didn't tolerate any signs of alcohol or tobacco use. If Roy heard about one of Noel's friends drinking or smoking, he tried to forbid his son from hanging out with the boy. "You can't ruin the family name," Roy told Noel, echoing the lessons Uncle Nicholas once said to Roy.[52]

Noel did engage in some questionable behavior. As one of their family friends recalled, "Noel pushes his dad a lot." Roy caught wind of him drinking on a couple occasions. Noel's argument, he recalled, was "You do it. Why can't I?" Of course, that didn't exactly fly with the war hero. They butted heads, with Roy becoming angry at Noel anytime he heard rumors about his son's misbehavior. Roy couldn't possibly know all that Noel did in high school, but people around town would tell him if Noel was seen buying alcohol or attending a party. Noel remembered some rough early mornings when he was awoken by his father to answer for some accusation. "I don't think my sisters had to deal with that," Noel remembers.[53]

The greatest perk of being the youngest and only male sibling was that Noel had the pleasure of traveling with his dad. As Noel matured into his teenage years, Roy began to take his son along as his travel companion. The pair would mostly fly, but they also took some long road trips in Roy's El Camino. Noel was fifteen when they drove to Virginia and spent nearly two weeks on the road. He credits the trip with helping him learn to drive.[54]

Roy liked to have some fun with his kids, sometimes at their own expense. He used to drive Yvette to school in an old red pickup truck that she found embarrassing. Roy "never bought anything brand new," his daughter recalled. "He had this old jalopy of a truck, and I hated it because I was embarrassed." She despised the old vehicle so much that she asked her father, "When you pick me up, can you pick me up in the car, please?" But when the school bell rang and Yvette walked out, "he'd be outside of his truck with the window down going, 'Yoohoo! Yvette, over here!' honking the horn." "He was teaching me a lesson," she remembered. "You should never be embarrassed at what you have." Roy got a major kick out of such antics. He had enjoyed schoolyard pranks ever since he was a kid himself.[55]

As for Roy and Lala, they were close but independent. She had her own interests and group of friends. Plus, she often played the role of both parents when her husband was traveling. Still, they embraced traditional gender roles. Lala was a supportive wife who enabled her husband's itinerant lifestyle, despite so many of those trips taking him away from the family. She respected his vision of his duty. In return, he trusted her with making major decisions about the children while he was away.[56]

They were also a very private couple. In public, they didn't cover each other with constant kisses and hugs. Theirs was more of a quiet intimacy. Roy would flirt with her in front of the kids, teasing that she had almost dumped him when they were young. Denise remembered, "Dad would say silly things like he was trying to court Mom and Mom was trying to quit him," referring to Roy's pursuit of Lala in the 1950s. They would tease and flirt, sharing inside jokes about their past. They were old-fashioned. One could see it when it came time to dance. "My mother always loved dancing with him," said Noel. "My mother didn't dance with me at my wedding. She said the only man that she would dance with was my father."[57]

The family loved having meals together. They were "really big breakfast eaters," described Yvette of her parents. Lala did most of the meal preparation. When Roy did cook on his own, he made odd dishes that filled his children with wonder and disgust. Roy "liked anything" his daughter remembered. "He would mix pudding and ice cream and cereal and yogurt," said Yvette. "I mean just weird things. . . . I think he'd do it more for the shock value."[58]

There is little to suggest that Roy took much heed of his physician's continuous orders to lose weight. For years, even before he left the Army, every doctor he saw said he was too heavy. The reasons were his diet, age, and disability. Roy loved to eat, and he liked beer, especially when he was hanging out with his best friends. He struggled to manage his weight, which was all the more difficult for a man with his injuries and travel schedule. But he was committed to his exercise routine. Almost every day that Roy was in El Campo, he walked the path around Friendship Park. People would see him out there every morning, rain or shine, in the heat or the cold. He was religious about walking that unshaded path around the playgrounds, picnic shelters, and ball fields. He'd spend hours there, walking and thinking. His walks were some of the only time he truly spent alone.[59]

Financially, Roy and his family were healthier in the late 1980s. After the problem with the Social Security office, Roy was never again removed from the disability rolls. Those payments, along with his Medal of Honor stipend, allowed the Benavidez family to live a fairly comfortable life in small-town Texas. El Campo was an affordable place to live, and they lived modestly. They only had one credit card, an American Express, and they always paid it off at the end of the month. "They had no debt," Yvette remembered. "Their mentality was if we didn't have money to get it, we weren't going to buy it." "They were very simple people," recalled a friend. "They weren't flamboyant in their decor or their furnishings." When the kids really wanted an expensive item, they could ask for it for Christmas.[60]

Roy took trips with his family that were much different from his typical journeys. "My dad was actually a big proponent of family vacations," said Yvette. They would pack up a red cooler with sandwiches and drinks and enjoy a family picnic at rest stops along the way. They went out west to Yellowstone and Utah. They also traveled to Big Bend National Park in western Texas. On other trips, they went to Alaska; Hawaii; Seattle; Washington, DC; and Philadelphia. Roy wanted them to "see the sights," exposing his children to the iconic places of the country he loved so much.[61]

At home, Roy didn't watch much television, mostly news shows like *60 Minutes* and *Nightline*. He also enjoyed Benny Hill specials and some sitcoms. He didn't like movies, especially those about the Vietnam War, except for the John Wayne film *The Green Berets*, which depicted America's involvement in Vietnam as overwhelmingly positive. He listened to country music, having first fallen in love with the genre during his days as a migrant laborer. He particularly liked Johnny Cash, Charley Pride, and Freddy Fender, the Tejano country singer born in South Texas just two years after Roy. He also read a lot. "He always had a book in his hand," remembers Yvette. It was common for him to read thrillers by authors such as John Grisham and Tom Clancy, whom he met on several occasions. Roy enjoyed comic strips like *Beetle Bailey* and *Hägar the Horrible*.[62]

He loved when people would visit. Those who knew him best stopped by El Campo whenever they were nearby. Roy "kept his inner circle very tight," described one of his friends. But those who were in that circle received his full attention. When "it was time to visit," recalled one of his buddies, "there was no outside obstacles like a television or the phones. It was all on whoever was visiting him." They would sit and talk about current events or the military. He shared memories of combat with those who served. "He had a hell of a memory," said one of his military buddies. Roy would often offer to help his friends and their families if they needed a letter of recommendation for a job or school. His name carried a lot of weight in Texas. As Roy once told a reporter, "I can't snap my fingers and get something done, but it [his endorsement] does open a few doors."[63]

His best friends at the time were other veterans, especially Hispanic ones who had been Airborne or members of the Special Forces. At this stage in his life, his best friend was probably Benito Guerrero, a veteran of the 82nd Airborne who was born near San Antonio the same year as Roy. Guerrero was also a decorated noncommissioned officer, like Roy. They had served together at Fort Sam Houston during Roy's final months in the

Army. The two men shared similar backgrounds based on their Texas upbringings and experiences in the Army and war. Both were very involved with veterans' causes, and they became tight friends in the 1980s and 1990s, when they and other Hispanic Airborne veterans would spend a great deal of time at the Drop Zone Cafe outside of Fort Sam Houston in San Antonio, an Airborne bar, popular with Hispanic veterans who would gather near the base to enjoy beers, tacos, and war stories.[64]

Roy's home life was peaceful and he was surrounded by his family and close friends. He was happy and relaxed in his daily routine. He enjoyed the slow days in El Campo, running small errands and eating suppers with his family. At home, he could be himself and enjoy his family's little world. But at any moment, the phone in the den might ring again, and the hero would pack up and head back out on the road.

CHAPTER 13

TO BE AN AMERICAN

Roy always received a lot of mail. Ever since he was awarded the Medal of Honor, his mail and post office boxes were stuffed with letters. They came from every state in America and even overseas, sent from veterans, students, and everyday people who'd heard Roy's story and wanted to share the impact he had on their lives. Some wrote just to thank Roy for his service. Others requested any number of things—a picture, an autograph, or an appearance at some event. The requests came from as far away as Norway and Belgium. His home address was unlisted, so people had to search. Some found it. Others just sent letters to the El Campo Post Office or even the *El Campo Leader-News*. At the end of the 1980s, he was receiving up to fifty letters per week.[1]

Roy did his best to answer them all. Letter-writing was a private part of his life that few people knew much about. Roy sent hundreds, perhaps even thousands, of letters every year. If there was one person who appreciated how much mail Roy received,

it was his daughter Yvette. For years, Roy paid her to help cata-
log the correspondence. She would organize the letters by state
and file them in a cabinet, affixed with a small note indicating
Roy's answer.[2]

As time wore on, and Roy's fame began to fade, the letters
started coming less from fans of the military and more from people who turned to Roy for other reasons. These were people who
had found something meaningful in words Roy had said or in
what they believed he represented. They were folks who needed
not an autograph or picture but rather direction or hope.

People—especially young men—wrote to Roy to solicit his
advice for their own lives. One such letter came from the small
town of Delaware, Ohio. A young man wrote to Roy with the
dilemma of being "torn between my duty to my country and
the wishes of my mother." The eighteen-year-old wanted to join
the Army, but his mother was set against it. He wrote to Roy,
"not only to applaud your book and patriotism but also to ask
your advice on a dilemma that I'm faced with. . . . I would
greatly appreciate it if you could give me some sort of advice
on this issue." There is no record of what Roy wrote back to the
conflicted young man.[3]

In 1987, Roy received a handwritten letter from an
eighth-grade girl at Bonnette Junior High School near Houston
who had heard him speak at her school. The girl revealed that
her mother had been killed in a car accident some years earlier.
The driver, she wrote to Roy, was her stepfather, who at the time
"was on tranquilizers mixed with qualudes [sic] and alcohol." "I
suffered from this," the girl told Roy, and "hold my step father
responsible." She had responded to Roy's anti-drug message. "I
now know how important it is to not be messed up with drugs,"
she insisted. "I also want to be a very moral citizen, like (from
hearing you speak today) I think you are. I want to think [sic] you
for doing your very best at defending our country and opening

your heart to us. This means a great deal to me and my friends as well. . . . Your bravery and courage will also help us as well as our posterity."[4]

That same year, Roy received a bundle of cards from students at Killough Middle School in Houston, another place he had recently spoken. "Your story was incredible!" wrote one student. "It really touched me. I try to listen to what you said about 'will power,' and that it could do anything." "Listening to you it brought tears to my eyes," penned another. "I respect you for caring so much for your country and flag." "You also said," wrote another, "that 'we are the future leaders of the world' and that had a strong impact on me." "The color of our skin didn't matter to you just the color of the flag," wrote a student named Natasha. "To me, you are my favorite hero." They thanked him, expressed interest in learning more about the war, and told him they were looking forward to the movie about his life.[5]

The following year, Roy sent a letter and picture to a veteran who wrote to say that he was dying of cancer. "I'm more afraid now than I ever was in combat," the man told Roy. "Your letter maid [sic] me feel better than I've felt in the last six months. . . . I have your picture over my bed, and when I hurt real bad I just look up at a real brother, and it helps me a lot. I just hope a little of your bravery rubs off on me." The man told Roy in 1988 that "any day now, can be my last," but it turned out that he would live another twenty-three years, longer than Roy himself.[6]

For a brief period, Roy became pen pals with a young man who was struggling with his father's deployment to South Korea. Roy never spoke at the young man's school, but the boy somehow got ahold of Roy's address and wrote to share that he had found comfort and inspiration in Roy's book. In doing so, he also mentioned having a hard time with his father being sent to live so far away. Roy wrote back to the boy, comforting him by reminding him that his dad was involved in something important, and that the country needed them both to remain strong while they were apart. The boy's father wrote independently to Roy, thanking him "for your kindness." The father continued, "He found strength to go on by the heroism you exhibited in your book."[7]

Very few people close to Roy mentioned his extensive correspondence with his admirers. The author Pete Billac did write that Roy "likes the ones from kids best," but that was about it. Although Roy may have told friends that he received a lot of mail, no one knew quite how much. When Roy was at home, he spent much of his life in his den, surrounded by military memorabilia, opening those letters and reading their contents. This was a different experience for the hero, one set far apart from the glory of his days on the road. He didn't talk much about those letters or their meaning. But he kept them, and he answered nearly all of them. People were always telling Roy what he meant to them. Few ever stopped to consider what they all meant to him.[8]

When Roy wasn't at home answering mail, he was out on the road—off to speak at Lackland Air Force Base; the Texas Association of Mexican American Chambers of Commerce; Hispanic Heritage celebrations in Florida, California, and Texas; and seemingly every branch of the American Legion in his home state. There was no discernable pattern to these engagements beyond the theme of patriotism. Roy went everywhere. He was at Flag Day in Richmond, Virginia; the Midwest Hispanic Conference in Merrillville, Indiana; and American Heritage Week in Rock Island, Illinois. In the spring of 1992, he was in Colorado, where he spoke to an estimated 3,500 students. For a while, he traveled with a replica of the Vietnam Veterans Memorial wall, appearing with the model monument in Michigan, Wisconsin, Maryland, and Tennessee.[9]

In the late 1980s and early 1990s, Roy spoke at fewer events honoring him specifically and more at ceremonies celebrating the military more broadly. He also often spoke at Hispanic heritage events or celebrations of the big three patriotic American holidays—Memorial Day, the Fourth of July, and Veterans Day. Those holidays were special days for Roy, moments in time when it was normal to be such a staunch patriot. He embodied the spirit of these holidays every day of his life, but people seemed to appreciate that attitude most on the days when the main streets of America filled with flag-waving marchers in patriotic parades. "Roy P. Benavidez is what the Fourth of July is all about," wrote a Texas journalist in 1989. "Veterans Day is about Master Sgt. Roy P. Benavidez," agreed an El Paso reporter the following year.[10]

Out of all his speaking events, Roy's greatest joy remained his visits with young people at schools. He was especially invested in Hispanic-serving schools. "They need positive role models," he told an Abilene reporter about Latino students. "That's what I'm trying to be." His presence was an important symbol of Hispanic pride and achievement at a time when Hispanics were severely underrepresented in all aspects of American public life, despite being the fastest growing minority group in the country. Roy was an example for young Latino students, a hero of their ilk and a powerful symbol of Hispanic contributions to the United States. Years later, a Latino activist based in California remembered Roy's 1987 visit with Hispanic students in Santa Ana. "The children stood in awe to see his chest full of medals," the witness recalled, "and hanging down from his neck was the Congressional Medal of Honor."[11]

In 1991, Roy experienced one of the great honors of his life when a committee of Houston educators decided to name a new school after him. Roy had no idea it was coming. One day, he received an unexpected phone call informing him that a new $4.1 million facility would be dedicated in his honor. Roy was chosen because the school was expected to serve a large Hispanic population (85 percent), and the naming committee wanted to select a Hispanic icon. "He cares about kids," one of the educators explained. "He espouses what we believe in for our kids. He's a role model." They held a naming ceremony the following May, filled with band performances, the pledge of allegiance, and the singing of patriotic songs. Roy, of course, was also asked to speak. Roy P. Benavidez Elementary School is still in use today on the west side of Houston.[12]

In 1993, Roy started a fund to help Latino students in El Campo. His "Hispanic Education Scholarship Fund" kicked off that year with a banquet and raffle. The proceeds went toward scholarships of $300 each to local students who were enrolling in college. In 1993, the fund distributed ten such scholarships, increasing its total to fifteen in 1994 and twenty-five by 1995, when its annual event raised roughly $7,500.[13]

Meanwhile, Roy continued working to spread his own story. He still wanted a movie, and in 1992, he partnered with a company named Bronze Bishop Films to produce a one-hour documentary on his life. This small firm was in the business of "developing film and television projects which speak to the declining moral values in America." The proposal included Roy as an executive producer along with several individuals who had experience in the film industry. Their intent was to tell Roy's backstory and show "never before seen footage" of the 1981 Medal of Honor ceremony before ending the film with clips of Roy talking with schoolchildren. They thought the film could be shown on PBS and perhaps some cable channels. Unfortunately, it was never made. The proposal was probably about as close as Roy ever got to creating a feature film about his life.[14]

In 1993, the White House called Roy to ask if he would stand in for President Bill Clinton in presenting the Presidential Medal of Freedom to actress Martha Raye, who had entertained American soldiers during World War II, the Korean War, and the Vietnam War. Roy flew to Los Angeles with Jose Garcia for the ceremony. Pictures of Roy standing next to the woman nicknamed "Colonel Maggie" were printed in newspapers across America.[15]

In 1994, the Associated Press picked up the story of Roy meeting the family of Leroy Wright at Fort Bragg in North Carolina. Roy had previously corresponded with Wright's widow, but they had never before met in person. "Everywhere I go I mention your husband," Roy told He Ja Wright. That same year, Roy was back in the news when he served as a guest judge for the Mrs. America Pageant with *The Brady Bunch* actress Florence Henderson. Wherever Roy visited, local newspapers interviewed him and printed stories about his speaking engagements. Roy was still constantly in the media, especially in Texas. As the *San Antonio Express-News* observed, "Few national heroes have had more written about them than Roy Benavidez."[16]

Roy also worked on two more books. The first, *The Last Medal of Honor*, was published in 1990 by Pete Billac. A prolific author of books on widely ranging topics, Billac interviewed Roy extensively as part of his research. Roy happily participated, eager as he was to spread his story to as many people as possible. In public, Roy promoted the book, traveling across Texas for a handful of events where he autographed copies. Roy said that some of the book's sales revenue would be contributed to help build a new memorial for women veterans of the American war in Vietnam and to aid homeless Vietnam veterans.[17]

The book recounts Roy's heroics from May 2, 1968. It quotes heavily from written testimony provided by both Roy and Brian O'Connor in 1980, along with that of a handful of helicopter pilots who had been involved in the action. Billac spent a lot of time with Roy and clearly liked him a lot. The book is an admirable but somewhat brief and winding montage of Roy's heroics, supplemented with some short descriptions of other people's wartime heroics and reprinted copies of letters Roy received. It also includes an alarming diagram of Roy's body showing the locations his wounds.[18]

The Last Medal of Honor didn't receive much attention outside of a handful of positive reviews in Texas. A reviewer in Victoria praised it as "a story of blood and guts . . . and the courageous and selfless sacrifice that forged a hero and allowed him to tell his version of the Vietnam War. One that we can be proud of." The *El Paso Herald-Post* carried a very brief review from a local reader who called it "excellent," praising its "fine job portraying the life of a South Texas Indian/Hispanic orphan who suffered racial harassment while growing up." Another syndicated columnist wrote about Roy and the meaning of courage but did little to evaluate the book beyond describing the day of Roy's battle on May 2, 1968. Roy's hometown *El Campo News-Leader* offered the most extensive review, but even that was decidedly neutral.[19]

In 1995, Roy released a much more popular book titled *Medal of Honor*. This book was coauthored by John R. Craig, an Air Force veteran and journalist based out of Houston. He also ran a literary management company. H. Ross Perot, the Texas billionaire who at the time was between two high-profile presidential campaigns, agreed to write the foreword. Perot used the space to celebrate the "opportunities" provided by the United States. "I find Roy's life one with which I can empathize," Perot wrote, "and one that should make all Americans proud of the opportunities America offers to those strong enough to seize the chance." "As a fellow Texan," Perot concluded, "I have known about and admired Roy's courage and his fulfillment of the American dream."[20]

Medal of Honor was the best writing Roy ever published about his life. It's a straightforward biography, opening with the early details of his childhood before moving into his time in the Army. Like Roy's public persona, the book is serious but funny, with descriptions of poverty and battlefield action interspersed with tales of soldiers' jokes and military hijinks. It's true to reality, except the part about the timing of the death of Roy's mother, which he never publicly acknowledged. It's also imbalanced, dominated by Roy's time in the service, with few details about his life after Vietnam, except a brief chapter on his pursuit and receipt of the Medal of Honor. But even there, he downplayed his own role in the process, focusing instead on the unnamed Special Forces buddies who he said encouraged him to pursue the medal. Roy was always careful to say it had been others who had sparked his pursuit. To reveal otherwise might have led some to cast him as a glory hound. The book ends after a short discussion of Roy's fight to retain his disability benefits in 1983.[21]

In the book, Roy discusses his family's history in Texas. He didn't know many details of their land ownership or movements, but he understood the basic story. In some of the final writings of his life, Roy described his relatives who fought for Texas in its "war for independence." "In spite of the loyalty of the Bena-vides brothers," he wrote, "they were in danger after the war was won." More than lamentation, this heritage was a point of pride for Roy. "The Benavideses," he emphasized in the 1995 mem-oir, "were *vaqueros*, cowboys who had practiced their craft for two hundred years before the *gringos* came to sit at their feet and learn to be cowboys."[22]

In an epilogue, Roy offered perhaps his most thoughtful and challenging critique of the American war in Vietnam. "A great deal of the work that my buddies and I did was lost," he lamented. "The Vietnam conflict was a tragedy that should not have happened," he insisted, "because in my opinion the majority of the South Vietnamese did not understand or support individ-ual freedom. They were ill-prepared as fighters to wage war." Roy did not seriously question the basic premise of the global war to stop communism. His ideological conformity with the United States government and its military at that time prevented him from ever doing so publicly. He focused on the "soldiers who had died [so] that others might be free." And he insisted on honoring America. "I believe," he argued, "that only in America could I, a young Hispanic-Indian American, have risen to my place." It was for that reason, he insisted, that he gave speeches so often, and why he was so dedicated to sharing his experiences with others. It is young people who matter most, Roy wrote. "Only through the transfer of knowledge from generation to generation will free men survive."[23]

Roy hustled to promote his book. He personally shipped over one hundred copies to media outlets across the country, asking them to review the book. As with many of his efforts to publicize his story, Roy did not receive the response he desired. The book was only lightly reviewed, but it did impact a lot of people in ways Roy could not have expected.[24]

In the months after *Medal of Honor* was published, letters responding to Roy's book arrived in El Campo from across the United States and even from as far away as Germany, Korea, and Australia. The first edition included the address of Roy's post office box in El Campo where readers could write him directly. A Kentucky man wrote to share, "Your book inspired me. It lets me know that absolutely nothing can conquer the human spirit." A Vietnam veteran living in Chicago penned, "Your book made me cry and affected me greatly." The son of another veteran from Nevada wrote to say, "Your book has given me a lift and inspiration." A woman in Toronto called the book "truly inspirational" and sent along some poetry she had been inspired to write. A teacher in Germany wrote to say, "I enjoyed it [the book] very much. It touched me very much. . . . Thank you for speaking out for what you believe in," and, "Please know, Mr. Benavidez, that you are one of my heroes." A twenty-year-old community college student with cerebral palsy praised Roy's book as a "true testimony of the American spirit." He wrote, "The main reason I wrote this letter to you is to let you know that although I will never serve in the military the military has been an inspiration to me." A high school senior shared the impact the book had on him: "I am also very proud and grateful to you for serving our country in a very dangerous and controversial era." The young man attributed his decision to join the Army ROTC at the University of Texas to Roy's example. "I have been thinking about this for a long time," he wrote, "and I think your book pushed me over the edge." A high school student in Idaho wrote to share that he was her favorite author. "Because of you," the eleventh grader insisted, "many teenagers' lives have changed for the better. . . . Thank you for instilling in me more patriotism, for speaking against drugs, gangs, and dropping out of school." A fourteen-year-old in Florida wrote to tell him, "It was the best book I have ever read." A California man told Roy, "You are what makes me proud to be an American."[25]

Roy's latest book came out amid another busy time on the road. In 1995 and 1996, he spoke at dozens more events: the Oklahoma American GI Forum annual meeting; the Wright-Patterson Air Force Base Hispanic Heritage Month awards luncheon; Hispanic Heritage Month at Peterson Air Force Base; Hispanic Heritage Month for the Army Corps of Engineers in Philadelphia; the Army's 221st birthday celebration in San Antonio; a Latino veterans conference in Woodburn, Oregon; the San Jose American GI Forum Cinco de Mayo parade; Armed Forces Week at the National Security Agency; and an event at the Misawa Air Base in Japan. He spoke to students, cadets, and Hispanic groups; inmates, pilots, and police; even insurance underwriters. "He is an unabashed patriot, and a pleasure to talk to," wrote a Rhode Island journalist who saw Roy speak in 1996. "Like that medal he wears, you have to salute him."[26]

THROUGHOUT THESE BUSY YEARS, ROY'S HEALTH DECLINED. HE turned sixty years old in 1995, hardly an elderly man but also much older than his mid-40s, when he commenced his itinerant lifestyle. Roy was a war hero, but he was also an aging man saddled with hypertension, reduced lung capacity, and chronic severe pain. He was on the road too much to adequately manage his poor condition. And when he was gone, he was wrapped up in the moment, sharing stories, talking to thousands of people, and eating and drinking sometimes late into the night. Roy had escaped battle alive on May 2, 1968, but the wounds he sustained in that battle haunted him forever and increasingly began to slow him down.

In 1993, Yvette was at a routine optometrist visit when the doctor asked her, "How's your dad doing with the diabetes?" Yvette was "flabbergasted," she remembers, blurting out, "What?!" "Oh yeah," the doctor told her, "I diagnosed him about five years ago." Yvette told her family. They obviously knew that Roy had major long-term health problems, but they did not know about this. It was evident that their father had not been taking good care of himself, or at least not taking the diabetes diagnosis seriously.[27]

Roy had never had a great relationship with his own health. It is likely that he simply didn't know much about the seriousness of his conditions beyond the daily physical limitations. "He didn't do any research like we would do research today," explained Denise, "and try to figure out—doctor our own selves." It's also important to consider just how many problems Roy was facing. It was hard to keep up. He had pain everywhere, and the doctors' orders were a maddening maze of prescriptions and instructions. He didn't completely ignore their directions. He took dozens of pills every day, and he walked his mileage at Friendship Park. He would drive himself to regular appointments at the VA in Houston, but otherwise he thought he had a good handle on his health.[28]

Roy's inability, even at times unwillingness, to properly manage his own health was also related to the war. Roy's experiences with battle left him with a unique perspective about death and his own mortality. "I think he thought he was invincible," remembers Yvette, "that if he could do two tours in Vietnam and come back, almost die, intestines hanging out, you know, all that, that 'nothing's going to happen to me.'" For a man who had survived Roy's experiences in combat, the diagnosis of diabetes seemed deferrable. Roy had certainly navigated much more pressing health problems. Yvette explains that her dad's mindset was, "'with everything in life that I've been through, I've earned it.' That's how I feel he felt." Most days, he didn't feel any worse than on others. Every day was a gift anyway, so he just kept living.[29]

When it came to diabetes, Yvette thought Roy was "ignorant about the disease and the progression of it." Roy also didn't want his family to dwell on his health care. They had their own lives and interests. His kids were mostly out of the house or about to move off on their own, getting married and progressing in their careers. He became a grandfather in 1992. "I think he just didn't want to burden us with it," Denise explains. "It was just his own personal matter." "We'd ask how he is," and he would respond, "Oh, I'm fine. Don't worry about me." Roy was never truly "fine" by most people's standard. He was always sick and wounded. His family had little reason to think any one problem was much worse than the issues they saw him face every day. When their father, a man celebrated across the world for his superhuman feats, told them he was feeling okay, they believed him, and he just might have believed it himself.[30]

Things changed in 1997. That January, Roy and Noel traveled to Washington, DC, for Bill Clinton's second presidential inauguration. On their second night in the city, Noel, twenty-four years old at the time, went to the hotel bar to eat dinner and hang out with some acquaintances while his father was out with his Medal of Honor buddies. When Noel returned to their shared room, Roy was asleep. During the night, he remembered hearing his father get up "a couple of times, but I didn't think nothing of it."[31]

The next morning, the day of the inauguration, Noel looked over to find his father sitting upright on the edge of the bed. "He was just all bruised, his abdomen, his ribcage, that area," remembered Roy's son. Noel asked his dad if he was alright, and Roy brushed him off, just as he always did when his children asked about his health. "Don't worry about it. I'm fine. Don't worry about it." Noel began to get ready for the day. He shaved and showered and was walking out of the hotel bathroom to get dressed when he saw his dad still sitting there. Something was wrong. When Noel noticed Roy's speech "getting a little distorted," he called his mom who told her son to put Roy on the phone. They argued, but Roy dismissed her concerns, saying, "I'm just a little slow moving." They finished dressing and prepared for the day ahead.[32]

When they went downstairs, some of the other Medal of Honor recipients began to notice Roy's appearance. "He was really sluggish," Noel remembered. "He was pale. I'd never seen this side of him before. And his speech kept slurring off and on." Roy's buddies began asking him, "Roy, you don't look too good. What's wrong?" Roy blamed his appearance on a lingering cold. Lucian Adams, a famous World War II hero and Latino Medal of Honor recipient from Texas, asked Noel about Roy's condition. Shortly thereafter, Adams's daughter told Noel that Roy needed to go to a hospital. Another Medal of Honor recipient who was a doctor came over and looked at Roy. "You need to go to the hospital, Roy," the fellow hero told him. Roy responded, "I'm not going to no damn hospital," Noel recalls. "I'll go home before I go to a hospital."[33]

One of the military men in the crew suggested that the Walter Reed Army Medical Center "would accept him ASAP," remembered Noel, but Roy insisted that he fly home. Noel called the airline and arranged a flight back to Houston later that day. They went to the airport, where Roy had a bite to eat and started to feel a bit better. But he became very fidgety on the flight. He experienced serious discomfort as the plane rose and began getting aggravated. The flight attendants finally let him stand up and he began to relax. Roy was picked up at Hobby Airport by Yvette and her husband, Rene, who observed that Roy was "having difficulty breathing." "I remember," said Yvette, "just he sat in the back [of the car] and he was just still talking, but his voice sounded weak and he just looked really bloated." They took him to his doctor in El Campo and he was diagnosed with pneumonia, possibly stemming from a case of the flu.[34]

From that point, Roy's life was deluged by an avalanche of health problems. His chronic health problems worsened, and his organs began to show signs of failure. He was in constant pain, he had trouble breathing, and his legs began weeping from the diabetes, which he had never managed well. "That was the worst of it," remembers Denise, "to see the legs, fluid just pumping out of the pores of his legs, and he'd be soaking wet in his sweats and the sheets and everything and they'd try to wrap him up in towels and bandages to stop the weeping. It was horrific." He most likely had some type of kidney disease related to his diabetes. He was retaining water in his belly and would become bloated to the point where his kids felt it necessary to take him to the VA hospital in Houston. At one point, his regular doctor in El Campo told his children that he had congestive heart failure. Roy didn't have long to live.[35]

"It was just a roller-coaster ride after that," Noel remembers. "It was very tense." Roy was in and out of the VA hospital. All the kids pitched in to help. Noel and his wife moved back to

El Campo from Houston. Denise and Yvette were already living nearby. The children helped Lala by taking turns taking care of their father. It was incredibly time-consuming, emotional, and stressful. They were losing him and were spending hours driving back and forth between Houston and El Campo in an endless, circuitous process that offered only temporary help with no end in sight.[36]

Still, Roy somehow kept going. His health no longer allowed for such a rigorous travel schedule, but he managed to keep some of his speaking commitments in 1997, even after his health scare. In April, he flew to Bismarck, North Dakota, to speak with the National Guard Association of North Dakota and the Bismarck VFW. In September, he went to Alaska, where he spoke at Fort Richardson, the University of Alaska, and a local middle school. That Veterans Day, in November, he spoke in New Jersey at a Vietnam veterans memorial service.[37]

Back at home, the constant trips to the Houston VA hospital took a serious toll on the family. Lala also went, but it was the kids who usually drove their parents to the visits. They were all exhausted, and Roy was going through a lot of "psychological issues at that time," remembers Yvette, "because I think he knew then 'this is the end.'" He was still in good enough spirits that he "cracked jokes," but he was definitely "frustrated," recalls Denise. "He just wanted to escape," says Yvette. The people in the hospitals wanted Roy to see a psychiatrist. They also wanted to prescribe antianxiety medication because "I think he was starting to have panic attacks," explained Yvette. "I think fear was settling in. . . . He didn't want to take the medicine. He didn't want to see the psychiatrist." "He was getting to be very combative with everyone there at the hospital," said Denise, "to where they were starting to strap him down."[38]

The family began having significant problems with the Houston VA. Roy was no one's version of a dream patient, but his treatment there was certainly unbecoming of a veteran, especially for one of the most celebrated war heroes in the United States. Roy did not enjoy having needles inserted into his arms, and he tried to remove them, which led the hospital staff to begin re-straining him to the bed. "We would walk in, and he'd be re-strained, and that was really hard to see," remembers Yvette. One of Denise's friends who worked at the Houston VA once checked in on Roy and discovered that he was also being given drugs for sedation. When Noel heard this and tried to get the responsible physician on the phone, the doctor blew him off during a golf match. "I was furious," Noel said.[39]

At the same time, the hospital staff was allowing all sorts of visitors into Roy's room. While once visiting his father, Noel found a crowd of "just random people," explains Yvette, "want-ing to talk to him, [and asking for] autographs." Noel would have to tell the staff not to allow visitors who wanted to meet the hero. The family also found a sharp object sitting out in the open in their father's room and were concerned about his access to the item given his current mental state. He could have grabbed it and hurt somebody, even himself. Then one day, Roy's Medal of Honor wristwatch went missing. It's a unique watch given only to Medal of Honor recipients, and someone at the hospital had taken Roy's while he was admitted. Incredulous, the family in-quired about the issue and the watch was returned anonymously, but it further eroded their relationship with the Houston VA. "I felt like they were not taking his health care seriously enough for us," Yvette recalls.[40]

In May of 1998, after months of questionable treatment in Houston, the family finally had enough and decided against ever sending him back. With some assistance from Roy's military buddies, they arranged to have him transported by ambulance from Houston to BAMC in San Antonio, back to the hospital where he was treated after both tours in Vietnam. The Houston

VA, concerned about a possible public relations nightmare for their treatment of the famous veteran, urged the family to keep Roy in Houston, but his family and friends refused. His friends essentially "came and kidnapped Dad," Denise says, and took him to BAMC, where he remained until his next release. They decided to take him to BAMC for future stays. He would certainly have more privacy in San Antonio, as the Army could better restrict access to his room.[41]

BAMC was better for Roy and his family. San Antonio is about twice as far from El Campo as Houston, but the improved care was worth the trip. The family took him to San Antonio when excessive fluid collected in his body and needed to be drained. Typically, these visits involved an eight- or nine-hour outpatient procedure that took most of the day. Sometimes he would stay overnight, and his family would lodge at the Fisher House, a residence near BAMC that provides shelter for military families whose loved ones are in the hospital. Roy's military buddies in the San Antonio area also helped. His good friend Benito Guerrero lived in San Antonio and would sometimes meet the family halfway between El Campo and San Antonio to drive Roy to BAMC.[42]

But Roy's health continued to spiral downward. He developed anemia, and his kidneys began to show signs of failure. "They couldn't put a time on it," Noel remembered of the doctors' answers. "They couldn't say, 'He's going to die in a year. . . . He's going to die in three months.' . . . They just said they were going to do the best they can and we're going to have to do the best we can."[43]

In October of 1998, doctors informed Roy that they would need to amputate his right leg at the knee. His diabetes had caused severe nerve damage in his leg and left him exposed to infection and further tissue damage. He received the amputation, then started rehab and was fitted for a prosthetic leg. Roy experienced "phantom pains" in the missing leg. What a cruel twist. Roy could never escape pain. For the last thirty years of his life, he lived every day in pain, feeling it even in the leg that was no longer there.[44]

A couple weeks after his amputation, a reporter from the *San Antonio Express-News* visited Roy to write another feature story about the famous Texan. Roy at the time was rehabbing in Methodist Hospital Northeast, having just come off another surgery a few days before. The article offered a grim update for fans of Roy Benavidez. The author opened the piece with an anecdote about Roy emitting "a long, high-pitched moan" due to the pain coming from his amputated leg. Roy was shown in a wheelchair sitting by a window talking to another vet. Another image showed him using a walker with the help of a physical therapist, his face grimacing in obvious pain. "He has a long road ahead," the author told readers. "He wants to continue inspiring kids to stay off drugs and get an education, a mission he'd gladly undertake, if only his body cooperates with his mind and spirit." Still, Roy's patriotism rang through the interview. "I'm proud to be an American," he told the reporter.[45]

That article was reprinted in newspapers across Texas in early November, just before Veterans Day. The coverage upset some of Roy's friends and family who didn't like the depiction of him as weak or suffering. One family friend wrote a letter to the editor of the newspaper because "she didn't like to see Dad like that," remembers Denise. "No one did, but it was the reality of it all."[46]

Letters started coming to the hospital. The news coverage had alerted readers to Roy's situation, and some of those readers began sending cards and notes to his room at Northeast Methodist. Roy received cards and handwritten notes from all over the country—East Chicago, Indiana; Omaha, Nebraska; Manchester, Maine; Hoover, Alabama; Latrobe, Pennsylvania; West Point, New York; and, of course, from all over Texas. The mail came from as far away as Australia and South Korea. Some of the people had heard Roy speak and referenced a moment from their memories. Others mentioned his book. Many thanked him for his service to the country. Nearly all wished him a speedy recovery.[47]

The most touching letters came from students, some of whom Roy had visited. Teachers asked entire classes to make get-well cards using craft paper and crayons. These projects came to Roy in the hospital, signed by dozens of students who left brief messages of encouragement. Students drew flags, soldiers, and tanks on the cards. One young Hispanic student wrote, "I never had a hero but you are my first hero."[48]

Other students wrote essays or filled out worksheets explaining the meaning of the flag and answering the question, "What does it mean to be an American?" Kids in grades 1 through 8 sent these projects to Roy in the hospital. Being an American "means we help," wrote a second grader. "It means to share." "In America we get all kinds of choices," declared a first grader. For another, being an American "means I can go to school here, and keep some of my friends." A lot of the first graders wrote that the flag makes them think of veterans.[49]

An entire class of fifth graders from Orange Grove, Texas, wrote to share that they were learning about Roy and the Vietnam War. They were ten and eleven years old, and they sent juvenile but heartwarming messages. "You will be a hero for all of us for the rest of our lives," one of the students told him. "I think you are way cool," wrote another. "I think you are the bravest man in the world," one student told him. "You are a true hero," another student penned. "I am also very sorry that that [sic] they cut off your leg." A ten-year-old Hispanic girl wrote, "I'm proud of you for doing what you did. . . . P.S. you're my hero!" They wished him well and invited him to visit their class when he got out of the hospital. He would have loved to go.[50]

Roy lay in his hospital bed recovering from surgery. He laid there in pain, aided by medications designed to keep him comfortable. After he lost his leg, his family knew he wouldn't live much longer. The letters he received were a bridge from the past to the future. Roy had once been like some of those at-risk kids. That's why he was so motivated to speak with Hispanic youths about their direction in their life. It was that orphan boy, grown up into a heroic man, who said such encouraging messages to the kids he met across America. Some might have disagreed with his approach, but in the end, that's what he most wanted to be, a role model for the Hispanic youths of Texas, someone who could help children find a path toward a happy, productive life.

That Veterans Day of 1998 was a rare one, among the very few when Roy Benavidez was not out somewhere marching in a parade or delivering a speech. He still had several outstanding speaking engagements and was upset about missing them while he recovered in the hospital. But in some ways, the audiences came to him that year. In the hospital, he had those letters, the mail from young students, the ones he wanted to reach most, the ones he always called the "future leaders of America."[51]

Chris Barbee remembered Roy expressing frustration during those days that he couldn't make a speaking event in Philadelphia where he was supposed to deliver a talk to students. Of course he couldn't go. He was bedridden, sick, and medicated, having recently lost his leg. But he was concerned about missing his favorite events, the speeches when he was out on the road talking to young people. He never wanted to stop. He never grew too tired of being on the road. And even as late as November 17, 1998, he was still holding out hope for a movie. "Hopefully soon," he responded to one admirer that day in a letter, "we can make a movie about my life, and then we'll be able to show America what I'm really all about."[52]

Roy remained in the hospital for a few weeks after the story ran in the *San Antonio Express-News*. His closest friends and family came to see him. By then, Roy knew he was dying. Jose Garcia saw Roy near the end and remembered Roy asking him, "Do me a favor. Look after my family." Roy said something similar during a visit with Chris Barbee. When Barbee visited Roy, he saw his good friend lying in bed, disheveled and barely able to speak. Roy grabbed Barbee by the front of his shirt and pulled him closer as he struggled to say something. Barbee couldn't quite make it out, but he thought Roy was asking him "to look after his family." "Okay, Roy," Barbee told him. "There was a sense of relief and he let go of my shirt," remembered Barbee. "That was our last conversation."[53]

ROY BENAVIDEZ DIED AT 1:33 P.M. ON NOVEMBER 29, 1998. He was sixty-three years old. His death was caused by sepsis and respiratory failure stemming from aspiration pneumonia. He also had anemia and chronic liver disease, and his heart and kidneys were failing. In some regard, it was a miracle that he lived as long as he did. He had carried the wounds of May 2, 1968, from that day until his last.[54]

In Texas, the news was broadcast over the radio and local television. Governor George W. Bush ordered all flags across the state flown at half-mast. "Roy was a great Texan," said the governor, "a Medal of Honor winner, a man of great courage and determination." Just down the road at Fort Sam Houston, over one hundred soldiers were eating a meal in a busy mess hall when news of Roy's death came on the television. "Every soldier in the room stopped eating and sat staring at the big-screen tv," one of the soldiers wrote to Lala. "Not a sound was made. . . . That's the kind of respect your husband deserved." Later that week, Dan Rather offered an obituary on the national *CBS Evening News*.

Rather said: "Somebody once told Roy Benavidez they thought his one-man rescue mission was extraordinary. He replied, 'No that's duty.' And that's a hero."[55]

Roy's obituary appeared in newspapers from Miami to Seattle. All the obituaries mentioned the Congressional Medal of Honor and described the actions that earned him the award. "Because of Benavidez and others like him, our lives are free, our nation lives and our world is blessed," wrote a Hispanic columnist in Texas. Some mentioned his work speaking at schools. Many of the articles quoted him as recently saying, "I am proud to serve my country, serve it well."[56]

Condolences addressed to Lala and "family" poured in from across the United States. People wanted to share how much Roy had touched their lives and express their sympathy and grief. Many of the cards were sent by people who had heard Roy speak. They said wonderful things about him. One of the letters was from a Latino soldier stationed in Alaska who had just seen Roy the previous year. "He was a strong yet humble, caring man," he wrote. "Roy has been a true role model for me and he makes me proud to be a soldier and proud to be an American." One couple made a donation on Roy's behalf to the Houston elementary school that bears his name. Others passed along their prayers and blessings. The cards and letters came from all over—Anaheim, Wichita, Shreveport, Honolulu, Denver, Chicago, Kansas City, Nashville, New Jersey, New Hampshire, and more. Many of the writers had never met Roy, but they thanked him and Lala for his service and expressed their sympathies that he was gone.[57]

There were services in El Campo and San Antonio. Unbeknownst to Roy's family, he had already made arrangements to be buried at Fort Sam Houston National Cemetery instead of in El Campo with much of the rest of his family, including Uncle Nicholas and Aunt Alexandria. He wanted to be buried on base, at a place where Army men did their jobs. His buddies would join him there one day, and so too, eventually, would Lala.[58]

A rosary service was held on the evening of Tuesday, December 1, at St. Robert Bellarmine Catholic Church in El Campo, where Roy, Lala, and all their children were married. The crowd was standing room only, and overflowed into the parish hall. Passersby paid their respects to Roy, who lay in a coffin draped in the American flag and surrounded by flowers, the logo of the 82nd Airborne, and the battlefield cross of his helmet resting on his rifle. Roy's good friend Chris Barbee fought back tears as he delivered an emotional eulogy to his buddy of more than twenty years. "It was his willingness to stand up and be counted that made him special," Barbee said. "And that trait endeared him to people all over this country."[59]

After the El Campo ceremony, members of the Special Forces Association escorted Roy's body back to San Antonio. On that Wednesday, he lay in an open casket at the Fort Sam Houston Main Post Chapel. Soldiers came to pay their respects. Roy was a legend in the Special Forces community. "There's no one in Special Forces who doesn't know Roy Benavidez by reputation," said a major general from Fort Bragg who came for the funeral.[60]

On Thursday, December 3, Roy's funeral was held at the historic San Fernando Cathedral in San Antonio, the oldest church in Texas. It's a big, beautiful Roman Catholic cathedral built in the French Gothic style, with cream-colored limestone walls, stained-glass windows, and twin bell towers. That morning, more than a thousand mourners came to San Fernando Cathedral. It was a bright, sunny day in San Antonio with temperatures in the upper seventies. The church was packed. Members of the media wanted to bring in cameras, but they were stopped by Roy's friends and family who preferred a private affair. The attendees had driven from far and wide. A group of veterans who'd met Roy a decade before in Chicago drove through the night to attend. The priest leading the service noted how both Roy and Jesus had been "willing to give it all up for the sake of others." "I hope and pray that all of us learn that important lesson," he said. Another of Roy's friends described him as "a real flesh and blood hero to all of us—and then some." It was an emotional and powerful affair, "the type of funeral," Chris Barbee said, "that a Medal of Honor recipient should get."[61]

After the event at San Fernando, a motorcade drove to Fort Sam Houston National Cemetery for the burial. It was a traditional military service. The pallbearers, firing squad, and buglers were Green Berets from Fort Campbell in Kentucky. Roy's family sat in the front row underneath a collapsible tent. After the chaplain made his remarks, the cadets offered a twenty-one-gun salute and the bugler played "Taps." The soldiers collected and folded the flag draping Roy's casket, and a major general from Fort Bragg presented it to Lala. The men lowered Roy's body into the ground where it remains today. Roy's grave is located near the entrance of the cemetery, in the shade of an oak tree, underneath a towering pole holding aloft an American flag.[62]

EPILOGUE

WHEN ROY DIED, LETTERS POURED INTO EL CAMPO FROM every corner of America. Thousands of people wanted to share with Lala and her children just how much Roy had touched their lives and to express their condolences and grief. The people who sent cards and letters came from all walks of life. The secretary of the Army wrote, "We hope that you and your family find solace and inspiration from the memory of who he was and all that he gave to the nation." A group of Hispanic fifth-grade students in Laredo wrote to Lala, "We wanted you to know how sorry we were and to let you know our prayers are with you and your family." The letters and cards ranged from sad to inspiring. Some of the writers had met Roy and shared stories of seeing him speak. Others had only heard of him in the news but felt compelled to express their sorrow at the loss of such an important American hero. Together, these messages helped give shape to the meaning of the life of Roy Benavidez. With the passage of time, the letters began to slow. When that happened, Roy started to become a different type of symbol, no longer a living hero but one from the past, and the honorifics started all over again.[1]

In 1999, the United States Army named a new complex at Fort Bragg after Roy. The $14 million Roy P. Benavidez Special Operations Logistics Complex was dedicated on August 16, less than nine months after his passing. Lala flew to North Carolina along with her daughters, their husbands, and Denise's children to attend the ceremony. It was a homecoming of sorts for Lala, who had lived at Bragg for much of the 1960s, and Denise, who had been born there. Lala cut the opening ribbon, and her grandsons helped reveal the sign for the new complex.[2]

In July of 2000, Roy's memory was celebrated as part of a two-act play called *Veteranos: A Legacy of Valor*, which ran for five nights at the Los Angeles Theatre Center. Roy was one of four Hispanic Medal of Honor recipients whose stories were dramatized in the play. "This is the first time within the Latino Hollywood community," the show's executive producer declared, "where our veterans are celebrated and honored by their own." Noel flew to California for a performance. "I could hear people sniffling in the audience," he told a reporter about the emotional show. "One woman just started bawling." The play came to Texas in 2002, with performances in Houston and San Antonio. The actor Emiliano Torres played Roy in the production.[3]

On May 2, 2001, the thirty-three-year anniversary of Roy's heroic actions in Cambodia, the Texas Legislature honored him with a posthumous Texas Legislative Medal of Honor, making him only the third person ever to receive that award (Audie Murphy would get his in 2013). Lala and her children attended this ceremony, too. Texas governor Rick Perry said, "We sometimes use the term 'hero' too loosely. But in the case of Roy Benavidez, there is no other word." "Our family is proud," Yvette told a reporter, "and we know our father is, too." One of the legislators commented on Roy's impact as a speaker and role model for young people, suggesting that "Roy saved more than those eight lives."[4]

On July 21, 2001, the United States Navy christened a new ship named the USNS *Benavidez* during a ceremony in New Orleans. Lala served as the ship's sponsor and enjoyed the honor of cracking a champagne bottle against the bow. Denise and Yvette were the matrons of honor, with Noel a guest of honor. Each of Roy and Lala's children brought their own spouses and kids. The Navy put up the whole family at the Hilton Riverside near the French Quarter. A special dinner the night before paid further tribute to Roy and his family. Some of Roy's other family and friends also came to the event, including his brother Roger, his cousins, and his friends Ben Guerrero, Jose Garcia, and Steve Sucher. A vice admiral in the Navy offered remarks, promising, "The ship you see before you will stand for the same ideals held by Roy Benavidez." "The way it's built," said Yvette, "you can tell that nothing is going to bring it down—just like my dad." The USNS *Benavidez* is a noncombat logistics ship. It made its maiden voyage in 2004 and is still in service to the United States Navy.[5]

Later that same summer, the Hasbro toy company released a limited-edition Roy Benavidez GI Joe. It was part of a special series of GI Joes depicting famous Medal of Honor recipients. The image on the cover of the box shows Roy in soldier's camouflage firing an automatic weapon next to a helicopter. The twelve-inch collectable comes with accessories including a map, two machine guns, extra ammunition, a radio, and a knife. He's wearing a Green Beret uniform with his name stitched on the outside, an outfit no one in his B-56 unit would have ever worn into combat. An expert on the matter might say the apparel and weaponry is inaccurate. Roy's Medal of Honor citation is printed on the inside flap. The doll retailed for thirty dollars.[6]

Noel thought his dad would have been "tickled pink" about the GI Joe. "He'd be cracking jokes about it." Yvette kidded that her dad "is looking down smiling, saying, 'I am not a doll. I am an action figure.'" Whatever one calls it, Roy's GI Joe was the first ever produced to resemble a Hispanic hero. The director of marketing for GI Joes said, "Roy's courage was unparalleled, and we are deeply honored and humbled to create a figure in his likeness." "It's a morale booster," Noel said, "that Hasbro is finally recognizing a Hispanic." The syndicated Hispanic columnist Victor Landa agreed, suggesting, "Many of these figures are going to end up surrounded by candles on impromptu *altares*— alters." "It's a cultural thing that would take more than one column to explain," Landa wrote. "Let's just say that it has to do with hopes and loyalties."[7]

In the fall of 2000, the city of Cuero, Texas, broke ground on the site for a bronze statue of Roy. A group led by Roy's cousin hired a Dallas-based sculptor to complete the monument. They raised the money themselves, relying on individual donations through a handful of fundraising tactics. They sold inscribed bricks to be laid on a walkway approaching the statue. Their efforts were bolstered by members of the West Point class of 1982, who donated several thousand dollars to honor the man they heard speak more than twenty years earlier. The organizers also sold raffle tickets and held a dance at the local VFW. It took four years and cost a reported $50,000 to erect the six-foot-eight-inch sculpture across from Cuero High School. "It's a beautiful statue," Lala said at the unveiling. "It looks just like Roy." The monument is still there today. It shows Roy leaning over a raised knee with his rifle in his hands.[8]

Roy's image can also be seen today at the Reagan Presidential Library in Simi Valley, California, in a permanent exhibit called "Honoring American Heroes." The exhibit features the two men Ronald Reagan presented with the Medal of Honor. The first is a World War II veteran named William J. Crawford, who was initially thought to be dead and awarded the medal posthumously in 1944. Crawford was later rescued alive from German captivity, but he never received a formal ceremony until Reagan held one for him in 1984. Roy is the other. His Medal of Honor is on loan to the library. It's displayed in a case in that hall of heroes along with a picture of Reagan and Roy from the day of his ceremony in the Pentagon.[9]

Roy's story continues to be told in a variety of forums. In 2015, the military historian Eric Blehm published *Legend: A Harrowing Story from the Vietnam War of One Green Beret's Heroic Mission to Rescue a Special Forces Team Caught Behind Enemy Lines*, a book that provided extensive details about Roy's May 2 mission, including more information about the pilots involved. Two years later, Roy's daughter Yvette published a children's book about her father's life and military service. Another military buff has also written a children's book about Roy's heroic actions. In 2019, the Army released a graphic novel as part of its "Medal of Honor" series that offered an illustrated depiction of Roy's 1968 heroics.[10]

Roy's name dots a smattering of other venues. There is a Roy P. Benavidez Elementary School in San Antonio, in addition to the one in Houston. Colorado Springs has a Roy P. Benavidez Park. In May of 2017, the Texas Legislature passed a bill designating a portion of Highway 71 as the "Master Sgt. Roy P. Benavidez Memorial Highway." Fort Moore in Georgia (formerly Fort Benning) has a MSG Roy P. Benavidez NCO Academy. El Paso has a Roy P. Benavidez United States Army Reserve Center. The city of Eagle Pass, Texas, has a Roy P. Benavidez Recreation Center. Several Airborne and American Legion chapters have renamed their groups in memory of Roy.[11]

Roy continues to be considered for other honors. When the Department of Defense recently decided to rename American military bases that carry the names of Confederate soldiers, Roy's name was a common suggestion for new honorees. Most who proposed Roy's name suggested it be used as a replacement for

Fort Hood in Texas or Fort Bragg in North Carolina, where Roy trained and spent several years of his life. Among those who advocated for renaming bases after Roy were the League of United Latin American Citizens, the Congressional Hispanic Caucus, *Texas Monthly*, and Congressman Joaquin Castro. The Army instead chose General Richard E. Cavazos, its first Hispanic brigadier general and a friend of Roy, for Fort Hood, and the name Fort Liberty for Fort Bragg. But the Army did rename a street for Roy: Fort Liberty includes a road named Benavidez Street.[12]

There is one elusive honor that Roy's supporters have been unable to secure. Many years ago, in El Campo, Chris Barbee suggested naming a local elementary school, Northside Elementary, after Roy. It seemed appropriate. The school was located in Roy's hometown, and he loved speaking with kids. Named for a mere area on a map, Northside Elementary seemed like a good candidate to carry the name of a local hero. Plus, it was only about a mile from Roy's old house. But Barbee abandoned the effort after learning about the onerous process of gathering hundreds of signatures of registered voters.[13]

In 2015, Roy's daughter Yvette helped reignite the push to rename Northside Elementary after her father. She was inspired, in part, by looking through her father's old papers and coming across a cache of letters written by Northside students in 1980 asking President Jimmy Carter to approve Roy's medal upgrade. Northside Elementary students were also in the choir that sang on the night Roy was welcomed home after receiving the Medal of Honor.[14]

Yvette worked with a handful of other local citizens to collect the signatures needed for the school board to consider their proposal. They gathered support by convincing local businesses to publicly display the petition. Yvette also garnered assistance from outsiders who understood the importance of her father.

Marcus Luttrell, of *Lone Survivor* fame, wrote a letter of support. So, too, did a historian writing a biography of her father. Additional backers wrote letters and emails of support to school board members.[15]

After four years, the name of the elementary school finally went to a vote before the El Campo Board of Trustees in November of 2019. The choice before the board was to rename the school Roy Benavidez Elementary or keep the current name of Northside Elementary. Much to Yvette's chagrin, the board voted 4–2 against changing the name to Roy Benavidez Elementary. The school board members who voted no refused to speak with a reporter who'd asked about their decision. The *Victoria Advocate* editorial board called the school board's decision "a shame." Yvette was hurt and disappointed, but, she said, "this just means his name is meant for something bigger."[16]

In some form or another, Roy's memory continues to live. The push to rename a military base in his honor brought his name back into the mainstream news, especially in Texas. In June of 2020, the *Dallas Morning News* ran a feature explaining Roy's importance to a new generation of Texans. There also remains talk of a possible film, but today's filmmakers face many of the same challenges as Roy did in his own efforts to convince a major studio to produce a movie about his life. As recently as 2020, the director Edward James Olmos testified to Congress that "the film and television studios do not want to give us the opportunity to create a superhero because they are content with their belief that Latinos must be feared and kept in their place." Olmos—an actor and director whose credits include *Stand and Deliver*, *Selena*, and *Battlestar Galactica*—had long dreamed of making a film based on Roy Benavidez. But "Hollywood does not want to make a movie," he concluded, "about the life of a real-life superhero who happens to be Mexican American."[17]

To this day, the story of Roy's valor continues to appear in newspaper columns citing the example of his bravery on May 2, 1968, and people still watch clips of his speeches on YouTube. The story of his valor is still regularly shared on dozens of websites and podcasts, and every Memorial Day and Veterans Day inspired speakers tell their audiences about the tale of Roy's courage. They usually focus on the fighting and his ability to overcome poverty, embracing the same messages that Roy once did in speaking about his own journey. He remains an icon in the Special Forces community and a role model for young Latinos, whether they're interested in the military or not. The progeny of ancestors who could never assimilate, he became a bona fide American hero through his wartime heroics, courage, and willingness to fight for not only his country but himself.

Today, Roy's offspring manage his estate and continue to help curate his legacy. His kids are regularly invited to participate in events honoring their father's military service. Yvette maintains a Roy P. Benavidez Facebook page that draws hundreds of "likes" for every post. Strangers routinely contact her to share memories of hearing her father speak decades ago or to express their appreciation for his military service. Roy's children deal with all sorts of requests, interactions, and even promises. They are honorable and generous stewards, continuously willing to share their father and his memory with people all over the world. Especially since Lala's passing in 2019, it is they who have taken up the mantle from their father of managing and interpreting his messages and importance for the many others who find power in his story.

His life will always make up so much of theirs. They know that; they didn't ask for it, but they, like him, understand their role as an extension of their father's commitment to his country. That responsibility to their father's memory could be seen as both a burden and a gift. Managing their father's legacy has left them with rich rewards and deep disappointments, as they navigate the promises and ambitions of those who come seeking to engage with some aspect of his memory. They are lucky to have witnessed the ways their father touched so many of their fellow citizens. Their dad remains a cherished national treasure. He was truly a great American, just as he always wanted to be.

ACKNOWLEDGMENTS

I COULD NOT HAVE WRITTEN THIS BOOK WITHOUT THE SUPPORT of Roy's family, especially his children, Denise, Yvette, and Noel. From our first e-mail correspondence in 2015 to our most recent meal at the Lone Star Café in El Campo, they have welcomed me into a piece of their lives. We've been on road trips to rural cemeteries, eaten Texas barbeque, and shared difficult, emotional moments. They invited me into their homes and gave me so many contacts of people who knew their father. I was so grateful to get to meet their mother, Lala, and their Uncle Eugene, both of whom are no longer with us. Thank you to everyone in the Benavidez family for answering my endless array of texts, emails, and calls about all the big and small details related to your family history. And thank you for your patience, your grace, and your generosity. I admire you all so deeply and hope that this book makes you and your families proud.

My own family lived through this book with me and supported me along the way. My partner, Fan Lee, learned about this book near the time we met, and she has offered years of support and encouragement along the way. It must be a difficult thing living with a writer whose attention can turn to their work at any minute. We would be walking the dogs or watching a show when my mind would suddenly wander off to another time and place. I know it's not always fair or very charming, but she entertained me by engaging in discussions of far-flung topics such as Cambodian diplomacy in the 1960s or Hispanic life in Texas in the 1920s, neither of which has much to do with our immediate existence. Her support allows me to pursue my passions and makes my dreams possible. Thank you, Fan, for living with this book and for supporting me as I completed this work during a turbulent time in our lives. On the other side, I look forward to a life with you and our new daughter, Billie. I must also thank Billie as she has spent many hours of her young life sitting and lying next to me as I finish revisions. I can't think of a better writing companion as I finished this book. She is so happy and calm (at least in the mornings), and she gives me such a great sense of purpose and hope.

My mother, Peg Thoms, who taught me how to read and dream, has also lived with this book for some time. For years, she's listened to me talk about my hopes and challenges with this book. I began learning how to tell stories while sitting in her lap as a boy as she read me the books that filled me with a love of literature. Sid Fleischman, one of my favorite childhood authors, once said, "The books we enjoy as children stay with us forever— they have a special impact." He was so right. I know I'll never forget the adventures of Jingo and Jack that my mother read to me on that little tan couch in our house on Sharon Avenue. I thank her for her ear and for helping support the life I have built. None of this would be possible without her.

Thank you to my brother, Dave; sister-in-law, Jess; and nephew, Bo. You have also lived through this process with me and provided much-needed support along the way. Thank you for listening and believing in me. I have never been as excited to meet anyone as I was Bo. He brings me so much optimism for the future. I love you all. Thanks to Dad, Linda, Janet, Derek, my uncles Paul and Bob, and all members of the Sturkey and Thoms families. Although we don't see each other often, I feel your support and am bolstered by your examples. I am also so grateful for my mother-in-law, Sue, who has helped our family so much over the past months. It's unimaginable where we'd be without her. Thanks also to my father-in-law, Chen, and sister-in-law, Fay, for their support. Many thanks also to my Labrador retrievers, Fonny and Mumbo, who sat at my feet while I wrote much of this book. They were my companions for many hours when I was otherwise alone. Their patience and zest for life has brought me such joy, and they demanded that I take much-needed breaks. Thanks also to my best friends who help fill my life with joy and laughter through hobbies and dinners that are unrelated to history.

I owe many professional debts. The research for this book has been supported by the Dolph Briscoe Center for American History, National Endowment for the Humanities, and the University of North Carolina's College of Arts and Sciences, Institute for the Arts and Humanities, and the Office of the Executive Vice Chancellor and Provost. Most of my research was conducted at the Briscoe archives, where the wonderful staff hosted me for many hours over the past years. Special thanks to Margaret Schlankey at the Briscoe and historians Daina Ramey Berry, María Hammack, and Jessica Pliley who helped keep me company in Austin. I also appreciate my hometown friends Mike Szymecki and Greg Gianelli who helped show me around Austin and Houston. Thanks also to the talented staffers at the LBJ Library, the Reagan Library, the Texas State Library and Archives, the Catholic Archives of Texas, the Vanderbilt TV News Archive, the Jimmy Carter Library & Museum, the Colorado State University Archives & Special Collections, and the staff at the office of the Wharton County Clerk, especially Pamela Brandstetter, who spent an afternoon helping me locate records. Steve Branch at the Reagan Library and Aryn Glazier at the Briscoe provided much-needed assistance with images. Thank you to Kate Blackmer, who made the maps for this book.

Many thanks to those who knew Roy and spent hours talking with me about him—his children, Chris Barbee, Eugene and David Benavidez, Michael Benavidez, Benny Aleman, Jose Garcia, Buddy Gee, Joe Munoz, Sister Elizabeth Riebschlaeger, George Shepard, and Steve Sucher. Deborah Lattimore transcribed my interviews. She is wonderful to work with. Other much-needed research help was provided by Jay Driskell, Eric Burke, and Jaaz Catterall, who helped organize thousands of images. I'd still be organizing my research if not for Jaaz. Thanks to Joyce Loftin, Jennifer Parker, Sharon Anderson, David Culclasure, and Michael Williams for making my research trips possible. And thank you to Jennifer Marquardt for taking me into Cambodia and accompanying me across so much of that beautiful county. Rob Thompson provided helpful suggestions in response to random problems, and Kyle Rable lent his invaluable expertise to several chapters. Andrew Wiest helped me better understand the war.

At the University of North Carolina, I was blessed to work with such wonderful colleagues. The faculty and students have all elevated my abilities as a historian and writer. I'd like to offer a special thanks to Katie Turk, Erik Gellman, Jennifer Standish, Ron Williams, Kathleen Duval, Joe Glatthaar, Ben Waterhouse, Miguel La Serna, Lou Perez, Fitz Brundage, Susan Pennybacker, Lisa Lindsay, Matt Andrews, Chad Bryant, Zaragosa Vargas, Jerma Jackson, Antwain Hunter, Lauren Jarvis, Wayne Lee, Lloyd Kramer, Nancy Andoh, Alma Huselja, Carter Kurtz, Lan Li, Madeleine McGrady, Tess Megginson, Cristian Walk, Tim Marr, Bill and Marcie Ferris, Doug Zinn, Melanie Feinberg, Seth Kotch, Jacqueline Lawton, Michelle Robinson, Carolina Sá Carvalho, Ariana Vigil, Daniel Wallace, Lyneise Williams, and Lingyu Wang for reading and engaging with sections or ideas from this book. A manuscript workshop with Marcia Chatelain, Scott Nelson, Brandon Proia, and Kevin

Boyle also greatly enhanced this book. Greg Downs helped a lot with the introduction. Thanks to you all for your brilliance and generosity. My new colleagues at the University of Pennsylvania welcomed this project and offered helpful remarks that benefited this manuscript in the final stage of revisions. The last push to complete this book would not have been possible without the newest members of our family's community: Allie, Marc, and Clark Getty.

My talented agent, Lauren Sharp, fought for this book, and I will toast her when it is published. I am so grateful for her calm, grit, and professionalism. Thank you to my editor, Brian Distelberg, who believed in this project and has always believed in me. I couldn't ask for a better agent-editor partnership. Lauren and Brian are at once professional, deeply intelligent, and profoundly compassionate. Thank you both for putting your faith in this story. The team at Basic Books has been wonderful. Many thanks to Alex Cullina for so many portions of this project and to Kristen Kim, whose sharp and insightful line editing greatly improved the prose and structure of the final version. I am also so grateful to Melissa Veronesi, Elisa Rivlin, and Lillian Duggan for turning this Word document into a book.

ABBREVIATIONS OF SOURCES

Benavidez Guard File: Texas National Guard Records, Texas Military Department, Military Personnel Records, Austin, TX.

BMR: Official Military Personnel File of Roy P. Benavidez, Series: Official Military Personnel Files, 1912–1998, Record Group 319: Records of the Army Staff, 1903–2009, National Archives at St. Louis, St. Louis, MO.

GWS Records: Records of the Great Western Sugar Company, Agricultural and Natural Resources Archive, Colorado State University, Fort Collins, CO

LBJ: LBJ Presidential Library, Austin, TX.

Medal: Roy P. Benavidez, with John R. Craig, *Medal of Honor: One Man's Journey from Poverty and Prejudice* (Washington, DC: Potomac Books, 1995).

MOH Film: Medal of Honor Presentation to Master Sergeant Benavidez and President Reagan's Remarks at the Pentagon and Oval Office Photo Op., February 24, 1981, Reagan Library, www.youtube.com/watch?v=le8YfYf5meQ, accessed December 19, 2019.

NSF-Cambodia: National Security File-Country File, Cambodia, Papers of Lyndon Baines Johnson President, 1963–1969, LBJ Presidential Library, Austin, TX.

NSF-Vietnam: National Security File-Country File, Vietnam, Papers of Lyndon Baines Johnson President, 1963–1969, LBJ Presidential Library, Austin, TX.

RBP: Roy P. Benavidez Papers, 1943–2007, Dolph Briscoe Center for American History, The University of Texas at Austin, Austin, TX.

Reagan Library: Ronald Reagan Presidential Library, Simi Valley, CA.

Reagan MOH Photos: Roll #C00822–C00838, White House Photographic Office Collection, 1981, Reagan Library, Simi Valley, CA.

Sanborn: Sanborn Maps Company, Digital Sanborn Maps, 1867–1970, ProQuest, Ann Arbor, MI.

Texas State Archives: Texas State Library and Archives Commission, Austin, TX.

Three Wars: Roy P. Benavidez, with Oscar Griffin, *The Three Wars of Roy Benavidez* (San Antonio, TX: Corona, 1986).

NOTES

Prologue

1. The description of these events is derived from notarized eyewitness testimonies included in BMR; Roy Benavidez Medal of Honor Citation, United States Army Center of Military History, www.cmohs.org/recipients/roy-p-benavidez; Benavidez quoted in *Medal*, 139; and Eric Blehm, *Legend: A Harrowing Story from the Vietnam War of One Green Beret's Heroic Mission to Rescue a Special Forces Team Caught Behind Enemy Lines* (New York: Crown, 2015), especially 111–179.

2. BMR; Blehm, *Legend*, especially 111–179; *Medal*, quoted on 139; and Roy P. Benavidez and Oscar Griffin, *The Three Wars of Roy Benavidez* (San Antonio, TX: Corona, 1986), 1–5.

3. Statement of Personal History, 9/1/70, BMR; "Triple volunteer" quoted in Gordon L. Rottman, *US MACV-SOG Reconnaissance Team in Vietnam* (Oxford, UK: Osprey, 2011), 13; and *Medal*, 81–105.

4. Statement of Personal History, 9/1/70, BMR; and Memo, Joint Chiefs of Staff to Deputy Secretary of Defense, Washington, DC, December 3, 1968, #15a, box 93, folder: "Cambodia 5E (3) 11/68–1/69," NSF-Vietnam.

5. Intelligence Memo, CIA, 5/10/66, #6a, box 92, folder: Cambodia 5E (1)b 5/66–1/68 [1 of 2], NSF-Vietnam.

6. Cable, William Westmoreland MACV 40588, #80a, box 92, folder: Cambodia 5E (1)a 5/66–1/68 [2 of 2], NSF-Vietnam; and Memo, Earl G. Wheeler to General Westmoreland, #80, box 92, folder: Cambodia 5E (1)a 5/66–1/68 [2 of 2], NSF-Vietnam.

7. Memo, Walt Rostow to the President, 12/27/1967, #31, box 92, folder: Cambodia 5E (1)a 5/66–1/68 [1 of 2], NSF-Vietnam.

8. Blehm, *Legend*; John L. Plaster, *Secret Commandos: Behind Enemy Lines with the Elite Warriors of SOG* (New York: New American Library, 2005); Rottman, *US MACV-SOG*; and Lt. Col. Fred S. Lindsey, *Secret Green Beret Commandos in Cambodia: A Memorial History of MACV-SOG's Command and Control Detachment South (CCS)* (Bloomington, IN: Author House, 2012).

9. Memo, Earle Wheeler to Deputy Secretary of Defense, 12/3/68, #15a, box 93, folder: Cambodia 5E(3) 11/68–1/69, NSF-Vietnam; and *Medal*, quoted on 133.

10. *Medal*, 129–131, quoted on 130.

11. Statement of Personal History, 9/1/70, BMR; Clinical Record, May 12, 1968, box 4Zc194, folder 54, RBP; Roy Benavidez Medal of Honor Citation; *Medal*, quoted on 139–140; and Blehm, *Legend*, especially 111–179.

12. Roy Benavidez Medal of Honor Citation; and *Medal*, 133–145.

13. Statement of Personal History, 9/1/70; Physical Evaluation Board Proceedings, 8/4/76; Roy Benavidez Service Record, 10/24/73, BMR; and Roy Benavidez Medal of Honor Citation.

14. Noel Benavidez, interview by William Sturkey, El Campo, TX, December 5, 2015, transcript in author's possession; Noel Benavidez, interview by William Sturkey, El Campo, TX, August 2, 2018, transcript in author's possession; Shannon Crabtree, "Benavidez to Be Honored with Stamp This Friday," *El Campo Leader-News*, box 4Zc194, folder 59, RBP; and Roy quoted in Bob Kerr, "In This Case, Salute the Medal and the Man," *Providence Journal-Bulletin*, Monday May 13, 1996, B, box 4Zc199, folder 36, RBP.

15. "Texas Press Group Honors Countian as Texan of 1981," *Wharton Journal-Spectator*, June 25, 1981, A3; "State Leaders to Honor Benavidez in Austin Tuesday," *El Campo Leader-News*, March 28, 1981, box 4Zc194, folder 59, RBP; "Hall of Honor Planned," *Port Arthur News*, April 2, 1981, 7A; H.R. No, 371, Box 2.325, RBP; Frank Stransky, "Sgt. B Gets EP Key," *El Campo Leader-News*, October 5, 1988, 4-A; and Certificates located in box 2.325, RBP, and box 4Zc195, folder 9.

16. West Point Association of Graduates, History of Class Gifts, www.westpointaog.org/giving/your-impact/class-giving/history-of-class-gifts, accessed October 7, 2023; Christening Program, *USS-Benavidez*, July 21, 2001, New Orleans, LA, box 4Zc200, folder 31, RBP; Blehm, *Legend*, 276; and Yvette Garcia, email to author, November 7, 2022.

17. John McCain with Mark Salter, *Why Courage Matters: The Way to a Braver Life* (New York: Random House, 2004), 2–12; Caspar W. Weinberger, *Fighting for Peace: Seven Critical Years in the Pentagon* (New York: Warner Books, 1990), 56; and Kelley Shannon, "War Hero Recalled for Acts of Bravery," *McAllen Monitor*, December 4, 1998, 1C.

18. Neil Foley, *Mexicans in the Making of America* (Cambridge, MA: Belknap/Harvard University Press, 2014), 179–199.

19. "Ballad of Roy Benavidez" was written by Leonardo Carrillo, a professor at Corpus Christi University. "Stories," *El Campo Leader-News*, July 29, 1981, 2; "Corrido De Roy Benavidez," box 4Zc194, folder 56, RBP; and José Pablo Villalobos and Juan Carlos Ramírez-Pimienta, "'Corridos' and 'la Pura Verdad': Myths and Realities of the Mexican Ballad," *South Central Review*, vol. 21, no. 3 (Fall 2004), 129–149.

20. *Medal*, quoted on 46, 170, and 171.

21. "Walking roadmap," quoted in "'Walking Roadmap' Re-ups for 5," *San Antonio Express*, January 2, 1974, BMR; and Jose Garcia, "Roy P. Benavidez Quotes," 2002, document in author's possession.

22. Ronald Reagan, "Remarks on Presenting the Medal of Honor to Master Sergeant Roy P. Benavidez," Arlington, VA, February 24, 1981, www.presidency.ucsb.edu/documents/remarks-presenting-the-medal-honor-master-sergeant-roy-p-benavidez, accessed September 17, 2017; and Colin L. Powell with Joseph E. Persico, *My American Journey* (New York: Random House, 1995), 258.

23. Social Security Administration to Roy Benavidez, February 22, 1983, box 4Zc194, folder 53, RBP.

24. Medical Board Proceedings, Roy P. Benavidez, June 10, 1976, box 4Zc194, folder 53, RBP; and *Medal*, quoted on 163.

Chapter 1: Rawhide

1. Salvador and Teresa Benavidez wedding photo, October 7, 1934, in author's possession; 1930 US Census, DeWitt County, Texas, Population Schedule, Precinct 5, Sheet 19B, Dwelling 423, Family 423, Benavidez family, digital image, Ancestry .com; and 1930 US Census, DeWitt County, Texas, Population Schedule, Cuero, Sheet 9B, Dwelling 233, Family 237, Perez family, digital image, Ancestry.com.

2. *Medal*, 1.

3. US Census, DeWitt County, Texas, Population Schedule, Cuero, Sheet 9B, Dwelling 233, Family 237, Perez family, digital image, Ancestry.com.

4. *Medal*, 1–3; DeWitt County Historical Commission, *The History of DeWitt County, Texas* (Dallas, TX: Curtis Media, 1991), 143–145; "Lindenau Marker Dedicated," *Victoria Advocate*, October 16, 1979, 6B; and personal observations made on May 20, 2015. For more, see Texas Dance Hall Preservation, Inc., https://texas dancehall.org.

5. *Medal*, 1–3; 1930 US Census, DeWitt County, Texas, Population Schedule, Precinct 5, Sheet 19B, Dwelling 423, Family 423, Benavidez family, digital image, Ancestry .com; and 1930 US Census, DeWitt County, Texas, Population Schedule, Cuero, Sheet 9B, Dwelling 233, Family 237, Perez family, digital image, Ancestry.com.

6. Texas Historical Records Survey, "Inventory of the County Archives of Texas: DeWitt County, No. 62," January 1940, Texas State Library and Archives Commission (TSLAC), Austin, TX; A. Ray Stephens, *Texas: A Historical Atlas* (Norman, OK: University of Oklahoma Press, 2010), 24–25; DeWitt County Historical Commission, *History of DeWitt County, Texas*, 59; and personal observations.

7. Sam W. Haynes, *Unsettled Land: From Revolution to Republic, the Struggle for Texas* (New York: Basic Books, 2022), 25–95; T. R. Fehrenbach, *Lone Star: A History of Texas and the Texans* (Cambridge, MA: Da Capo, 2000, orig., 1968), 132–173; and DeWitt County Historical Commission, *History of DeWitt County*, quoted on 11.

8. Ana Carolina Castillo Crimm, *De León: A Tejano Family History* (Austin, TX: University of Texas Press, 2003), 113–118, 145–151; Victor M. Rose, *Victor Rose's History of Victoria* (San Antonio, TX: Lone Star Printing, 1961, orig., 1883), 10–15 and 104–106; A. B. J. Hammett, *The Empresario Don Martin De Leon* (Kerrville, TX: Braswell, 1971); and Stephen L. Hardin, "Plácido Benavides: Fighting Tejano Federalist," in Jesús F. de la Teja, ed., *Tejano Leadership in Mexican and Revolutionary Texas* (College Station, TX: Texas A&M University Press, 2010), 57–74.

9. Randolph B. Campbell, *An Empire for Slavery: The Peculiar Institution in Texas, 1821–1865* (Baton Rouge: Louisiana State University Press, 1989), 10–49; Alwyn Barr, *Black Texans: A History of African Americans in Texas, 1528–1995* (Norman, OK: University of Oklahoma Press, 1996, 2nd ed., orig., 1973), 13–38; and Haynes, *Unsettled Land*, Austin quoted on 75.

10. Hammett, *The Empresario*; Crimm, *De León*, 145–151; and Hardin, "Plácido Benavides," 57–74. Plácido later submitted claims for reimbursement that help reveal the extent of his financial and material contributions. These can be found in the

Republic Claims records available through the Texas State Libraries and Archives Commission Records: www.tsl.texas.gov/apps/arc/repclaims/records.

11. Crimm, *De León*, 145–151; Hammett, *The Empresario*, 80–81; Hardin, "Plácido Benavides," 57–74; and Fehrenbach, *Lone Star*, 174–189.

12. Crimm, *De León*, 167–171; Hardin, "Plácido Benavides," 57–74; and Arnoldo De León, *They Called Them Greasers: Anglo Attitudes Toward Mexicans in Texas, 1821–1900* (Austin, TX: University of Texas Press, 1983), 1–13, 49–62, quoted on 3 and 7.

13. David Montejano, *Anglos and Mexicans in the Making of Texas, 1836–1986* (Austin, TX: University of Texas Press, 1987); and Hammett, *The Empresario*, quoted on 27.

14. Montejano, *Anglos and Mexicans*; Hammett, *The Empresario*, quoted on 27; and Crimm, *De León*, 152–184.

15. Crimm, *De León*, 164–169; Rose, *Victor Rose's History of Victoria*, 106–107; Hammett, *The Empresario*, 78; and William D. Carrigan and Clive Webb, *Forgotten Dead: Mob Violence Against Mexicans in the United States, 1848–1928* (New York: Oxford University Press, 2013).

16. Richard Griswold del Castillo, *The Treaty of Guadalupe Hidalgo: A Legacy of Conflict* (Norman, OK: University of Oklahoma Press, 1990), especially 62–107, 100,000 figure on 62; and Donald B. Dodd, ed., *Historical Statistics of the States of the United States: Two Centuries of the Census, 1790–1990* (Westport, CT: Greenwood, 1993), 87. This count includes Tejanos, but white settlers constituted the vast majority of newcomers.

17. Frederick Law Olmsted, *A Journey Through Texas* (New York: Dix, Edwards, 1857), quoted on 245.

18. Foley, *Mexicans in the Making of America*, 13–38; Crimm, *De León*, 152–213; and Armando C. Alonzo, *Tejano Legacy: Rancheros and Settlers in South Texas, 1734–1900* (Albuquerque, NM: University of New Mexico Press, 1998), 145–159.

19. Alonzo, *Tejano Legacy*, 145–159, 259–270; and Montejano, *Anglos and Mexicans*, 24–74.

20. Montejano, *Anglos and Mexicans*, 24–74, quoted on 60.

21. Montejano, *Anglos and Mexicans*, 24–74; Benjamin Heber Johnson, *Revolution in Texas: How a Forgotten Rebellion and Its Bloody Suppression Turned Mexicans into Americans* (New Haven, CT: Yale University Press, 2003), 7–37; Alonzo, *Tejano Legacy*, 227–270; and John Weber, *From South Texas to the Nation: The Exploitation of Mexican Labor in the Twentieth Century* (Chapel Hill: University of North Carolina Press, 2015), 15–40.

22. Fehrenbach, *Lone Star*, 507–521, quoted on 510; Monica Muñoz Martinez, *The Injustice Never Leaves You: Anti-Mexican Violence in Texas* (Cambridge, MA: Harvard University Press, 2018), especially 76–119; and Crimm, *De León*, Benavides quoted on 179, "widow" on 240.

23. 1850 US Census, Victoria County, Texas, Free Inhabitants, City Unlisted, pg. 242, Dwelling 180, Family 180, Benavidez family, digital image, Ancestry.com; Crimm, *De León*, 197; and Texas, Memorials and Petitions, 1834–1929, Petition for Land, Nicholas Benavidez, January 30, 1854, digital image, Ancestry.com.

24. Historical Grantor/Grantee Indexes of Texas land found using Courthouse direct.com.

25. Rose, *Victor Rose's History of Victoria*, 106; Texas, County Tax Rolls, 1837–1910, Hidalgo County, 1868, Eugenio Benavides, digital image, Family search.org; 1870 US Census, Hidalgo County, Inhabitants, Precincts 3 and 4, pg. 17,

Dwelling 130, Family 112, Benavidez family, digital image, Ancestry.com; and Montejano, *Anglos and Mexicans*, 50–74.

26. Alonzo, *Tejano Legacy*, 95–143, 161–181, percentage on 163.

27. Alonzo, *Tejano Legacy*, Hidalgo example on 267; Martha Menchaca, *The Mexican American Experience in Texas: Citizenship, Segregation, and the Struggle for Equality* (Austin, TX: University of Texas Press, 2022), 90; and Montejano, *Anglos and Mexicans*, 72–73, quoted on 72, Hidalgo example on 52.

28. "From the Rio Grande and Mexico," *Galveston Daily News*, September 30, 1869, 2; and Alonzo, *Tejano Legacy*.

29. Warranty Deed, Nicholas Benavides to Thaddeus Rhodes, September 7, 1876, book DR, vol. B, pg. 256, Hidalgo County Clerk, available at: https://hidalgo.tx.publicsearch.us/.

30. Hoyt Hager, "Mexican-American to Lead," *Corpus Christi Caller*, May 19, 1970, 16B; Myra McIlvain, "Texas' Magic Valley," *Hondo Anvil Herald*, March 5, 1981, 13; Thaddeus Rhodes, Appointments of U.S. Postmasters, 1832–1971, Records of the Post Office Department, Record Group No. 28, Series M841, Roll Number 124, National Archives, Washington, DC, digital image, Ancestry.com; and "Relampago Park, Marker to Be Dedicated," *The Monitor* (McAllen, TX), May 13, 1981, 25.

31. Murphy Givens, "Mexico Blamed Texas for Banditry on the Border," *Corpus Christi Caller-Times*, July 17, 2013, 9A; Alonzo, *Tejano Legacy*, 131, 137, 177 for tax sale, 222–223, 250–251; *Reports Of The Committee Of Investigation Sent In 1873 By The Mexican Government To The Frontier Of Texas* (New York: Baker & Godwin, 1875); and 1880 U.S. Census, Non-population Schedules, Texas, 1850–1880, Agricultural Production Schedule, Relampago Rancho, pg. 1, Enumeration District No. 63, Rhodes Family, digital image, Ancestry.com. Land transactions available through Hidalgo County Clerk: https://hidalgo.tx.publicsearch.us/.

32. Texas, Death Certificates, 1903–1982, Wharton County, 1963, Jul.–Sept., no. 54273, Salvador Benavidez, died July 13, 1963, digital image, Ancestry.com; DeWitt County, Texas, marriage certificate no. 825 (1900), Salvador Benavidez and Ysabel Cisneros, DeWitt County Clerk, Cuero, Texas; 1900 US Census, DeWitt County, Texas, Population Schedule, Precinct 1, Sheet 6, Dwelling 108, Family 109, Cisneros family, digital image, Ancestry.com; 1920 US Census, DeWitt County, Texas, Population Schedule, Justice Precinct 3, Sheet 11B, Dwelling 188, Family 194, Benavidez family, digital image, Ancestry.com; and St. Michael Parish, Cuero, TX, Roll #111, Book #5, starting May 3, 1908, Baptismal Record, Salvador Benavidez, October 11, 1912, digital image, Familysearch.com.

33. DeWitt County Historical Commission, *History of DeWitt County*, 29–30; James E. Sherow, *The Chisholm Trail: Joseph McCoy's Great Gamble* (Norman, OK: University of Oklahoma Press, 2018), 13–29; and William Cronon, *Nature's Metropolis: Chicago and the Great West* (New York: Norton, 1991), 207–259.

34. US Bureau of the Census, *1880 Census of the Population: Vol. 3, Report on the Productions of Agriculture, Report on Cattle, Sheep, and Swine* (Washington, DC: Government Printing Office, 1883), 21; and Historical Commission, "The Chisolm Trail: A Guide for Heritage Travelers," pamphlet produced by the Chisholm Trail Heritage Museum, Cuero, TX, 2017.

35. F. S. Stockdale, "The Proposition," *San Antonio Daily Express*, August 27, 1871, 2; "Western Texas and Its Railway," *San Antonio Express*, July 21, 1874, 2; DeWitt

County Historical Commission, *History of DeWitt County*, 28 and 57; US Bureau of the Census, *1880 Census: Vol. 1, Population, Table II: Population of Each State and Territory by Counties*, 79; US Bureau of the Census, *1910 Census of the Population: Vol. 3, Population Reports by States, Nebraska-Wyoming* (Washington, DC: Government Printing Office, 1913), 781, and *1910 Census, Vol. 1, Population*, 244. Hispanic or Latino residents were classified as white.

36. DeWitt County Historical Commission, *History of DeWitt County*; and US Bureau of the Census, *1910 Census, Vol. 1, Population*, 135.

37. Texas Historical Records Survey, "DeWitt County," 9–12; US Bureau of the Census, *1910 Census, Vol. 7, Agriculture Reports by States, with Statistics for Counties, Nebraska-Wyoming, Alaska, Hawaii, Porto Rico*, 637–638, 660–661, 682–683.

38. US Bureau of the Census, *1910 Census, Vol. 7, Agriculture Reports by States*, 637–638 and 660–661; Neil Foley, *The White Scourge: Mexicans, Blacks, and Poor Whites in Texas Cotton Culture* (Berkeley, CA: University of California Press, 1997), 16–39, quotes taken from 36–38; and Weber, *From South Texas to the Nation*, 11–40.

39. *Medal*, 3; Foley, *White Scourge*, 17–92; David Eugene Conrad, *The Forgotten Farmers: The Story of Sharecroppers in the New Deal* (Urbana, IL: University of Illinois Press, 1965), 1–18; and Montejano, *Anglos and Mexicans*, 169–178.

40. US Bureau of the Census, *1910 Census, Vol. 7*, 637–638, 660, and 682; President's Commission on Migratory Labor, *Migratory Labor in American Agriculture* (Washington, DC: Government Printing Office, 1951), 144–151; and Foley, *White Scourge*, 141–162.

41. Foley, *White Scourge*, 141–162; and Eugene Benavidez, interview by William Sturkey, Richmond, TX, December 18, 2016, transcript in author's possession.

42. Weber, *From South Texas to the Nation*, 41–71.

43. Weber, *From South Texas to the Nation*, 41–71; Foley, *White Scourge*, 40–63; Foley, *Mexicans in the Making of America*, 39–63; and Menchaca, *Mexican American Experience in Texas*, 75–112, covenant on 106.

44. DeWitt County Historical Commission, *History of DeWitt County*, 52; Charles C. Alexander, *The Ku Klux Klan in the Southwest* (Lexington, KY: University Press of Kentucky, 1965), 36–54 and 107–128, membership figures on 53; and Martinez, *Injustice Never Leaves You*, 172–226.

45. Texas, Death Certificates, 1903–1982, DeWitt County, 1918, Oct.–Dec., no. 48983, Isabel Cisneros, died November 16, 1918, digital image, Ancestry.com; Texas, Death Certificates, 1903–1982, DeWitt County, 1918, Oct.–Dec., no. 49024, Rafaela Benavidez, died November 21, 1918, digital image, Ancestry.com; Texas, Death Certificates, 1903–1982, DeWitt County, 1918, Oct.–Dec., no. 55349, Eugenio Benavidez, died December 7, 1918, digital image, Ancestry.com; and Alison Medley, "Here's How Houston Handled the Horrific Spanish Flu Pandemic 100 Years Ago," *Houston Chronicle*, March 13, 2020, www.chron.com/local/article /Here-s-how-Houston-handled-the-horrific-Spanish-15126650.php.

46. DeWitt County, Texas, marriage certificate no. 103 (1919), Salvador Benavidez and Angelita Cisneros, DeWitt County Clerk, Cuero, Texas; Texas, Death Certificates, 1903–1982, Wharton County, 1946, July–Sept., no. 39101, Angelita Benavidez, died August 3, 1946, digital image, Ancestry.com; 1920 US Census, DeWitt County, Texas, Population Schedule, Justice Precinct 3, Sheet 11B, Dwelling 188, Family 194, Benavidez family, digital image, Ancestry.com; and Texas, Death

Certificates, 1903–1982, DeWitt County, 1921, Jan.–Mar., no. 980, Gumecinda Garcia, died January 22, 1921, digital image, Ancestry.com.

47. Reverse Index to Deeds, DeWitt County, H. W. Wallace to Salvador Benavides, book 76, page 604, courthousedirect.com.

48. Robb Walsh, *The Tex-Mex Cookbook* (Berkeley, CA: Ten Speed, 2004); Guadalupe San Miguel Jr., *Tejano Proud: Tex-Mex Music in the Twentieth Century* (College Station, TX: Texas A&M University Press, 2002), 3–36; and Wilhelmina Beane, *Texas Thirties* (San Antonio, TX: Naylor Company, 1963), 4.

49. DeWitt County Historical Commission, *History of DeWitt County*, 108–110 and 202; Henry Wolff Jr., "Inn's History Traced," *Victoria Advocate*, September 15, 1982, 6; and Mike Forman, "Where the Mustangs Roamed," *Victoria Advocate*, July 24, 2001, 17H.

50. Salvador and Teresa Benavidez wedding photo; St. Michael Parish, Cuero, TX, Roll #111, Book #4, starting June 17, 1908, Marriages, pg. 24, Nicholas Benavidez and Alexandria Gonzalez, January 18, 1924, digital image, Familysearch.com; and St. Michael Parish, Cuero, TX, Roll #111, Book #1, Communions, starting June 1919, Teresa Perez, April 17, 1924, digital image, Familysearch.com.

51. Coahuila, Mexico, Civil Registration Births, 1861–1930, pg. 116, Teresa Perez, born July 12, 1911, digital image, Ancestry.com; and *Medal*, 1–3, quoted on 2 and 1.

52. *Medal*, quoted on 2; 1920 US Census, DeWitt County, Texas, Population Schedule, Yorktown, Sheet 14B, Dwelling 327, Family 347, Perez family, digital image, Ancestry.com; and 1930 US Census, DeWitt County, Texas, Population Schedule, Cuero, Sheet 9B, Dwelling 233, Family 237, Perez family, digital image, Ancestry.com.

53. *Medal*, quoted on 2.

54. DeWitt County, Texas, marriage certificate no. 289 (1934), Salvador Benavidez and Teresita Perez, DeWitt County Clerk, Cuero, Texas; Our Lady of Guadalupe, Cuero, TX, Box #5, Roll #105, Book #1, September, 5 1925, pg. 41, Salvador Benavidez and Teresa Perez, October 7, 1934, digital image, Familysearch.com; and US Department of Commerce, *State Personal Income: 1929–1982* (Washington, DC: US Department of Commerce, Bureau of Economic Analysis, 1984), 8.

55. *Medal*, 1–4.

56. Texas State Department of Health, certificate of birth number 14231 (orig., August 5, 1935, amended January 24, 1968), Roy Benavidez, Bureau of Vital Statistics, DeWitt County, copy in author's possession; Our Lady of Guadalupe, Cuero, TX, Box #5, Roll #105, Book #1, starting September 5, 1925, Registrum Baptismorum, pg. 158, #3023, Raul Benavidez, November, 1935, digital image, Familysearch .com; and Our Lady of Guadalupe, Cuero, TX, Box #5, Roll #105, Book #1, starting September 5, 1925, Registrum Baptismorum, pg. 219, #3267, Rogelio Benavidez, December, 1937, digital image, Familysearch.com.

57. *Medal*, 4–5; Pauline R. Kibbe, *Latin Americans in Texas* (Albuquerque, NM: University of New Mexico Press, 1946), 126; and Helen Bynum, *Spitting Blood: The History of Tuberculosis* (New York: Oxford University Press, 2012).

58. *Medal*, 4–5; and DeWitt County, Texas, Probate Record, Minute Book Z, Application of Salvador Benavidez Jr. to Adjudged a Tuberculosis Patient, 320–321, DeWitt County Clerk, Cuero, Texas.

59. Texas State Tuberculosis Sanitorium Booklet, Texas Disability History Collection, University of Texas at Arlington Libraries, Special Collections, https://library.uta.edu/txdisabilityhistory/doc/20066962; "State Tuberculosis Sanatorium,"

Grand Prairie Daily News, August 21, 1936, 3; "Texas Tuberculosis Fight Unchallenged," *Austin American-Statesman*, June 21, 1931, 20.

60. DeWitt County, Texas, Probate Record, Minute Book 27, Application of Salvador Benavidez Jr. to Adjudged a Tuberculosis Patient, 57–58, DeWitt County Clerk, Cuero, Texas.

61. *Medal*, quoted on 4.

62. *Medal*, quoted on 4–5; and Texas, Death Certificates, 1903–1982, DeWitt County, 1938, Oct.–Dec., no. 49750, Salvador Benavides, died November 7, 1938, digital image, Ancestry.com.

Chapter 2: Fields

1. "Cuero Population," *Victoria Advocate*, June 5, 1940, 4; Mrs. George J. Schleicher, "Historical Sketch of Cuero," July 14, 1923, Vertical Files—Cuero, Dolph Briscoe Center for American History, Austin, TX; Texas Historical Records Survey, "DeWitt County," 19; DeWitt County Historical Commission, *History of DeWitt County*, 88–94; and Sheets 1–12, Cuero, TX, April 1922, Sanborn.

2. Harry C. Putman, "Your Thanksgiving Dinners Come from Here," *Texas Preview*, November 1951, Vertical Files—Cuero, Briscoe Center; "Cuero's Turkey Trot Carnival," *Houston Post*, October 6, 1912, 11; "That Cuero Turkey Trot," *Austin Statesman*, November 30, 1912, 4; and Isabella Kruse Schaffner, *Turkeys in Texas: A History of the Turkey Industry in Texas* (San Antonio, TX: Naylor, 1954).

3. "Governors Party to Cuero," *Austin Statesman*, November 19, 1913, 4; Putman, "Your Thanksgiving Dinners"; Scott W. Wright, "It's Turkey Time in Cuero," *Austin American-Statesman*, October 14, 1995, A1; "1936 Turkey Trot to Be Centennial Feature," *Cuero Record*, Vertical Files—Cuero, Briscoe Center; and "Cuero's Turkey Trot Declared Best Ever Held," *Austin American*, November 12, 1940, Vertical Files—Cuero, Briscoe Center.

4. "Mountain Lion Is Seen Near Cuero," *Victoria Advocate*, May 11, 1936, 3; and Joy W. Arnold, "Interesting Facts about Cuero and Territory," *Cuero Record*, December 31, 1935, Vertical Files—Cuero, Briscoe Center.

5. Linda Gordon, *Pitied but Not Entitled: Single Mothers and the History of Welfare, 1890–1935* (New York: Free Press, 1994).

6. *Medal*, 4–5; Gordon, *Pitied but Not Entitled*; and US Census Bureau, *1940 Census of the Population: Vol 3, The Labor Force* (Washington, DC: Government Printing Office, 1943), 526.

7. Our Lady of Guadalupe, Cuero, TX, Box #5, Roll #105, Book #1, starting September 5, 1925, Matrimoniorum Registrum, pg. 47, Pablo Chavez and Erenea Aguilar, June 14, 1936, digital image, Familysearch.com; Texas, Death Certificates, 1903–1982, DeWitt County, 1937, April–June, no. 25560, Erania Aguilar, died May 3, 1937, digital image, Ancestry.com; and DeWitt County, Texas, marriage certificate no. 831 (1940) Pablo Chavez and Theresa Perez [*sic*], DeWitt County Clerk, Cuero, Texas.

8. *Medal*, 4–7, quoted on 4 and 6.

9. *Medal*, 6.

10. *Medal*, 7.

11. *Medal*.

12. *Medal*.

13. *Medal*, 7–8; Sister Elizabeth Riebschlaeger, interview by William Sturkey, San Antonio, TX, August 2, 2018, transcript in author's possession; and Sheets 1 and 5, Cuero, TX, April 1922, Sanborn.

14. *Medal*, 6–9; and *Three Wars*, quoted on 76 and 77.

15. *Three Wars*, quoted on 76.

16. *Medal*, 6–9.

17. *Medal*, 8.

18. *Medal*, 8–10; and *Three Wars*, quoted on 76–77.

19. *Medal*, 8–10; and *Three Wars*, quoted on 76–77.

20. 1940 US Census, Wharton County, Texas, Population Schedule, Other Places, Sheet 7A, Family 148, Benavidez family, digital image, Ancestry.com.

21. Alonzo, *Tejano Legacy*, 115–118; and Foley, *White Scourge*, 145.

22. Our Lady of Guadalupe, Cuero, TX, Box #5, Roll #105, Book #1, starting September 5, 1925, Matrimoniorum Registrum, pg. 60, Pablo Chavez and Teresa Perez, October 29, 1943, digital image, Familysearch.com; Our Lady of Guadalupe, Cuero, TX, Box #5, Roll #105, Book #1, starting September 5, 1925, Registrum Baptismorum, pg. 351, #3794, Maria Guadalupe Chavez, November 6, 1943, digital image, Familysearch.com; and Our Lady of Guadalupe, Cuero, TX, Box #5, Roll #105, Book #1, starting September 5, 1925, Matrimoniorum Registrum, pg. 60, Pablo Chavez and Teresa Perez, October 29, 1943, digital image, Familysearch.com.

23. Eugene Benavidez, interview; and *Medal*, quoted on 5.

24. 1940 US Census, Wharton County, Texas, Population Schedule, Other Places, Sheet 7A, Family 148, Benavidez family, digital image, Ancestry.com; and Texas, Death Certificates, 1903–1982, Wharton County, 1940, April–June, no. 30651, Salvador Benavidez, died June 19, 1940, digital image, Ancestry.com.

25. Eugene Benavidez, interview.

26. Eugene Benavidez, interview.

27. Wharton County Historical Commission, *Wharton County Pictorial History, 1846–1946* (Austin, TX: Eakin, 1993); Paul N. Spellman, *Images of America: Wharton* (Charleston, SC: Arcadia, 2010), 25–42; and Stephens, *Texas*, 24–25.

28. Wharton County Historical Commission, *Wharton County Pictorial History*, 78–86; Frank P. Lund, "The Danevang Colony," *Houston Post*, November 6, 1911, 18; and Allan O. Kownslar, *The European Texans* (College Station, TX: Texas A&M University Press, 2004), 69–77. Purchase agreements found in the collections of the Danish Heritage Museum of Danevang, Danevang, TX.

29. Conrad, *Forgotten Farmers*, 64–82; Foley, *White Scourge*, $50 million on 178; Keith J. Volanto, *Texas, Cotton, and the New Deal* (College Station, TX: Texas A&M University Press, 2005), especially 125–141, nonowner figures on 7; and US Bureau of the Census, *1940 Census of the Population: Vol. 3, The Labor Force*, 360–377.

30. US Bureau of the Census, *1940 Census of the Population: Vol. 3, The Labor Force*, 476–495.

31. US Census Bureau, "Cotton Ginning—Crop of 1900," Census Bulletin No. 98, September 28, 1901, 2.

32. President's Commission on Migratory Labor, *Migratory Labor in American Agriculture*, 1–19; and Selden C. Menefee, "Mexican Migratory Workers of South Texas," Works Progress Administration, Division of Research (Washington, DC: Government Printing Office, 1941).

33. Weber, *From South Texas to the Nation*, 41–75; Zaragosa Vargas, *Proletarians of the North: A History of Mexican Industrial Workers in Detroit and the Midwest, 1917–1933* (Berkeley, CA: University of California Press, 1993), 13–55, quoted on 18; and Candy Hamilton, *Footprints in the Sugar: A History of the Great Western Sugar Company* (Ontario, OR: Hamilton Bates, 2009), 255–350, labor agent figures on 291.

34. President's Commission on Migratory Labor, *Migratory Labor in American Agriculture*, 3; *Medal*, 14–19; and US Census Bureau, *1940 Census of the United States: Agriculture, Vol. II, Part 2*, 528–529.

35. Eugene Benavidez, interview; *Medal*, quoted on 16; and Menefee, "Mexican Migratory Workers," 13–26.

36. Bert Nelson, "History of the Fort Collins Factory District, The Great Western Sugar Company, 1903–1955," box 33, folder 50, GWS Records; Hamilton, *Footprints in the Sugar*, 255–350; Weber, *From South Texas to the Nation*, 60–66; Menefee, "Mexican Migratory Workers," x; William John May Jr., *The Great Western Sugarlands: The History of the Great Western Sugar Company and the Economic Development of the Great Plains* (New York: Garland, 1989); and US Census Bureau, *1930 Census of the Population: Volume 3, Population, Reports by States* (Washington, DC: Government Printing Office, 1932), 291.

37. Mae M. Ngai, *Impossible Subjects: Illegal Aliens and the Making of Modern America* (Princeton, NJ: Princeton University Press, 2004), 17–75; Natalia Molina, *How Race Is Made in America: Immigration, Citizenship, and the Historical Power of Racial Scripts* (Berkeley, CA: University of California Press, 2013), especially 19–42; and Montejano, *Anglos and Mexicans*, 182–191.

38. Ngai, *Impossible Subjects*, 400,000 on 72; and Foley, *White Scourge*, 250,000 on 175.

39. Foley, *White Scourge*, quoted on 207; and Deborah Cohen, *Braceros: Migrant Citizens and Transnational Subjects in the Postwar United States and Mexico* (Chapel Hill, NC: University of North Carolina Press, 2011).

40. Cohen, *Braceros*, 500,000 on 30; Carl Allsup, *The American G.I. Forum: Origins and Evolution* (Austin, TX: University of Texas Press, 1982), 112–127; and Henry A. J. Ramos, *The American GI Forum: In Pursuit of the Dream, 1948–1983* (Houston, TX: Arte Público, 1998), 65–85.

41. Eugene Benavidez, interview; Menefee, "Mexican Migratory Workers," 19–26; Steven F. Mehls, *The New Empire of the Rockies: A History of Northeast Colorado* (Denver, CO: Bureau of Land Management, 1984), quoted on 142; United States Beet Sugar Association, *The Beet Sugar Story* (Washington, DC: United States Beet Sugar Association, 1959); various images found in box 8, folder 26, GWS Records; *Great Western Sugar Exhibit*, Loveland Museum, Loveland, CO; and US Census Bureau, *1940 Census: Agriculture, Vol. 1, Part 6*, 224.

42. United States Department of Labor, "Wartime Wages, Income, and Wage Regulation in Agriculture," Bulletin no. 883 (Washington, DC: Government Printing Office, 1946), 12; and President's Commission on Migratory Labor, *Migratory Labor in American Agriculture*, 119–135.

43. *Medal*, 16–18, quoted on 17; Menefee, "Mexican Migratory Workers," 19–26; Rubén Donato, *Mexicans and Hispanos in Colorado Schools and Communities, 1920–1960* (Albany, NY: State University of New York Press, 2007), 13–28; President's Commission on Migratory Labor, *Migratory Labor in American Agriculture*, 137–151, quoted on 154; and various images found in box 1, folder 16, and box 8, folder 7, GWS Records.

44. Donato, *Mexicans and Hispanos*, 29–88, quoted on 56.

45. *Medal*, 16–18.

46. *Medal*, 16–18; Eugene Benavidez, interview; and Menefee, "Mexican Migratory Workers," 26–35.

47. Volanto, *Texas, Cotton, and the New Deal*, quoted on 9; *Medal*, 16–18, quoted on 17; and Eugene Benavidez, interview.

48. *Medal*, 16–18; and Eugene Benavidez, interview.

49. President's Commission on Migratory Labor, *Migratory Labor in American Agriculture*, 78–83, quoted on 85 and 16.

50. Texas Historical Commission, *Texas in World War II* (Austin, TX: Texas Historical Commission, 2005); and Joanne Rao Sánchez, "The Latinas of World War II: From Familial Shelter to Expanding Horizons," in Maggie Rivas-Rodríguez and Emilio Zamora, eds., *Beyond the Latino World War II Hero: The Social and Political Legacy of a Generation* (Austin, TX: University of Texas Press, 2009), 5 percent on 76.

51. By 1954, 95 percent of Great Western Sugar Company beets were harvested by machines. GW Sugar Company, "GW," fiftieth anniversary publication, 1955, box 36, folder 1, GWS Records. By 1964, 78 percent of United States cotton was harvested by machines. Foley, *White Scourge*, 207.

52. Ira Katznelson, *Fear Itself: The New Deal and the Origins of Our Time* (New York: Liveright, 2013), and especially 148–182 and 227–275; and President's Commission on Migratory Labor, *Migratory Labor in American Agriculture*, 3–5, quoted on 5.

53. *Medal*, 16–18; Eugene Benavidez, interview; and US Census Bureau, *1950 Census of the Population: Vol. 1, Number of Inhabitants* (Washington, DC: Government Printing Office, 1952), 43–28.

54. *Medal*, 19–20; and Eugene Benavidez, interview.

55. *Medal*, 19; and US Census Bureau, *1900 Census of the Population: Vol. 1, Population, Part 1* (Washington, DC: United States Census Office, 1901), 786.

56. *Medal*, 19–21, quoted on 21; and Eugene Benavidez, interview.

57. Eugene Benavidez, interview; and Montejano, *Anglos and Mexicans*, 225–228.

58. *Medal*, quoted on 22 and 14.

59. *Medal*, quoted on 16.

60. Texas, Death Certificates, 1903–1982, DeWitt County, 1946, July–Sept., no. 40526, Teresa Perez Chavez, died September 25, 1946, digital image, Ancestry.com; *Medal*, 11–13; and Texas, Death Certificates, 1903–1982, DeWitt County, 1945, April–June, no. 25025, Bellatres Chavez, died June 25, 1945, digital image, Ancestry.com.

61. *Medal*, quoted on 11.

Chapter 3: A Leap of Faith

1. US Census Bureau, *1950 Census of the Population: Vol. 1, Number of Inhabitants*, 43–28; *The WPA Guide to Texas* (Austin: Texas Monthly Press, 1986, orig., 1940), 647; and Wharton County Historical Commission, *Wharton County Pictorial History*, 110–132.

2. Eugene Benavidez, interview.

3. Eugene Benavidez, interview; and *Medal*, 12.

4. *Medal*, 12–13.

5. *Medal*, 12–14.

6. *Medal*.

7. Texas, Death Certificates, 1903–1982, Wharton County, 1963, Jul.–Sept., no. 54273, Salvador Benavidez, died July 13, 1963, digital image, Ancestry.com; and *Medal*, 12–15.

8. *Medal*, 14.

9. *Medal*, 14–15, quoted on 14.

10. *Medal*, 15.

11. Mario T. García, *Mexican Americans: Leadership, Ideology, & Identity, 1930–1960* (New Haven, CT: Yale University Press, 1989); and Philis M. Barragán Goetz, *Reading, Writing, and Revolution: Escuelitas and the Emergence of a Mexican American Identity in Texas* (Austin, TX: University of Texas Press, 2020), 125–169.

12. Benjamin Márquez, *LULAC: The Evolution of a Mexican American Political Organization* (Austin, TX: University of Texas Press, 1993), 15–38; "Lulacs Now Boast 5,000," *Valley Morning Star*, October 3, 1937, 7; García, *Mexican Americans*, 25–61; and Aaron E. Sánchez, *Homeland: Ethnic Mexican Belonging Since 1900* (Norman, OK: University of Oklahoma Press, 2021), 41–67.

13. Márquez, *LULAC*, 15–38, quoted on 20; and Sánchez, *Homeland*, 100–109, quoted on 104.

14. Márquez, *LULAC*, 15–38; and Sánchez, *Homeland*, 100–109. For more on the labor-based leftist Mexican American organizations of the era, see García, *Mexican Americans*, 145–227.

15. Márquez, *LULAC*, 15–38; "Lulacs Now Boast 5,000," quoted on 7; and Sánchez, *Homeland*, 43.

16. Sánchez, *Homeland*, 47–67.

17. Darlene Clark Hine, *Black Victory: The Rise and Fall of the White Primary in Texas* (Columbia, MO: University of Missouri Press, 2003, orig., 1979); and Kibbe, *Latin Americans in Texas*, 227–229.

18. Montejano, *Anglos and Mexicans*, 262–271, 60 percent on 247–249, quoted on 193.

19. Montejano, *Anglos and Mexicans*.

20. Montejano, *Anglos and Mexicans*, 15–16.

21. Montejano, *Anglos and Mexicans*, 21.

22. Montejano, *Anglos and Mexicans*, 22.

23. *Medal*, 14, quoted on 21.

24. *Medal*, quoted on 21.

25. *Medal*, quoted on 21 and 22.

26. *Medal*, 12–22, quoted on 19; Albert C. Gregurek Questionnaire, box 4Zc197, folder 4, RBP; and Eugene Benavidez, interview.

27. *Medal*, 12–22, quoted on 19.

28. *Medal*, 21–23, quoted on 22.

29. *Medal*, quoted on 23; and Dub King, "Worley Impresses with Knockout," *Fort Worth Star-Telegram*, February 13, 1948, 13.

30. *Medal*, 21–23; "Wharton County Sheriffs, 1846–1996," list on display at the Wharton County Historical Museum in Wharton, Texas; and "T. W. 'Buckshot' Lane," obituary, *Victoria Advocate*, July 12, 1991, 12A.

31. Buck Lane to J. J. Herrera, Wharton, TX, May 14, 1949, digital image, Houston Metropolitan Research Center at Houston Public Library, https://texashistory .unt.edu/ark:/67531/metapth249334/m1/1/, accessed December 14, 2020; and John J. Herrera Papers Finding Aid, Houston Metropolitan Research Center, Houston Public Library, Houston, TX.

32. *Medal*, quoted on 22; and Eugene Benavidez, interview.

33. *Medal*, 23–24; and Eugene Benavidez, interview.

34. *Medal*, 23–24.

35. *Medal*, 23–24, quoted on 24; and BMR.

36. *Medal*, 24–29, quoted on 24; and Vera Schramm Questionnaire, box 4Zc197, folder 4, RBP.

37. *Medal*, 25.

38. *Medal*, 25; and "Rev. A. F. Haddock—Obituary," *Victoria Advocate*, May 28, 1988, 12.

39. *Medal*, quoted on 29.

40. *Medal*, 29–31, quoted on 30 and 61; and 1940 US Census, San Patricio County, Texas, Population Schedule, Justice Precinct 1, Sheet 15b, Dwelling 4, Family 385, Coy family, digital image, Ancestry.com.

41. *Medal*, 29–30 and 63, quoted on 30 and 63, respectively.

42. *Medal*, 29–30.

43. *Medal*; Yvette Garcia, interview by William Sturkey, El Campo, TX, December 4, 2015, transcript in author's possession; and Denise Prochazka, interview by William Sturkey, El Campo, TX, July 16, 2016, transcript in author's possession.

44. Allsup, *American G.I. Forum*, 15–20; Richard Griswold Del Castillo, "The War and Changing Identities: Personal Transformations," in Richard Griswold Del Castillo, ed., *World War II and Mexican American Civil Rights* (Austin, TX: University of Texas Press, 2008), 50; and Sánchez, "Latinas of World War II," 63–89.

45. Ronald Takaki, *Double Victory: A Multicultural History of America in World War II* (Boston, MA: Little, Brown, 2000), quoted on 83; and Griswold Del Castillo, "War and Changing Identities," quoted on 51.

46. Takaki, *Double Victory*, quoted on 89, 87–88, and 83; and Maggie Rivas-Rodriguez, "Introduction," in Maggie Rivas-Rodriguez, ed., *Mexican Americans & World War II* (Austin, TX: University of Texas Press, 2005).

47. Richard Steele, "The Federal Government Discovers Mexican Americans," in Griswold Del Castillo, *World War II*, 19–33, quoted on 24; and Foley, *Mexicans in the Making of America*, 64–95. For testimonies of wartime discrimination toward Mexican Americans, see Appendix G: "Affidavits of Mexican Americans Regarding Discrimination in Texas During World War II," in Griswold Del Castillo, *World War II*, 189–206.

48. Macario García, Medal of Honor Citation, Congressional Medal of Honor Society, www.cmohs.org/recipients/marcario-garcia; and Michael A. Olivas, "The 'Trial of the Century' That Never Was: Staff Sgt. Macario Garcia, the Congressional Medal of Honor, and the Oasis Café," *Indiana Law Journal*, vol. 83, no. 4 (Fall 2008), 1391–1403.

49. Allsup, *American G.I. Forum*, 30–38; Ramos, *American GI Forum*, 1–17; and Ernest Morgan, "A Man of Controversy," *Corpus Christi Caller-Times*, December 18, 1966, 4B for Martin Luther King comparison.

50. Allsup, *American G.I. Forum*, 33–38; and Ramos, *American GI Forum*, 1–17.

51. Allsup, *American G.I. Forum*, 36–51.

52. Ramos, *American G.I. Forum*, 1–64, Raul Yzaguirre quoted on vii.

53. Steven Rosales, *Soldados Razos at War: Chicano Politics, Identity, and Masculinity in the U.S. Military from World War II to Vietnam* (Tucson, AZ: University of Arizona Press, 2017), 54–71 and 118–136.

54. *Medal*, 21–31, quoted on 21–22.

55. Glen Ross, "Texas National Guard Traces History to Battle of Alamo," *El Paso Times*, March 4, 1951, 33; "Ainsworth Says Security Costs Less Than War

Loss," *Corpus Christi Caller-Times*, September 6, 1949, 24; and Annual Report of the Adjutant General, August 31, 1950, box 401-899, folder 20, Texas Adjutant General's Department Texas National Guard Records, Texas State Archives.

56. "Gen. K. L. Berry Freezes Discharges from All the Texas National Guard," *Hood County News-Tablet*, July 27, 1950, 4; "Regular Armed Force Service Only Guard Release Excuse," *Corpus Christi Caller-Times*, January 19, 1951, 8; and Bruce A. Olson, "Texas National Guard," *Texas State Historical Association Handbook of Texas*, www.tshaonline.org/handbook/entries/texas-national-guard, accessed June 7, 2021.

57. "Members of America's Defense Team—Ad," *Waxahachie Daily Light*, February 1, 1950, 4; "Audie Joins Guard, Sworn in as Captain," *Fort Worth Star-Telegram*, July 15, 1950, 1; and copy of Audie Murphy poster on display at Texas Military Forces Museum, Austin, TX.

58. *Medal*, quoted on 30; and Benavidez Guard File.

Chapter 4: Cold Warrior

1. *Medal*, 31; Benavidez Guard File; and William C. Barnard, "Many Air Fields Are Reactivated," *Longview Sunday News-Journal*, April 11, 1948, 2.

2. Melvyn P. Leffler, *A Preponderance of Power: National Security, the Truman Administration, and the Cold War* (Stanford, CA: Stanford University Press, 1992); and Odd Arne Westad, *The Global Cold War: Third World Interventions and the Making of Our Times* (Cambridge, UK: Cambridge University Press, 2005), 8–38.

3. Benavidez Guard File; Annual Report of the Adjutant General, August 31, 1950, box 401-899, folder 20, Texas Adjutant General's Department Texas National Guard Records, Texas State Archives; and *Medal*, 30–31.

4. *Medal*, 30–35, quoted on 30; and "Recruiting Training Is Investigated," *Billings Gazette*, April 16, 1951, 7.

5. *Medal*, quoted on 30 and 31.

6. *Medal*.

7. *Medal*, 30–33, quoted on 32; BMR; and US Department of Commerce, *State Personal Income*, 9.

8. *Medal*, 30–33, quoted on 31.

9. *Medal*, 31–32.

10. *Medal*, 32; Benavidez Guard File; and Art Keinarth Questionnaire, box 4Zc197, folder 4, RBP.

11. *Medal*, 32–33.

12. *Three Wars*, 87.

13. *Medal*, 32–33, quoted on 33.

14. *Medal*, 34; Muhammad Ali and Richard Durham, *The Greatest: My Own Story* (New York: Random House, 1975), 162; and personal observations made on December 5, 2015.

15. Benavidez Military File; and 1955 Military Pay Chart, Defense Finance and Accounting Service, www.dfas.mil/Portals/98/MilPayTable1955.pdf, accessed November 2, 2021.

16. Bruce Cumings, *The Korean War: A History* (New York: Modern Library, 2010), killed statistic on 35; and Bruce Cumings, *Korea's Place in the Sun: A Modern History* (New York: Norton, 2005), especially 237–298.

17. Fredrik Logevall, *Embers of War: The Fall of an Empire and the Making of America's Vietnam* (New York: Random House, 2012), 3–91, two million on 81.

18. Logevall, *Embers of War*, 67–91.

19. Ho Chi Minh, "Speech at the Tours Congress" and "Speech at the Founding of the Communist Party of Indo-China," in Jack Woods, ed., *Ho Chi Minh: Selected Articles and Speeches, 1920–1967* (New York: International, 1969), 13–14 and 26–28; and Logevall, *Embers of War*, 67–120.

20. "The Vietnamese Declaration of Independence," in Robert McMahon, ed., *Major Problems in the History of the Vietnam War: Documents and Essays* (Lexington, MA: Heath, 1990), 35–36; Ho Chi Minh, "Speech Delivered in the First Days of the Resistance War in South Viet Nam," in Woods, *Ho Chi Minh*, 34–35; and Logevall, *Embers of War*, 67–120.

21. Logevall, *Embers of War*, 123–701.

22. *Medal*, 37.

23. *Medal*, 37–39, quoted on 38.

24. *Medal*, 38.

25. *Medal*, 38.

26. Edwin R. Andrews, "Your Soldier Sons," *Honolulu Star-Bulletin*, December 24, 1955, 4–5; and *Medal*, quoted on 35.

27. *Medal*, xv and 38–39.

28. *Medal*, 38–40.

29. Record of Assignments, BMR; and *Medal*, 40–41.

30. *Medal*, 40; and Tony La Russa quoted in Bill Pennington, *Billy Martin: Baseball's Flawed Genius* (Boston: Houghton Mifflin Harcourt, 2015), xi and 110–113.

31. *Medal*, 41.

32. *Medal*, 41.

33. *Medal*.

34. Record of Assignments, BMR; *Medal*, 43; and Richard E. Ecker, *Korean Battle Chronology: Unit-by-Unit United States Casualty Figures and Medal of Honor Citations* (Jefferson, NC: McFarland, 2005), 186.

35. Record of Assignments, BMR; *Medal*, 43; and Cumings, *Korea's Place in the Sun*, 299–341.

36. *Medal*, 43 and 44.

37. *Medal*, 45.

38. *Medal*, 46–48.

39. *Medal*, 46.

40. *Medal*, 61.

41. Record of Assignments, BMR; 180,000 from Walter Trohan, "Yank Troops Abroad Drain on Taxpayers," *Chicago Daily Tribune*, March 11, 1958, 1; Hope M. Harrison, *Driving the Soviets Up the Wall: Soviet-East German Relations, 1953–1961* (Princeton, NJ: Princeton University Press, 2003), 49–138, 500,000 on 102; and *Medal*, quoted on 55.

42. *Medal*, 56–59, quoted on 56; *Three Wars*, 84–86 and 89–96; and BMR.

43. Commanding Officer to Roy Benavidez, APO 742, September 27, 1957, BMR.

44. *Medal*, 56–62, quoted on 61 and 56, respectively.

45. *1955 El Campo Ech-O*, digital images, Ancestry.com.

46. BMR.

47. *Medal*, 62–63, quoted on 62.

48. *Medal*.

49. *Medal*.

50. BMR; 1958 Military Pay Chart, Defense Finance and Accounting Service, www.dfas.mil/Portals/98/MilPayTable1958.pdf, accessed November 2, 2021; and *Medal*, 62–63, quoted on 63.

51. *Medal*, 62–64, quoted on 63.

52. *Medal*, 63–65, quoted on 64; and Roy and Lala Benavidez wedding photos, June 7, 1959, copy in author's possession.

53. *Medal*, 63–65, quoted on 64.

54. BMR; and *Medal*, 63–66, quoted on 64 and Westmoreland on 66.

55. BMR; 1958 Military Pay Chart; and *Medal*, quoted on 67.

56. *Medal*, 67–69.

57. *Three Wars*, 113–115, quoted on 114; *Medal*, 67–69; and 82nd Airborne Division, Certificate of Completion, May 12, 1961, box 4Zc194, folder 56, RBP.

58. William MacDougall, "Paratroopers Set for Battle," *Los Angeles Times*, March 26, 1962, 2; and Leroy Thompson, *The All Americans: The 82nd Airborne* (New York: David & Charles, 1988).

59. Serhii Plokhy, *Nuclear Folly: A History of the Cuban Missile Crisis* (New York: Norton, 2021); Harrison, *Driving the Soviets*; Frederick Kempe, *Berlin, 1961: Kennedy, Khrushchev, and the Most Dangerous Place on Earth* (New York: Putnam, 2011); Odd Arne Westad, *The Cold War: A World History* (New York: Basic, 2017); and Neil Sheehan, *A Bright Shining Lie: John Paul Vann and America in Vietnam* (New York: Random House, 1988), figures on 43.

60. BMR; GED Completion Certificate, November 11, 1963, box 4Zc194, folder 52, RBP; and *Medal*, quoted on 66.

Chapter 5: Land Mine

1. *Three Wars*, 9–19, quoted on 10.

2. *Three Wars*, 9–20.

3. *Three Wars*, quoted on 22–24; "Marines Jam Base to See Hope's Show," *Los Angeles Times*, December 25, 1968, 5; "LBJ Sends His Thanks to Bob Hope," *Miami Herald*, December 30, 1965, 1; and Hedda Hopper, "Hope's Tour May Include Son's Base," *Los Angeles Times*, August 23, 1965, C23.

4. Logevall, *Embers of War*, 217–546, de Lattre quoted on 283, Eisenhower quoted on 339 and 365; and Dulles quoted in Lloyd Gardner, "Introduction," and Memo, Department of State, March 27, 1952, "Draft—Indochina Section of NSC Paper," William Appleman Williams et al., eds., *America in Vietnam: A Documentary History* (New York: Norton, 1989), 121–127 and 133.

5. Logevall, *Embers of War*, 547–619, killed statistics on 607 and 619; Memo, Department of State, March 27, 1952, $1.2 billion on 125; and Ho Chi Minh, "Appeal Made After the Successful Conclusion of the Geneva Agreements," in Woods, *Ho Chi Minh*, 91–93.

6. Logevall, *Embers of War*, 615–701, quoted on 669.

7. Logevall, *Embers of War*, 615–701, $300 million on 669, 250,000 on 677; and "The SEATO Treaty" and "SEATO in Power," in Williams et al., *America in Vietnam*, 174–178 and 180–182.

8. Logevall, *Embers of War*, 615–701, Eisenhower quoted on 675; "Text of Eisenhower-Diem Statement," *New York Times*, May 12, 1957, 25; "The Text of

President Diem's Address to Congress," *New York Times*, May 10, 1957, 12; and "An Asian Liberator," *New York Times*, May 10, 1957, 13.

9. Logevall, *Embers of War*, 674–701; and Sheehan, *Bright Shining Lie*, 192–196.

10. Logevall, *Embers of War*, 674–701, quoted on 679; and William J. Jordan, "Ferment in Asia Worries U.S.," *New York Times*, November 12, 1960, 2.

11. "Kennedy Attacks Nixon 'Weakness,'" *New York Times*, August 25, 1960, 1; and John F. Kennedy, "Inaugural Address," Washington, DC, January 20, 1961, John F. Kennedy Presidential Library and Museum, www.jfklibrary.org/archives /other-resources/john-f-kennedy-speeches/inaugural-address-19610120, accessed July 19, 2021.

12. Logevall, *Embers of War*, 702–714, 11,000 on 705; and Sheehan, *Bright Shining Lie*, 35–125.

13. Sheehan, *Bright Shining Lie*, 173–199, torture techniques on 102–103.

14. David Halberstam, "The Buddhist Crisis in Vietnam," *New York Times*, September 11, 1963, 14; "Diem, Nhu Suicides," *Los Angeles Times*, November 2, 1963, 1; and Logevall, *Embers of War*, 16,000 on 705.

15. "Transcript of President Johnson's Address . . .," *New York Times*, November 28, 1963, 20; and Fredrik Logevall, *Choosing War: The Lost Chance for Peace and the Escalation of War in Vietnam* (Berkeley, CA: University of California Press, 1999), especially 75–192, quoted on 77.

16. Logevall, *Choosing War*, 193–299; and "Statement by Secretary McNamara," August 6, 1964, box 76, folder: Gulf of Tonkin ('64–67) (2), NSF-Vietnam.

17. Paul Hendrickson, *The Living and the Dead: Robert McNamara and Five Lives of a Lost War* (New York: Knopf, 1996), especially 76–118; William C. Westmoreland, *A Soldier Reports* (New York: Da Capo, 1989, orig., 1976), 119–143; and Phillip B. Davidson, *Vietnam at War: The History, 1946–1975* (New York: Oxford University Press, 1988), 387–423.

18. Neil Sheehan et al., *The Pentagon Papers: The Secret History of the Vietnam War* (New York: Bantam, 1971), especially 307–458, eighteen to twenty thousand and one hundred thousand on 384; Lyndon B. Johnson, "Peace Without Conquest," Baltimore, MD, April 7, 1965, Lyndon B. Johnson Presidential Library, www.presidency.ucsb.edu/documents/address-johns-hopkins-university -peace-without-conquest, accessed July 19, 2021; and Logevall, *Embers of War*, 180,000 on 714.

19. AP, "U.S. Battalions Pull Back in Vietnam Battle," *Los Angeles Times*, November 17, 1965, 1; and Harold G. Moore and Joseph L. Galloway, *We Were Soldiers Once . . . and Young* (New York: Ballantine, 1992).

20. Moore and Galloway, *We Were Soldiers*, 234 on xxiv; Sheehan, *Bright Shining Lie*, 573–580; Davidson, *Vietnam at War*, 360–363, 1,200 on 362; *American Military History, Vol. II: The United States Army in a Global Era, 1917–2008* (Washington, DC: US Army Center of Military History, 2010), 311–314; and William Anderson, "U.S. Victory Seen in Viet Fight," *Chicago Tribune*, November 20, 1965, S6.

21. BMR; *Medal*, 70–71.

22. Eric Michael Burke, "A Brief Tactical Survey and Military Bibliography of the American War(s) in Vietnam," unpublished manuscript in author's possession.

23. W. P. Davidson and J. J. Zasloff, "A Profile of Viet Cong Cadres," June 1966, RM-4983-ISA/ARPA, box 237, folder: A Profile of Vietcong Cadres, NSF-Vietnam;

J. M. Carrier and C. A. H. Thomson, "Viet Cong Motivation and Morale," May 1966, RM-4830-ISA/ARPA, box 237, folder: Viet Cong Motivation and Morale, 5/66, NSF-Vietnam; and *American Military History, Vol. II*, 294–297.

24. W. P. Davidson and J. J. Zasloff, "A Profile of Viet Cong Cadres," June 1966, RM-4983-ISA/ARPA, box 237, folder: A Profile of Vietcong Cadres, NSF-Vietnam; J. M. Carrier and C. A. H. Thomson, "Viet Cong Motivation and Morale," May 1966, RM-4830-ISA/ARPA, box 237, folder: Viet Cong Motivation and Morale, 5/66, NSF-Vietnam; *American Military History, Vol. II*, 294–297; and Le Ly Hayslip with Jay Wurts, *When Heaven and Earth Changed Places: A Vietnamese Woman's Journey from War to Peace* (New York: Plume, 1990).

25. *Medal*, quoted on 76; and *Three Wars*, quoted on 27.

26. *Medal*, quoted on 75 and 71, respectively. For more, see Gregory A. Daddis, *No Sure Victory: Measuring U.S. Army Effectiveness and Progress in the Vietnam War* (New York: Oxford University Press, 2011).

27. *Three Wars*, quoted on 26; and *Medal*, 73–80, quoted on 81.

28. *Medal*, 73–80; and *Three Wars*, 29–43, quoted on 26 and 15, respectively.

29. *Medal*, 73–80, quoted on 74; and *Three Wars*, 32–35.

30. *Medal*, 73–74; and *Three Wars*, 29–32.

31. *Medal*, 82–85, quoted on 83; and *Three Wars*, 39–43, quoted on 39, 41, and 42.

32. *Medal*, 77; and *Three Wars*, 46–49.

33. *Medal*, 75; and *Three Wars*, 60–62, quoted on 61.

34. *Medal*, quoted on 77, quoted on 80; *Three Wars*, quoted on 39; Sheehan, *Bright Shining Lie*, 49–125, quoted on 90; and Andrew Wiest, *Vietnam's Forgotten Army: Heroism and Betrayal in the ARVN* (New York: New York University Press, 2008), especially 11–64, two hundred thousand on 7.

35. *Medal*, 77–79; and *Three Wars*, 50–60.

36. *Medal*, 77–79; and *Three Wars*, 50–60.

37. *Medal*, 79–80, quoted on 79; *Three Wars*, 61–65, quoted on 62 and 64; and Nick Turse, *Kill Anything That Moves: The Real American War in Vietnam* (New York: Picador, 2013), especially 144–191.

38. AP, "33 Refugees Die in Massacre," *Spokane Chronicle*, January 19, 1966, 20; *Medal*, 79–80; and *Three Wars*, 61–65.

39. *Three Wars*, 61–65, quoted on 63, 64, and 65.

40. BMR; *Medal*, 85; and *Three Wars*, 33–36.

41. *Medal*, 84–85.

42. BMR; *Medal*, 87–91, quoted on 87; and *Three Wars*, 69–72.

43. BMR; *Medal*, 87–91, quoted on 87; and *Three Wars*, 69–72.

44. "Vietnam's Reds Win Success in Years of War," *Philadelphia Tribune*, March 24, 1966, 14; *Medal*, 87–89; and *Three Wars*, 74–75, quoted on 74.

45. *Medal*, 87–89; and *Three Wars*, 74–75.

46. *Medal*, 87–89, quoted on 88 and 89; and *Three Wars*, 74–75.

47. *Medal*, 90–91, quoted on 90 and 91.

48. *Medal*, 87–94; and *Three Wars*, 79–83, quoted on 82.

49. *Medal*, 93–98, quoted on 94; and *Three Wars*, 79–83.

50. *Medal*, 93–98, quoted on 94; and *Three Wars*, 79–83.

51. *Medal*, 93–98, quoted on 95; and *Three Wars*, 79–83.

52. *Medal*, 93–98; and *Three Wars*, 79–83.

53. *Medal*, 93–98; and *Three Wars*, 79–83 and 97–100.

Chapter 6: Sojourn

1. BMR; and *Medal*, quoted on 99.

2. John G. Norris, "Army Shortly Will Open 3 New Training Centers," *Washington Post*, April 9, 1966, A11; "New Army Training Centers to Turn Out 30,000 a Month," *Atlanta Journal* and *Atlanta Constitution*, April 10, 1966, 2; "Carriers Find Short Cut to Viet Jungles," *Daily Independent* (Kannapolis, NC), October 16, 1966, 3A; Don Gray, "Fort Bragg Gets Ready for Recruits," *Charlotte Observer*, May 8, 1966, 1C for fifty thousand; and Don King, "Guardsmen Brave Heat, Dust, Noise—And Red Bugs," *Rocky Mount Telegram*, June 26, 1966, quoted on 1B.

3. Davidson, *Vietnam at War*, troop figures on 395 and bombing tonnage on 394; Oleg Hoeffding, "Bombing North Vietnam," December 1966, RM-5213-ISA, box 237, folder 7, NSF-Vietnam; and "Mr. Johnson's Terms for Withdrawal from Vietnam," *The Guardian*, September 6, 1966, 9.

4. Márquez, *LULAC*, 39–85; Allsup, *American G.I. Forum*, 98–141; Foley, *Mexicans in the Making of America*, 148–179; and *Medal*, quoted on 101.

5. "Hispanics in the Army," US Army, www.army.mil/hispanics/history.html#: ~:text=More%20than%2080%2C000%20Hispanic%2DAmericans,the%20 Siege%20of%20Khe%20Sanh, accessed February 27, 2023; Steven Rosales, *Soldados Razos at War: Chicano Politics, Identity, and Masculinity in the U.S. Military from World War II to Vietnam* (Tucson, AZ: University of Arizona Press, 2017), 90–136; and Lorena Oropeza, *¡Raza Sí! ¡Guerra No!: Chicano Protest and Patriotism During the Viet Nam War Era* (Berkeley, CA: University of California Press, 2005), 58–66, Garcia quoted on 62, entertainer on 63.

6. Oropeza, *¡Raza Sí!*, 1–10 and 80–201; Allsup, *American G.I. Forum*, 152; and David Montejano, *Quixote's Soldiers: A Local History of the Chicano Movement, 1966–1981* (Austin, TX: University of Texas Press, 2010), especially 117–143.

7. Lea Ybarra, ed., *Vietnam Veteranos: Chicanos Recall the War* (Austin, TX: University of Texas Press, 2004), quoted on 211. Also see George Mariscal, ed., *Aztlán and Viet Nam: Chicano and Chicana Experiences of the War* (Berkeley, CA: University of California Press, 1999); Charley Trujillo, ed., *Soldados: Chicanos in Viêt Nam* (San Jose, CA: Chusma House, 1990); and Gil Dominguez, ed., *They Answered the Call: Latinos in the Vietnam War* (Baltimore, MD: PublishAmerica, 2004).

8. *Medal*, quoted on 99.

9. *Medal*, quoted on 100; and *Three Wars*, 97–98.

10. Morton Mintz, "Curb Sought on Darvon Painkiller," *Washington Post*, April 26, 1976, A1; and Robert C. Wolfe, Marcus Reidenberg, and Raul H. Vispo, "Propoxyphene (Darvon®) Addiction and Withdrawal Syndrome," *Annals of Internal Medicine*, vol. 70, no. 4 (April 1969), 773–776.

11. *Medal*, quoted on 100; and *Three Wars*, 1,500 and quoted on 99.

12. *Medal*, 100–101; and *Three Wars*, 98–99.

13. *Medal*, 100–101, doctor quoted on 100; and *Three Wars*, 98–99.

14. *Medal*, 100–101; and *Three Wars*, 98–99.

15. *Medal*, quoted on 101; and *Three Wars*, 99–100.

16. *Medal*, 100–103; and *Three Wars*, 99–100 and 116–120.

17. *Medal*, 100–103, quoted on 101; and *Three Wars*, 99–100 and 116–120.

18. *Medal*, 100–103, quoted on 101; and *Three Wars*, 99–100 and 116–120.

19. *Medal*, 100–103, quoted on 102; and *Three Wars*, 99–100 and 116–120, quoted on 119.

20. *Medal*, 100–103, quoted on 103; and *Three Wars*, 99–100 and 116–120, quoted on 119.

21. *Medal*, 100–103; and *Three Wars*, 99–100 and 116–120, quoted on 120.

22. Byron Sheppard to Roy Benavidez and Earle Burns, Fort Bragg, NC, November 5, 1966, and W. H. Pierce to Roy Benavidez, Fort Bragg, NC, November 5, 1966, BMR.

23. Charles M. Simpson III, *Inside the Green Berets: The First Thirty Years* (Novato, CA: Presidio, 1983), 19–75; and Everett Parker, "Green Berets Demonstrate Preparedness," *Orlando Evening Star*, December 10, 1966, 15.

24. Hanson W. Baldwin, "Green Beret Men—How They Work," *San Antonio Express/News*, August 7, 1966, 4; sales figures taken from Jack Smith, "Green Berets Offer Vietnam 'Hero Image,'" *Los Angeles Times*, March 11, 1966, Part II, 1; "Obituary: Barry Sadler," *Palm Beach Post*, November 7, 1989, 4B; and Christian G. Appy, *American Reckoning: The Vietnam War and Our National Identity* (New York: Viking, 2015), 119–130, *Saturday Evening Post* quoted on 120.

25. *Medal*, quoted on 103.

26. *Medal*, 103–105; and *Three Wars*, 120–122.

27. "John F. Kennedy Center for Special Warfare," *News & Observer*, May 28, 1965, 10; and Plaster, *Secret Commandos*, 7.

28. Plaster, *Secret Commandos*, 5–23.

29. BMR; *Medal*, 107–109, quoted on 107; *Three Wars*, 123–127; Shelby L. Stanton, *Green Berets at War: U.S. Army Special Forces in Southeast Asia, 1956–1975* (London: Arms and Armour, 1985), 167–170.

30. *Medal*, 107–109, quoted on 108; *Three Wars*, 123–127; Ted Gress, "U.S. Is Training New Breed of Warrior," *Lebanon Daily News*, June 1, 1966, 21; Plaster, *Secret Commandos*, quoted on 7; and Donald Duncan, *The New Legions* (New York: Random House, 1967), 117–199.

31. *Medal*, quoted on 108; *Three Wars*, 123–127; and Blehm, *Legend*, 57–59.

32. BMR; and Cpt. Lawrence O. Dover to Roy Benavidez, Fort Bragg, NC, November 1, 1967, box 4Zc194, folder 52, RBP.

33. Hal Hendrix, "Green Beret Men Called Work Horses of Command," *Miami Herald*, March 9, 1966, 1-BW; and Westad, *Global Cold War*, 143–152.

34. Hendrix, "Green Beret Men"; and Georgie Anne Geyer, "Green Beret Rumors Buzz," *Boston Globe*, December 22, 1966, 14.

35. *Medal*, 110–113, quoted on 112.

36. Memo, Secretary of Defense to the President, November 1, 1967, #2a, "A Fifteen Month Program for Military Operations in Southeast Asia," box 75, folder: Primarily McNamara Recommendations re Strategic Actions [1 of 2], NSF-Vietnam.

37. Memo, Joint Chiefs of Staff to the Secretary of Defense, October 17, 1967, #3b, "Increased Pressures on North Vietnam," box 75, folder: Primarily McNamara Recommendations re Strategic Actions [1 of 2], NSF-Vietnam; and John Prados, *The Blood Road: The Ho Chi Minh Trail and the Vietnam War* (New York: Wiley, 1999).

38. Prados, *Blood Road*, 296–297.

39. David P. Chandler, *The Tragedy of Cambodian History: Politics, War, and Revolution Since 1945* (New Haven, CT: Yale University Press, 1991), 14–45.

40. Chandler, *Tragedy of Cambodian History*, 46–121; William J. Rust, *Eisenhower & Cambodia: Diplomacy, Covert Action, and the Origins of the Second Indochina War* (Lexington, KY: University Press of Kentucky, 2016); and Norodom Sihanouk, *My War with the CIA: The Memoirs of Prince Norodom Sihanouk* (New York: Pantheon, 1972), 92–93.

41. Chandler, *Tragedy of Cambodian History*, 99–107; and Sihanouk, *My War with the CIA*, 107–113, quoted on 113 and 131.

42. Chandler, *Tragedy of Cambodian History*, 140; Memo, James C. Thomson Jr. to the President, December 28, 1964, #145, "United States Relations with Cambodia," box 236, folder: Memos 8/64–6/65, vol. III, NSF-Cambodia; and Henry Raymont, "Cambodia Recalls Envoy," *New York Times*, December 13, 1963, 1.

43. Peter Grose, "Cambodia Given Apology on Raids," *New York Times*, March 22, 1964, 1; Richard Eder, "U.S. Voices Regret on Cambodian Raid," *New York Times*, September 24, 1966, 1; Peter Grose, "Cambodia Charge Conceded by U.S.," *New York Times*, October 29, 1964, 1; and Seymour Topping, "Cambodia Breaks Tie with the U.S.," *New York Times*, May 4, 1965, 1.

44. Topping, "Cambodia Breaks Tie"; Memo, White House Situation Room to the President, April 26, 1965, #140, box 236, folder: Memos 8/64–6/65, vol. III, NSF-Cambodia; Memo, White House Situation Room to the President, May 3, 1965, #135 and CIA Intelligence Memo, April 29, 1965, #138, both located in box 236, folder: Memos 8/64–6/65, vol. III, NSF-Cambodia; and Kenton J. Clymer, "The Perils of Neutrality: The Break in U.S.-Cambodian Relations, 1965," *Diplomatic History*, vol. 23, no. 4 (Fall 1999), 609–631.

45. CIA Intelligence Cable, December 19, 1966, #8, "Discussion by Cambodian Government Representatives of Report on Negotiations with National Front for Liberation of South Vietnam," box 237, folder: Cables vol. IV, 10/65–9/67, NSF-Cambodia.

46. CIA Intelligence Memo, June 13, 1966, #43, "Cambodia and the Vietnamese Communists: A New Phase?," box 237, folder: Memos vol. IV, 10/65–9/67, NSF-Cambodia.

47. CIA Intelligence Memo, December 30, 1967, #7, "Transport of Arms and Other Commodities into South Vietnam Through Ratanakiri Province," box 92, folder: Cambodia 5/66–1/68 [1 of 2], NSF-Vietnam.

48. CIA Intelligence Memo, July 26, 1967, #5, "Cambodia and the Vietnamese Communists," box 92, folder: Cambodia 5E(1)b 5/66–1/68, NSF-Vietnam; CIA Intelligence Memo, September 5, 1967, #4, "Cambodia and the Vietnamese Communists," box 92, folder: Cambodia 5E(1)b 5/66–1/68, NSF-Vietnam; Memo, Secretary of State to American Embassy in Canberra, November 29, 1967, #86, box 92, folder: Cambodia 5/66–1/68 [2 of 2], NSF-Vietnam; and Chandler, *Tragedy of Cambodian History*, 122.

49. Memo, American Embassy Saigon to Secretary of State, October 1967, #108, "Cambodia," box 92, folder: Cambodia 5/66–1/68 [2 of 2], NSF-Vietnam.

50. Memo, American Consulate in Hong Kong to Secretary of State, December 30, 1967, #8, and Memo, White House Situation Room to the President, December 31, 1967, #2, both located in box 92, folder: Cambodia 5/66–1/68 [1 of 2],

NSF-Vietnam; and "Angry Sihanouk Shuts Cambodia to U.S. Newsmen 'Permanently,'" *Washington Post*, November 25, 1967, A8.

51. "ICC Says It Found No Rockets in Cambodia," *Washington Post*, September 16, 1967, A10; Arthur J. Dommen, "Cambodia Issue Seen as Largely Unsettled," *Los Angeles Times*, January 14, 1968, E16; Chalmes M. Roberts, "Policing of Cambodian Border Beset by Variety of Problems," *Washington Post*, January 6, 1968, A11; and Bernard Nossiter, "U.S. Set Back by ICC Ruling on Cambodia," *Los Angeles Times*, February 7, 1968, 16.

52. Memo, American Consulate in Hong Kong to Secretary of State, December 30, 1967, #8, box 92, folder: Cambodia 5/66–1/68 [1 of 2], NSF-Vietnam.

53. Memo, American Consulate in Hong Kong to Secretary of State, December 30, 1967, #8, box 92, folder: Cambodia 5/66–1/68 [1 of 2], NSF-Vietnam; Sihanouk Speech, undated, #32c, box 237, folder: Misc. Cables & Memos, 1/67–12/68 [2 of 2], NSF-Cambodia; and CIA Intelligence Memo, December 23, 1967, #44, "Comments of Soviet Member of United Nations," box 92, folder: Cambodia 5/66–1/68 [1 of 2], NSF-Vietnam.

54. Text of Cable from General Westmoreland, December 5, 1967, #80a, box 92, folder: Cambodia 5/66–1/68 [1 of 2], NSF-Vietnam; and Westmoreland, *Soldier Reports*, 180–184, quoted on 184.

55. Memo, Earle G. Wheeler to the Secretary of Defense, December 16, 1967, #62a, "Operations in the Triborder Area," box 92, folder: Cambodia 5/66–1/68 [2 of 2], NSF-Vietnam.

56. Memo, Earle G. Wheeler to the Secretary of Defense.

57. Memo, Secretary of State to Ambassador Canberra, November 29, 1967, #86, box 92, folder: Cambodia 5/66–1/68 [2 of 2], NSF-Vietnam; CIA Intelligence Memo, July 26, 1967, #5, "Cambodia and the Vietnamese Communists," box 92, folder: Cambodia 5E(1)b 5/66–1/68, NSF-Vietnam; *Medal*, 112–113; and Sihanouk Speech, December 27, 1967, #32a, box 237, folder: Misc. Cables & Memos 1/67–12/68, NSF-Cambodia.

58. *Three Wars*, quoted on 128; Robert M. Gillespie, *Black Ops, Vietnam: The Operational History of MACVSOG* (Annapolis, MD: Naval Institute Press, 2011), forty-four thousand on 142; Davidson, *Vietnam at War*, 473–528, eighty-four thousand and forty-five thousand on 475; and Statement by General Westmoreland, April 7, 1968, #24, box 96, folder: Talks with Hanoi, 6G (3) 4/1–10/68 [1 of 3], NSF-Vietnam.

59. Davidson, *Vietnam at War*, 529–574; Don Oberdorfer, *Tet!: The Turning Point in the Vietnam War* (Baltimore, MD: Johns Hopkins University Press, 2001, orig., 1971), 157–196; and Nguyen Co Thach quoted in Barbara Crossette, "Recalling Tet," *New York Times*, January 31, 1988, 1.

60. Davidson, *Vietnam at War*, 529–574; Walter Cronkite, "Report from Vietnam," *CBS Evening News*, February 27, 1968, transcript: www.digitalhistory.uh.edu/active_learning/explorations/vietnam/cronkite.cfm, accessed November 24, 2021; Editorial, "After the Tet Offensive," *New York Times*, February 8, 1968, 42; and Louis Harris, "War Support Spurts After Tet Attacks," *Washington Post*, February 12, 1968, A1.

61. Tom Wells, *The War Within: America's Battle over Vietnam* (Berkeley, CA: University of California Press, 1994), 223–286; "Anti-U.S. Protests Bring Street Fights,"

Washington Post, February 19, 1968, A9; and "LBJ Is Burned in Effigy at War Protest in Manila," *Washington Post*, January 24, 1968, A15.

62. *Medal*, quoted on 116.

63. *Medal*, 112–120; and *Three Wars*, quoted on 128.

Chapter 7: Fearless

1. *Medal*, 116–119, quoted on 117–118.

2. *Medal*, quoted on 109–111 and 118; and Lindsey, *Secret Green Beret Commandos*, 138.

3. *Medal*, 118–120, quoted on 118; *Three Wars*, 131–135; and Blehm, *Legend*, 103–105.

4. *Medal*, 118–120, quoted on 120; *Three Wars*, 131–135; and Blehm, *Legend*, 103–105.

5. BMR; Blehm, *Legend*, 93–110; Rottman, *US MACV-SOG*, 10 percent on 61; Plaster, *Secret Commandos*, 28–30; and Gillespie, *Black Ops*, 91–130.

6. Gillespie, *Black Ops*, 122; and Lindsey, *Secret Green Beret Commandos*, 54–55.

7. CIA Report, August 1967, #104a, "Communist Use of Cambodia in Support of the War in Vietnam," box 92, folder: Cambodia May 66–Jan. 68 [2 of 2], NSF-Vietnam; and Memo, CIA, March 7, 1968, #1a, "Recent Uses of Cambodian Territory," box 92, folder: 5E(2)a Jan. '68–Oct. '68 [1 of 2], NSF-Vietnam.

8. Gillespie, *Black Ops*, recon statistics on 123 and 151, respectively.

9. Rottman, *US MACV-SOG*, 11–54; Stanton, *Green Berets at War*, 205–213; and Plaster, *Secret Commandos*, 50–71.

10. Personal observations made on October 3, 2017.

11. Lindsey, *Secret Green Beret Commandos*, 109–117.

12. Rottman, *US MACV-SOG*, 26–43; and Plaster, *Secret Commandos*, 61–62.

13. Gillespie, *Black Ops*, 44; Plaster, *Secret Commandos*, 37; and Jeffrey J. Clarke, *Advice and Support: The Final Years, 1965–1973* (Washington, DC: US Army Center of Military History, 1988), 32–39, 69–74, and 195–207.

14. Gillespie, *Black Ops*, 44; Plaster, *Secret Commandos*, 37; Clarke, *Advice and Support*; George Shepard, interview by William Sturkey, Chapel Hill, NC, November 5, 2018, transcript in author's possession.

15. Clarke, *Advice and Support*, 32–39, 69–74, and 195–207.

16. *Medal*, 121–131; *Three Wars*, 131–135; and Plaster, *Secret Commandos*, quoted on 51.

17. *Medal*, 121–124, quoted on 121; *Three Wars*, 136–140; and Lindsey, *Secret Green Beret Commandos*, 91.

18. *Medal*, 121–124; *Three Wars*, 136–140; Lindsey, *Secret Green Beret Commandos*, 91; and COMUSMACV to RUHKA/CINCPAC, April 1968, #5a, "Operations near Cambodian Border," box 237, folder: Miscellaneous Cables & Memos 1/67–12/68 [1 of 2], NSF-Cambodia.

19. *Medal*, 122–123, quoted on 123; and *Three Wars*, 136–140.

20. Memo, Earle Wheeler to Deputy Secretary of Defense, 12/3/68, #15a, box 93, folder: Cambodia 5E(3) 11/68–1/69, NSF-Vietnam; and Lindsey, *Secret Green Beret Commandos*, 90–94.

21. Rottman, *US MACV-SOG*, 51–61; Gillespie, *Black Ops*, 91–130; Lindsey, *Secret Green Beret Commandos*, 52–83; and Richard R. Burgess and Rosario M. Rausa, *US Navy A-1 Skyraider Units of the Vietnam War* (New York: Osprey, 2009).

22. COMUSMACV to RUHKA/CINCPAC, April 1968, #5a, "Operations near Cambodian Border," box 237, folder: Miscellaneous Cables & Memos 1/67–12/68 [1 of 2], NSF-Cambodia; and Memo, Deputy Secretary of Defense, December 3, 1968, #15a, box 93, folder: Cambodia 5E(3) 11/68–1/69, NSF-Vietnam.

23. Plaster, *Secret Commandos*, quoted on 50.

24. Plaster, *Secret Commandos*.

25. Plaster, *Secret Commandos*, 50–71; and Memo, Earle Wheeler to Deputy Secretary of Defense, 12/3/68, #15a, box 93, folder: Cambodia 5E(3) 11/68–1/69, NSF-Vietnam.

26. *Medal*, 122–124, quoted on 123–124.

27. *Medal*.

28. *Medal*, 124–125; and *Three Wars*, quoted on 141 and 142.

29. *Three Wars*, quoted on 154.

30. *Medal*, 121–131; *Three Wars*, 124–125; Lindsey, *Secret Green Beret Commandos*, 118–120. Background information taken from various documents found on Ancestry.com.

31. *Medal*, 121–131, quoted on 130; and Rottman, *US MACV-SOG*, 26.

32. *Medal*, quoted on 124–128; and *Three Wars*, 141–149.

33. *Medal*, 128–131, quoted on 129; and *Three Wars*, 149–153.

34. *Medal*, 128–131, quoted on 129; and *Three Wars*, 149–153.

35. *Medal*, 128–131, quoted on 129; and *Three Wars*, 149–153.

36. *Medal*, 130–131; and *Three Wars*, 152–153.

37. *Medal*, 130–131; and *Three Wars*, 152–153.

38. The battle action from May 2, 1968, that follows is derived from Roy Benavidez Medal of Honor Citation; Brian O'Connor Eyewitness Statement, July 24, 1980, box 4Zc194, folder 2, RBP; Roger Waggie, Statement Concerning Events of May 2, 1968, April 29, 1976, BMR; Leroy Wright, Distinguished Service Cross Citation, and Lloyd F. Mousseau, Distinguished Service Cross Citation, both available through Vietnam Veterans Memorial Fund, www.vvmf.org; Ralph Drake, Recommendation for Award, May 12, 1975, BMR; Jerry Cottingham Statement, February 4, 1975, BMR; Jesse Naul to James W. Mason, Dallas, TX, March 31, 1975, BMR; Ronald Radke to James W. Mason, February 23, 1975, BMR; James C. Fussell to James W. Mason, October 27, 1975, BMR; Michael Grant to James W. Mason, Ft. Carson, CO, October 8, 1975, BMR; William Darling, Witness Statement, February 28, 1977, BMR; Chandler Carter, Witness Statement, April 7, 1977, BMR; Fact Sheet, Request for Upgrade of the Distinguished Service Cross to the Congressional Medal of Honor for MSG Roy Benavidez, BMR; *Medal*, 133–145; *Three Wars*, 177–223; Blehm, *Legend*, 110–222; and Lindsey, *Secret Green Beret Commandos*, 140–147.

Chapter 8: Home

1. Pete Billac, *The Last Medal of Honor: The True Story of Green Beret Sergeant Roy P. Benavidez and His Six-Hour Battle in Hell* (New York: Swan, 1990), 82; and *Medal*, 147.

2. Telegram, Maj. Gen. Kenneth G. Wickham to Hilaria Benavidez, May 5, 1968, BMR; Memo, CG USARV LBN RVN to RUEOAFA/CAS DIV DA, May 5, 1968, BMR; and *Medal*, 147.

3. *Medal*, 145.

4. Jerry Cottingham, Statement, February 4, 1975, BMR; Roger Waggie, Statement Concerning Events of May 2, 1968, April 29, 1976, BMR; *Medal*, 145; and Blehm, *Legend*, 220.

5. *Three Wars*, 224–231; *Medal*, 144–148; Roger Waggie, Statement Concerning Events of May 2, 1968, April 29, 1976, BMR; William R. Darling, Statement, February 28, 1977, BMR; and Blehm, *Legend*, 224–225.

6. Lindsey, *Secret Green Beret Commandos*, 140–147; and *Three Wars*, 224–231, quoted on 225.

7. Blehm, *Legend*, 221–224; and *Medal*, quoted on 145.

8. *Three Wars*, quoted on 225–226; and *Medal*, 147.

9. *Three Wars*, quoted on 226–227; and *Medal*, 147.

10. Michael Grant, Statement, October 7, 1975, BMR; and William R. Darling, Statement, February 28, 1977, BMR.

11. *Medal*, 147; *Three Wars*, 226; and Brian O'Connor, Eyewitness Statement, July 24, 1980, box 4Zc194, folder 2, RBP.

12. Record of Assignments, BMR; *Three Wars*, quoted on 227 and 228; and *Medal*, 148.

13. Record of Assignments, BMR; *Three Wars*, quoted on 227 and 228; and *Medal*, 148.

14. Jerry Cottingham, Statement, February 4, 1975, BMR; CIA Intelligence Memo, August 2, 1968, #21, box 93, folder: Cambodia 5E(3) 11/68–1/69, NSF-Vietnam; Lindsey, *Secret Green Beret Commandos*, 147–229.

15. Memo, Author unknown, "The Cambodian Border Problem," September 24, 1968, #17a, box 237, folder: Misc. Cables & Memos 1/67–12/68 [1 of 2], NSF-Cambodia; CIA Intelligence Cable, October 31, 1968, #14, box 237, folder: Misc. Cables & Memos 1/67–12/68 [1 of 2], NSF-Cambodia.

16. James H. Willbanks, *Vietnam War Almanac: An In-Depth Guide to the Most Controversial Conflict in American History* (New York: Skyhorse, 2013), 260–263; and Erik B. Villard, *Combat Operations: Staying the Course October 1967 to September 1968: The U.S. Army in Vietnam* (Washington, DC: US Army Center of Military History, 2017), 529–595, sixty thousand on 530, deceased figures on 589.

17. Villard, *Combat Operations*, 673–680, deceased statistics on 673.

18. Frank Newport and Joseph Carroll, "Iraq Versus Vietnam: A Comparison of Public Opinion," Gallup, August 24, 2005, https://news.gallup.com/poll/18097/iraq-versus-vietnam-comparison-public-opinion.aspx, accessed May 24, 2022; Memo, Art McCafferty to Walt Rostow, May 22, 1968, #5, "Achievements of the Tet Offensive," box 152, folder: Captured Documents, NSF-Vietnam; and Secretary of State to American Embassy Wellington, April 1968, box 96, folder: Talks with Hanoi, 6G(3) 4/1–10/68 [3 of 3], NSF-Vietnam.

19. Telegram, Department of State to American Embassy in Paris, May 7, 1968, #6GG, box 96, folder: Talks with Hanoi 6G (6) 5/68–9/68, NSF-Vietnam; and CIA Report, "The Vietnam Situation," June 6, 1968, #20a, box 76, folder: Strategic Reconsiderations After Tet (4/68–12/68), NSF-Vietnam.

20. Physical Evaluation Board Proceedings, July 7, 1976, BMR.

21. *Three Wars*, 227–229; and *Medal*, 148–149.

22. Ralph R. Drake, "Commander's Recommendation for Promotion," June 3, 1968, BMR; and 1968 Military Pay Chart, Defense Finance and Accounting Service, https://www.dfas.mil/Portals/98/MilPayTable1968.pdf, accessed April 22, 2022.

23. *Three Wars*, 227–229, quoted on 229; and *Medal*, 148–149.

24. Department of the Army, "Award of the Purple Heart," May 3, 1968, box 4Zc194, folder: 62, RBP; *Three Wars*, 227–229; *Medal*, 148–149; Award of the Distinguished Service Cross, Benavidez, Roy, July 24, 1968, BMR; Lloyd F. Mousseau, Distinguished Service Cross Citation, Leroy Wright, Distinguished Service Cross Citation, Larry McKibben, Distinguished Service Cross Citation, all available through the Vietnam Veterans Memorial Fund, www.vvmf.org/Wall-of-Faces.

25. Army Regulation 600-8-22, "Military Awards," 3-10 Distinguished Service Cross, 58, Department of the Army, https://armypubs.army.mil/epubs/DR_pubs/DR_a/pdf/web/ARN18147_R600_8_22_admin2_FINAL.pdf, accessed April 23, 2022; and Home of Heroes: Medal of Honor & Military History, https://homeofheroes.com/distinguished-service-cross/vietnam-war, accessed November 3, 2022.

26. Gillespie, *Black Ops*, 120; and Lindsey, *Secret Green Beret Commandos*, 21–27.

27. Award of the Distinguished Service Cross, Benavidez, Roy, July 24, 1968, BMR; Leroy Wright, Distinguished Service Cross Citation and Lloyd F. Mousseau, Distinguished Service Cross Citation, both available at the Vietnam Veterans Memorial Fund, www.vvmf.org; and *Three Wars*, quoted on 231.

28. *Three Wars*, 228–231, quoted on 229; and *Medal*, 148–149.

29. "'Westy's' Driver Awarded Second Highest Medal," *Baytown Sun*, September 11, 1968, 3; *Medal*, 148–149, quoted on 149; and *Three Wars*, 228–231.

30. "'Westy's' Driver." Image reprinted in *Medal*, insert between 110–111.

31. Roger Waggie to Roy Benavidez, South Vietnam, September 16, 1968, box 4Zc194, folder 35, RBP; and Blehm, *Legend*, 225–227.

32. Record of Assignments, BMR.

33. Health Record, box 4Zc194, folder 61, RBP; Blehm, *Legend*, 228–229; and Larry McKibben, Distinguished Service Cross Citation, Vietnam Veterans Memorial Fund, www.vvmf.org/Wall-of-Faces/36931/LARRY-S-MCKIBBEN.

34. Record of Assignments, BMR; *Medal*, 152; *Three Wars*, 235; and Clinical Record, March 20, 1969, box 4Zc194, folder 54, RBP.

35. *Medal*, 152; *Three Wars*, 235; and Record of Assignments, BMR.

36. *Three Wars*, 235–236; and Record of Assignments, BMR.

37. "Hearings before a Subcommittee of the Committee on Appropriations," House of Representatives, 20th Cong., 2nd sess., Part 2 (Washington, DC: Government Printing Office, 1968), 216–218; "There Goes Our Cavalry," *New York Daily News*, May 26, 1968, 106; Fort Riley Historical Society, Custer House Museum—Fort Riley, Kansas," www.fortrileyhistoricalsociety.org/custer-house.html; and various updates published in the *Manhattan Mercury* and *Salina Journal* between 1969 and 1972.

38. Bill Stone, "Veterans Paid Peaceful Tribute," *Wichita Eagle*, November 12, 1969, 1–2A.

39. *Medal*, 152; and *Three Wars*, 235–236.

40. Robert R. Linvill, Statement on Application for WO-1, July 30, 1970, BMR; Brig. Gen. J. A. Seitz to Adjutant General of the Army, Junction City, KS, July 20, 1971, BMR; Col. J. F. Wilhm, Letter of Recommendation, Fort Riley, KS, August 20, 1971, BMR; and Col. Richard Cavazos, Letter of Recommendation, Fort Riley, KS, January 13, 1972, BMR.

41. Willbanks, *Vietnam War Almanac*, 276–287.

42. William Beecher, "Raids in Cambodia by U.S. Unprotested," *New York Times*, May 9, 1969, 1; and Willbanks, *Vietnam War Almanac*, statistics on 290.

43. Lewis Gulick, "U.S. Seeks Ties with Cambodia," *Washington Post*, April 13, 1969, 1; Gene Roberts, "Wider Use of Cambodia by the Enemy Reported," *New York Times*, September 29, 1968, 1; Joseph Lelyveld, "India Hints a Shift on Cambodia Issue," *New York Times*, January 7, 1968, 1; A. D. Horne, "U.S., Cambodia Resume Relations," *Washington Post*, July 3, 1969, A1; Chandler, *Tragedy of Cambodian History*, 178–183.

44. Chandler, *Tragedy of Cambodian History*, 159–191; and Ben Kiernan, *How Pol Pot Came to Power: Colonialism, Nationalism, and Communism in Cambodia, 1930–1975*, Second Edition (New Haven, CT: Yale University Press, 2004, orig., 1985), 249–288.

45. "Go, Cambodia Tells Reds," *Chicago Tribune*, March 14, 1970, S1; Henry Kamm, "Cambodia Ending Neutralist Stance," *New York Times*, May 7, 1970, 1; Terrence Smith, "U.S. and Cambodia Sign Military Assistance Pact," *New York Times*, August 21, 1970, 1; and Kiernan, *How Pol Pot Came to Power*, 297–393.

46. Wells, *The War Within*, 403–470, 1,350 on 425; and Robert D. McFadden, "College Strife Spreads," *New York Times*, May 8, 1970, 1.

47. Kiernan, *How Pol Pot Came to Power*, 297–393, Hanoi Radio quoted on 299; Chandler, *Tragedy of Cambodian History*, 192–235; Sydney H. Schanberg, "Cambodia: Communist Pressure Steadily Growing," *New York Times*, June 21, 1970, 145; and James P. Sterba, "Cambodia Incursion by U.S. Appears to United Foe," *New York Times*, June 29, 1970, 1.

48. Record of Assignments, BMR; *Medal*, 152–153, quoted on 152; and *Three Wars*, 235–237.

49. Record of Assignments, BMR; *Medal*, 152–153; and *Three Wars*, 235–237.

50. Patrick Cassidy to President, DA Enlisted Promotion Selection Board E-8, San Antonio, TX, August 27, 1974, BMR.

51. James H. Hollingsworth to DA Enlisted Promotion Selection Board E-8, San Francisco, November 15, 1973, BMR; James T. L. Dandridge to DA Enlisted Promotion Selection Board E-8, Fort Sam Houston, TX, November 13, 1973, BMR; and Fred R. White to DA Enlisted Promotion Selection Board E-8, Fort Sam Houston, TX, December 11, 1973, BMR.

52. BMR.

53. James H. Willbanks, *Abandoning Vietnam: How America Left and South Vietnam Lost Its War* (Lawrence, KS: University Press of Kansas, 2004).

54. *Medal*, 153.

55. Enlistment Paperwork and article located in BMR.

Chapter 9: Honor

1. Roy Benavidez to Henry González, Fort Sam Houston, TX, February 25, 1974, box 4Zc194, folder 18, RBP. Marine Jay Vargas had received the Medal of Honor on May 14, 1970, for actions conducted in Vietnam on April 30–May 2, 1968, www .cmohs.org/recipients/jay-r-vargas.

2. "Military Awards for Valor-Top 3," Department of Defense, https://valor .defense.gov/Description-of-Awards; United States Army, "Recommendation Process" and "Statistics & FAQs," www.army.mil/medalofhonor/index.html, accessed March 17, 2023; and National Medal of Honor Museum, https://mohmuseum .org/the-medal/#:~:text=Through%20education%2C%20leadership%2C%20 and%20inspiring,Forces%20since%20the%20Civil%20War, accessed March 17, 2023.

3. Congressional Medal of Honor Society, Statistics & FAQs, www.cmohs.org /medal/faqs, accessed May 23, 2021; and United States Army, "Recommendation Process" and "Statistics & FAQs."

4. Lindsey, *Secret Green Beret Commandos*, 21–27; and Gillespie, *Black Ops*, 120–121.

5. *Medal*, 152.

6. *Medal*, 152–155; *Three Wars*, 235–240; and Blehm, *Legend*, 233–235.

7. *Medal*, 152–155; *Three Wars*, 235–240, quoted on 239; and Blehm, *Legend*, 233–235.

8. *Medal*, 152–155; *Three Wars*, 235–240; and Blehm, *Legend*, 233–235.

9. Ralph Drake to Commander Fifth US Army, Fort McClellan, AL, April 9, 1974, box 4Zc194, folder 15, RBP.

10. Army Regulation 15-185, Army Board for Correction of Military Records, Department of the Army, March 31, 2006.

11. *Medal*, 152–155, quoted on 153; *Three Wars*, 235–240; and Blehm, *Legend*, 233–235.

12. US Public Law 93-469, 93rd Cong., 2d sess. (October 24, 1974), 1422.

13. James Markham, "South Vietnam, a Year After Truce, Is Still Racked by Indecisive War," *New York Times*, January 27, 1974, 1; John A. Finney, "House Bars Rise in Vietnam Aid," *New York Times*, April 5, 1974, 77; and Philip A. McCombs, "Vietnam Fighting Heaviest Since Truce," *Washington Post*, August 20, 1974, A1.

14. Kevin M. Kruse and Julian E. Zelizer, *Fault Lines: A History of the United States Since 1974* (New York: Norton, 2019), especially 7–25.

15. Robert S. Bell to Commander, US Army Forces Command, Alexandria, VA, August 28, 1974, box 4Zc194, folder 4, RBP.

16. *Three Wars*, 241–249; and affidavits from Jerry Cottingham, Raymond Stipsky, Jesse Naul, Ronald Radke, James Fussell, Michael Grant, and John Crist in BMR. Jerry Ewing statement in box 4Zc194, folder 16, RBP.

17. Patrick Cassidy to Henry González, San Antonio, TX, July 4, 1975; and Patrick Cassidy to Harold G. Moore, San Antonio, TX, May 17, 1976, both located in box 4Zc194, folder 12, RBP.

18. Texas, Death Certificates, 1903–1982, Wharton County, 1975, Apr.–Jun., no. 39335, Nicholas Benavides, died May 1, 1975, digital image, Ancestry.com; and *Medal*, 153.

19. Sister Anna Theresa Hussey to Commander, San Antonio, TX, August 15, 1976, BMR.

20. Extracts of Special Orders No. 116, June 16, 1975; Patrick Cassidy to President, DA Enlisted Promotion Selection Board (E8), San Antonio, TX, August 27, 1974; 1974 Military Pay Chart, Defense Finance and Accounting Service, www .dfas.mil/Portals/98/MilPayTable1974.pdf, accessed June 11, 2022; and various course completion certificates, all located in BMR.

21. Patrick Cassidy to President, DA Enlisted Promotion Selection Board (E8), San Antonio, TX, August 27, 1974; and Disposition Form, "Ability to Perform Duty in Primary MOS . . . ," October 20, 1975, BMR.

22. Cpt. Curtis P. Miller to Roy Benavidez, Fort Sam Houston, Texas, March 11, 1976, BMR; and Disposition Form, "Reclassification Hearings," March 23, 1976, BMR.

23. Disposition Form, "MSG Roy Benavidez," May 7, 1976, BMR.

24. Francis J. Calverase to Roy Benavidez, Alexandria, VA, July 8, 1976, BMR; and William C. Moore to Joseph Martin, June 22, 1977, box 4Zc194, folder 2, RBP.

25. Physical Evaluation Board Proceedings, August 4, 1976, BMR.

26. Physical Evaluation Board Proceedings, August 4, 1976, BMR.

27. Physical Evaluation Board Proceedings, August 4, 1976, BMR.

28. Physical Evaluation Board Proceedings, August 4, 1976, BMR.

29. Physical Evaluation Board Proceedings, August 4, 1976, BMR.

30. Physical Evaluation Board Proceedings, August 4, 1976, BMR.

31. Medical Board Proceedings, June 10, 1976, BMR.

32. Physical Evaluation Board Proceedings, August 4, 1976, BMR.

33. James Windsor to Roy Benavidez, Retirement Orders D41-3, Alexandria, VA, August 27, 1976, BMR; and "Oft-Decorated Solider Retires," *Victoria Advocate*, September 11, 1976, 1.

34. *Three Wars*, 250–251, quoted on 251.

35. *Three Wars*, 254.

36. *Three Wars*, 254.

37. Joseph D. Martin to Roy Benavidez, Philadelphia, PA, June 16, 1976, box 4Zc194, folder 22, RBP.

38. Carlos C. Ogden to Joseph D. Martin, June 22, 1976; Joseph D. Martin to Roy Benavidez, Philadelphia, PA, undated; Joseph D. Martin to Roy Benavidez, Philadelphia, PA, June 28, 1976; and various letters all located in box 4Zc194, folder 22, RBP.

39. Joseph D. Martin to John Young, Philadelphia, PA, October 15, 1977; and various letters all located in box 4Zc194, folder 22, RBP.

40. William C. Moore to Joseph D. Martin, June 22, 1977; and Dudley Bunn to Joseph D. Martin, June 1, 1977, both located in box 4Zc194, folder 22, RBP.

41. Chris Barbee, interview by William Sturkey, El Campo, TX, December 5, 2015, transcript in author's possession; and Chris Barbee, Interview Questions.

42. "Oft-Decorated Solider Retires"; and Barbee interviews.

43. Barbee interviews.

44. Barbee interviews; and Fred Barbee to George Mahon, March 15, 1977, box 4Zc194, folder 37, RBP.

45. Memo, "For the Record," August 27, 1979, box 4Zc194, folder 48, RBP.

46. Steve Sucher, interview by William Sturkey, Gonzales, TX, December 4, 2015, transcript in author's possession.

47. Barbee, interview; Noel Benavidez, interviews; Garcia, interview; Prochazka, interview; Yvette Garcia and Denise Prochazka, interview by William Sturkey, El Campo, TX, August 1, 2018, transcript in author's possession; and Joe Munoz, interview by William Sturkey, San Marcos, TX, July 18, 2016, transcript in author's possession.

48. Barbee, interview; Noel Benavidez, interviews; Garcia, interview; Prochazka, interview; Garcia and Prochazka, interview; and Joe Munoz, interview.

49. Barbee, interview; Noel Benavidez, interviews; Garcia, interview; Prochazka, interview; Garcia and Prochazka, interview; and Joe Munoz, interview.

50. Sucher, interview.

51. Sucher, interview.

52. Sucher, interview.

53. Sucher, interview.

54. Fred Barbee, "Roy Benavidez . . . *Sometimes Patience Wears Thin*," *El Campo Leader-News*, February 22, 1978, 5-A.

55. *Three Wars*, 255–260, quoted on 257 and 259; and Sucher, interview.

56. Max Krochmal, *Blue Texas: The Making of a Multiracial Democratic Coalition in the Civil Rights Era* (Chapel Hill, NC: University of North Carolina Press, 2016), especially 153–170.

57. "Fact Sheet" and Robert S. Young to Roy Benavidez, September 22, 1978, located in box 4Zc194, folder 5, RBP.

58. Melvin Price to J. J. Pickle, Washington, DC, January 11, 1979; and J. J. Pickle to Roy Benavidez, Washington, DC, January 17, 1979, both located in box 4Zc194, folder 28, RBP.

59. Joe Wyatt Jr. to Roy Benavidez, Washington, DC, April 23, 1979, box 4Zc194, folder 36, RBP.

60. George Bush to Sam Wilson, Houston, TX, June 29, 1979, box 4Zc194, folder 9, RBP.

61. Ruben Bonilla Jr. to *El Campo Leader-News*, Corpus Christi, TX, June 4, 1979, box 4Zc194, folder 3, RBP; and Ruben Bonilla Jr. to the President, location unknown, April 1, 1980, box 4Zc194, folder 49, RBP.

62. *Medal*, 126–127 and 145, quoted on 127; Joe Wyatt Jr. to Roy Benavidez, Washington, DC, June 15, 1979, box 4Zc194, folder 36, RBP; and Rodolfo Montalvo to Henry Joe Wyatt, Nuremberg, Germany, June 5, 1979, box 4Zc194, folder 36, RBP.

63. Joe Wyatt Jr. to Robert L. Nelson, Washington, DC, September 12, 1979; William Clark to Joe Wyatt Jr., Washington, DC, October 24, 1979; Memo, Vernon R. Hull, "Reconsideration of Medal of Honor," February 21, 1980; and ABCMR Memorandum of Consideration, "Roy Benavidez, March 5, 1980," all located in BMR.

64. Steve Sucher, "Sgt. Benavidez' Medal Reviewed for 6th Time," *El Campo Leader-News*, January 19, 1980, 1.

65. *Three Wars*, 261–262.

66. *Three Wars*, quoted 261.

67. *Three Wars*, quoted on 262.

68. *Three Wars*, quoted on 262; and Blehm, *Legend*, 244–248.

69. *Three Wars*, quoted on 262; and Blehm, *Legend*, 244–248.

70. Sucher, interview; Mary Barrineau, "Texan to Receive Medal," *Dallas Times Herald*, reprinted in *Honolulu Star-Bulletin*, February 22, 1981, A-18; and Hearing on H.R. 8386, 96th Cong., 2nd sess., November 21, 1980 (Washington, DC: Government Printing Office, 1980).

71. A. T. Webber Jr. to John Tower, Houston, TX, September 11, 1978, box 4Zc194, folder 34, RBP.

72. A. T. Webber Jr. to John Tower, Houston, TX; and "Feature Story Aids MOH Effort," *El Campo Leader-News*, February 25, 1981, 1.

73. *Howitzer, 1951*, United States Military Academy Yearbook, West Point, NY, 188 and 250; Matt Schudel, Edward C. Meyer obituary, *Washington Post*, October 18, 2020, C10.

74. Vernon Hull to Roy Benavidez, Alexandria, VA, March 12, 1980; and Vernon Hull to Chief of Staff, Army, Alexandria, VA, March 31, 1980, both located in box 4Zc194, folder 20, RBP.

75. United States Army Chief of Staff to Joint Chiefs of Staff, May 6, 1980, box 4Zc194, folder 24, RBP; Chris Barbee, "Benavidez Earns Nation's Highest Honor," *El Campo Leader-News*, February 25, 1981, 1; and Sucher, interview.

76. United States Army Chief of Staff to Joint Chiefs of Staff, May 6, 1980, box 4Zc194, folder 24, RBP; Chris Barbee, "Benavidez Earns Nation's Highest Honor," *El Campo Leader-News*, February 25, 1981, 1; and Sucher, interview.

77. Schudel, Edward C. Meyer obituary.

78. Barbee, "Roy Benavidez."

79. Brian O'Connor, Congressional Medal of Honor Eyewitness Statement, July 24, 1980, box 4Zc194, folder 2, RBP.

80. Felix Sanchez, "Carter Approves, but El Campo Man Still Awaits Medal," *Corpus Christi Caller-Times*, November 27, 1980, 3B; Hearing on H.R. 8386, 96th Cong., 2nd sess., November 21, 1980 (Washington, DC: Government Printing Office, 1980); and Summary: H.R. 8386, 96th Cong., 2nd sess. (1979–1980), www.congress.gov/bill/96th-congress/house-bill/8386, accessed July 1, 2022.

81. *Three Wars*, 265–266; and "Texas Veteran May Receive Medal as Christmas Present," *Wichita Falls Times*, November 30, 1980, 12A.

Chapter 10: A Hero

1. Prochazka, interview.

2. *Medal*, quoted on 161.

3. *Three Wars*, 265–278, quoted on 273; Barbee, interview; Steve Sucher, "Nation's Eyes Focusing on 'Sgt. B,'" *El Campo Leader-News*, February 21, 1981, 1.

4. *Three Wars*, 274–276.

5. *Three Wars*, 274–276.

6. *Three Wars*, 274–276.

7. "Short Stories," *El Campo Leader-News*, January 31, 1981, 1; "Students Proud of Alum . . . ," *El Paso Times*, December 21, 1980, 17-B; "DeMolays Honor Benavidez," *El Campo Leader-News*, February 14, 1981, 1; "Short Stories," *El Campo Leader-News*, January 31, 1981, 1; and Allen E. Schoppe to Roy Benavidez, Sugar Land, Texas, January 26, 1981, Box 4Zc194, folder 59, RBP.

8. Sam Donaldson and David Ensor, "Benavidez/Cong. Medal of Honor," #70221, *ABC World News Tonight*, February 22, 1981.

9. Memo, Stuart Eizenstat and Ellen Goldstein to the President, "Enrolled Bill H.R. 8386 Relief of Roy P. Benavidez," December 17, 1980, Collection: Office of the Executive Clerk, Series: Tom Jones's Enrolled Bills Files, 1977–1980, folder: H. R. 8366—Relief of Roy P. Benavidez, 12/18/80, container 125, Jimmy Carter Presidential Library, Atlanta, GA; Weinberger, *Fighting for Peace*, 52.

10. Weinberger, *Fighting for Peace*, 52–56, quoted on 56.

11. Robert M. Collins, *Transforming America: Politics and Culture During the Reagan Years* (New York: Columbia University Press, 2007), 7–27; and Appy, *American Reckoning*, 283–248.

12. Art Hoppe, "We'll All Be Paved," *Daily Times-Advocate* (Escondido, CA), October 20, 1965, 2A.

13. Carl Greenberg, "Reagan Lauds Vietnam Policy," *Los Angeles Times*, June 26, 1971, A3; and "U.S. Is Criticized in Vietnam's Fall," *New York Times*, August 19, 1975, 13.

14. "Vietnam Was 'Noble Cause,' Reagan Says," *Atlanta Constitution*, August 19, 1980, 1.

15. "Reagan Calls Vietnam War a 'Noble Cause,'" *Los Angeles Times*, August 18, 1980, A2; Editorial, "Reagan: His VFW Speech Renews His Old Image of Recklessness," *Detroit Free Press*, August 20, 1980, 8A; and Douglas Dowie, "Reaction Surprises Reagan as He Lauds Viet War 'Nobility,'" *Muncie Evening Press*, August 19, 1980, 14.

16. Patrick Hagopian, *The Vietnam War in American Memory: Veterans, Memorials, and the Politics of Healing* (Amherst, MA: University of Massachusetts Press, 2009), Reagan "purge" on 38; Jimmy Carter, "Address at Commencement Exercises at the University of Notre Dame," South Bend, IN, May 22, 1977; and Republican Party Platform of 1980, www.presidency.ucsb.edu/documents/republican-party -platform-1980, accessed November 1, 2022.

17. David Hoffman, "How Reagan Views Foreign Policy," *Miami Herald*, May 27, 1980, 10A; Howell Raines, "Reagan Is Welcomed on Notre Dame Trip," *New York Times*, May 18, 1981, A1; Steve Neal, "Reagan Rips Russ Leaders," *Chicago Tribune*, January 30, 1981, 1; and Bernard Gwertzman, "President Sharply Assails Kremlin," *New York Times*, January 30, 1981, A1.

18. "The Signposts Are Missing," *Los Angeles Times*, July 16, 1980, Part II, 6; Collins, *Transforming America*, 193–234; and H. W. Brands, *Reagan: The Life* (New York: Doubleday, 2015), especially 249–273.

19. *Three Wars*, quoted on 263; and Prochazka, interview.

20. Steve Sucher, "Nation's Eyes"; Entitlements Informal Briefing, February 23, 1981, box 4Zc195, folder 13 RBP; and Medal of Honor Pension Application, February 24, 1981, box 4Zc194, folder 39, RBP.

21. *Medal*, 156–160; *Three Wars*, 261–271, quoted on 264; and Chandler D. Carter, Witness Statement, April 7, 1977, and Drake statements in BMR; and *Three Wars*, quoted on 264.

22. *Three Wars*, 261–271; and O'Connor quoted in "After a Long Delay, the Medal of Honor," *Hartford Courant*, February 24, 1981, A2.

23. *Medal*, 156–160, quoted on 158.

24. *Three Wars*, 261–271.

25. Appts. File and Diary Notes, Box I: 588, Folder 2, Caspar W. Weinberger Papers, LOC; *Medal*, 158; and *Three Wars*, 263–264.

26. Reagan MOH Photos.

27. *Three Wars*, 261–271, quoted on 267.

28. Reagan MOH Photos; Reagan's Daily Diary, February 24, 1981, Reagan Library, www.reaganlibrary.gov/digital-library/daily-diary; and *Three Wars*, quoted on 268.

29. Reagan's Daily Diary, February 24, 1981; *Three Wars*, quoted on 268; *Medal of Honor*, quoted on 161 and 158; and Department of the Army to Mr. and Mrs. Joseph Martin, Washington, DC, box 4Zc197, folder 15, RBP.

30. Reagan's Daily Diary, February 24, 1981; and MOH Film.

31. "The Weather," *Washington Post*, February 25, 1981, C2; Reagan MOH Photos; MOH Film; Lou Cannon, "President Awards Medal, Says Troops Weren't Permitted to Win in Vietnam," *Washington Post*, February 25, A2; Robert C. Toth, "Officers Urged to Be Faithful to Military in Their Fashion," *Philadelphia Inquirer*, February 28, 1981, 1A; and Powell, *American Journey*, 258.

32. Reagan MOH Photos; and MOH Film.

33. Reagan MOH Photos; and MOH Film.

34. Reagan MOH Photos; and MOH Film.

35. Reagan MOH Photos; and MOH Film.

36. Reagan MOH Photos; MOH Film; and Reagan, "Remarks on Presenting."

37. Reagan MOH Photos; MOH Film; and Reagan, "Remarks on Presenting."

38. Reagan MOH Photos; MOH Film; Reagan, "Remarks on Presenting"; *Three Wars*, quoted on 270; and *Medal*, 158–161.

39. Reagan MOH Photos; MOH Film; Reagan, "Remarks on Presenting"; *Three Wars*, quoted on 270; and *Medal*, 158–161.

40. Douglas Brinkley, ed., *The Reagan Diaries, Volume I: January 1981–October 1985* (New York: Harper Collins, 2009), 21.

41. Powell, *American Journey*, 258.

42. "President Reagan Lauds Vietnam Vets," *Nashua Telegraph*, February 25, 1981, 3; "Reagan Extends Overdue 'Gratitude' to Vietnam Veterans," *Frederick News* and *Frederick Post*, February 26, 1981, D-8; "Reagan: Viet Vets Overlooked 'Too Long,'" *Pacific Stars and Stripes*, February 27, 1981, 1; Arthur Wiese, "Benavidez Remembered 'Buddies' at Ceremony," *Houston Post*, February 25, 1981, box 4Zc194, folder 39, RBP; and *Three Wars*, quoted on 267.

43. Reagan MOH Photos; MOH Film; and Reagan's Daily Diary, February 24, 1981.

44. *Three Wars*, quoted on 270; MOH Film; "Sergeant to Be Honored for Vietnam Valor," *Los Angeles Times*, February 24, 1981, A5; and Reagan's Daily Diary.

45. "Commissioners Recognize Roy Benavidez," *El Campo Leader-News*, February 25, 1981, 2-A; Chris Barbee, "Medal of Honor Recipient Returns Home," *El Campo Leader-News*, February 28, 1981, 1; and "Benavidez Welcomed," *Victoria Advocate*, February 26, 1981, 1.

46. *El Campo Leader-News*, February 25, 1981, 1A–3A.

47. "Commissioners Recognize Roy Benavidez"; Barbee, "Medal of Honor Recipient"; "Benavidez Welcomed"; and personal observations in El Campo High School gymnasium made on August 7, 2017.

48. "Commissioners Recognize Roy Benavidez"; Barbee, "Medal of Honor Recipient"; and "Benavidez Welcomed."

49. "Commissioners Recognize Roy Benavidez"; Barbee, "Medal of Honor Recipient"; and "Benavidez Welcomed."

50. Proclamation, Office of the Mayor of Galveston, TX, "Roy Benavidez Day," March 22, 1981, box 4Zc195, folder 9, RBP; "State Leaders to Honor Benavidez in Austin Tuesday," *El Campo Leader-News*, March 28, 1981, 1; and "Legislature Honors Army Hero," *Austin American-Statesman*, April 1, 1981.

51. "Cesar, This Is the Plan," *El Campo Leader-News*, April 15, 1981, 9; Lyndell Williams to Roy Benavidez, Austin, TX, May 27, 1981, box 4Zc194, folder 65; and "WCJC Awards Benavidez Degree," *El Campo Leader-News*, March 14, 1981, 2.

52. Numerous invitations found in box 4Zc194, various folders; Robert Williams, "Benavidez Speaks at Virginia Tech," *The Cadet*, June 10, 1981, 10; and "Short Stories," *El Campo Leader-News*, May 23, 1981, 2.

53. Sara Marsh, "War Hero Urges Students to Set Sights High," *Munster Times*, November 19, 1993, B1; and Garcia, "Benavidez Quotes."

54. Munoz, interview.

55. Munoz, interview.

56. Garcia, "Benavidez Quotes"; Noel Benavidez, interviews; and Chris Barbee Interview Questions, December 5, 2015, document in author's possession.

57. Memo, Secretary of Defense to the President, "Master Sergeant (Retired) Roy P. Benavidez," April 14, 1981, and Memo, Ronald Reagan to Caspar Weinberger, "Recruiting Duties for Roy Benavidez," April 23, 1981, both located in WHORM Subject file ND007, Rec ID 019016SS, Reagan Library; and Munoz, interview.

58. *Three Wars*, quoted on 284.

59. "New Wheels for 'Sgt. B,'" *El Campo Leader-News*, April 8, 1981, 2A; "A Gift from Texas," *El Campo Leader-News*, May 13, 1981, 2A; and "A Hero Says 'Thanks,'" *Honolulu Advertiser*, December 2, 1981, A15.

60. Foley, *Mexicans in the Making of America*, 179–199, elected officials data on 189; and Geoffrey Godsell, "Hispanics in the US," *Christian Science Monitor*, April 28, 1980, 3.

61. Phil Gailey, "Courting Hispanic Voters Now a Reagan Priority," *New York Times*, May 19, 1983, B12; and Roger Langley, "Reagan Appoints More Hispanics," *The Californian*, September 23, 1981, 8. For more on the history of the Latino vote, see Benjamin Francis-Fallon, *The Rise of the Latino Vote: A History* (Cambridge, MA: Harvard University Press, 2019); and Geraldo Cadava, *The Hispanic Republican: The Shaping of an American Political Identity, from Nixon to Trump* (New York: Ecco, 2020), 204–233.

62. "Leaders Eat Feast by Texan," *Corpus Christi Times*, June 10, 1981, 2C; Ronald Reagan, "Remarks at White House Hispanic Heritage Week Ceremony," Washington, DC, September 15, 1982; Ronald Reagan, "Remarks at Cinco de Mayo Ceremonies," San Antonio, TX, May 5, 1983; Ronald Reagan, "Remarks at the American G.I. Forum 35th Annual Convention," El Paso, TX, August 13, 1983; Ronald Reagan, "Remarks at White House Luncheon," Washington, DC, April 17,

1984, all located in box 183, folder: 10/31/84 Hispanic Stamp Presentation, Speechwriting: Research Office, Reagan Library.

63. Victory '82 Fundraising Dinner Program, June 15, 1982, box 4Zc194, folder 67, RBP; and "Reagan Stumps for Clements," *Victoria Advocate*, June 16, 1982, 1.

64. Don Brown, "Candidates Debate Issues at Rally," *Victoria Advocate*, October 21, 1982, 1; and Mrs. John W. Griffin, "Wyatt Used Benavidez," *Victoria Advocate*, October 27, 1982.

65. Wiese, "Benavidez Remembered 'Buddies'"; and *Three Wars*, quoted on 267.

66. *Howitzer, 1982*, United States Military Academy Yearbook, West Point, NY, 88–90; "Paving the Way," *Victoria Advocate*, January 12, 2004, 3A; and Ann Rundle, "New Jersey Man Helps Benavidez Memorial," *Victoria Advocate*, June 16, 2003, 3A.

67. Travis Post #76, "Newsletter," November 1981, box 4Zc194, folder 66, RBP; and Pamphlet, "America We Love You," Travis Post #76, box 4Zc200, folder 40, RBP.

68. Burnet letters located in box 4Zc197, folder 18, RBP.

69. Hagopian, *Vietnam War in American Memory*, 79–165.

70. Hagopian, *Vietnam War in American Memory*, 140–165; "Benavidez to Represent Texas," *ECLN*, November 10, 1982, 1D; and Dee Goodin, "Medal of Honor Winner Notes Absence of Elected Officials," *Johnson City Press-Chronicle*, November 24, 1982, 1.

71. Noel Benavidez, interviews; Garcia, interview; Prochazka, interview; and Roger P. Benavidez, obituary, *Victoria Advocate*, March 16, 2015, A4.

72. Noel Benavidez, interviews; Garcia, interview; Prochazka, interview; and Roger P. Benavidez, obituary, *Victoria Advocate*, March 16, 2015, A4.

73. Noel Benavidez, interviews; Garcia, interview; Prochazka, interview; and Roger P. Benavidez, obituary, *Victoria Advocate*, March 16, 2015, A4.

74. Noel Benavidez, interviews; Garcia, interview; Prochazka, interview; and Roger P. Benavidez, obituary, *Victoria Advocate*, March 16, 2015, A4.

75. Noel Benavidez, interviews; Garcia, interview; Prochazka, interview; Roger P. Benavidez, obituary, *Victoria Advocate*, March 16, 2015, A4; and Munoz, interview.

Chapter 11: Security

1. Department of Health and Human Services Social Security Administration to Roy Benavidez, Washington, DC, February 22, 1983, box 4Zc194, folder 53, RBP.

2. Department of Health and Human Services Social Security Administration to Roy Benavidez, Washington, DC, February 22, 1983, box 4Zc194, folder 53, RBP; and US House of Representatives, *Hearing Before the Select Committee on Aging*, 98th Cong., 1st sess. (Washington, DC: Government Printing Office, 1983), 42.

3. Roy P. and Hilaria C. Benavidez, Social Security Award Certificate, Social Security Administration, July 25, 1977, box 4Zc194, folder 62, RBP. MOH recipients' pay increased from $100 to $200 by Veterans' Disability Compensation and Survivors' Benefits Act of 1978, Public Law 95-479, 95th Cong., 2nd sess. (October 18, 1978).

4. US Public Law 96-265, 96th Cong., 2nd sess. (June 9, 1980), 441–481; and Susan Gluck Mezey, *No Longer Disabled: The Federal Courts and the Politics of Social Security Disability* (Westport, CT: Greenwood, 1988), 71–87.

5. Ronald Reagan, "A Time for Choosing," Los Angeles, CA, October 27, 1964, Ronald Reagan Presidential Library, www.reaganlibrary.gov/reagans/ronald-reagan /time-choosing-speech-october-27-1964, accessed November 5, 2022; and Kruse and Zelizer, *Fault Lines*, 88–112.

6. Collins, *Transforming America*, 29–91; and Ronald Reagan, *An American Life* (New York: Simon & Schuster, 1990), 316.

7. *Hearing Before the Select Committee on Aging*, "purge" on 10, quoted from *Roanoke Times & World-News*, June 12, 1983; Mezey, *No Longer Disabled*, 82; Annual Statistical Report on the Social Security Disability Insurance Program, 2016, Social Security Office of Retirement and Disability Policy, www.ssa.gov/policy/docs /statcomps/di_asr/2016/sect01b.html#table3, accessed August 11, 2022.

8. *Medal*, 163; and *Three Wars*, 279–282, quoted on 281 and 278.

9. *Medal*, 164; Social Security Administration, Amended Notice of Hearing, May 11, 1983, box 4Zc194, folder 68, RBP; and *Three Wars*, quoted on 281 and 282.

10. *Medal*, quoted on 164; Social Security Administration, Amended Notice of Hearing, May 11, 1983, box 4Zc194, folder 68, RBP; and *Three Wars*, quoted on 281 and 282.

11. Spencer Rich, "Vietnam-Era Hero Falls Victim to Cuts In Social Security," *Washington Post*, May 27, 1983, A1; and Tom Brokaw and Jamie Gangel, "Medal of Honor Winner's Problems," #530675, *NBC Nightly News*, May 27, 1983.

12. William Lowther, "A Medal for Roy Benavidez," *Reader's Digest*, April 1983, 121–125; and Conchita Thompson to Roy Benavidez, Los Angeles, CA, April 12, 1983, box 4Zc199, folder 28, RBP; and *Medal*, quoted on 164.

13. "Veteran Fighting Denial of Benefits," *New York Times*, May 28, 1983, 25.

14. *Medal*, 165.

15. Letters reprinted in *Hearing Before the Select Committee on Aging*, 27–40; Kenneth Fryer to Roy Benavidez, Louisville, KY, June 1, 1983, box 4Zc199, folder 1, RBP; Doug Leonard to Roy Benavidez, (town illegible) New Hampshire, May 30, 1983, box 4Zc199, folder 13, RBP; and James W. Ross to Roy Benavidez, Slippery Rock, PA, July 1, 1983, box 4Zc197, folder 15, RBP.

16. James M. Johnson to Roy Benavidez, Scotch Plains, NJ, June 22, 1983, box 4Zc199, folder 14, RBP.

17. *Hearing Before the Select Committee on Aging*, quoted on 18.

18. Jacklyn Kearns to President Ronald Reagan, Cresskill, NJ, May 27, 1983, and Irene Mansfield to President Ronald Reagan, location unknown, May 31, 1983, both located in *Hearing Before the Select Committee on Aging*, 36–37; and *Three Wars*, 286. Dozens more such letters located in box 3, Willkie, Wendell Files at the Reagan Library, but remain confidential as of this writing due to the personal information they divulge.

19. "So Much for Heroes," *Los Angeles Times*, June 3, 1983, E4; and "Congress Must Call a Halt to Purge of the Disabled," *Philadelphia Inquirer*, June 7, 1983, A14.

20. Reagan, "Remarks at Cinco de Mayo Ceremonies"; and "Veteran Fighting Denial of Benefits."

21. "Reagan Tells of Concern for Vietnam Hero," *Los Angeles Times*, May 27, 1983, A2; "Disabled War Hero Wants Pay, but Reagan Offers 'Charity,'" *Atlanta Constitution*, May 31, 1983, 3A; and *Three Wars*, 284–285.

22. Jennifer Mittelstadt, *The Rise of the Military Welfare State* (Cambridge, MA: Harvard University Press, 2015), 94–119.

23. Mittelstadt, *Rise of the Military Welfare State*, quoted on 9, figure on 153.

24. VA History, US Department of Veterans Affairs, www.va.gov/HISTORY /VA_History/Overview.asp, accessed March 1, 2023.

25. *Disabled American Veterans*, October 1981, 4–11; and Myra MacPherson, "Pulling the Rug from Under Vietnam Vets Again," *Washington Post*, March 15, 1981, D1 and D4.

26. "Chief Defends Vets' Rights," *VFW*, May 1982, 28–30; and Memo, Paralyzed Veterans for America, "Cuts in the Veterans Administrative Budget," March 20, 1981, box 10, folder: VA, Carleson, Robert B. Files, Reagan Library.

27. "The Overblown VA," *Arizona Republic*, March 12, 1981, A6; and "Touching the Untouchable," *Wall Street Journal*, February 23, 1982, 34.

28. "Legion Blasts V.A. Proposed Budget Cut," *Okmulgee Daily Times*, October 25, 1981, 3; MacPherson, "Pulling the Rug," NVLC director quoted on D4; Bernard Weinraub, "Veterans Call Cutbacks 'Another Betrayal,'" *New York Times*, May 4, 1981, B11; and Pat Morrison and Eric Malnic, "Hospital Evicts 40 VA Protestors Without Strife," *Los Angeles Times*, June 10, 1981, 1.

29. US Public Law 97-35, 97th Cong., 1st sess. (August 13, 1981), 353–933, especially 353–605; US Public Law 96-398, 96th Cong., 2nd sess. (October 7, 1980), 1564–1613; Christian G. Appy, *Working-Class War: American Soldiers & Vietnam* (Chapel Hill, NC: University of North Carolina Press, 1993); and Gerald N. Grob, "Public Policy and Mental Illness: Jimmy Carter's Presidential Commission on Mental Health," *Millbank Quarterly* 83, no. 3 (September 2005), 425–456.

30. "Veterans Groups Hail Choice for VA Chief," *Washington Post*, July 10, 1981, A6; Ellen Hume, "Man Who Accused Jane Fonda of Treason Picked to Head VA," *Los Angeles Times*, May 1, 1981, B7; and "Ex-California Official Is Chosen to Head VA," *Boston Globe*, May 1, 1981, 10.

31. "VA Chief to Seek to Recover Medical Funds Given Veterans for Non-Service Connected Bills," *Atlanta Daily World*, November 5, 1981, 1.

32. "V.A. May Abandon Free Care for Veterans over 65," *New York Times*, January 11, 1982, B14; 12 million in Betty Cuniberti, "Battle in Veterans Administration," *Los Angeles Times*, August 5, 1982, J1; and Mike Feinsilber, "VA to Reconsider Plans for $2.7B in Construction," *Boston Globe*, February 22, 1982, 1.

33. American Legion Press Release, box 67, folder 2, Meese, Edwin III Files, Reagan Library; "DAV Hotline!," *DAV*, April 1982, 4–5; and Cooper T. Holt to Robert P. Nimmo, Washington, DC, March 5, 1982, box 67, folder 2, Meese, Edwin III Files, Reagan Library.

34. Turse, *Kill Anything That Moves*, 94; "Veterans' Diseases Associated with Agent Orange," US Department of Veterans Affairs, www.publichealth.va.gov /exposures/agentorange/conditions, accessed August 17, 2022; "teenage acne" quoted in Cuniberti, "Battle"; and Mike Feinsilber, "Agent Orange Pay Would Total Billions," *The Tennessean*, November 19, 1981, 6.

35. Mike Royko, "2 Views of Federal Spending," syndicated column, *Chicago Sun-Times*, May 28, 1982, 2; Veterans Administration to H. P. Goldfield, Washington, DC, June 11, 1982, box 67, folder 5, Meese, Edwin III Files, Reagan Library;

WJLA-TV Investigative Reports, box 67, folder 3, Meese, Edwin III Files, Reagan Library; and Jack Anderson, "VA Chief Target of U.S. Probes over Spending," *Washington Post*, June 10, 1982, F12.

36. Mike Royko, "2 Views of Federal Spending," syndicated column, *Chicago Sun-Times*, May 28, 1982, 2; Veterans Administration to H. P. Goldfield, Washington, DC, June 11, 1982, box 67, folder 5, Meese, Edwin III Files, Reagan Library; WJLA-TV Investigative Reports, box 67, folder 3, Meese, Edwin III Files, Reagan Library; and Jack Anderson, "VA Chief Target of U.S. Probes over Spending," *Washington Post*, June 10, 1982, F12.

37. "NACV Calls for Nimmo's Resignation or Removal," *Stars and Stripes*, June 24, 1982, 8; "VFW Urges Reprimand of Nimmo," *Boston Globe*, August 19, 1982, 4; "Nimmo—An Embarrassment," *Stars and Stripes*, June 17, 1982, 8; "House Members Seek VA Chief's Ouster," *Los Angeles Times*, July 1, 1982, A2; and Cuniberti, "Battle."

38. Memo, MRC to EJF, "Follow-Up on Nimmo Memorandum," June 10, 1982, box 67, folder 6, Meese, Edwin III Files, Reagan Library.

39. "Robert Nimmo Quits as VA Head," *Chicago Tribune*, October 5, 1982, 3; and "Disability Pay Wasted, VA Chief Says," *Chicago Tribune*, November 22, 1982, 3.

40. Ronald Reagan, "Remarks of the President at Veterans Day Observance," Washington, DC, November 11, 1982, www.reaganlibrary.gov/public/2020-12/40-833-5716612-005-022-2020.pdf.

41. Robert Pear, "Reagan Aide Hails Shift on Disability," *New York Times*, June 8, 1983, A17; and "Disability-Review Program Eased Again by Reagan to Retain More Beneficiaries," *Wall Street Journal*, June 8, 1983, 6.

42. Dan Rather and Lem Tucker, "Social Security Disability Payments," #291380, *CBS Evening News*, June 7, 1983.

43. C. Fraser Smith, "What Drives Public Policy?," *Baltimore Sun*, June 12, 1983, K1; Robert Pear, "U.S. Plans to Ease Disability Criteria in Social Security," *New York Times*, June 7, 1983, A1; and "Disabled Need Justice," *News & Observer*, June 11, 1983, 4A.

44. C. Fraser Smith, "What Drives Public Policy?," *Baltimore Sun*, June 12, 1983, K1.

45. "Not Fair Enough for the Disabled," *New York Times*, June 14, 1983, A22; Robert Pear, "Reagan Aide Hails Shift on Disability," *New York Times*, June 8, 1983, A17; and "Congress Must Call a Halt to Purge of the Disabled," *Philadelphia Inquirer*, June 7, 1983, 14A.

46. *Hearing Before the Select Committee on Aging*, 8–19.

47. *Hearing Before the Select Committee on Aging*.

48. *Hearing Before the Select Committee on Aging*, 20–40.

49. *Hearing Before the Select Committee on Aging*, 41–59.

50. *Hearing Before the Select Committee on Aging*.

51. "Quotation of the Day," *New York Times*, June 21, 1983, B1.

52. Judge Waldo E. Ximenes, Decision in the Case of Roy Benavidez, July 8, 1983, in author's possession.

53. Tom Brokaw, "Benavidez/Social Security," #5311600, *NBC Nightly News*, July 12, 1983; and "War Hero Wins Fight for Benefits," *Atlanta Constitution*, July 13, 1983, 1A.

54. Spencer Rich, "War Hero Told He Won't Lose Disability Aid," *Washington Post*, July 13, 1983, A2; *Hearing Before the Select Committee on Aging*, 539–541 and 662–664; and Mezey, *No Longer Disabled*, 121–145.

55. "County Museum Association Unveils New Photo Display," *ECLN*, July 28, 1982, 2A; and *Three Wars*, 272–275.

56. Constitution of the Community Action Committee of El Campo, Texas, July 17, 1980, box 4Zc197, folder 10, RBP; and "CAC Surveys Progress Made in Community," *ECLN*, January 23, 1982, 2A.

57. Barbee, interview.

58. "El Campo Salutes Hometown Hero," *Victoria Advocate*, May 15, 1983, 1 and 14; and personal observations on May 20, 2015.

59. Kathryn Moore, "Letter to the Editor," *Victoria Advocate*, June 7, 1983, 4A.

60. Mary Barrineau, "A Hero Without Hometown Honors," *Westward Magazine*, August 7, 1983.

61. "Coverage Outrageous," *El Campo Leader-News*, June 1, 1983, box 4Zc194, folder 1, RBP.

62. Letters to the editor in *Victoria Advocate*, June 11, 14, and 17.

63. Letters to the editor in *Victoria Advocate*, June 11, 14, and 17.

64. *San Antonio Express* citation; *Hearing Before the Select Committee on Aging*, 64; and Judge Ximenes, Decision.

65. Barrineau, "Hero."

66. Barrineau, "Hero"; and Ken Hammond, "Hero," *Texas Magazine*, January 31, 1982, 9.

67. Barrineau, "Hero"; and Ken Hammond, "Hero," *Texas Magazine*, January 31, 1982, 9.

Chapter 12: Glory Days

1. *Real People*, "Episode 5," November 9, 1983, Amazon video; Conchita Thompson to Roy Benavidez, Los Angeles, CA, April 12, 1983, box 4Zc199, folder 28, RBP; and "TV Cameras Visit El Campo," *El Campo Leader-News*, April 23, 1983, 1 and 2.

2. *Real People*.

3. *Real People*.

4. *Real People*.

5. *Real People*; and TV Ratings Guide, www.thetvratingsguide.com/2020/03/1983-84-ratings-history.html, accessed September 7, 2022.

6. Jose Garcia, interview by William Sturkey, Taft, TX, August 4, 2018, transcript in author's possession; and Benny Aleman, interview by William Sturkey, Austin, TX, July, 19, 2016, transcript in author's possession.

7. Jack Chielli, "A Real Hero Reflects on Vietnam Experience," *Vineland Times-Journal*, March 29, 1984, 1; "164 Texans Remembered in Ceremony," *Victoria Advocate*, July 21, 1984, 2D; Greg Hitt, "Medal of Honor Winner Tells Vets He Knows the Problems They Face," *Kansas City Times*, June 15, 1984, B12; "Ground Broken for Reserve Center," *Corpus Christi Times*, November 14, 1984, 2A; and Dean Juipe, "Roy Benavidez," *El Campo Leader-News*, October 30, 1985.

8. 1984 calendar in box 4Zc197, folder 6, RBP.

9. Garcia, interview.

10. Garcia, interview.

11. Garcia, interview.

12. Garcia, interview.

13. Barbee, interview.

14. *Real People.*

15. Appy, *American Reckoning*, 221–250, quoted on 237; and Hagopian, *Vietnam War in American Memory*, 49–78, quoted on 74.

16. Joseph Darda, *How White Men Won the Culture Wars: A History of Veteran America* (Oakland, CA: University of California Press, 2021), 121–151.

17. John Kelso, "Busy Hero," *Longview News-Journal*, June 30, 1989, 1 and 10.

18. Roy Benavidez to the President, El Campo, TX, October 14, 1982; and Fred F. Fielding to Roy Benavidez, Washington, DC, December 20, 1982, both located in WHORM Subject file PR014-09, Rec ID 116004CU, Reagan Library.

19. Roy Benavidez to Bill Dean, El Campo, TX, February 26, 1983; and Ellen Levin to Roy Benavidez, New York City, March 15, 1983, both located in box 4Zc199, folder 16, RBP.

20. Garcia, interview; and Garcia, "Benavidez Quotes."

21. Garcia, interview; Garcia, "Benavidez Quotes"; Aleman, interview; and MSG Roy Benavidez speech 1991, YouTube, www.youtube.com/watch?v=_oUtJxE4s js&ab_channel=dtss1000, accessed November 10, 2022.

22. Garcia, "Benavidez Quotes"; and Juipe, "Roy Benavidez."

23. Bob Hamilton, "As I See It . . . ," newspaper clip, box 4Zc196, folder 13, RBP; Barrineau, "Hero"; Hammond, "Hero"; and Billac, *Last Medal of Honor*, 195.

24. MSG Roy Benavidez speech 1991.

25. Garcia, "Benavidez Quotes."

26. Hammond, "Hero"; and *Medal*, quoted on 31.

27. Jack Ingram, "Hero Lauded," *El Campo Leader-News*, March 20, 1985, 4A.

28. Memo, Office of the Assistant Secretary of Defense, "After Action Report," undated, box 183, folder: 10/31/84 Hispanic Stamp Presentation, Speechwriting: Research Office, Reagan Library; and William Garland, "Officials Pack Reception to Laud Dr. Garcia," *Corpus Christi Times*, March 27, 1984, 3A.

29. Joyce Gemperlein, "A Hero's Burial for an Unknown—Vietnam Soldier," *Philadelphia Inquirer*, May 29, 1984, A1; and UPI, "Reagan Honors Viet Unknown," *Indianapolis News*, May 29, 1984, 12.

30. Ronald Reagan, "Hispanic Stamp Presentation," Washington, DC, October 31, 1984, transcript, box 183, folder: 10/31/84 Hispanic Stamp Presentation, Speechwriting: Research Office, Reagan Library; 20c Hispanic Americans single, Smithsonian National Postal Museum, https://postalmuseum.si.edu/object /npm_1999.2004.371, accessed September 11, 2022; and Harrison Rainie, "Ron Tougher on Gerry," *New York Daily News*, November 1, 1984, C5 and C21.

31. Dominic Sama, "Commemorative Issuance Muddled by Politics," *Philadelphia Inquirer*, November 18, 1984, S13; Jimmy Packard, "Hispanic Stamp Released," *Richmond Times-Dispatch*, November 11, 1984, N7; Fran Murphey, "Politics Permeates Even Stamp World," *Akron Beacon Journal*, November 5, 1984, B2; George W. Brown, "2 New Stamps in Presidential Election," *Asbury Park Press*, October 21, 1984, I10; and Samuel A. Tower, "Saluting Hispanics," *Washington Post*, November 18, 1984, E11.

32. Francis-Fallon, *Rise of the Latino Vote*, 344–379, quoted on 370–371.

33. Congressional Medal of Honor Society National Headquarters Bulletin, January 18, 1985, box 4Zc197, folder 23; Barbee, interview; and Chris Barbee, "Capital Warm Despite Cold," *El Campo Leader-News*, January 30, 1985, 1D.

34. AP, "Politicians, Not Soldiers, Lost Vietnam War, Medal Winner Says," (Longview, WA) *Daily News*, April 25, 1985, 13A.

35. Press Release, Corona Publishing Company, November 9, 1986, box 4Zc199, folder 31, RBP; and Betsy Blaney, "Oscar Griffin," obituary, *Boston Globe*, December 3, 2011, B10.

36. *Three Wars*, 14–17, quoted on 15.

37. Photographer unknown, *Roy and Westmoreland*, June 13, 1986, box 3T4.3, RBP; UPI, "Vietnam Veterans," *Times-Press* (Streator, IL), June 14, 1986, 16; and Westmoreland, *Soldier Reports*, 286.

38. Kirkus Reviews, October 15, 1986, www.kirkusreviews.com/book-reviews/a /roy-p-oscar-griffin-benavidez/the-three-wars-of-roy-benavidez, accessed September 13, 2022; and David Sedeno, "Viet Vet Still Fighting," *Victoria Advocate*, December 7, 1986, 1D; and Mike Cox, "Soldier's Personal, Military Battles Defy Comparison," *Austin American-Statesman*, November 11, 1986, Onward, 9.

39. Roy Benavidez, "Hispanic Veterans Due Support," *Corpus Christi Caller-Times*, November 22, 1986, 17A; "Benavidez Looks at Death," *Daily Star*, November 13, 1986, 1 and 18F; and "An Embattled Chicano," *Miami News Vista*, January 3, 1987, 20.

40. Larry and Diane Smith to Roy Benavidez, August 3, 1987, and Ruben Salazar to Luis Valdez, Eagle Pass, TX, August 18, 1987, both located in box 4Zc195, folder 5, RBP; Hugo Clemente to Roy Benavidez, El Paso, TX, April 24, 1987, box 4Zc199, folder 41, RBP; and George Bush to Roy Benavidez, Washington, DC, January 4, 1987, box 4Zc197, folder 10, RBP.

41. Jose Garcia to Julius Gates, Houston, TX, March 18, 1988, box 4Zc197, folder 10, RBP; and Paul McCarthy to Roy Benavidez, New York City, April 14, 1989, box 4Zc199, folder 16, RBP.

42. John Broder, "When Drums Begin to Roll . . .," *Los Angeles Times*, January 20, 1989, 26; and John Kelso, "Medal of Honor," *Austin American-Statesman*, June 26, 1989, B1 and B4.

43. Ruben R. Salazar to Luis Valdez, Eagle Pass, TX, August 18, 1987, box 4Zc195, folder 5, RBP; and Rolf G. Schmitz to Joseph B. Wilkinson Jr., Los Angeles, CA, September 4, 1985, box 4Zc198, folder 12, RBP.

44. Memo, LULAC to Hall of Fame Honoree, March 31, 1987, "Hispanic Hall of Fame," box 4Zc199, folder 41, RBP; Ronald White to Roy Benavidez, West Point, NY, July 5, 1987, box 4Zc199, folder 16; Panama Itinerary, June 27, 1988, box 4Zc196, folder 26, RBP; and Memorial Day Program, May 30, 1987, Silvis, IL, box 4Zc196, folder 21, RBP.

45. Billac, *Last Medal of Honor*, book blurb.

46. Barbee, interview; Broder, "When Drums Begin to Roll"; Chris Barbee, "President's Inauguration Yields Lasting Memories," *El Campo Leader-News*, January 26, 1989, box 4Zc194, folder 59, RBP; and Paula Schwed and David Marziale, "Washington Puts on Its Best for Bush," *Daily Journal*, January 21, 1989, 1 and 2.

47. Garcia, interview.

48. Prochazka, interview; Garcia, interview; Benavidez interviews; and Munoz, interview.

49. Prochazka, interview; Garcia, interview; Benavidez interviews; and Munoz, interview.

50. Prochazka, interview; Garcia, interview; Benavidez interviews; Munoz, interview; and "Mrs. Benavidez," obituary, *Victoria Advocate*, October 21, 1990, 12A.

51. Prochazka, interview; Garcia, interview; Benavidez interviews; and Munoz, interview.

52. Prochazka, interview; Garcia, interview; Benavidez interviews; and Munoz, interview.

53. Prochazka, interview; Garcia, interview; Benavidez interviews; and Munoz, interview.

54. Prochazka, interview; Garcia, interview; Benavidez interviews; and Munoz, interview.

55. Prochazka, interview; Garcia, interview; Benavidez interviews; and Munoz, interview.

56. Prochazka, interview; Garcia, interview; Benavidez interviews; and Munoz, interview.

57. Prochazka, interview; Garcia, interview; Benavidez interviews; and Munoz, interview.

58. Prochazka, interview; Garcia, interview; Benavidez interviews; and Munoz, interview.

59. Prochazka, interview; Garcia, interview; Benavidez interviews; and Munoz, interview.

60. Prochazka, interview; Garcia, interview; Benavidez interviews; and Munoz, interview.

61. Garcia, interview.

62. Prochazka, interview; Garcia, interview; and Noel Benavidez, interview.

63. Munoz, interview; Aleman, interview; and Dean Juipe, "Roy Benavidez: All Out Every Day for America," newspaper clipping, box 4Zc194, folder 59, RBP.

64. Noel Benavidez, interview; "Five Top NCOs Named," *San Antonio Express*, May 11, 1976, 6; and "Benito Guerrero," obituary, *San Antonio Express-News*, June 19, 2010, www.legacy.com/us/obituaries/sanantonio/name/benito-guerrero -obituary?id=7149306, accessed March 10, 2023.

Chapter 13: To Be an American

1. John Kelso, "Medal of Honor," *Austin American-Statesman*, June 26, 1989, B1 and B4.

2. Garcia, interview.

3. Jared Reagh to Roy Benavidez, Delaware, OH, undated, box 4Zc196, folder 24.

4. Heather Townsend to Roy Benavidez, Deer Park, TX, November 25, 1987, box 4Zc195, folder 14, RBP.

5. Letters in box 4Zc196, folder 20, RBP.

6. C. C. Josey to Roy Benavidez, White City, OR, August 8, 1988, box 4Zc194, folder 64, RBP.

7. John Groves to Roy Benavidez, APO, SF, September 10, 1988, box 4Zc199, folder 3, RBP.

8. Billac, *Last Medal of Honor*, 97.

9. Various clippings found in box 4Zc196, folder 17, RBP; "Benavidez Is Guest Speaker for the Kiwanis Club," *Fort Bend Star*, December 29, 1993, 3; "Hero to Participate," *Victoria Advocate*, July 26, 1990, 17; "Patrick AFB," *Florida Today*, September 23, 1991, 2B; and Gerry Bueker to Chris Barbee, Aurora, CO, May 18, 1992, box 4Zc194, folder 57, RBP.

10. Elizabeth Conner, "Veteran Symbolizes Fourth," *Victoria Advocate*, July 4, 1989, 1A; and Joe Olvera, "Veteran's Day Honors the Men Who Fought for the United States," *El Paso Times*, November 11, 1990, 3G.

11. Roy Jones II, "Decorated Soldier Urges Hispanics to Graduate," *Abilene Reporter-News*, September 26, 1992, 1A and 10A; and David Reyes, "Honors for a Few Good Soldiers . . . ," *Los Angeles Times*, November 8, 1998, B1 and B6.

12. Chris Barbee, "HISD Names Elementary for Roy Benavidez," *El Campo Leader-News*, August 28, 1991; and Roy P. Benavidez Elementary School Dedication Ceremony Program, May 19, 1992, box 194, folder 59, RBP. For more, see the school website at www.houstonisd.org/benavidez.

13. "Banquet Deemed a 'Total Sellout,'" *El Campo Leader-News*, undated, box 4Zc194, folder 17, RBP.

14. Biography of a Patriot, Proposal, 1992, box 4Zc195, folder 14, RBP.

15. AP, "Raye Awarded Medal of Freedom," *Victoria Advocate*, November 17, 1993, 3C.

16. AP, "Honored Veteran Meets Rescuer's Kin," *Charlotte Observer*, July 30, 1994, 6C; 1994 Mrs. America Pageant Program, box 4Zc195, folder 7, RBP; and "'Medal of Honor' Story for Everyone," *San Antonio Express-News*, April 23, 1995, 1.

17. "Medal Winner to Be in McAllen . . . ," *The Monitor* (McAllen, TX), August 15, 1990, 14A; Dale Roverson, "Benavidez Seeking Support for Plan to Aid U.S. Troops," *Victoria Advocate*, January 10, 1991, 8B.

18. Billac, *Last Medal of Honor*.

19. Lois Scott, "Vietnam Hero Tells His Story," *Victoria Advocate*, September 23, 1990, 5; Frank Stransky, "Book Tells the Story of Medal of Honor Soldier," *El Paso Herald-Post*, July 16, 1990, B6; Joel Kirkpatrick, "War Hero Benavidez Still Can't Define Courage," *Galveston Daily News*, March 31, 1990, 12A; and Dale Robertson, "Book Relates Battle in Hell," *El Campo Leader-News*, May 30, 1991, 6A.

20. Shannon Crabtree, "New Book Recounting Benavidez's Story Out Feb. 1," *El Campo Leader-News*, January 25, 1995, 3A; H. Ross Perot, "Foreword," in *Medal*, vii–viii.

21. *Medal*.

22. *Medal*, 3.

23. *Medal*, quoted on 168, 170, and 171.

24. Roy's letters to publishers are located in box 4Zc197, folder 7, RBP.

25. Mitch Shanklin to Roy Benvaidez, Auburn, KY, February 12, 1995, box 4Zc199, folder 1; Michael Catalano to Roy Benavidez, Chicago, IL, March 5, 1995, box 4Zc198, folder 16; Norman Hoggatt to Roy Benavidez, Carson City, NV, box 4Zc199, folder 12; Donna Ikeda to Roy Benavidez, Toronto, Canada, May 6, 1996, box 4Zc197, folder 9; Timothy Berg to Roy Benavidez, Stuttgart, Germany, July 24, 1995, box 4Zc198, folder 13; Brandon Brewer to Roy Benavidez, Peoria, AZ, July 18, 1995, box 4Zc199, folder 24; Justin Gorczynski to Roy Benavidez, San

Antonio, TX, March 6, 1995, box 4Zc195, folder 2; Jennifer Rick to Roy Benavidez, Idaho Falls, ID, October 22, 1996, box 4Zc198, folder 15; Elijah Ingraham to Roy Benavidez, Ormond Beach, FL, September 24, 1995, box 4Zc198, folder 11; and D. Buckmaster to Roy Benavidez, Citrus Heights, CA, box 4Zc199, folder 27, all located in RBP.

26. Myra Fincher to Roy Benavidez, WPAFB, OH, August 21, 1995, box 4Zc196, folder 24; Maria Cruz to Roy Benavidez, Philadelphia, PA, September 8, 1995, box 4Zc197, folder 15; Brian Orban, "In the Eyes of a Hero," *Northern Light*, November 1, 1996, 6; and additional invitations found in box 197, folder 17, all located in RBP.

27. Garcia and Prochazka, interview.

28. Garcia and Prochazka, interview.

29. Garcia and Prochazka, interview.

30. Garcia and Prochazka, interview.

31. Noel Benavidez, 2018 interview.

32. Noel Benavidez, 2018 interview.

33. Noel Benavidez, 2018 interview.

34. Noel Benavidez, 2018 interview; and Garcia and Prochazka, interview.

35. Noel Benavidez, 2018 interview; and Garcia and Prochazka, interview.

36. Noel Benavidez, 2018 interview; and Garcia and Prochazka, interview.

37. Bob Link, "Hero Brings Message," *Bismarck Tribune*, April 13, 1997, 1A; "Around Anchorage," *Anchorage Daily News*, September 18, 1997, D2; and Colleen Dee Berry, "Horror of 'Nam Came Home," *Courier-News*, November 12, 1997, A1 and A14.

38. Garcia and Prochazka, interview.

39. Garcia and Prochazka, interview; and Noel Benavidez, 2018 interview.

40. Garcia and Prochazka, interview; and Noel Benavidez, 2018 interview.

41. Garcia and Prochazka, interview; Noel Benavidez, 2018 interview; "Hero Needs Help," *The Sentinel* (Carlisle, PA), May 25, 1998, B3; and Tom Waddill, "Vietnam War Hero Benavidez Is Listed Stable," *Victoria Advocate*, May 8, 1998, 8A.

42. Garcia and Prochazka, interview; and Noel Benavidez, 2018 interview.

43. Garcia and Prochazka, interview; and Noel Benavidez, 2018 interview.

44. Garcia and Prochazka, interview; and Noel Benavidez, 2018 interview.

45. Sig Christenson, "Veteran Faces New Struggle," *San Antonio Express-News*, November 8, 1998, 1B and 5B.

46. Garcia and Prochazka, interview.

47. Letters can be found in box 4Zc198, folders 1–9 and box 4Zc196, folders 1–6, RBP.

48. Letters can be found in box 4Zc198, folders 1–9 and box 4Zc196, folders 1–6, RBP. Specific reference taken from card in 4Zc196, folder 5.

49. Letters in box 4Zc196, folders 4–6, RBP.

50. Letters in box 4Zc196, folder 3, RBP.

51. Noel Benavidez, 2018 interview.

52. Barbee, interview; and Roy Benavidez to John Garcia, San Antonio, TX, November 17, 1998, box 4Zc198, folder 20, RBP.

53. Garcia, interview; and Barbee, interview.

54. Texas State Department of Health, certificate of death, reg. file # 02 09666 (Dec. 10, 1998), Roy Benavidez, Bureau of Vital Statistics, San Antonio Metropolitan District, copy in author's possession.

55. Kelly Shannon, "Last Farewell to a Soldier and a Hero," *Corpus Christi Caller-Times*, December 4, 1998, A13; Barbee, interview; Garcia and Prochazka, interview; Patricia Smith-Newsome to Mrs. Benavidez, San Antonio, TX, December 8, 1998, box 4Zc198, folder 2; and Dan Rather, "Benavidez Death," #379838, *CBS Evening News*, December 4, 1998.

56. Louis Lerma, "Benavidez Gave His Life to Serving America," *Galveston Daily News*, December 2, 1998, A14; Richard Estrada, "Benavidez Personified Patriotism," *El Paso Times*, December 7, 1998, 11A.

57. Hiram Benitez to Mrs. Benavidez and the Benavidez Family, Eagle River, AK, December 16, 1998, box 4Zc198, folder 4, RBP; Diana DeLaRosa to Noel Benavidez, Houston, TX, December 10, 1998, box 4Zc198, folder 8, RBP; and other cards box 4Zc198, folders 1–8, RBP.

58. Garcia and Prochazka, interview; and Noel Benavidez, 2018 interview.

59. Barbee, interview; Barbee Eulogy, December 1, 1998, El Campo, TX, box 4Zc195, folder 22, RBP; and pictures from the ceremony located in box 3T4.3, RBP.

60. "The Passing of an American Hero," *The Drop*, Spring, 1999, 4–7, quoted on 5.

61. Personal observations made on numerous occasions; Barbee, interview; and AP, "Veterans Turn Out to Say Goodbye to Roy Benavidez," *Victoria Advocate*, December 4, 1998, 1.

62. Roy Benavidez Funeral Program, box 4Zc195, folder 22, RBP; pictures from the ceremony located in box 3T4.3, RBP; and personal observations made on numerous occasions.

Epilogue

1. Louis Caldera to Mrs. Roy P. Benavidez, Washington, DC, December 3, 1998; and Sympathy Card located in box 4Zc198, folder 1, RBP. Other cards and letters located in folders 1–9, box 4Zc198, RBP.

2. Chris Barbee, "U.S. Army Complex Named in Honor of Benavidez," *El Campo Leader-News*, August 25, 1999, 3A; and "Roy P. Benavidez Special Operations Logistics Complex Ribbon Cutting and Dedication Ceremony" program, August 16, 1999, box 4Zc200, folder 4, RBP.

3. "Play Honors Latino Vets," *Los Angeles Times*, July 27, 2000, 52; Scott Huddleston, "San Antonians May See Play About Benavidez, Other Veterans," *San Antonio Express-News*, October 26, 2000, 1B; Chris Barbee, "Benavidez Featured in Wortham Play," *Wharton Journal-Spectator*, June 8, 2002, box 4Zc194, folder 58, RBP; and "Veteranos: A Legacy of Valor" program, box 4Zc200, folder 38, RBP.

4. Invitation to Texas Medal of Honor Presentation to Roy Benavidez, box 4Zc200, folder 4, RBP; Juan B. Elizondo Jr., "Patriotic Texan Wounded in '68 Rescue Is Given Legislative Medal of Honor," *Austin American-Statesman*, May 3, 2001, B1 and B5; and "Local Military Hero Wins Legislature's Top Honor," *Victoria Advocate*, May 3, 2001, 1 and 12.

5. Christening, USS Benavidez, Program, July 21, 2001, box 4Zc200, folder 31, RBP; Buddy Gee, "Navy Christens USNS *Benavidez*," *El Campo Leader-News*, July 25, 2001, 7A; Cristina McGlew, "A Hero Both on the Battlefield and Off," *Sealift*,

August 2001, box 4Zc200, folder 35, RBP; and Ann Rundle, "Ship Sails with Local Hero's Name," *Victoria Advocate*, July 29, 2001, 1A and 8A.

6. Stephanie L. Jordan, "Another Honor for Roy Benavidez," *Corpus Christi Caller-Times*, July 22, 2001, 1 and 9; and Rundle, "Ship Sails."

7. Rundle, "Ship Sails"; AP, "G.I. Joe, the Hispanic Hero," *Albuquerque Tribune*, August 20, 2001, 1. Roy Benavidez G.I. Joe in author's possession.

8. Melony Overton, "Cuero to Honor War Hero with Life-Sized Bronze Statue," *Victoria Advocate*, September 27, 2000, 4; Ann Rundle, "Building a Memorial to a Hero," *Victoria Advocate*, August 28, 2002, 1; "Area Veterans Day Events," *Victoria Advocate*, November 11, 2004, 4D; "Dance Will Raise Money for Memorial," *Victoria Advocate*, February 7, 2002, 5A; "Paving the Way"; AP, "Vietnam War Hero Honored with Statue," *Austin American-Statesman*, 13, 2004, B5; and personal observations made on multiple occasions.

9. Personal observations made at the Reagan Library and Presidential Museum, Simi Valley, CA, June 19, 2019.

10. Blehm, *Legend*; Yvette Benavidez Garcia, *Tango Mike Mike: The Story of Master Sergeant Roy P. Benavidez* (self-published by author, 2017); and *Medal of Honor: Roy Benavidez* (Arlington, VA: United States Army, 2019).

11. Roy P. Benavidez Elementary School website: https://www.southsanisd.net /BES, accessed August 22, 2018; and "State Highway to Be Dedicated to Special Forces Veteran," *Victoria Advocate*, March 19, 2019, A6.

12. Alex Horton, "Army Should Remove Ft. Hood's Confederate Namesake for a Legendary Hispanic Soldier," *Washington Post*, July 31, 2019, www.washingtonpost.com/history/2019/07/31/army-should-remove-ft-hoods -confederate-namesake-legendary-hispanic-soldier-group-says; Emily Caldwell, "Panel Gathering Input on New Military Base Names," *Marion Star*, October 4, 2021, A4; Sig Christenson, "Castro and Other Hispanic Lawmakers Renew Call to Rename Fort Hood for Roy Benavidez," *San Antonio Express-News*, April 13, 2021, www.expressnews.com/news/local/article/Castro-and-other-Hispanic -lawmakers-renew-call-to-16098856.php; Sarah Kuta, "Nine Army Bases Honoring Confederate Leaders Could Soon Have New Names," *Smithsonian Magazine*, May 26, 2022, www.smithsonianmag.com/smart-news/these-are-the-9-new-name s-recommended-for-army-bases-honoring-confederate-leaders-180980160; and Rachael Riley, "These 9 Fort Bragg Roads Will Be Renamed," *Fayetteville Observer*, April 5, 2023, www.fayobserver.com/story/news/military/2023/04/05 /fort-bragg-officials-renaming-nine-roads-on-post/70069513007.

13. Bianca Montes, "Hero," *Victoria Advocate*, November 11, 2015, A1, A4, and A5.

14. Montes, "Hero."

15. Samantha Douty, "El Campo ISD Rejects Naming School After War Hero," November 23, 2019, A1 and A3; "School Board's Decision Insult to War Hero," *Victoria Advocate*, December 6, 2019, A6; and Yvette Garcia, email to author, November 7, 2022.

16. Douty, "El Campo ISD"; "School Board's Decision"; and Garcia, email to author.

17. David Tarrant, "Who Was Roy Benavidez?," *Dallas Morning News*, June 9, 2020, www.dallasnews.com/news/2020/06/09/who-was-roy-benavidez-the-man

-whose-name-some-say-should-replace-confederate-generals-at-fort-hood/#:~ :text=Texas%20native%20Roy%20Benavidez%2C%20a,U.S.%20president%20 would%20later%20say; and US House, "Diversity in America: The Representation of People of Color in the Media," September 24, 2020, 116th Cong. (Washington, DC: Government Printing Office, 2022), 13–20, www.govinfo.gov /content/pkg/CHRG-116hhrg42635/html/CHRG-116hhrg42635.htm, accessed February 24, 2023.

INDEX

ABCMR. *See* Army Board for
    Correction of Military Records
absent without leave (AWOL), 101
acculturation, 68–69
Adams, Lucian, 352
administrative work, 137–139, 141–142
adoption, 46–51, 56–61, 220
African Americans, 18–20, 31–32, 79
aircraft, 188
    American A-1H Skyraiders, 168
    helicopters and, 167–174
American A-1H Skyraiders, 168
American GI Forum, 81–82,
    134–135, 230
American Legion, 81, 247, 250–251,
    289, 291
amputation, 356–359
ancestors
    of Benavidez, Teresa, 35–37
    Benavidez family and, 9, 17–20,
        23–27, 35, 59, 65–67, 73–74,
        347
    stories about, 65–66
    worldview affected by, 67
anti-war movement, 136–137,
    158–159, 208
Apocalypse Now (film), 249
Appy, Christian, 290, 313
Armed Forces Expeditionary Medal, 5
Army, US. *See also* Army Special Forces;
    specific wars

administrative position with,
    137–139, 141–142
assignment, after Vietnam War,
    203–204
basic training for, 90–91, 94–95
Berlin assignment and, 100–102
career goals with, 93–94
education in, 95, 109, 144–145
82nd Airborne and, 108
enlistment to, 89–90, 93–94
honorable discharge from, 103–104
infantry training for, 95–96
jump school and, 106–108, 107
    (photo), 139–141
Korea assignment and, 96–99
military police training at, 103–104
re-enlistments to, 103–104, 106,
    211–212
retirement from, 5, 224–227
after return from Korea, 99–100
17th Infantry Regiment and, 97–98
wages from, 90, 104, 221, 287
Army Airborne School, 106–108, 107
    (photo)
Army Board for Correction of Military
    Records (ABCMR), 216–217, 238
Army Commendation Medal, 5
Army of the Republic of Vietnam
    (ARVN), 114–115, 124–125
Army Special Forces
    B-56 unit of, 162–174, 194

Army Special Forces *(continued)*
  education in, 144–146
  emergency extraction of Wright's
    team and, 183–189
  first duties with, 147
  Green Berets and, 141–147, 155–156,
    161–174, 183–189
  Training, 141–147
  Wright's mission and, 174–189
ARVN. *See* Army of the Republic of
  Vietnam
AWOL. *See* absent without leave

B-56 unit, 162–174, 194
"Ballad of Roy Benavidez" (Carrillo), 8
ballads ("canciones rancheras"), 34
La Bamba (film), 328–329
BAMC. *See* Brooke Army
  Medical Center
Barbee, Chris, 232, 252, 268, 300,
  329–330, 362
  El Campo Leader-News and,
    229–230, 246
  Northside Elementary and, 370
  photograph of, 312 (photo)
  Roy's last days and, 359–360
  speaking engagements and, 310–313
Barbee, Fred, 252, 264
  El Campo Leader-News and, 229–230,
    234–236, 240–241
  photograph of, 312 (photo)
  "Roy Benavidez...*Sometimes Patience
    Wears Thin*" by, 234–236, 240–241
baseball, 95–96
basic training
  for Army, 90–91, 94–95
  for Texas National Guard, 86–87
Battle of Dien Bien Phu, 113
Battle of Ia Drang, 118–119
Bay of Pigs invasion, 108
Benavides, Eugenio, 24–26
Benavides, Nicholas, 20, 24–25, 65
Benavides, Plácido, 17–19, 84
Benavidez, Alexandria
  background on, 47, 59, 63–65
  Roy's adoption by, 46–51, 220
Benavidez, Angelita, 33

Benavidez, Denise, 172, 209–210,
  232–233, 245, 275–276
  birth of, 133
  photograph of, 210 (photo)
Benavidez, Hilaria "Lala" Coy, 141,
  172, 210 (photo)
  background on, 102
  death of, 372
  early romance with, 77–78, 99–100,
    101–103
  formal courtship with, 102, 103–104
  in Fort Bragg, 109 (photo)
  marriage to, 105–106, 107 (photo),
    274–275, 331–334
  pregnancy and, 109, 127–128,
    209–210
  Roy's death and, 360–362
  Roy's hospitalization and, 127–129,
    191–192, 199
Benavidez, Nicholas, 96–97
  background on, 47, 56, 59, 63–64
  Coy family and, 102
  death of, 220
  Roy's adoption by, 46–51, 56–61, 220
  Roy's fighting and, 72–76
  on Roy's joining the Army, 47, 56, 59,
    63–64, 89–90
  as sheriff of Wharton County, 74–75
Benavidez, Noel, 233, 239, 256,
  332–334, 368
  birth of, 209–210
  photograph of, 210 (photo)
  on Roy's health decline, 352–354, 355
Benavidez, Raul Perez "Roy." *See also*
  specific topics
  adoption of, 46–51, 56–61, 220
  Barbees photographed with, 312
    (photo)
  in Berlin, 100 (photo)
  birth of, 37
  buildings and landmarks named
    after, 343–344, 366, 369–371
  death and funeral of, 360–363
  family life and children of, 133–134,
    205, 209–210, 275–276, 331–337
  father's death and, 38
  at Fort Gordon, 104 (photo)

GI Joe figure of, 7, 367–368
in Green Beret uniform, 146 (photo)
in "Honoring American Heroes"
    exhibit, 368–369
at Houston Astro-dome, 267 (photo)
at jump school, 106–108, 107 (photo),
    139–141
The Last Medal of Honor and, 345–346
lives saved by, 186–189, 193–194
marriage of, 105–106, 107 (photo),
    274–275, 331–334
Medal of Honor and, 346–348
memory of, 365–373
in Meritorious Service Medal
    ceremony, 224 (photo)
mother's death and, 60–61
nicknames for, during Vietnam War,
    46–51, 56–61, 239
public persona of, 5–9, 317–321
Reagan photographed with, 258
    (photo), 260 (photo), 263 (photo)
on *Real People*, 308 (photo)
ship named after, 367
statue of, 368–369
as "Texan of the Year," 6, 266
The Three Wars of Roy Benavidez by,
    324–328
Westmoreland photographed with,
    325 (photo)
Benavidez, Rogelio, 37, 42, 47–48,
    57–58, 75
Benavidez, Salvador, Jr.
    background on, 15–17, 27–38
    birth of, 27, 30
    death of, 38
    marriage to Teresa and, 15–17, 34–38
    photo of, 36 (photo)
    tuberculosis and, 37–38, 60
Benavidez, Salvador, Sr.
    background on, 17, 27, 29–30, 32–33
    Roy's relationship with, 65–66, 97
Benavidez, Teresa Perez
    ancestors of, 35–37
    background on, 15–17, 34–38
    Chavez, P., and, 41–42, 46–47
    death of, 60–61
    domestic work and, 41

after husband's death, 39–42
marriage and, 15–17, 34–38,
    41–43, 46–47
photo of, 36 (photo)
remarriage of, 41–43, 46–47
separation of Roy from,
    46–48, 60–61
Benavidez, USNS (ship), 367
Benavidez, Ysabel Cisneros, 27,
    29–30, 32–33
Benavidez, Yvette, 209–210, 233,
    331–333, 367–368
    birth of, 205
    children's book by, 369
    letter correspondence and, 339–340
    Northside Elementary and, 370–371
    photograph of, 210 (photo)
    on Roy's health decline, 350–351,
        353, 354
Benavidez family. *See also* childhood;
    family life; *specific family members*
    ancestors and, 9, 17–20, 23–27, 35,
        59, 65–67, 73–74, 347
    familial duty and, 32–33, 67
    farming and, 29–31, 33–34, 36–37
    homes of, 64, 133, 225, 274–275
    letters to, 365–366
    Medal of Honor ceremony and, 245,
        255–257, 262–263
    property ownership and, 24
    Roy's death and, 360–363
    Texas settlement and, 17–25
Benavidez Street, 370
Bentsen, Lloyd, 230, 236, 244
Berlin Crisis, 100–102, 108
Billac, Pete, 342, 345–348
Blehm, Eric, 369
Bob Hope Vietnam Christmas Show, 12
Bonnette Junior High School, 340–341
books and writing
    by Benavidez, Yvette, 369
    book ideas and, 315–316, 320
    The Last Medal of Honor and, 345–346
    Medal of Honor and, 346–348
    The Three Wars of Roy Benavidez and,
        324–328
boxing, 73–74

Bracero Program (1942) (Mexican Farm Labor Program), 52–53, 80
Brokaw, Tom, 299
Bronze Bishop Films, 344
Brooke Army Medical Center (BAMC), 198–199, 202–203, 355–357
Brown, George W., 322
Buddhist Crisis, 116–117
buildings and landmarks, named after Benavidez, Roy, 343–344, 366, 369–371
Burch, J. Thomas, 297–298
Bush, Barbara, 229, 330
Bush, George H. W., 6, 7, 237, 257, 329–330
Bush, George W., 7, 360

Cambodia
    background and historical context of, 148–157
    China and, 149–152, 154, 208–209
    Cold War and, 148–150
    communism in, 3, 148–152, 196, 207–209
    creation of, 113
    Daniel Boone missions and, 2, 3–5, 163–174
    environment and wildlife in, 164–165
    France and, 149
    Ho Ngoc Tao, 166–167
    Khmer Rouge and, 209
    Lon Nol and, 207–209
    NLF in, 153–155, 196
    Phnom Penh protests and, 150–151, 208–209
    Pol Pot and, 209
    SEATO and, 149
    Sihanouk and, 149–157, 196, 207
    Sihanouk Trail and, 148–150, 152–154
    Soviet Union and, 151, 154–155
    Vietnam War and, 2–5, 148–157, 163–198, 206–209, 326
"canciones rancheras" (ballads), 34
Cannon, Howard, 228
capitalism, 100, 113

Cardwell, Crockett, 28
Carrillo, Leonardo, 8
Carter, Chandler, 253
Carter, Jimmy, 250, 251, 370
    Medal of Honor and, 229, 237, 244
    SSDI and, 280, 286
Cassidy, Patrick F., 209–210, 219–221
Castro, Joaquin, 370
Catholicism, 34, 46, 65, 123, 129, 362
cattle farming, 28–29
Cavazos, Richard E., 206, 370
chauffeur driving job
    for Cassidy, 209–210
    for Linvill, 203–205
    for Westmoreland, 106, 201
Chavez, Bellantres, 60–61
Chavez, Lupe, 96
Chavez, Maria Guadalupe, 61
Chavez, Pablo, 41–42, 46–47
Chicano Movement, 135–136
childhood, 226
    adoption and, 46–51, 56–61, 220
    boxing and, 73–74
    in Colorado, 50–55
    cotton picking in, 55–56
    in Cuero, 39–44, 47–48
    discipline, 65
    education, 43–44, 57–58, 69–70
    in El Campo, 63–78, 83–84
    fighting during, 72–76
    juvenile corrections facility and, 75–76
    labor and jobs in, 44–45, 64, 70–72, 73, 76–78
    mother's death and, 60–61
    racism and, 58–60, 70–73
    religion during, 65, 76–77
    running away during, 47–48
    separation from mother in, 46–48, 60–61
China
    Cambodia and, 149–152, 154, 208–209
    Vietnam and, 150, 208–209
CIDGs. See Civilian Irregular Defense Groups

Cisneros, Henry, 270
Civilian Irregular Defense Groups
    (CIDGs), 166
  extraction of, 183–189
  mission and assignment of, 174–183
civil rights, 82, 134–136
Civil Rights Act (1964), 134
Civil Rights Movement, 134–136
Civil War, 28, 214, 288
Clements, Bill, 6, 264–265, 272
Clinton, Bill, 298, 344–345, 351–352
Cold War, 90–91
  Berlin Crisis and, 100–102, 108
  Cambodia and, 148–150
  82nd Airborne in, 108
Colorado
  childhood in, 50–55
  Fort Carson, 95–96
Combat Infantryman Badge, 5
communism
  in Cambodia, 3, 148–152, 196,
    207–209
  capitalism and, 113
  "domino theory" and, 85–86, 93,
    121, 324–325
  Korean war and, 85–86, 91
  Reagan on, 251–252
  Soviet Union and, 251–252
  spread of, 113–114
  Vietnam War and, 3, 92–93, 109,
    113–115, 251
Community Action Committee of El
    Campo, 300
Cottingham, Jerry, 253
cotton
  farming, 30–31, 48–50
  mill, 42
  picking, 55–56
cowboys, 45–46, 66
Coy family, 102
Craig, John R., 346–348
Craig, Michael, 1–2, 184, 193
Crawford, William J., 368–369
Cronkite, Walter, 157
Cuban Missile Crisis, 108
Cuero, Texas, 39–44, 47–48
cultural assimilation, 68–69

Danevang, Texas, 48
Daniel Boone missions, 2, 3–5, 163–174
  Medal of Honor and, 214–215
  Roy's emergency extraction and,
    183–189
  shutting down, 195–196
  Wright's mission, 174–189
Danish immigration, 48
Darvon, 137–138
D- Day invasion, 108
"Decade of the Hispanic," 270–271
The Deer Hunter (film), 249
DeWitt County, Texas, 16–17, 27–30,
    33–34, 39–44, 47–48
diabetes, 350–357
"Dickie" (soldier), 123–124
disability. See also Social Security
    Disability Insurance
  eligibility for disability benefits, 224
  health and, 5, 221–222, 224,
    279–286, 294–304
  military disability pay and, 280
Distinguished Service Cross, 5,
    200–201, 209, 218, 230
DMZ. See Vietnamese
    Demilitarized Zone
documentary, 344
domestic work, 41
"domino theory," 85–86, 93, 121,
    324–325
Donaldson, Sam, 248
Drake, Ralph, 194, 200, 253
  Medal of Honor and, 215–216,
    218–219, 226, 241
  on Real People, 308
Dulles, John Foster, 112–113

education
  in Army, 95, 109, 144–145
  in Army Special Forces/Green
    Berets, 144–146
  childhood, 43–44, 57–58, 69–70
  financial funding and scholarships
    for, 344
  GED exam and, 109
  Latino/Hispanic community and,
    31–32, 344

education *(continued)*
　literacy and, 70
　quitting school and, 76
　racial discrimination and, 69–70
　school speaking engagements and,
　　266–268, 273, 308–309, 310,
　　340–341–344
　Wharton County Junior College
　　and, 266
82nd Airborne, 108
Eisenhower, Dwight, 114–115
El Campo, Texas
　childhood in, 63–78, 83–84
　Community Action Committee
　　of, 300
　El Campo High School celebration,
　　263–265
　Northside Elementary in, 370–371
　retirement in, 225–226, 231
　return to, 96–97, 99–100, 225–226
　Roy's criticism within community of,
　　299–305
　after Vietnam War, 127–130
El Campo Leader-News, 266, 346
　Barbees and, 229–230, 234–236,
　　240–241, 246
　on Medal of Honor, 234–236,
　　240–241, 246, 264
　"Roy Benavidez…*Sometimes Patience
　　Wears Thin*" and, 234–236,
　　240–241
emergency extractions, 4
　aftermath of, 191–195
　helicopters and, 167–174
　of Wright's CIDG team and,
　　183–189
Ensor, David, 248
eyewitness testimony, 216, 217, 219,
　　226, 231, 237–240, 243

fame, 5–7, 280
　LULAC Hispanic Hall of Fame
　　and, 329
　Medal of Honor and, 299–305,
　　313–315
　publicity and, 299–304, 309
　speaking engagements and, 311–312

familial duty, 32–33, 67
family life. *See also* childhood
　children and, 133–134, 205,
　　209–210, 275–276, 331–337
　family vacations and, 335
　in Fort Riley, 203–206
　in Fort Sam Houston, Texas,
　　209–211, 220–225
　friends and, 336–337
　health and, 334–335, 350–360
　at home, 331–337
　major life changes and, 220–225
　marriage and, 274–275, 331–334
　after Medal of Honor ceremony,
　　274–277
　military service and, 109, 133,
　　158–159
　moving back to El Campo, 225–226
　retirement and, 224–227, 231
　Roy's health decline and, 350–360
　speaking engagements and, 275–277
　during Vietnam War, 172
famine, 91
fan mail, 283–284, 327–328, 339–342,
　　348–349, 357–359
farming
　Benavidez family and, 29–31,
　　33–34, 36–37
　cattle and, 28–29
　cotton, 30–31, 48–50
　cotton picking and, 55–56
　labor and, 29–31, 48–56
　migrants and, 49–55
　property ownership and, 23
　sharecropping and, 29–30,
　　36–37, 49–50
　sugar beets, 50–51, 53–54
fascism, 82, 86
fighting, in childhood, 72–76
film idea, 315–316, 320, 328–329,
　　344, 371
finances, 335
financial funding and scholarships,
　　344
financial inequality, 21–25, 316,
　　319
Firestone Tire store job, 76–78, 87

Fonda, Jane, 290
Ford, Gerald, 217, 229
Fort Bragg, North Carolina, 106–109,
    109 (photo), 248
    administrative position at, 137–139,
        141–142
    Green Berets and Army Special
        Forces Training in, 141–147
    return to, 133–147
    Roy P. Benavidez Special Operations
        Logistics Complex in, 366
Fort Carson, Colorado, 95–96
Fort Chaffee, Arkansas, 102–103
Fort Devens, Massachusetts, 203
Fort Gordon, Georgia, 103–104
"For the relief of Roy P. Benavidez"
    bill, 244
Fort Knox, Kentucky, 86–87
Fort Ord, California, 93–95, 109
Fort Riley, Kansas, 99–100, 203–206
Fort Sam Houston, Texas, 209–211,
    220–225
Fournier, Nelson, 193
France, 91–93, 112–113, 149

García, Héctor, 81, 135, 228, 321
Garcia, Jose, 310–312, 328, 360
García, Macario, 80–81
Gatesville State School for Boys, 75–76
General Educational Development
    (GED) exam, 109
Geneva Accords, 113–114, 149,
    153–154, 211
Germany, 80–82, 100–102, 108. See also
    World War II
GI Joe figure, 7, 367–368
González, Henry B., 213, 219–220,
    228, 235–236
Good Conduct Medals, 5
Great Depression, 36, 46, 52
"Greatest Generation," 67, 82
Great Society programs, 280–281
Great Western Sugar Company, 50–51
Green Berets
    Army Special Forces and, 141–147,
        155–156, 161–174, 183–189
    education in, 144–146

emergency extraction of Wright's
    team and, 183–189
in Latin America, 146–147
popular culture and, 142
Roy, in Green Beret uniform, 146
    (photo)
Vietnam War and, 2, 155–156,
    161–174, 183–189
Griffin, Oscar, 324
Guerrero, Benito, 336–337
Gulf of Tonkin Resolution, 117

Haddock, Art, 76–77, 87
Hagopian, Patrick, 313
Hall of Heroes, 257
Hanoi, Vietnam, 115, 134, 198,
    208, 290
Hauser, Jean, 301
Hayes (Captain), 245
health. See also Social Security
    Disability Insurance
    amputation of Roy's leg and, 356–359
    BAMC and, 198–199, 202–203,
        355–357
    battle wounds and, 11–12, 127–131,
        137–138, 186–189, 193, 198–199,
        221–224, 232–233
    criticism of SSDI and Roy's, 284,
        299–305
    decline in, 350–360
    diabetes and, 350–357
    disability and, 5, 221–222, 224,
        279–286, 294–304
    family life and, 334–335, 350–360
    influenza pandemic and, 32–33
    kidney failure and, 356–357
    lifespan and, 37
    medical exam and, 222–224
    mental, 233–235, 289–290
    Omnibus Budget Reconciliation Act
        and, 289–290
    Physical Evaluation Board and,
        222–224
    physical therapy and, 129–131,
        137–140, 144
    religion and, 129–130
    in retirement, 224, 232–235

health *(continued)*
    Roy's first hospitalization in Vietnam
      War and, 127–131
    Roy's second hospitalization in
      Vietnam War and, 189, 191–195,
      198–199, 202–203
    self-medicating and, 137–138
    shrapnel and, 223, 232–233
    SSDI appeal process and, 281–282,
      296–299
    travel and, 359
    tuberculosis and, 37–38, 60
    VA and hospitalization in Houston,
      354–356
Heckler, Margaret, 295
helicopters, 167–174
Henderson, Florence, 345
heroes
    Hall of Heroes, 257
    "Honoring American Heroes" exhibit
      and, 368–369
    patriotism and, 313–314
    politics and, 270–272, 313
    popular culture and, 313–314
"A Hero Without Hometown Honors"
    (Dallas Times Herald), 304
Herrera, John J., 74
Hidalgo County, Texas, 24–27
Hispanic community. *See* Latino/
    Hispanic community
Hispanic Education Scholarship
    Fund, 344
Hispanic Heritage Week, 271, 310
Ho Chi Minh, 91–93, 113, 115
Ho Chi Minh Trail, 148, 156–157
Hollingsworth, James, 210–211
homes, of Benavidez family, 64, 133,
    225, 274–275
Ho Ngoc Tao, 166–167
honorable discharge, 103–104
"Honoring American Heroes" exhibit,
    368–369
Hope, Bob, 112
House Committee on Aging, 296–299
housing, for migrants, 54, 56
Houston Astro-dome, 265–266, 267
    (photo)

ICC. *See* International Control
    Commission
I Corps Tactical Zone, 119–120
immigration
    Danish, 48
    immigrant labor and, 51–52
    to Texas, 28–29
Immigration Act (1952), 51–52
income. *See* wages and income
Indochina, 91–93, 112–113
infantry training, 95–96
influenza pandemic, 32–33
inheritance, 22–23
intergenerational wealth, 22–23, 26–27
International Control Commission
    (ICC), 153–154
Iran Hostage Crisis, 249

Jackson, Lula, 42
Japan
    transport and hospitalization in,
      195
    World War II and, 91, 92
Jim Crow era, 10, 31–32, 58–60
jobs. *See* labor and jobs
Johnson, Lyndon B.
    Great Society programs and, 281
    "Peace Without Conquest" speech
      by, 118
    Vietnam War and, 3, 117, 118, 135,
      148, 158, 250
jump school, 106–108, 107 (photo),
    139–141
juvenile corrections facility, 75–76

Kennedy, John F., 115–116, 117, 159
Kent State University shootings, 208
Khmer Rouge, 209
kidney failure, 356–357
Killough Middle School in
    Houston, 341
King, Martin Luther, Jr., 158
KKK. *See* Ku Klux Klan
Korea, 96–99, 112–113
Korean war, 85–86, 90–91, 291
Ku Klux Klan (KKK), 32, 54
Kyle, Chris, 7

labor and jobs
administrative work and, 137–139,
141–142
chauffeur driving job, 106, 201,
203–205, 209–210
in childhood, 44–45, 64, 70–72,
73, 76–78
cotton farming and, 30–31, 48–50
cotton picking and, 55–56
domestic work and, 41
farming and, 29–31, 48–56
Firestone Tire store job, 76–78, 87
immigrants and, 51–52
Latino/Hispanic community and,
9–10, 49–55, 80
migrants and, 49–57
racism and, 29
Social Security and, 41, 57
World War II and, 52–53, 56–57
land redistribution, 21–26, 59
Lane, T. W. "Buckshot," 74
Lantos, Tom, 298
Laos, 113, 148, 166
The Last Medal of Honor (Billac),
345–346
Latin America, 146–147
Latino/Hispanic community. *See also*
racial discrimination; racism
acculturation and, 68–69
Chicano Movement and, 135–136
Civil Rights Movement and,
134–136
cultural assimilation and, 68–69
"Decade of the Hispanic" and,
270–272
education and, 31–32, 344
Hispanic Education Scholarship
Fund for, 344
Hispanic Heritage Week, 271, 310
icons and role models for, 7–8, 268,
320, 329, 343–344
immigrant labor and, 51–52
in Jim Crow era, 31, 58–60
labor and, 9–10, 49–55, 80
lifespan and, 37
LULAC and, 67–69, 81, 134–135,
237, 329

Mexican American Generation
and, 67–70
Mexican American Movement
and, 79–80
migrant labor from, 49–57
politics and, 270–271, 322–323
population of, 69
Roy as role model for, 343
speaking engagements and, 269–272
Texas and, 270–272
VA and, 81
Veteranos and, 366
veterans from, 81, 135–137, 321–322
voting and, 270–271, 322–323
in World War II, 78–81
League of United Latin American
Citizens (LULAC), 67–69, 81–82,
134–135
Hispanic Hall of Fame, 329
Medal of Honor and, 237
Legend (Blehm), 369
León, Martín de, 18–20
letters
fan mail and, 283–284, 327–328,
339–342, 348–349, 357–359
pen pals and, 341–342
after Roy's death, 365–366
Lindenau Rifle Club, 16, 34–35, 103
Linvill, Robert, 203–206
literacy, 70
Logevall, Fredrik, 114
Lon Nol, 207–209
LULAC. *See* League of United Latin
American Citizens
Luttrell, Marcus, 7, 370–371

MACV-SOG. *See* Military Assistance
Command, Vietnam-Studies and
Observations Group
March, John, 254
marriage
of Benavidez, Roy and Lala,
105–106, 107 (photo), 274–275,
331–334
of Benavidez, Teresa Perez, 15–17,
34–38, 41–43, 46–47
family life and, 274–275, 331–334

Martin, Billy, 95–96
Martin, Joseph D., 227–229, 238–239
Marxism, 146
Mazak, Stefan "Pappy," 162
McCain, John, 7
McGuire rigs, 4, 167–168, 170, 172–174
McKibben, Larry, 184–189, 193, 200,
    203, 254
McNamara, Robert, 147–148
Medal of Honor, 5, 7, 11, 369
    appeals for Roy's receipt of, 213–220,
        225–231, 235–243
    approval for Roy's receipt of, 243–244
    Barbee, F., and support for, 229–230,
        234–236, 240–241
    Benavidez family during ceremony
        of, 245, 255–257, 262–263
    benefits attached to, 252–253
    Cassidy's support and, 219–220
    ceremony, for Roy, 245–249, 252–264
    citation, 272–273
    Daniel Boone missions and, 214–215
    description and background on,
        214–215
    Drake's support and, 215–216,
        218–219, 226, 241
    eligibility period for receiving,
        217, 244
    extending statute of limitations
        for, 244
    eyewitness testimony and, 216, 217,
        219, 226, 231, 237–240, 243
    fame and, 299–305, 313–315
    family life after receiving, 274–277
    for García, M., 80–81
    LULAC and, 237
    Martin, J. D., and, 227–229, 238–239
    Meyer's support and, 241–243
    for Murphy, 82, 320
    O'Connor's support and,
        239–240, 243
    politics and, 217–218, 235–236,
        270–272
    publicity and, 229–230, 234–236,
        240–241, 246, 248, 262–274
    Reagan and, 248–249, 252, 255–262,
        263 (photo), 271, 322–324
    reconsideration for appeal, 242–243
    rejections for Roy's appeals, 222,
        225–226, 236, 238–239
    self-promotion after receiving,
        314–319
    stipend, 226, 253, 280
    support and allies of Roy's appeal
        for, 215–216, 218–219, 226–231,
        235–238
    Vietnam War recipients, 214–215
    Wyatt's support and, 237–238,
        242–243
Medal of Honor (Benavidez, Roy and
    Craig, John. R.), 346–348
"Medal of Honor" graphic novel
    series, 369
medals and awards, 7, 11, 101, 199–200.
    See also Medal of Honor
    ABCMR and, 216–217, 238
    Armed Forces Expeditionary
        Medal, 5
    Army Commendation Medal, 5
    Combat Infantryman Badge, 5
    Distinguished Service Cross, 5,
        200–201, 209, 218, 230
    Good Conduct Medals, 5
    National Defense Service Medal, 5
    Parachutist Badge, 5
    Presidential Medal of Freedom,
        344–345
    procedures to upgrade, 216–217
    Purple Heart Medal, 5, 199–200
    Republic of Vietnam Campaign
        Medal, 5
    Senior Army Decorations Board and,
        229, 231, 238
    Texas Legislative Medal of Honor,
        366–367
    Vietnam Service Medal, 5
medical exam, 222–224
Meese, Ed, 256
Memorial Day parade, 329
Memorial Day tribute, 321–322
mental health, 233–235, 289–290
Mental Health Systems Act (1980), 290
Meritorious Service Medal, 224–225,
    225 (photo)

Mexican American Generation, 67–70
Mexican American Movement, 79–80
Mexican-American War, 20–21
Mexican Constitution, 18–19
Mexican crab story, 66
Mexican Farm Labor Program (1942)
    (Bracero Program), 52–53, 80
Mexico, 17–21
Meyer, Edward C., 241–243, 257
migrants
    discrimination against, 54
    farming and, 49–55
    housing for, 54, 56
    labor and, 49–57
    racism against, 54–55
Military Assistance Command,
    Vietnam-Studies and Observations
    Group (MACV-SOG), 3–4,
    162–174, 200, 214–215
military disability pay, 280. See
    also Social Security Disability
    Insurance
military patrolling, 122–127
military police training, 103–104
military service. See also Army; veterans;
    specific wars
    American GI Forum and, 81–82,
    134–135, 230
    basic training and, 86–87,
    90–91, 94–95
    faith in, 269
    family life and, 109, 133, 158–159
    Latino service in World War
    II, 78–81
    LULAC and, 81–82
    racism and, 80–81, 99
    Roy's first interest in, 78–84
    Roy's reasons for joining, 10
    speaking engagements for military
    installations and, 310, 330 (photo),
    342–343, 354
    Texas National Guard and, 2, 6,
    83–84, 85–90
    wages from, 90, 104, 221, 287
Mittelstadt, Jennifer, 287
Montejano, David, 23
Moore, Harold, 220, 222

Moore, Kathryn, 301–302
Mousseau, Lloyd, 171, 193, 200, 254
    extraction of, 183–189
    mission of, 174–183
movie idea, 315–316, 320, 328–329,
    344, 371
Murphy, Audie, 82, 87–88, 320
Mustang Mott, 34
My Lai massacre, 218
My War with the CIA (Sihanouk),
    150

National Defense Service Medal, 5
National Hispanic Leadership
    Conference, 271
National Liberation Front (NLF)
    in Cambodia, 153–155, 196
    membership of, 120–121
    tactics of, 120
    in Vietnam War, 120–127,
    153–157, 196
Native Americans, 17, 35
Ngo Dinh Diem, 114–117
nicknames, 171, 239
Nimmo, Robert, 290–294
"Nine Rules" cards, 325–326
1960s, 134–136
Nixon, Richard, 115–116
    Vietnam War and, 206, 208, 250
    Watergate scandal and, 218
NLF. See National Liberation Front
Northside Elementary, 370–371

O'Connor, Brian, 171, 194–195, 215
    extraction of, 183–189
    Medal of Honor and, 239–240, 243
    mission of, 174–183
    reunion with, 253–254, 262–263, 263
    (photo)
Ogden, Carlos, 228
Olmos, Edward James, 371
Olmsted, Frederick Law, 21
Omnibus Budget Reconciliation Act
    (1981), 289–290
Operation Rolling Thunder, 118, 134
Ortiz, Eusebia, 35
Overseas Service Bars, 5

Panama, 329
Parachutist Badge, 5
Paris peace negotiations, 197–198
patriotism, 68–69, 265
 heroes and, 313–314
 speaking engagements and, 267–270,
  317–320, 342–343
"Peace Without Conquest" speech
 (Johnson), 118
pen pals, 341–342
Perez, Agapito, 35
Perez, Manuel, 35
Perry, Rick, 366
philanthropy, 344
Phnom Penh, 150–151, 208–209
Physical Evaluation Board, 222–224
physical therapy, 129–131, 137–140,
 144
Pickle, J. J., 222, 236–237
politics, 10–11
 anti-war sentiment and, 158–159
 heroes and, 270–272, 313
 Latino/Hispanic community and,
  270–271, 322–323
 Medal of Honor and, 217–218,
  235–236, 270–272
 in 1960s, 134–136
 Reagan and, 248–252, 322
 speaking engagements and, 270–272
 Vietnam War and, 195–198,
  206–209, 217–218, 235–236,
  249–252, 324–327
 voting and, 270–271, 322–323
 Watergate scandal and, 218
Poll Tax, 82
Pol Pot, 209
popular culture, 335–336
 Green Berets and, 142
 heroes and, 313–314
 Vietnam War and, 249, 313–314,
  328–329
Powell, Colin, 7, 11, 262
Presidential Medal of Freedom,
 344–345
probate process, 22–23
Project Sigma, 162–163
property ownership

auctions, sales, and, 24–26
 farming and, 23
 intergenerational wealth and,
  22–23, 26–27
 land redistribution and, 21–26, 59
 probate process and, 22–23
 settlement and, 20–26, 59
 sharecropping and, 29–30
 taxes and, 22–23, 24, 26–27
publicity, 345
 fame and, 299–304, 309
 Medal of Honor and, 229–230,
  234–236, 240–241, 246, 248,
  262–274
 Real People and, 307–309, 308
  (photo), 313
 about Roy's death, 360–361
 on Roy's SSDI, 282–286,
  295–296, 309
 self-promotion and, 314–319, 348
 for *The Three Wars of Roy
  Benavidez*, 327
public persona, 5–9, 317–321
public speaking. *See* speaking
 engagements
Purple Heart Medal, 5, 199–200

racial discrimination, 9–10, 226, 247
 education and, 69–70
 in Jim Crow era, 10, 31–32, 58–60
 "Mexican American Generation"
  and, 67–70
 against migrants, 54
 structural disadvantages of, 69–72
racial segregation, 58–60, 68, 319
racism, 247, 304
 childhood and, 58–60, 70–73
 financial inequality and, 21–25,
  316, 319
 Jim Crow era and, 10, 31–32, 58–60
 KKK and, 32, 54
 labor and, 29
 land redistribution, property
  ownership, and, 21–25
 against migrants, 54–55
 military service and, 80–81, 99
 settlement and, 18–24

sidestepping issue of race and, 319–320
veterans and, 80–81
violence and, 20, 32
railroads, 28
Rather, Dan, 360–361
Raye, Martha, 344–345
Reagan, Ronald, 5, 6, 11, 12
Benavidez family's meeting with, 255–257
on communism, 251–252
Gacia, H., and, 321
on Great Society programs and social welfare, 280–281
Hispanic Heritage Week and, 271
Latino/Hispanic veterans and, 321–322
Medal of Honor and, 248–249, 252, 255–262, 263 (photo), 271, 322–324
Memorial Day tribute and, 321–322
patriotism and, 269
politics and, 248–252, 322
Roy's photographs with, 258 (photo), 260 (photo), 263 (photo)
second inauguration for, 323–324
on Soviet Union, 251–252
SSDI and, 280–286, 294–296
VA and, 286–294
veterans and, 248–251, 286–294
Vietnam War and, 248–252, 259–260
Real People (television show), 307–309, 308 (photo), 313
reconnaissance, 2, 3–5, 163–174. *See also* Daniel Boone missions
refugees, 125–126
religion, 183
Buddhist Crisis and, 116–117
during childhood, 65, 76–77
health and, 129–130
religious persecution and, 116–117
in Vietnam, 123
repatriation, 52
Republic of Vietnam Campaign Medal, 5
retirement
from Army, 5, 224–227

in El Campo, 225–226, 231
family life and, 224–227, 231
health in, 224, 232–235
Revolutionary War, 288
Rhodes, Thaddeus, 26
romantic interests, 77–78, 99–100
"Roy Benavidez Day," 6, 264, 265, 300–301
"Roy Benavidez...*Sometimes Patience Wears Thin*" (Barbee, F.), 234–236, 240–241
Roy P. Benavidez Elementary School, 343–344, 369
Roy P. Benavidez Special Operations Logistics Complex, 366
running away, 47–48
Ryan, Nolan, 265–266

Sama, Dominic, 322
San Fernando Cathedral, 362–363
Santa Anna, Antonio López de, 18–19
scholarships, 344
school speaking engagements, 266–268, 273, 308–309, 310, 340–341–344
Scott, Willard, 329
SEATO. *See* Southeast Asia Treaty Organization
self-medicating, 137–138
Senior Army Decorations Board, 229, 231, 238
settlement
property ownership, land redistribution, and, 20–26, 59
racism and, 18–24
Tejanos and, 19–20
Texas settlers and, 17–25
17th Infantry Regiment, 97–98
sharecropping, 29–30, 36–37, 49–50
shrapnel, 223, 232–233
Sihanouk, Norodom, 149–157, 196, 207
Sihanouk Trail and, 148–150, 152–154
Sisisky, Norman, 298
slavery, 18–20
social change, of 1960s, 134–136
Social Security, 11–12, 41, 47
Social Security Administration, 11–12, 279–283, 298–299

Social Security Disability
Insurance (SSDI)
appeal process and, 281–282,
296–299
Carter, J., and, 280, 286
criticism of Roy's health and, 284,
299–305
discontinuation of Roy's, 11–12,
279–286, 294–299
eligibility review process for,
279–286, 294–299
income and, 280
letters to Roy about, 283–284
military disability pay and, 280
payments, 280
publicity on, 282–286, 295–296, 309
Reagan and, 280–286, 294–296
resentment over, 300–304
Roy's call for moratorium on
disability reviews for, 297–299
Roy's testimony in appeal for,
296–299
veterans and, 11–12, 279–286,
294–305
winning appeal for, 296–299
social welfare, 12, 280–281. *See also*
Social Security; Social Security
Disability Insurance
Southeast Asia Treaty Organization
(SEATO), 114, 149
Southwest Region Recruiting
Command, 269
Soviet Union, 151, 154–155, 251–252
speaking engagements, 6–7, 220–221
Barbee, C., and, 310, 312–313
at El Campo High School, 265
fame and, 311–312
family life and, 275–277
Garcia, J., and, 310–312
health decline and, 354
at Hispanic Heritage Week, 271
Latino/Hispanic community and,
269–272
at Memorial Day parade, 329
Memorial Day tribute, 321–322
for military installations, 310, 330
(photo), 342–343, 354

patriotism and, 267–270, 317–320,
342–343
politics and, 270–272
Roy's public persona during, 5–9,
317–321
schedule and, 310, 349
for schools, 266–268, 273, 308–309,
310, 340–341–344
travel and, 309–312, 321, 329, 333
on Veterans Day, 310, 354, 359
at Virginia Tech, 266
wages, perks, and, 267, 270, 315
at West Point, 272–273
SSDI. *See* Social Security Disability
Insurance
statue, of Benavidez, Roy, 368
Sucher, Steve, 233–234, 252
Sugar Act (1937), 53–54
sugar beet farming, 50–51, 53–54

Tam Ky, Vietnam, 119–127
taxes
Poll Tax and, 82
probate process and, 22–23
property ownership and, 22–23,
24, 26–27
Teague, Olin E., 222, 228, 236
Tejanos, 19–25
Tejeda, Frank, 272–273
Tet Offensive, 156–158, 163–164
"Texan of the Year," 6, 266
Texas. *See also* El Campo, Texas
Cuero, 39–44, 47–48
Danevang, 48
DeWitt County, 16–17, 27–30,
33–34, 39–44, 47–48
Fort Sam Houston, 209–211,
220–225
Hidalgo County, 24–27
immigration to, 28–29
Latino/Hispanic community and,
270–272
Mexico and, 17–21
San Fernando Cathedral in, 362–363
settlers and settlement of, 17–25
slavery in, 18–20
statehood of, 20

University of Texas and, 266
  Wharton County, 48–49, 74–75, 266
Texas Legislative Medal of Honor,
  366–367
Texas National Guard, 2, 6
  background on, 83–84
  basic training, 86–87
  Roy's decision to join, 84, 85–86
  Roy's service to, 85–90
Texas Revolution, 18–20, 27, 68
The Three Wars of Roy Benavidez
  (Benavidez, Roy, and Griffin),
  324–328
To Hell and Back (film), 88, 320
To Hell and Back (Murphy), 320
Tower, John, 240–241
travel
  family vacations and, 335
  health and, 359
  for speaking engagements, 309–312,
  321, 329, 333
Treaty of Guadalupe Hidalgo, 20–21
Trujillo, Rafael, 108
Truman, Harry, 80–81
tuberculosis, 37–38, 60
Turkey Trot, 40–41, 42

United States Military Academy, 329
University of Texas, Austin, 266

VA. *See* Veterans Administration
Valdez, Luis, 329
Veteranos (play), 366
veterans
  American Legion and, 81, 247,
  250–251, 289, 291
  benefit cuts for, 287–294
  history of benefits for, 288
  Latino/Hispanic, 81, 135–137,
  321–322
  Nimmo and, 290–294
  Omnibus Budget Reconciliation Act
  and, 289–290
  racism and, 80–81
  Reagan and, 248–251, 286–294
  Social Security and, 11–12
  SSDI and, 11–12, 279–286, 294–305

as victims, 314
  Vietnam Veterans Memorial and,
  273–274, 287
  Vietnam War veterans, 135–137,
  214–215, 248–251, 259–263,
  271–274, 287, 292–294
  from World War II, 80–83, 288, 291
Veterans Administration (VA), 230
  Latino/Hispanic community and, 81
  military veteran benefit cuts by,
  287–294
  Nimmo and, 290–294
  Reagan and, 286–294
  Roy's health decline and, 354–356
Veterans Day, 205, 310, 354, 359
Veterans of Foreign Wars (VFW), 81,
  250–251, 291–293
Victoria (colony), 18, 20–21
Viet Cong. *See* National
  Liberation Front
Viet Minh, 91–93, 113, 120
Vietnam
  ARVN and, 114–115, 124–125
  China and, 150, 208–209
  division of, 113
  France and, 91–93, 112–113
  Hanoi, 115, 134, 198, 208, 290
  Ho Chi Minh and, 91–93, 113, 115
  Ngo Dinh Diem and, 114–117
  religion in, 123
  Roy's arrival in, 111–112, 118–119
  Viet Minh and, 91–93, 113, 120
  violence in, 116–117
Vietnamese Demilitarized Zone
  (DMZ), 119–120
Vietnam Jump Wings, 5
Vietnam Service Medal, 5
"Vietnam syndrome," 217–218, 249, 269
Vietnam Veterans Memorial,
  273–274, 287
Vietnam Veterans Memorial Fund, 287
Vietnam War, 1–2
  anti-war movement and, 136–137,
  158–159, 208
  background and historical context of,
  91–93, 112–117, 148–157
  Battle of Dien Bien Phu and, 113

Vietnam War *(continued)*
    Battle of Ia Drang and, 118–119
    blame for failures of, 325–327
    Cambodia and, 2–5, 148–157,
        163–198, 206–209, 326
    casualties of, 128, 196–197
    CIDG and, 166, 174–189
    communism and, 3, 92–93, 109,
        113–115, 251
    Daniel Boone missions and, 2, 3–5,
        163–189, 195–196
    "Dickie" and, 123–124
    Eisenhower and, 114–115
    end of, 211
    expansion of, 134
    family life during, 172
    France and, 91–93, 112–113
    Green Berets and, 2, 155–156,
        161–174, 183–189
    Gulf of Tonkin Resolution and, 117
    Ho Chi Minh Trail and, 148,
        156–157
    Johnson and, 3, 117, 118, 135, 148,
        158, 250
    The Last Medal of Honor on, 345–346
    Latino/Hispanic veterans from,
        135–137
    MACV-SOG and, 3–4, 162–174,
        200, 214–215
    McKibben and, 184–189, 193
    Medal of Honor and, 347–348
    Medal of Honor recipients from,
        214–215
    military patrolling in, 122–127
    My Lai massacre and, 218
    Nixon and, 206, 208, 250
    NLF in, 120–127, 153–157, 196
    Operation Rolling Thunder and,
        118, 134
    Paris peace negotiations and, 197–198
    politics and, 195–198, 206–209,
        217–218, 235–236, 249–252,
        324–327
    popular culture and, 249, 313–314,
        328–329
    Project Sigma in, 162–163
    public polling on, 197

    Reagan and, 248–252, 259–260
    reconnaissance and, 2, 3–5, 163–174
    refugees, 125–126
    "Roy Benavidez…*Sometimes Patience
        Wears Thin*" on, 234–236, 240–241
    Roy's emergency extraction of Wright
        and CIDG team, 183–189
    Roy's first assignment in, 109–127
    Roy's first hospitalization and return
        from, 127–131
    Roy's second assignment in, 156,
        158–159, 161–174
    Roy's second hospitalization and
        return from, 189, 191–195,
        198–199, 202–203
    Sihanouk and, 149–157, 196, 207
    Sihanouk Trail and, 148–150,
        152–154
    in Tam Ky, 119–127
    Tet Offensive and, 156–158, 163–164
    The Three Wars of Roy Benavidez on,
        324–328
    veterans, 135–137, 214–215,
        248–251, 259–263, 271–274, 287,
        292–294
    violence in, 118–127, 128, 172–174,
        176–189
    "Wag" and, 125
    Wright and, 4, 171–172, 174–189
violence, 10
    fighting and, 72–76
    racism and, 20, 32
    in Vietnam, 116–117
    in Vietnam War, 118–127, 128,
        172–174, 176–189
    during World War II, 80
Virginia Tech, 266
voting
    Latino/Hispanic community and,
        270–271, 322–323
    politics and, 270–271, 322–323
    Poll Tax and, 82

"Wag" (soldier), 125
wages and income, 36
    from Army and military service, 90,
        104, 221, 287

for cotton picking, 56
finances and, 335
at Firestone Tire store, 76–77, 87
Medal of Honor stipend and, 226, 253, 280
speaking engagement perks and, 267, 270, 315
SSDI and, 280
for sugar beet farmers, 54
Waggie, Roger, 192–193, 202, 308
Warrant Officer Candidate School, 205–206
Watergate scandal, 218
Webber, Absalom Theodore "AB," 241–242, 243
Weinberger, Caspar, 7, 249, 254, 256, 259
welfare state, 12, 280–281
Westmoreland, William, 3, 106, 155, 157, 201–202, 325–326 (photo)
West Point speaking engagement, 272–273
Wharton County, Texas, 48–49, 74–75, 266. *See also* El Campo, Texas
Why Courage Matters (McCain), 7

Wilson, Sam, 237
work ethic, 29
worldview, 67
World War II, 42, 55
African Americans in, 79
Crawford and, 368–369
García, M., and, 80–81
Japan and, 91, 92
labor and, 52–53, 56–57
Latino service in, 78–81
veterans from, 80–83, 288, 291
violence during, 80
Wright, Leroy, 4, 171–172, 200, 239, 254
death of, 181–182, 185–186, 193
extraction of CIDG team and, 183–189
meeting family of, 345
mission and assignment for, 174–189
writing. *See* books and writing
Wyatt, Joe, Jr., 237–238, 242–244, 264–265, 308

Yaqui Indians, 35
Young, John, 228, 231, 236

William Sturkey is an associate professor of history at the University of Pennsylvania. He is the author of *Hattiesburg*, a finalist for the Benjamin L. Hooks National Book Award and winner of the 2020 Zócalo Book Prize, and the coeditor of *To Write in the Light of Freedom*. He lives in Philadelphia, Pennsylvania.